The Jews of Bielorussia during World War II

The Jews of Bielorussia during World War II

Shalom Cholawsky
Ein Hashofet, Israel

harwood academic publishers
Australia • Canada • China • France • Germany • India • Japan
Luxembourg • Malaysia • The Netherlands • Russia • Singapore
Switzerland • Thailand

Copyright © 1998 OPA (Overseas Publishers Association) Amsterdam B.V. Published in The Netherlands by Harwood Academic Publishers.

All rights reserved.

No part of this book may be reproduced or utilized in any form or by any means, electronic or mechanical, including photocopying and recording, or by any information storage or retrieval system, without permission in writing from the publisher. Printed in Singapore.

Amsteldijk 166
1st Floor
1079 LH Amsterdam
The Netherlands

British Library Cataloguing in Publication Data

Cholawsky, Shalom, 1914–
 The Jews of Bielorussia during World War II
 1. World War, 1939–1945 — Jewish resistance — Belarus
 2. World War, 1939–1945 — Jewish resistance — Belarus — Case studies
 I. Title
 940.5'337

ISBN 90-5702-193-5

Contents

Foreword		vii
Map of Belarus		x
Introduction		xi
Acknowledgements		xxix
Chapter 1	The Jews of Bielorussia under Soviet Rule: 1939–1941	1
Chapter 2	Operation Barbarossa: Nazi Preparations to Deal with the Jewish Population in the Occupied Territories to the East	35
Chapter 3	Nazi Policies in Western Bielorussia	47
Chapter 4	The Waves of Murder in Western Bielorussia	69
Chapter 5	The First Series of Aktzias	79
Chapter 6	Beginnings of the Underground	103
Chapter 7	The Underground in Battle	117
Chapter 8	The Resistance	159
Chapter 9	Revolt in the Ghetto	185
Chapter 10	Revolt in the Ghettos without Undergrounds	201

Chapter 11	Escape from the Ghetto	209
Chapter 12	On a Mission of Rescue and Revenge	239
Chapter 13	Underground and Judenrat	251
Chapter 14	The Non-Jewish Population's Attitude Towards the Jews During the Holocaust	271
Chapter 15	In Conclusion	287
Index		311

Foreword

This study fills a lacuna in the history of the fate of the Jews in Bielorussia during the Holocaust. The ghettos of Bielorussia were populated by a vibrant Jewish community, with its own particular traditions, its own unique characteristics justifying our detailed examination of its fate. In general, it may be said that every region, both in Eastern Europe and in other parts of the continent, differed from its neighbors. For Bielorussia that statement is of even greater validity. This region of forests and marshes, situated at the edge of the society and economy of the political unit to which it belonged (once Poland and *today Belarus*), contained villages and towns serving as centers for farming and forestry. The Bielorussians arrived at their self-awareness late and only partially, and the many Jews who lived there could not but feel themselves as being on a higher level of cultural development than the local society. There was, therefore, no assimilation. But the alienation which existed with its origin in a combination of religious and cultural motives on the one hand, and the simple economic fact that the Jews formed a middle stratum of craftsmen and petty traders on the other, was not extreme to the point of murderous hatred as it was in the Ukraine. That is not to say that the Bielorussians were a Jew-loving people or that we could plant a very thick forest of trees in honor of gentiles who went out of their way to help Jews. But there were such gentiles among them, and in a far larger proportion than among the Lithuanians to the northwest or the Ukrainians to the south. In the face of Nazi murderousness, the Jews had greater prospects of survival in the Bielorussian villages than in other regions.

The forest alters the picture we have of central or western Poland: Wild forest and not a grove of cultivated woods; a jungle-forest where only those privy to its secret knew its paths; where it was not possible to exist except in the few villages or the farms cleared from its midst.

Dr Cholawsky paints a broad picture of the area, the Jews within it and their special culture. This is the true Jewish town, rather than the product of nostalgic sentimentality. In the 1930s it was a town where the majority were already secular and Zionist, with Hebrew disseminated from the *Tarbut* school, and with strong Zionist movements. There was a great deal of poverty in it, but there were also many cultural enterprises. The townspeople were, as I have said, craftsmen, shopkeepers and traders for the most part, but there was also an important group of intellectuals and a few wealthy persons and among them industrialists and bigger traders.

The Soviet era, 1939–1941, enjoys a careful treatment at Dr Cholawsky's hands. It forms the background for the events which took place after the German invasion of the USSR. Nazi policies, though they may already be familiar to us in their broadest sense, are described in detail. This book's uniqueness, however lies in its description and analysis of the fate of the region's Jews, imprisoned into ghettos run by the 'Jewish Councils' or Judenrats, and sentenced to harsh extinction.

The battle for the lives of these Jews is the book's central theme. The Judenräte are revealed to have been for the most part, though not always, authentic Jewish leaders of the Jewish public, whom they attempted to help and rescue. There were also those who came to the point of armed resistance. The public responded and the proximity of the forest opened possibilities that did not exist in central and western Poland where there are no forests of this kind.

The book before us describes the organization for active resistance and for battle, and points to the fact that we have here a mass phenomenon and not something exceptional. That unique phenomenon is carefully examined, the author analyzes the motives, the paths taken and the results. In the end, many thousands went into the forest. Here the book's story concludes and we can only hope that Dr Cholawsky will continue his research and tell us what happened in the forest in both Western and Eastern Bielorussia and the armed resistance within it.

Here we have a special tribe of Jews, a special way of response, and an author who is not only an historian trained in his craft, but was also the commander of the first revolt in the region in Nieswiezh. He has written about that experience in another book: "Soldiers from the Ghetto", published by Moreshet in 1973. Dr Cholawsky has opened a window for us onto an important section of Jewry, whose heirs we are, as we are the heirs of all the Jews who died in the Holocaust, a Jewry that fought for its life as long as it could. The descriptions and analyses in this book will assist us in our attempt to understand that reality, and for that we thank the author.

Yehuda Bauer

Map of Belarus showing the border between East and West Belarus. This book concerns the Jews in West Belarus.

Introduction

The Jews of Bielorussia

Ever since the establishment of the first Jewish communities (after the Mongolian conquest) the Jews of Bielorussia had been affected by Bielorussia's lack of political independence. Political changes in this geographical area, a region of dispute and war between Russia, Poland and Lithuania, also affected the economic, social and cultural development of its Jews. Up until the fourteenth century, the Bielorussian Jews had been the subjects of the Lithuanian principalities; with growing Polish influence in the area they became an integral part of Polish Jewry and subject to the good graces of the Polish rulers. After Poland's partition in 1772 and until the end of World War I, they formed part of Russian Jewry. With Bielorussia's partition following the Riga Pact of 1920, the Bielorussian Jews found themselves once more divided.

Demographic Data

According to the first population census of independent Poland in 1921, the Jews numbered 2,850,000, 10.5 percent of the total population. This census did not include Upper Silesia, the city of Vilno and the Vilno, Troki, Oszmiana and Swieciany districts; from the end of the nineteenth century until the 1920s the Jewish population declined in these districts.

	1897 Census			1921 Census		
District	Population	Number of Jews	% Jews	Population	Number of Jews	% Jews
Pruzhany	135,741	17,611	13.0	82,272	10,630	12.9
Kobryn	180,397	25,048	13.9	127,639	17,116	13.4
Slonim	224,369	34,372	15.3	145,363	18,633	12.8
Lida	204,051	24,372	12.1	194,166	16,551	8.5
Pinsk	230,678	45,112	19.6	235,646	30,937	13.1
Novogrudok	245,055	30,405	12.4	197,283	12,194	6.2

The above table points to the declining numbers of Jews in these districts in 1887–1921. This decline was caused by the wave of immigration to the United States before World War I and the ensuing battles which destroyed many Jewish communities and drove a considerable section of the Jewish population from their homes. Of a Jewish population which had previously numbered about 30,000, only some 7,000 Jews were left in Pinsk during the War.[6] Emigration from the regions subject to Russian occupation increased. Previously, during the 1880s some 20,000 Jews annually emigrated from these regions and before World War I the number rose to some 70,000. The main emigration was from the districts of Polesie and Bialystok, Novogrudok, Vilno, Warsaw and Vohlynia.[7] Jewish re-immigration was relatively small. During the period of Polish independence, intensive Jewish emigration continued from the eastern districts of Bielorussia and Vohlynia. The largest Jewish emigration was from the Novogrudok region.

Natural Increase

In the nineteenth century, Jewish natural increase in the areas occupied by Poland (excluding the Prussian region) was greater than that of the Christian population. The reason was not due to the Jews' greater fertility, but in the lower mortality of Jewish children. The natural increase was still higher in the centers of Hasidic Judaism. The flow to the larger cities because of industrialization led to smaller families. The new social and political movements like Zionism and socialism that contested orthodoxy, also led to a decline in the natural increase.

The annual increase of the Polish Jews between the two world wars was 30,000: average annual emigration was 18,000. Actual natural increase came, therefore, to 12,000 persons annually.

In the 1931 census of independent Poland; its second, the Jews numbered 3,113,933: 9.8 percent of the population as a whole (31,915,779).[8] Some 452,400 of these Jews were in Western Bielorussia, according to the following distribution:

District	Jews
Bialystok	153,500
Vilno	108,900
Novogrudok	77,000
Polesie	113,000

If we add to this natural increase until 1939, some 485,000 Jews were living in Western Bielorussia at the onset of the German Polish war; in the Vilno, Novogrudok and Polesie districts they numbered some 323,000.

Economic Situation

The economic situation of the Jews of Western Bielorussia was influenced by Poland's economic development between the two world wars, the Polish government's colonialist policies in the eastern border areas, and the discriminatory policies adopted by the Polish government against the Jewish minority in Poland.

The years 1918–1932 showed the results of World War I and the war between Poland and the USSR (1920). These were years of galloping inflation. From 1923 to 1928 there was a temporary economic upswing, but 1928–1933 were years of depression as a result of the world economic crisis. From 1933 to 1939 there was a slow rise in industrial production, intensified poverty in the villages and constant growth in the numbers of urban unemployed.

One of the fundamental ills of the Polish economy was the lack of land for the ten million people living in the villages who held no more than five hectares per family: 45 percent of the land was owned by 13,000 large landlords.

The desperate village poverty, the large number of unemployed and the consequent declining purchasing power of the inhabitants, struck first and foremost at the livelihood of the Jews. The Jewish population was destitute, especially in the eastern regions. Trade declined because of the population's general impoverishment, the steep rise in taxes, the competition of agricultural and commercial cooperatives and, finally, a series of regulations inaugurated by the government authorities, especially for the eastern regions, which limited petty trade.

After World War I the eastern markets were closed to trade and to craft products. These facts worsened the situation of the Jews, especially in Western Bielorussia, Vohlynia and Galicia. Poverty outpaced productivity. About 80 percent of the Jewish population in the middle of the 1920s were poor.[9]

The unemployment rate among Jewish workers was higher than among non-Jewish workers. The process of impoverishment also affected commerce: wholesale businesses turned into retail shops and retailers turned into pedlars in the markets and streets.

In the eastern Polish districts many of the village 'householders' kept small home farms with a cow or goat, a small vegetable garden (cucumbers, onions, radishes, etc.) and a small fruit orchard. Agricultural products were very cheap. The Jews found it easier to survive in these districts.

Independent Poland's political regime worked against the Jews' economic status and Jewish trade was hurt badly; in eastern Poland, the Polish government conducted statist policies and discriminated against trade as compared to other economic sectors. The monopolies on the production of tobacco, spirits, alcohol and salt; the consumers' and producers' cooperatives in the 1930s; the high taxation; the law imposing a total Sabbath on Sundays; the propaganda against the 'Judaification' of trade; and the Polish settlers' taking over positions in business and in offices, all affected Jewish tradesmen.[10]

From 1931 to 1939 the numbers of Jews occupied in trade in Poland declined at an intensified pace. In the Vilno, Bialystok, Novogrudok and Polesie districts the Jews' share in trade declined from 72.7 to 65 percent in the period from 1933 to 1937. Hitler's ascent to power in 1933, and the German-Polish agreement of 1934, served as a sharp turning point for Poland's policies in general towards Jews in all spheres of life. On 4 June

1936, Polish Prime Minister Florian Slavoi Skladkovsky, while supposedly expressing his reservations in the Polish Sejm against acts of violence against the Jews, defined the government's attitude on the economic war against them by one word: "owszem," ("of course"). That was the green light for violent propaganda and the boycott of Jewish shops culminating in riots.

In 1935 there were pogroms in Grodno, Suvalki, Racionzh and Odzhibul (in the Opoczno district), and in Pszytyk in March 1936; Minsk-Mazowiecki in June 1936; in Brzesc in May 1937; in Czestochowa in June 1937. The wave of pogroms also spread to other localities, large and small. In December 1938 (after Kristallnacht in Germany), the head of '*Ozon*' (the party of National Unity that supported the government), General Stanislav Skwarczynski, announced in an address in the Sejm the preparation of new laws setting the numbers of Jews permitted in the various professions. Sejm delegate Kienc tendered a draft law curtailing Jewish civil rights. According to that proposal, the Jews would be deprived of the right of active or passive election; the right to work in certain institutions and companies; the right to send their children to the general elementary, secondary and higher schools; to teach in the schools; and to work in journalism, the cinema or the theatre. Those working in the free professions would be denied the right to possess real estate; to manage banks; and to open new enterprises in industry, crafts, commerce and transportation. Existing Jewish businesses would only be allowed to employ Jewish workers.[11]

Christians and Poles holding placards bearing the words: "Each man to his own community" and "Don't buy from Jews" stood in front of Jewish shops.

There was no room for error concerning the aim of the Polish government's policies and the sources from which it had drawn its inspiration.

Industry, Crafts and Agriculture

As early as the eighteenth century Jews had comprised about half of all craftsmen in the State of Poland. At the beginning of the nineteenth century, with the abrogation of the obligation for craftsmen to belong to guilds and the decrees against Jewish tavern-keeping, Jews streamed into commerce and crafts: shoemaking, tailoring, tinsmithing, watchmaking and metalworking.

In central, or 'Congress' Poland the proportion of manual laborers among the Jewish population had been about 74 percent during the first half of the nineteenth century.¹² We may assume that the proportion of manual laborers in Bielorussia at that time, was not much different.

The proportion of Jews among all craftsmen in independent Poland came to approximately 36 percent. In eastern Poland, Jews comprised 53 percent of those in industry and crafts.¹³ In Western Bielorussia, the proportion of Jewish to non-Jewish craftsmen was much higher: in the Bialystok district it was 76.1 percent, in the Vilno district it was 59.7 percent, in Novogrudok district it was 77 percent, and in Polesie it was 81.1 percent.¹⁴ At the beginning of the 1920s Pinsk Jews were occupied in 43 different kinds of crafts,¹⁵ and in 1933 95 percent of all craftsmen in the city were Jewish. That high rate had no parallel in any Jewish community between the two world wars, except for the USSR.

In the days of independent Poland the process of Jews being driven from their occupations, especially from the free professions, intensified, and many secondary school and university graduates were compelled to seek their livelihoods in physical labor.

Farming had been prevalent among Polish Jews from their beginnings in that country. In the middle of the eighteenth century, village Jews formed one-third of the Jewish population.¹⁶ Within the Pale of Settlement in 1897, 3.6 percent of the Jewish population were farmers. In the Minsk, Grodno, Kovno, Vilno and Suvalki districts, at the beginning of the century, Jews had cultivated vegetable gardens on land that had been bought or leased. In the course of time a kind of urban agriculture had developed by the purchase or leasing of plots of land in the vicinity of the towns.

According to the 1931 census, 135,200 Polish Jews, 4.3 percent of the Jewish population, earned their living from agriculture. In Polesie the proportion of Jews earning their living from agriculture came to seven percent.

In Western Bielorussia there were 32 villages of Jewish farmers with 720 families (6,800 persons) owing 6,198 hectares of land. Of the towns in the Vilno, Bialystok, Polesie and Novogrudok districts, 23 towns saw the rise of this 'urban agriculture', mostly on private and party leased land.¹⁸ However, only in those towns where the Jews owned land did Jews persist in agricultural occupations until the outbreak of World War II.

The Jewish farmers suffered from the lack of land. Seventy-five percent of the Jewish farmers had small holdings up to five hectares, the minimum area for an agricultural existence. The Polish government discriminated against Jewish farmers when granting loans from state credit institutions. In order to maintain themselves, Jewish farmers were compelled to take up supplementary occupations like craftmaking, trade and wagonry.

In the 1930s there were many cases of Jewish farms being attacked and burned, but the Jews defended their lives and property. The Polish paper, *Rolnik* (Farmer) of 6 June 1937 stated: "The Jewish ownership of land in Poland must be liquidated and as swiftly as possible ..."[19]

Public Service and Free Professions

The discriminatory policies of the Polish government were particularly outstanding in this sector. The proportion of Jews in the civil service came to only one percent. Jewish physicians formed 56 percent of all private physicians in Poland, but only 11.9 percent in the hospitals and health services. In the Bialystok, Novogrudok, Polesie and Vohlynia districts, Jews comprised between 73.1 and 78.4 percent of all medical doctors.

The most striking and impressive fact in the educational field is that Western Bielorussia and Vohlynia held about 75 percent of all the Hebrew schools and about 70 percent of all the Yiddish-language schools in Poland. These schools were maintained by the Jews themselves. The minimal support once given to these schools by municipal authorities was also withdrawn. The numbers of Jewish students in the Polish universities declined from 24.6 percent in 1921–22 to 8.2 percent in 1938–39. Jews were not accepted in the pharmacological, veterinarian and medical faculties of the Warsaw and Krakow universities. "Jews to the ghetto!" was the slogan raised by the non-Jewish students when, in 1935, they demanded 'ghetto benches' in the universities and other institutions of higher learning.[20]

On the eve of World War II, the Bielorussian Jews, as part of Polish Jewry in general, found themselves facing a rising antisemitic tide increasingly expressed in all spheres of life and this in the course of a process of general impoverishment. A greater proportion of the Jewish population began to turn to radical views and Jewish emigration increased. Between 1931 and 1938 Jews formed 64 percent of all emigrants from Poland to the countries of Europe. Numbering some 450,000, 140,000 of these went to Palestine.[21] More than 120,000 Jewish soldiers fought in the 1939 Polish-German War: 36,000 of them fell on the battlefields including those of Poznan, Modlin and Kutno.[22]

The Towns

While the Jews of Bielorussia have similar characteristics to those of other East European Jews, what distinguished them in particular is the high proportion of manual laborers. We should not exclude from these a certain group of shopkeepers and pedlars, who travelled about the villages throughout the week with their wagons. In the descriptions of witnesses from many towns we find the sentence: "Our town was a laboring town." The high moral level of Jewish family life, the elementary cell of national continuity, was maintained and reinforced in Eastern Europe Jewish parents' devotion to their children. Their concern for their health, studies and future were among their basic values.

The Eastern European Jews' centrality to their country's economy, their high degree of productivity in craft, industry and agriculture, the ramified institutions of Jewish autonomy ever since the 'Committee of the State of Lithuania' (The Committee of Four Countries — in the 16th to 18th centuries), their dynamic social and cultural lives — all these gave many Jews a sense of relative stability. "It was impossible to imagine that there was any other place in the world where Jews could conduct so normal a way of life as among us before the *Churban* (destruction).[23]

The 'Jewish Quarter' that in many countries turned into a ghetto, was here the 'Jewish street' where the Yiddish language reigned and where Jews were not deterred from conducting themselves according to their own customs and from appearing in their Jewish garb.

How did the Eastern European Jews overcome the limitations imposed upon them, as a barely-tolerated minority? They succeeded in this due to the *shtetl* (town) which some view as a unique way of life for these Jews. As early as the nineteenth century, Jews in many towns of eastern Poland had become almost the only representatives of the urban class. Urban commerce and a large part of the various crafts were concentrated in Jewish shops and workshops, while the urban Christians turned to the suburbs and carried on in semi-agricultural existences. It was in this way that the Jewish shtetl grew as a social and communal form, putting its stamp upon the organization of Jewish society in Eastern Europe. In the shtetls the Jews ceased being a tolerated, and in many cases an untolerated, minority of the large city. Here the Jew turned into a dominant factor, quantitatively and qualitatively. In many towns there were almost no Christian businessmen or craftsmen. The Christian minority was composed of a majority of farmers and a minority of officials. In the town, where there was a Jewish majority, many Jews had the feeling that the town's population and life was "one hundred percent Jewish;" but even in towns with a Christian majority, the Jew did not feel himself a minority in his shtetl. In a certain sense, the shtetl was for Jewish life what the village was for Christian life. The shtetl Jew knew that he was

Introduction

in exile ("Because of our sins we were exiled from our country"), but in his everyday life he felt "at home" wherever he was living. The shtetl Jew's attachment to nature, to fields and forests, was great. Jewish literature on the shtetl is replete with descriptions of nature. The variety of crafts in which the Bielorussian Jews occupied themselves was large: wood-turning, blacksmithing, metalworking, copperworking, tinsmithing, building, carpentry, soapmaking, ropemaking, bookbinding, pottery, leather-tanning, wheelmaking, harness-making, carving, tile-making, painting, beerbrewing, tailoring, shoemaking. They were furriers; they made hats and corsets; sewed sacks; did weaving, sewing, glazing, hoopmaking, and made jewelry. They were machinists, watchmakers, photographers, denticians, bakers, millers, oilpressers, candlemakers, shoepolish-makers, confectionists, sausage-makers, chimney sweeps, well-diggers. They repaired clay objects with wire. Among the nonprofessional occupations were the wagoneers, water-drawers, woodchoppers and porters. The free professions included the traditional teachers (melameds), the ritual slaughterers, synagogue attendants, cantors, scribes and musicians. "The Jewish population was composed mainly of ordinary people — workers, Jewish types like those Zalman Schneour described in histories: honest, laboring, strong and good-hearted, who were ready always to defend Jewish honor and did so in time of need."[24]

Surrounding the towns were Jewish villages which in addition to farming, were also occupied in crafts, shopkeeping and inn-keeping on the highways. Jewish families in the villages often gave their children a Jewish and a general education, won an honorable status in their gentile environment and established a cultural aristocracy within it.

Ways of Life

Bielorussian and Lithuanian Jews over the course of generations, joined together their ways of life and cultural creativity to create 'Lithuanian Jewry' (the 'Litwaks'). There were many centers of Bielorussian Jewry and of its cultural creativity, but the most central among them were Minsk and Vilno, as which here were conducted a wide range of intensive Jewish activities, and whose personalities and creations radiated over Bielorussia and Lithuania and far beyond it.

Bielorussian Jews were marked by their love of Torah study. Jews scrimped in their food and pawned their pillows and blankets for their children's education. Torah study was a challenge. The Bielorussian Jew's aspiration to be diligent and "rise in the Torah ladder" (*Shteigen in lernen*) was reflected upon by an elder from the Slobodka *yeshiva*: "If I knew that I would remain what I am, I would take my own life; but if I hadn't hoped to be like the Gaon of Vilno I would not have succeeded even in being what I am today."

An important step in Torah study in Bielorussia had been the establishment of the Volozhin *yeshiva* in 1802 by Rabbi Chaim, a student of the famous Gaon of Vilno. That *yeshiva* was a central site of Torah study in the Jewish world for close to 140 years (until 1940). The region included other *yeshivas* famous in the Jewish world: Vilno, Minsk, Slutzk, Bobruisk, Grodno, Slonim, Mir, Eishishok (Ejsyszki), Radun, Lida, Slobodka, Novogrudok and Baranowicze. The *yeshiva* students studied day and night, making do with little, they were frequently fed by the local Jewish population[25], and often slept on a bench in the study house, because "that was the way of the Torah".

This Jewry's culture, however, is not measured only by its spiritual creations but also, and perhaps mainly, by its way of life. Joshua Heschel writes:

"The pattern of life of a people is more significant than the pattern of its art. What counts most is not expression, but existence itself. To appraise adequately the East European period in Jewish history, I had to inquire into the life-feeling and life-style of the people. This led to the conclusions that in this period our people attained the highest degree of inwardness. I feel justified in saying that it was a golden age in Jewish history, in the history of the Jewish soul … That era was the Song of Songs of Jewish history during the last two thousand years."[26]

In Bielorussia, as in the other Jewish communities in Eastern Europe, the Jews cultivated an elaborate system of institutions for mutual aid based on the fulfillment of the commandments relating to man's relationship to man, enhancing the whole responsibility for the individual in his distress and preserving Jewish existence. They developed the *Hachnasat Orchim* (travelers' facilities), *G'milut Hassadim* (free loans), *Bikur Holim* (visitation of the sick), *Matan Be'seter* (charitable gifts-anonymous, in order not to embarrass the recipient), *Linat Lai'la* (night lodgings), *Hachnassat Kalah* (to provide the new and needy bride with the requisites for her wedding), *Yoldot Aniot* (to care for needy nursing mothers and pay for the circumcision), *Lechem Ani'im* (bread for the poor), *Ma'ot Hittim* (matzot for Passover), *M'angei Shabbat* (to provide the Sabbath's needs), *Pidyon Shvu'im* (to ransom prisoners), *Poalei Zedek* (to do justice), *Machzikei Yetomim* (care of orphans), and more. If the individual did not have a solution for his distress he had the weapon of "stopping the Torah reading," by going up to the synagogue rostrum, striking the table with his hand and calling out: "Sirs, I am holding up the Reading!" The Reading was stopped until the audience and its leaders promised that the evil would be corrected.

The Bielorussian Jews created an environment of their own and were influenced only to a very limited extent by their surroundings. Despite the severe social differences and tensions in the Jewish town society, it was an organic society spiritually and in its way of life. It could however not 'digest' the exception. There were hardly any cases of assimilation in the shtetl.

Lingual assimilation was also very rare. By law, the Polish language was studied in all the schools. Polish literature also impressed young Jewish students, but the Polish language as a spoken language was hardly adopted by Jewish youth in the region. The Bielorussian language in its Jewish dialect was only a language for communication with the neighborhood farmers and no more. The Jews felt themselves clearly superior to the Bielorussian culture. However, among Bielorussian Jewish intellectuals who had gained their education in Tzarist Russia, the great influences of the Russian language and literature was evident. In some intellectual homes in the larger cities, before World War I, parents desired that Russian become their children's first language so they would not fail to enter secondary school. A 'good education' included the governess speaking a foreign language, the study of French, and playing the piano. These intellectuals, however, formed only a thin stratum of the Jewish public. The Yiddish language in the region was replete with Slavsims which had taken hold and wandered with Jewish emigration to the far corners of the Jewish diaspora.

Bielorussian Jewry included a respectable stratum of great scholars, but Torah study was shared by wide sections of the people. The Jew carried out his dialogue with his Creator using "sayings" from the Psalms and, even if he did not always understand what the words meant, he knew how to put his sight at the right place in the quotation. Zalman Schneour's *The Jews of Shklov* and *Noah Pandre* grew out of Bielorussian Jewish life. The *Beit Hamidrash* (the study hall) and synagogue was a second home for many Jews. At the break of day the shoemaker went there, along with the tailor, the watchmaker, wagoneer, small shopkeeper, the rich businessman and the pauper. Some studied the 'daily page'. The common people, loved to study the Parables, *Ein Yaakov* and midrash. Here the Jew enjoyed the teachings, the eloquence and melody of a *maggid* who had just happened to stop by. This 'maggidism' was prevalent among the Bielorussian Jews and was an art, in its own right. The *maggid* combined Torah, melody and a moral lesson, with the aid of parables and the Agaddah, in a popular form understood by all who listened.

To some degree the Bet-Hamidrash also served as a meeting place, where daily matters, state affairs, politics and the like were discussed. However, Torah study was in the Jew's eyes the foundation of the world. The mother's lullaby was "Torah is more precious than s'chora (goods)". A Jew obtaining a Torah scholar as a son-in-law gave him his mezonot (food) for a number of years and sometimes all his life. Study was a kind of an aesthetic experience. Study was also casuistry and sometimes 'hair-splitting'. The Bielorussian Jew was marked by the 'Lithuanian sharpness' and the telling response, but not by these alone.

"Life came from the inner richness of their being, from the polarity of reasons and feeling, of joy and sorrow, from the mixture of intellectualism and mysticism ... There were many who did not trust words, and their deepest thoughts would find expression in a sigh. Sorrow was their second soul, and the vocabulary of their heart consisted of one sound: "oi" when there was more than the heart could say."[27]

Together with these attributes, Bielorussian Jews were endowed with a deep sense of practicality. The Bielorussian Jews strove to the point: he did not flutter in the upper spheres, did not rely on miracles. In this Jewry, as in Lithuanian Jewry in general, only few dealt with the mysticism of the Kabalah. The false messianic movements had taken very little hold. Hassidism had penetrated here during the 1770s but had been denounced by the Gaon of Vilno. Bielorussian Jews leaned towards realistic thinking and rejected 'masters of the sign,' fortune-tellers and 'faith healers'. Unlike Hassidim in other regions, the Habad Hassidim and disciples of the author of the *Tanya* diligently studied the Talmud and Commentaries. The cult of the 'Zaddik' as a wonder-worker was also not prevalent; their attitudes towards secular learning was not as hostile as in the other places. The heirs of the great Rabbi Aharon of Karlin did not seek wealth nor look for outer splendor like the Zaddikim of Vohlynia and the Ukraine. On the contrary, they maintained a tradition of taking money from their hassidim and distributing it to the poor among them. The great Rabbi Aharon stood at the side of the poorer population, as did those who came after him.

The Gaon of Vilno and his students waged a bitter war against Hassidism. The *mitnaged* (opponent of Hassidism) lived in a world of spiritual sobriety as compared to the Hassid's spiritual intoxication. During the last quarter of the nineteenth century, the bitterness of the war between the *Mitnagdim and Hassidim* abated, even though the differences in views and customs remained as they had been. The more restrained attacks against Hassidism coincided with the declining influence of religion among the non-Hassidic population.

The Enlightenment movement in Bielorussia (and also in Lithuania), unlike Germany and Galicia, was permeated by a national spirit and enriched the Hebrew language. The Enlightenment also created a Yiddish literature. It also brought on a wave, though small, of assimilation.

The Mussar (Ethics) movement put a deep stamp upon Bielorussian Jews. Israel Salanter (1810–1883), one of the movement's outstanding thinkers, feared the connection between Enlightenment and assimilation. As against the Enlightenment's call to "know the world", Rabbi Salanter called out: "Know Judaism! Know thyself!" ("Seventy years a man lives with himself and does not know himself"). Rabbi Salanter sought to bring the Jewish individual, by way of the Torah, to good deeds that would shape him into a better person. Here is the source of the great social sensitivity of the Mussar movement: "The other's physical needs are the concern of my soul."

The 'Hibat Zion' (pre-Zionist) movement reached the Jewish communities in Bielorussia. Political Zionism aroused strong emotions in the region which was the cradle of two great movements. The first, the Poalei Zion Socialist Zionist movement appeared there at the end of the nineteenth century (at Minsk in 1897), and then spread to Jewish centers throughout the world. The second was the Jewish Socialist Workers Party 'Bund' founded in Vilno in October 1897 and also spread to major Jewish communities. It was characteristic of Eastern European Jews that socialist Jewish parties, essentially secular in nature like Poalei Zion, the Bund and part of the Communists, included Jews who conducted traditional and even religious lives without their seeing any contradiction between their ways of life and their socialist views. Bielorussian Jewry produced a long and impressive line of famous Jewish personalities, party leaders and famous writers.

Eastern European Jewry placed its stamp on the character of Jewish parties throughout the world even until this very day. It was not only the political framework. Almost all the Jewish parties were messianic and utopian movements with some element of universalism. Every party cultivated activities in the social and economic fields; published a paper; established a youth movement; cultural institutions; economic enterprises; established a moral discipline; a spirit of volunteering and a 'final goal'. Zionist was not the program of a political movement alone, and although they did not actually join a political party it was shared by most of the Jewish people with the exception of the 'Bund' and Communists. In the people's eyes Zionism was the quintessence of Judaism: Palestine symbolized hope. The Jewish 'street' was Zionist even though in some places the 'Bund' was better organized and more militant.

In most towns, the parties revolved around some central person or group of persons and were aroused to activity as a result of special occurrences, like elections to the Zionist Congress, the Sejm (Polish parliament), or the municipalities. Some of the Jewish youth, though relatively few, were active within the ranks of the illegal Communist Party. The youth movements filled a particular role in the Bielorussian towns. These were first established in the 1920s. The largest movements in the region were Hashomer Hatzair, Hechalutz, Hechalutz Hatzair, Betar, Gordonia, Freiheit, Hanoar Hatzioni and Skif (the Bund). Many towns had a number of movements and the larger centers contained all of them. The youth movements aroused in young Jews the call to independence, activity, joy in living and self-fulfillment. In some towns they were at times more active than all the adult parties put together. In essence, they provided the realistic, though limited alternative to the reality of shtetl life.

A second weighty factor shaping Bielorussian Jewish life between the two world wars was Jewish education (in Hebrew and Yiddish): the heders, Talmud Torahs, Tachkemoni, Yavne, Yiueo (Yiddish schools) and, first and foremost, the network of Tarbut schools. The latter was the source of the phenomenon of Hebrew being spoken by many Bielorussian Jews: both in school and outside it and in the youth movements. The Hebrew schools also served as the reservoir of members for the youth movements.

The Bielorussian Jews between the two world wars were rich in welfare, cultural and educational institutions. In the town of Volkovisk, which had 5,130 Jews in 1921, for example, there was a Herzlia Hebrew High school; five Hebrew schools (Tarbut, Tachkemoni, Yavne, Talmud Torah, Kadima); a number of heders; a Yiddish school; a business school; and an old-age home; lodgings for travellers and the needy; a hospital; a small yeshiva; an orphanage; a bank; a 'peoples' bank; a business bank; a free loan society; eleven batei midrash; a synagogue; a Tarbut library; a people's library; two cemeteries; a Zionist Organization; parties: Hitachdut; Mizrachi; Poalei Zion; Bund; Hashomer Hatzair, Gordonia; Freiheit; Zukunft; and Betar.[29] Most of the institutions mentioned were found in many Bielorussian towns.

In the 1930s, and despite the growing unrest in Poland, the Bielorussian Jews demonstrated an astonishing vitality in the internal organization of their lives. Against the growing antisemitic hostility they organized, in some places, self-defense organizations, which included members of the Polish army reserves and older members of the youth movements. However, with the rise of Nazism and the Polish government's anti-Jewish policies, and in view of the critical political events in Europe, the sense of relative security collapsed completely and confusion grew. Two letters, by a husband and his wife, written in Pinsk in 1939 reflect these feelings.[30] In the wife's letter of May 20 1939 we read:

> Recent events in the world [the Nazi occupation of Czechoslovakia and Danzig] and especially our troubles and the humiliating distress deprive me ... of any interest in anything ... You are happy in blessed America ... You are at least sure about the morrow ... And we know what awaits us here, the Middle Ages are returning. They want to purify the world with our blood ... We are filled with despair and frustration ...

And the husband, after listing the antisemitic acts of discrimination by the government, writes:

> They have already taken off the white glove from their Antisemitism and are taking Hitler's path, and all their thoughts are how to find ways to push us out. And so, in this situation, what is our hope? I have come to the conclusion that we must save from the conflagration what can be saved, because we are in a situation before a great conflagration and all my desire is to save my children ... Here, however, is our real tragedy, because there is nowhere to send them ...

Notes

1. Nicholas Vakar, *Belorussia: The Making of a Nation* (Cambridge, Mass., 1956), p. 43; Ivan S. Lubachko, *Belorussia Under Soviet Rule, 1917–1957* (Lexington, 1972), pp. 1, 5.

2. Vakar, op. cit., pp. 74, 105; Lubachko, op. cit., p. 128.
3. Lubachko, op. cit., pp. 128–129. He estimates that in 1931 the national composition of the population in Bielorussia was as follows:

Belorussians	3,460,900	77.9%
Jews	450,000	10.2%
Poles	260,000	5.9%
Russians	101,000	2.3%
Lithuanians	70,400	1.6%
Ukrainians	60,200	1.3%
Germans	25,500	0.6%
Others	9,800	0.2%

4. Ibid., p. 132.
5. Vakar, op. cit., p. 14.
6. Bohdan Wasiutynski, *Ludnosc zydowska w Polsce w Wiekach XIX i XX* (The Jewish People in Poland in the Nineteenth and Twentieth Centuries) (Warsaw, 1930), pp. 5, 82. According to a Vilno region census held in 1919, the Jewish population there numbered 63,849, or 12.8 percent of the total.
7. Ya'akov Eliasberg, *Beolam Hahafechot* (In a World of Upheavals) (Jerusalem, 1965), pp. 12–20; Szyja Bronsztejn, *Ludnosc żydowska w Polsce w okresie miedzywojennym* (The Jewish People in Poland in the Inter-War Period) (Wroclaw-Warsaw, 1963), p. 92.
8. Jacob Leszczynski, "Dos Poilishe Yidentum Erev der Hitler-Katastrofe" (Polish Jewry on the Eve of the Hitler Catastrophe), *Allgemeine Encyclopedie* (Yiddish), cf. under "Yidn" (New York, 1963); Bronsztejn, op. cit., p. 112.
9. Bronsztejn, op. cit., p. 80. The weekly outlay for a Jewish family in a number of places came to 10 zloty. For this sum the following could be bought in Warsaw in 1932: 7 kilos of bread, 7 kilos of potatoes, 7 litres of milk, 5 eggs, 1 kilo of meat (veal) and 1 kilo of sugar.
10. Rafael Mahler, *Yehudei Polin bein shtei milchamot olam* (The Jews of Poland Between the Two World Wars) (Tel Aviv, 1969), pp. 118–137.
11. Artur Eisenbach, *Hitlerowska politika zaglady Zydow* (The Hitlerian Policy of the Annihilation of the Jews) (Warsaw, 1961), p. 117.
12. A. Manes, "Die Mizrach-Europaiesh Tkufe in der Yiddisher Geshichte" (The East European Period in Jewish History), *Allgemeine Encyclopedie*, cf. under "Yidn".
13. Bernard D. Weinryb, *The Jews in the Soviet Satellites* (Syracuse, 1953), p. 112.

14. Bronsztejn, op. cit., p. 220.
15. Azriel Shochat, "Toldot Kehillat Pinsk, 1581–1941" (The History of Pinsks Jewish Community, 1581–1941), in *Sefer Zikaron Pinsk* (Pinsk Book) (Tel Aviv, 1969), vol. 1, part 2, p. 208.
16. Shmuel Ettinger, *Toldot Am Yisrael Ba'et Hachadasha* (Tel Aviv, 1969), p. 28.
17. Mahler, op. cit., p. 182.
18. Shimshon Tapuach "Agrikultur bei Yidn in Poilen tswishn beide Welt-Milchomes" (Agriculture Among Jews in Poland Between the Two World Wars), in YIVO, *Shtudies Wegn Yidn in Poilen, 1919–1939* (New York, 1974), p. 372.
19. Ibid., p. 421.
20. Mahler, op. cit., p. 161.
21. Manes, op. cit., p. 404.
22. Ber Mark, Zycie i walka warszawskiego Getta (The Life and Struggle of the Warsaw Ghetto) (Warsaw, 1959), p. 21.
23. Yad Vashem (YV) testimony 03/2154 (Avraham Shpitkovsky).
24. Mordechai Bezdersky, testimony in *Sefer Zikaron Yanov al-yad Pinsk* (Yanov near Pinsk Memorial Book) (Jerusalem, 1969), p. 217.
25. But Rabbi Chaim Volozhyner abolished the custom of 'eating days', i.e., the allocation of yeshiva students to different householders who would feed them each day. Yeshiva students received weekly money allocations ('Wocher') instead of food. At the Mir yeshiva, students also received money allocations. In Eishishok, householders used to bring food to the students at the yeshiva.
26. Abraham Y. Heschel, *The Earth is the Lord's* (New York, 1949), pp. 10, 81.
27. Ibid., pp. 15–16.
28. Ze'ev Rabinowitz, *Hachassidut Halita'it Mireshit Ve-ad Yameinu* (Lithuanian Chassidism from the Beginning to Today) (Jerusalem, 1961), p. 59.
29. YV M-1/Q-512 (Raya Maretzka).
30. Shochat, op. cit., pp. 220–221.

Acknowledgements

My deep appreciation for Moreshet — Mordechaj Anielevich Memorial and for Awraham Herman Institute of Contemporary Jewry which assisted in publishing this book.

My great esteem for Prof. Yehuda Bauer — Head of the "Martyrs and Heroes Rememberance Authority-Yad Vashem" for his advice and devotion and Prof. Dalya Offer from Awraham Herman Institute of Contemporary Jewry for her assistance in bringing about the publication of this book.

Shalon Cholawsky

CHAPTER 1

The Jews of Bielorussia under Soviet Rule: 1939–1941

Soviet Political Measures in the Occupied Territories

The fate of Western Bielorussia had been determined by the non-aggression pact between the USSR and Germany on 23 August 1939; — the so-called "Ribbentrop-Molotov Pact." Clause two of the "secret additional codicil" to the non-aggression pact states:

> In the event of a new organization, territorial and political, of the territories pertaining to the state of Poland, the border of the areas of influence between Germany and the USSR will be approximately along the lines of the Narev-Visla-San rivers.[1]

On 1 September, 1939 the German armies invaded Poland spearheaded with tanks and supported by the air force in a swift campaign which defeated the Polish Army. The Germans' rapid advance eastward prompted the Soviets to occupy their share of the territory of the collapsing Polish state.

On 17 September 1939 the Red Army crossed the western Polish border. Russian Foreign Minister Molotov broadcast on the radio that day saying that, in view of the collapse of the Polish state, the Soviet government had instructed the Red Army to cross the border and take the population of Western Ukraine and Western Bielorussia under its protection.

On 28 September 1939 a "Border and Friendship Pact between Germany and the USSR" was concluded with the stipulation that the Bug River would be the border between Germany and the USSR. According to that agreement, Lithuania remained within the Soviet sphere of influence.

In October 1939 a treaty was signed by the USSR and Lithuania transferring the city of Vilna and its environs, including a population of 457,000 persons, most of whom were not Lithuanians, to Lithuania. The Soviet government justified this step by its consideration for the historic past and the aspirations of the Lithuanian people. Soviet forces continued to be stationed in Lithuania, as in the other Baltic countries, and Lithuania was granted quasi-independence.

The territories annexed to the Soviet Union included an area of 108,000 square kilometers in Western Bielorussia, with a population of 4.8 million inhabitants; 88,000 square kilometers in Western Ukraine, with a population of eight million; making a total of 196,000 square kilometers with 13 million inhabitants.[2]

The Soviet authorities in the annexed territories began to accelerate measures to Sovietize the whole area and, parallel to that, to "Bielorussianize" Western Bielorussia and "Ukrainize" Western Ukraine, giving national and political preferment to the Bielorussian and Ukrainian populations by granting them key positions and power.

On 22 October 1939, elections to the National Assembly were held in the annexed territories. A total of 926 delegates were elected to the Western Bielorussian National Assembly; of these 72 (7.77 percent) were Jews. (The Jewish population in general then totalled 8.5–9 percent).[3]

On 29 October 1939, the Western Bielorussian National Assembly convened in Bialystok and voted to unite Western Bielorussia with the Soviet Socialist Republic of Bielorussia. The National Assembly also voted to nationalize the large estates, industry and the banks.[4]

On 24 March 1940 elections were conducted in Western Bielorussia for the Supreme Soviet and the Soviet of Nations. Of the 298 persons elected to the Western Bielorussian Soviet, 9 were Jewish (4.5 percent of the total).[5]

An important link in the Sovietization process was the citizenship law of 29 November 1939, granting Soviet citizenship to the following categories of the population:

1. All persons who had lived in the regions of Western Bielorussia and Western Ukraine on the days of their annexation to the USSR (1–2 November 1939); and,
2. Anyone who arrived in these areas as a result of the exchange of population agreement between Germany and the USSR, as well as all those who had come from Vilna after its transfer to Lithuania.

This citizenship law served as the dividing line for the many refugees who came to the east from western, Nazi-occupied, Poland.

The Number of Jews in the Annexed Territories

According to the Polish population census of 1931 and the real natural increase until 1939, the number of Jews in Western Bielorussia on the eve of World War II came to approximately 485,000. The Jewish population in Vilna and its environs which had been transferred to Lithuania in October 1939 numbered 63,000. The Jewish population remaining within the area of Western Bielorussia (excluding the refugees) came to about 422,000 persons. The number of Jews in the Vilna (excluding the city of Vilna and its immediate environs), Novogrudok and Polesie districts was more than 260,000. The number of Jews in all the areas annexed by the USSR came to 1,309,000.

How the Jews Received the Russians

The Jewish population in Western Bielorussia received the Red Army with great joy. This spontaneous reaction included almost all sections of the population. The rumors of the Polish Army's collapse, the fall of the Polish state, and the deep-rooted fear of the German invasion, had left feelings of depression within the Jewish public as a whole. The sudden appearance of a mighty army backed by a tremendous power, promising the end of the war and the prevention of a German invasion, now led to a feeling of salvation. Jews sighed in relief. A veteran Hebrew teacher in Slonim relates:

> After the fall of Poland the Jewish population received the Soviet Army on its entry into the city with bread and wine, with a shower of flowers that were thrown at the soldiers, with drums and dances. The first tankist to roll into the city at the head of the file of tanks, paused for a moment by the Victoria Hotel, stood up on his tank and declared with great festivity: "The Red Army bears on its banner, for all the population without distinction of religion or nationality, equality and fraternity." The Slonim Jews threw themselves into the arms of the Soviet soldiers, embraced them and kissed them. The festivities continued three days. Liquor flowed like water and speeches were made in the spirit of Communism. Many believed that our salvation had come and that the Soviet Russians were our messiah. The gentiles whispered and said: "Now the Jewish government has come."[6]

The Jewish population still remembered the discriminatory policies towards the Jewish citizens that had been conducted by the Polish authorities and the Polish Army. The Red Army's courteous attitude towards the population, and towards children in particular, won the hearts of many: "They pat the children's heads." People from all sectors of the population burst into the streets, "kissed the cavalry horses. The Red Army whose attitude towards us is very friendly ..."[7]

A Jew from the town of Dereczyn related:

> "... It is hard to describe our joy. It seemed to us that this was the happiest day in our lives. All of the Jewish population, and also many non-Jews, came out to welcome the Soviet saviors ... They embraced and kissed every one who came to greet them. To the children they distributed red flags ... Our joy had no bounds ... Almost the days of the Messiah ..."[8]

The radio announced: "See, in Berlin — it is dark, in London dark. Here (these) light and happiness." However, there were also more sober persons who saw the lurking dangers. What is more, even among the large majority who rejoiced at the coming of the Red Army, there were dark forebodings that had been put off but not erased by the joy at the immediate salvation.

The way in which the Jewish population of Western Bielorussia and Western Ukraine received the Russians in September 1939 had implications for the Jews. As to how the local population later reacted towards the Jews, we should point out that we are speaking here of the attitude of the Jews in receiving the Red Army rather than the Soviet regime. We shall now examine the motives behind this reception by the Jewish population.

There were three basic motives:

1. ideological identification;
2. expectations of social changes among the socially depressed circles (this motive is only very partially correlated to ideological identification); and,
3. reliance upon the tremendous defense force providing protection from immediate troubles and long-range dangers.

Although we do not have statistics on the number of Jewish Communists in Western Bielorussia, we would not be mistaken in affirming that the circles among the Jewish population of this region identifying themselves ideologically with the Soviet regime were quite limited. We need not view all those who joined themselves ideologically with the regime as Communists. The Communists, too, were divided into two groups: those who were absorbed into the Soviet apparatus and continued to identify themselves with the regime, and Communists who had been active in the past, who had been imprisoned in Poland, and now became "undesirables" for the Soviet regime.[9]

The second group in particular included Jewish refugees from Western Poland. The Soviet regime eyed them with a great measure of suspicion as being tainted with the sin of Trotskyism, like most members of the Polish Communist Party in the past, and as the first candidates for imprisonment or deportation despite their past underground activities, their devotion and their achievements. They were left in a corner, depressed, laden with deep pain and disappointment.[10] The Jewish Communist who identified themselves with the Soviet regime formed only a narrow support for the expanding Soviet administration. In the town of David-Horodok "the main elements to celebrate the Soviet rule were the Jewish Communists ... the Communist rank and file was composed of 6–7 Jews and 3–4 Poles." In other places the numbers were even smaller.

For the "ordinary people" the coming of the Russians was an awakening. It seemed that the time of the poor and oppressed had finally come. In the poorer Jewish sections of the cities and towns bustling with work, poverty and Torah, expectations rose of change in social status and standards of living. The poor sensed that their time had come and that the era of the wealthy and their spacious homes had passed. It was these people who volunteered for the "peoples' militia," wore the hat with the ribbon giving them a kind of "government" status, and marched with rifles on their shoulders on the sidewalks of the city center with a confidence they had never known before.

"Shmuel-Yossel, one of the inhabitants of Michaliszok, who had received a "peoples' police" hat and a rifle, awoke early in the morning and came to the rich storekeeper for whom his sisters had worked for many years, banged on the door vigorously: "Open!" From within came the dull scared voice of the storekeeper: "Who's there?"

"Shmuel-Yossel!"

"What Shmuel-Yossel?"

"Shmuel-Yossel the government!" was the sure and laconic reply."[11]

The majority of the Jewish population viewed the Red Army as their salvation from immediate danger. The collapse of Polish rule had created ugly moods. In a considerable number of cities, the Jews could expect robbery and rioting on the part of the local population. In Slonim a new drive for recruits for the Polish Army was ordered in the course of which the windows of Jewish homes were shattered. Hooligans ran wild in the streets and Jews suffered murderous blows. There were stubborn rumors that the Poles were preparing a pogram against the Jews. The town of Lenin in Polesie was left abandoned for a number of days without any Polish government. Rumors spread that the neighborhood peasants were preparing to attack the town, to loot and do their worst. Young Jews organized for defense. No wonder, then, that Jews looked upon the Red Army as their savior and welcomed it with joy and flowers. The main thing, however, was that the Jews were freed of the deep fears gnawing at many Jewish hearts for their very lives in view of the German invasion of Poland.

"When I came home healthy and whole from the adventures of this miserable war, I was a happy man ... We were bathed in a feeling of security after days of confusion and depression. We thought that for us the war had already ended. We were under the protection of the Soviet Union, a tremendous power of 200 million inhabitants ... The Soviet Union was in our eyes in those days the most secure fortress of all against fascist expansion."[12]

A Jew of David-Horodok related:

> "A high ranking officer marching at the head of the [Red] Army, on seeing among those standing on the sidewalk old Velvel Raishkes, went up to him and said, "We have to live, old man, we have to live!" His words aroused indescribable enthusiasm. All those days people were intoxicated with joy and happiness."[13]

The officer's words to the old Jew would certainly have impressed those standing near because of the human touch in them, especially when this had been demonstrated by a soldier. But the enthusiastic response of the Jews of the town was for the stress of his remarks ("We have to live!") in all their simplicity and yet with tremendous weight, in view of the fears for their lives. Particularly pleased were the refugees from Poland who had begun to arrive in Western Bielorussia and who had already experienced the taste of German rule in the occupied territories.

The measure to which the problem of physical existence was the dominant one in the Jew's attitudes towards the Soviet regime, may be attested to by this sober example:

> "We knew what the Zionist movement could expect from the Soviet regime; we knew it would close the way to Eretz Israel for us, but we also knew that it first of all promised us our lives and, therefore, no wonder that when the rumor became true and we saw the first tanks of the Russian Army in the town, the whole town came to greet them with flowers and with a demonstration of our joy at their coming" ...[14]

In the later experiences of the Jews of Western Bielorussia who came under the Soviet regime, with all their difficulties, that existential moment remained in the balance. "However, after all the suffering ... we were sure of our lives."

There were, however, other and more careful reactions: "Already on September 17 [1939] most people were happy but the more deliberate among them were depressed."[16] One man from Dokszyce testified:

> "The Jews received the Soviet Russians indifferently. Some of them were afraid. It wasn't what we had wanted ... However, undoubtedly they were better than the Germans. On this there were no differences among Jews. Even though we were isolated from the world we received news of what was being done to Jews under the German occupation. They were suffering humiliation, hunger and the fear of death."[17]

The rumors of the "humiliation, hunger and fear of death," coming from the areas under German occupation, moved even the more cautious of the Jews to draw the conclusion: "They are better than the Germans." That was a very low common denominator but one that no one questioned.

Jewish Refugees from Polish Areas under German Occupation

With the outbreak of the German-Polish War, a stream of Polish refugees began to flow from western Poland eastward. At the end of that campaign some of the refugees returned to their homes but, at the same time, the eastward stream increased and exceeded the numbers of those returning.

On 28 September 1939, the day when the German-USSR "Borders and Friendship Agreement" was concluded in Moscow, another secret pact was also concluded, to the effect that "the Government of the USSR will put no difficulties in the way of the German nation or persons of German origin dwelling in the territories subject to its control, to emigrate, if they desire to do so, to Germany or to the territories within the sphere of its control …

A similar obligation is undertaken by the Government of the German Reich concerning persons of Ukrainian or Bielorussian origin populating the territories within the sphere of its control …"[18]

On 16 November 1939 the governments of Germany and the USSR agreed on the practical arrangements concerning this emigration. The Germans attempted to apply this secret agreement to Jews as well, and registered them as "Ukrainians of the Jewish faith" and "Bielorussians of the Jewish faith" in Radom, Piotrkov and Czestochowa. The Soviets, however, refused to recognize these Jews as "Bielorussians" or "Ukrainians" and refused them transit. The Germans encouraged the flight eastward and the Russians conducted searches along the border. Many Jews were trapped in the border area, worn-out from cold and hunger and many of them died.[19]

It would seem that until the middle of October 1939, Soviet policy towards the refugees was ambiguous but in the second half of October the Russians' attitude towards the refugees turned hostile. In February-March 1940, when the program to issue identity cards began, the hostile attitude of the Soviets towards the refugees became stronger. The reception of Soviet citizenship by the refugees should have enhanced the prestige of the Soviet regime in the annexed territories and also served as a foil against the propaganda of the Polish Government-in-Exile. The fact, however, that most of the refugees refused to receive Soviet citizenship served to justify the authorities' attitude towards them. The refugees were charged with dual loyalty and espionage. Family ties in countries like England, the USA and Palestine were considered to be ties with enemy countries. The refugees were not permitted to settle in the larger cities. Even those refugees who did accept Soviet citizenship received identification cards with the addition of "clause 11", which meant the denial of the right to live in the large cities and a ban on dwelling in the vicinity of the Russian-German border.

The numbers of Jewish refugees coming from western Poland to the east, according to Weinryb's estimate, totalled some 300,000,[20] but their number would seem to have been much larger. We may assume that the number of refugees (not including those who returned) came to no less than 500,000. "There was hardly a house without a refugee." It is assumed that some 250,000 refugees reached Western Bielorussia. Thus, with the coming of the refugees, and the separation of Vilna and its environs from Bielorussia and their annexation to Lithuania, the Jews of Western Bielorussia numbered more than 670,000.

At the beginning, the refugee stream flowed towards the larger cities. The Jewish population of Lvov, some 100,000 before the war, grew to 180,000. Vilna, with some 60,000 Jews before the war, grew to 70,000.[21] The refugees were, as a rule, well received by the Jewish inhabitants of Western Bielorussia, who provided generous aid in the form of food, housing, medicine, and other needs.

A Refugee Committee was established in Bialystok. In several places refugee kitchens were opened. However, in spite of all this aid, the refugees still faced problems of housing, work and food. Many of them slept in railway stations, and in the synagogues. Particularly hard was the lot of the intellectuals among the refugees. The refugees were also troubled by the authorities' suspicions towards them as spies because of their social origin. When part of the refugees turned to trade, the authorities thought this a reason to charge them with anti-Soviet activities. At the close of 1939, the authorities, in a public campaign, called on the refugees to volunteer for work inside Russia. Those refugees, however, who responded to this appeal, found the conditions very hard and attempted to leave. The refugees seemed in the authorities' eyes to be a foreign element who could not be adapted to Soviet conditions.

When the Soviets offered the refugees the choice of either receiving Soviet citizenship or returning to Nazi Germany, many of them refused citizenship. There were a number of reasons for this. Firstly, many were weary of their wandering abroad and wanted to go home. Because there was very little information of what was taking place in the Nazi-occupied territories, it seemed to them that the "first storm" had passed and that life in western Poland was beginning somehow to become settled. Secondly, family ties were strong and there were those who preferred to suffer together with the members of their families among the Germans rather than to live apart. Thirdly, many of the refugees looked upon their stay in eastern Poland as only a "night's lodging". They did not want to live under the conditions of the Communist regime, especially since the regime's attitude towards them was basically negative. Some dreamed of going some place outside Europe (the USA, Palestine, etc.) after the war. Receiving Soviet citizenship, as they understood it, meant divorcing themselves from the outside world. In their increasingly distrustful attitude towards the refugees, the Soviet authorities looked upon the matter of receiving Soviet citizenship as the final test. Deportations were the Soviet Russians' answer to a problem they could not solve.

The Population and the Soviet Government

Many of the Poles living in Western Bielorussia were "settlers" — Polish Army veterans who had come to the frontier region to plant their "Polish roots" and who had received preferential treatment by the Polish authorities. After the Red Army's entry into the region, many of the Poles toyed with the idea that the USSR had perhaps come to the aid of the Polish Army. However, after Molotov's announcement on 17 September 1939, those illusions evaporated. Once the Soviet regime had established itself in the annexed territories, the Poles' attitude towards it became hostile for having lent its hand once more to Poland being partitioned. The nationalization of the Poles' lands and the arrests which followed intensified these feelings. The Bielorussian population for the most part welcomed the Red Army. The national minority's previous feelings of discrimination during the Polish era were now compensated by the Bielorussian's higher prestige.

However, while the Bielorussians' attitude toward Bielorussianization was favorable, this was not true as far as the process of Sovietization was concerned, which aroused opposition within considerable sections of the population. The Soviets conducted themselves with care towards the Bielorussians. At the outset, they nationalized only the banks and the factories but did not compel the Bielorussian peasants to join the *kolkhozes*, though Soviet propaganda attempted to convince them to do so. Only 40 *kolkhozes* were established in the spring of 1940 in Western Bielorussia.[22] After pressure was applied by the Soviet authorities, 1,115 *kolkhozes* were established by the end of 1940. Private farming was reduced in status.

Also the NKVD (Soviet secret police) made arrests among the Bielorussian population, especially those who had worked for the Polish municipal and governmental institutions. Also arrested were Bielorussian Communists who had worked in the underground during the Polish era. These arrests served to intensify the opposition of sections of the Bielorussian population to the regime.

The Meeting Between Western Bielorussian Jews and Jews of the USSR

The joy of salvation felt by the Jewish population was enhanced by meeting their relatives from the Soviet Union from whom they had been separated ever since Bielorussia's partition in 1921. The Jews of Western Bielorussia were surprised at the Soviet Jews' attachment to Jewish tradition and culture. "At the head of the village council was a Jew named Gotein. He was in his forties, the son of a rabbi from the environs of Moscow, intelligent, and knew Hebrew perfectly."[23]

The Soviet Jews told of the equality of rights in their country and their hidden ties with West Bielorussian Jews. In *A Letter Home*, a Soviet-Jewish writer who had been born in Western Bielorussia, turned to the Jews of his native region with the following words:

> "*Mazal tov*" [good luck] to you, my liberated home! My precious towns! The leatherworkers of Simorgon, the builders of Iwieniec, the machinists of Rakov, the skin-beaters of Horodok, the poor people of Kamin, the villagers from Volma, my dear teachers! You have given me unbounded love for our people and its creations. From your mouths I have learned the colorful, strong language of the masses of the House of Israel.[24]

The Beginning of the Awakening

As the memory of the meeting with the Red Army waned, there was a growing readjustment among the Jewish population of its attitude towards the Soviet regime. The older population, to varying degrees, were afraid of what was to come. The young knew less and hoped for more: their feelings of relief at having been saved from the war had not yet evaporated. The slogans of equality and justice, the simple manners of the Russian people, the charm of the Russian songs and Russian films, all spoke to their hearts. There were new possibilities for study for young people and some went to the USSR for this purpose.

The Soviets divided the population into three groups:

1. Those loyal to the Soviet regime — the Communists;
2. Enemies of the regime; and
3. "Ordinary" citizens who had to be educated to loyalty to the regime.

The authorities imposed the laws of their regime systematically and cast a feeling of fear among the population. There was very strict discipline at work. Absence or lateness implied carelessness and meant months of imprisonment. The authorities began an intensive examination into the "pasts" and social origins of the population. According to their view social origin went together with political outlook. Non-voting meant an open declaration against the Soviet regime, and voting meant a vote in favor of the regime.[25] As the authorities entrenched themselves and introduced Soviet patterns of life, wide sections of the population found themselves on the margins, some because of hostile attitudes.

The Population and the Jews

Despite the criteria of acceptable social origins and public and political past imposed by the regime in employing workers, not a few among the Jewish population found the doors open to employment and to official positions that had been tightly closed in the days of the Polish regime. Jews found positions at various levels in the municipal administration, in government offices, in public services, and the postal service. Obtaining work was vital for survival.

Most of the Jews employed in the municipal government administrations did not identify themselves with the regime, or its methods and aims, though they felt compelled to conduct themselves with reasonable loyalty, at least superficially, in order to retain their position and for fear of being suspected of disloyalty to the regime and what that might imply. The regime's local base of power included mainly Jewish and Bielorussian Communists. Nonetheless, the Jewish population as a whole was identified by the non-Jews with the Soviet regime. The paradox lay in the fact that the Soviet authorities made great efforts for Sovietization not to be identified with the Jews. They were sensitive to the German propaganda stressing the connection between the Jews and the Bolshevik regime and avoided anything that might encourage that connection. However, the reception the Jews had accorded the Red Army on 17 September 1939, and their penetration into the Soviet administration, gave an intensified impetus to such an identification and thereby enhanced the already existing antagonism between the Jewish and non-Jewish societies and intensified the hostility.

The Polish population, possessed of a strong patriotic sense, looked upon the Soviet Russians as the natural heirs of the "*Moskals*" as the Russians had been called by the Poles for many generations. The talk about the changes that had taken place in Russia, describing the essential difference between Czarist Russia and the post-revolutionary government, fell on deaf Polish ears. Anybody identified with the Soviet regime seemed in their eyes to be taking part in the destruction of the Polish state. According to the report of the "Polish Delegation"[26] on Soviet rule in eastern Poland, the entire Jewish population in these regions had adopted to an orientation tying their future to the Red Army, thereby rupturing the already very weak ties between the Polish society and the Jews. According to this report the last two weeks of September 1939, when the Red Army was about to seize the territory between the Bug and the Vistula and even before the retreat of Polish Army units, had seen the formation of Soviet military forces with the Jewish influence. In addition, the report declared that the Jews had filled most of the positions available in Soviet offices, taken over the Soviet secret police, deported hundreds of thousands of Polish intellectuals to Russia, and it was only because of the Jews that a Polish underground had not been able to develop in the area of the Soviet occupation. Those Bielorussians, too, who considered themselves close to the Soviet authorities, never became accustomed to the sight of Jews holding positions in the administration. To a certain degree, they also saw themselves deprived of their own rightful positions because of the Jews. This antagonism towards the Jews was all the more apparent amongst the Bielorussian population that was hostile to the Soviet regime.

The Poles and Bielorussians viewed the status of the Jews as "Jewish chutzpa." At that time they could not give vent to their hatred, but repressed it and waited for an opportune moment. As we know, the Soviet authorities punished anyone using the expression "*Zhid*" which had not been punishable in Polish days. Many, however, found substitutes for that word in mocking forms of Jewish names.

In David-Horodok, during the elections to the National Assembly, slips were put into the ballot boxes with the inscriptions: "Death to the Bolsheviks and the Jews," "Down with the Soviet regime," and "Long live Hitler."[27]

As Sovietization intensified, more than a few non-Jewish inhabitants began to speak openly of the day to come when the Jews would pay twofold;

with the rumors of an imminent Russian-German war they did not hide their aspirations for vengeance against the Jews. Open antisemitism however had gone underground.

Jewish Livelihoods

The process of Sovietization in the economic field affected large sections of the general population. These processes were reflected in nationalization policies, loss of economic and social status and, as a result, unemployment; and fluctuations in the currency rates of exchange. The Bielorussians were less affected because they were a village population for the most part, with little or no land, working as day-laborers for Polish landlords. The Poles were most affected.

The Jewish population was hurt because of its special economic structure (see Introduction). During the first weeks after the Soviet occupation, large enterprises and wholesale trade had already been nationalized. Small shops and craftsmen, though not nationalized immediately, were "helped" by the authorities to go bankrupt.

One great economic blow was the equalization of the exchange rates of the ruble and the Polish zloty, at a time when the former's purchasing power was one-quarter of the latter's. On 1 January 1940, the zloty ceased to be legal tender. The Red Army and administration workers who had come from the USSR raided the shops and bought everything upon which they could lay their hands. The Jews were shocked at this mad rush which testified to the great shortage of basic commodities within the Soviet Union, especially of leather and textile products. They began to smile at the well-known Soviet slogan: "We have everything." Faith in the new rulers and their power was shaken. The gap between words and reality, an important element in the process of the awakening, stood out sharply.

The Soviets stood in long queues and bought anything they found without haggling. They even bought *Talithot* (prayer-shawls) without knowing what they were. The shops, of course, soon were empty and closed. When the local population sensed the great shortage in basic commodities that prevailed in the Soviet Union, they too began to hoard what they could: bread, soap, sugar, and the like and as a result the queues for commodities lengthened.

"The queue's length is determined by the importance of the commodity. People came early and some came earlier than the early ones. This competition led to people taking their places at midnight near shops that would open at a late morning hour … The Jewish shops were emptied of their goods … The farmers, who had been accustomed to seeing the Jewish stores well stocked, yearned for days gone by."[28]

Storekeepers who kept some of their goods were charged with speculation. The grain and flax dealers joined the government offices in charge of these fields as officials, but many storekeepers and traders suddenly lost their daily bread.

As a result of the currency's declining purchasing power, the peasants cut down on the marketing of their agricultural produce. Small manufacturing plants that had been nationalized were in any case doomed to liquidation because of the heavy taxes imposed upon them and the great difficulties in obtaining raw materials. Plant owners were accepted as workers or officials in their plants and after some time imprisoned, and some of them deported. Pharmacies and two-storied houses were also nationalized.[29] The "Free Loan" funds were also nationalized. Craftsmen who attempted to maintain their shops and to work by themselves were compelled to pay heavy taxes and found it difficult to obtain raw materials. They went to work in the cooperatives and cartels. Jews who tried office-work found it difficult since they did not know Russian nor how to read and write in Bielorussian, these being the two official languages, but they studied and eventually obtained positions. Sometimes Jews found themselves as government officials in the unenviable position of middlemen between the duties of their positions and the anger and even opposition of the population to economic policies, such as the peasants having to register their animal inventories. This situation certainly did nothing to alleviate the tensions between Jews and non-Jews. In every case where employment was offered, the candidate had to prepare a detailed history of his life. Wages were low, and the costs of clothing and shoes were very high.[30]

"Social origin" served as the main and decisive criterion for the Soviet authorities' attitudes towards the citizen. Former traders were defined as being "bourgeois origin," and "class enemies." These received identification cards with supplementary "clauses" preventing them from living in a large city or in the vicinity of the border, or from leaving their places of domicile without police permission. Members of wealthy or well-established families in many cases left their homes and "went into exile" to other places in order to disappear from the 'evil eye' of authority.

"Former capitalists" looked for places of work that would "justify" their existence as citizens, while the heavy barrier of 'social origin' barred them from employment. The paradox lay in the fact that anyone who did not work was considered to be an active opponent of the regime.

When work was not to be found and the need for a livelihood great, commerce remained. Everybody traded, Jews and Christians — they traded in everything: food commodities, salt, matches, clothes and shoes. There was also currency smuggling.

Of the 30,000 Jews who volunteered for work inside the USSR, 13,500 were sent to the Donbas mining region,[31] where there were very difficult conditions and low wages. However, the harsh work regime (in which absence or lateness were judged acts of sabotage and punished as such with anything from a 25 percent wage deduction up to six months imprisonment) deterred many from volunteering to work. The Soviet authorities organized raids, imprisonment and deportations. Jewish livelihoods disappeared. The Jewish population, the storekeepers and craftsmen, gave up the struggle for trade, craft or development, and their children were taken. There began to be the fear of the threat of hunger.[32] However, there were some Jews who sensed that the situation would get even worse and that people were complaining too early.

Despite the severity of the economic situation of wide sections of the Jewish population, there were still those that found their livelihoods, however meager, and settled for that. However, one of the important motives for the greater awakening against the regime was the heavy distress caused by the methods of intimidation and informing.

Many were invited to talks with the NKVD, but no one ever told of the contents of these discussions. The method was as follows: Some generally well-accepted person who was not suspected by anyone was invited for a talk. He was reminded of his "past sins" and given the choice: imprisonment and all that implied, or cooperation with the NKVD. They then made the man sign an undertaking not to reveal to any person the contents of the discussion. To our great sorrow there were those who took this work upon themselves. Since people did not know who the collaborator was, they feared everyone.[33]

In the city of Pinsk: "The archives had remained intact. The Russians brought translators who translated the documents. Investigations were begun, opening with 'We know everything' ... The city was in great fright.

People ceased talking even with acquaintances except about the weather alone ... They stopped telling jokes."[34]

People disappeared, and in most cases it was impossible to find any trace of them.

Religion

The Soviet authorities did not impose a ban on the Jewish population's religious life, but circumscribed it considerably. Jewish religion was subjected to strong attack and persecution. From time to time the Soviet press published articles making a mockery of Jewish holidays.[35] Heavy taxes were imposed on the synagogues. Many were closed and turned into workshops, clubs and store-rooms. "The artels were set up in the synagogues: The Kozimir synagogue became a bicycle artel; the shoemakers' synagogue — a shoemakers' artel, the Talmud Torah — for carpenters; the Kalte Shul was transformed by the authorities into a furniture warehouse and the "Mark Shul" — into a club.[36] A restaurant was opened in the building of the famous Volozhin *yeshiva*. Only one synagogue remained a place of prayer and Torah study. In Kleck, the *yeshivas* turned into a club. In Slonim, they took the Ark of the Torah out of the *yeshiva* building on Christmas and installed a Christmas tree. In Mir, 6,000 sacred writings were taken out and distributed as paper for the peasants' use and the *yeshiva* building was turned into a club. A resident of Volozhin related:

> The Soviet began to confiscate the property of the wealthy and well-off. That confiscation brought economic catastrophe on the Volozhin Jews ... but nothing disturbed the Volozhin Jews so much as the confiscation of the *yeshiva* building in order to turn it into a restaurant ... The *yeshiva* boys sat outside on the ground with their books in their hands and wept.[37]

In Janow, near Pinsk, the synagogue was turned into a stable. In Vilejka, the NKVD asked the Jews to sign a declaration that they did not oppose the closing of the synagogue. The authorities justified their turning synagogues into clubs by claiming that the "workers" and the youth demanded this ...

On the other hand, the Soviet authorities did not touch the Catholic and Orthodox churches. Christians continued to pray as if nothing had happened.[38]

For their most part, Jews attempted to observe Jewish customs quietly. Marriages were conducted secretly, hurriedly, in the presence of only a small audience. "The situation recalled the Marranos in Spain."[39] When the authorities closed the ritual bath in Volozhin, the Jews secretly dug a new bath. There were Jews who did not work on the Sabbath. There were towns where, because of fear, the number of synagogue visitors diminished, but there were also places where people persisted and even increased their attendance.

With the liquidation of the Jewish *kehilla* and its institutions, the synagogue became the only public meeting place for the local Jews and members of the movements, and the only shelter for Jewish refugees. Public prayer was also conducted in *minyans* (formal groups of ten worshippers), in private homes.

Culture and Education

The Soviet authorities systematically and speedily paralyzed the formerly intensive Jewish activities in the fields of culture and education. They closed the Hebrew schools and, in most cases, turned them into schools with Yiddish as the language of instruction, but with all studies about the Jewish people and its history eliminated. Yiddish received official status. Some parents still hoped that Yiddish would serve as a barrier to assimilation. The Jewish libraries were closed. The only Jewish newspaper appearing in Western Bielorussia was the *Bialystoker Shtern*, which was published in 5,000 copies.

It is estimated that some 30,000 pupils studied in the Jewish schools in Western Bielorussia. In Bialystok, a department for teacher-training was opened and, in Pinsk, half-year courses for Yiddish teachers were supposed to open in 1941–42. Four secondary schools and 39 elementary schools in the Yiddish language were opened with 6,000 pupils in Bialystok: the teachers were local Communists without pedagogic training. A Yiddish department was opened in Vilno University, headed by Noah Prilutzky. Reading rooms were opened, and evening courses were carried out. A state Jewish theater under the literary direction of R. Broderson was also opened in Bialystok. An itinerant Yiddish theater was formed in Slonim. A production of Halkin's "Bar Koch" drew large audiences.[40] The radio alloted an hour to Yiddish broadcasts. Jewish writers established a section within the general writers' organization. Of the 200 Jewish writers who had lived in Bialystok, only 40 remained and only some of them were accepted into the writers' association. The power to decide if a candidate was to be accepted into the association was in the hands of the Jewish Communists. Many of those rejected left for the frontier towns.

A delegation of Soviet Jewish writers came to Bialystok to establish cultural ties with the Western Bielorussian Jews (among the delegation's members were Peretz Markish, Leib Kwitko, Dobroshin, Sh. Halkin, Kushnirov and others), and Jewish writers from Western Bielorussia visited Minsk, Kiev and Moscow.

Z. Akselrod, the Soviet-Jewish poet, visited Bialystok, Vilno and Kovno and warned Jewish cultural workers in these places of the danger that the authorities might close the schools. He advised the pupils' parents to apply pressure on the authorities in order to prevent this closure. The Yiddish-language schools did, indeed, survive though most of them, in the course of time, went over to Russian as the language of instruction.

In the Hebrew Gymnasium in Pinsk, studies continued for two months in Hebrew and after that Ukrainian was introduced as the language of instruction, then Russian took its place and finally Yiddish. Study of the Bible, Eretz Israel and the Jewish people were removed. Celebration of Jewish holidays was banned. No vestiges of any Jewish religious education remained. The day of rest was moved from Saturday to Sunday. The students were even forbidden to dance the traditional "*sherele*" in a folk dance contest in the Minsk district.

Many troubles befell the Jewish teachers, and especially the Hebrew teachers: "At that time one of the teachers turned to his pupils with the following words: 'Children, I am speaking to you for the last time in Hebrew.' His lips trembled as he spoke and he burst into tears, and after him all the children in the class."[41]

Jewish Public Life

The Soviet regime in Western Bielorussia put an end to all organizations that bore any kind of independent Jewish character. The Jewish *kehilla*, the autonomous Jewish framework, was dismantled. All the parties, from the Zionists to the Bund, were disbanded and barred from the day the Soviets came. The same was true for all the Jewish youth movements.

Even organizations with a purely social and professional character, like "ORT" and "TOZ" that had continued to operate for a short time, were closed. Welfare institutions like the (Gemilut Hasadim) "Free Loan", (Bikur Cholim) "Sick Visits", (Linat Laila) "Night Lodging", and the like, were closed. Political life stopped. "Jewish public life ... has disappeared ... the former institutions, Zionist, Socialist, the cultural institutions, mutual aid bodies, are disbanding." With the establishment of the Soviet regime all national and cultural life in the town came to an end. All Jewish community life, with its political parties and cultural activities, was paralyzed. The *Tarbut* and other educational institutions were closed and their activities banned absolutely. Libraries were confiscated and books found not in accord with the Communist spirit were destroyed.[42]

Underground Activity

In the addition to small groups that identified themselves with the Soviet regime, there was a measure of adaptation to the regime among wider circles, for various reasons — economic, or out of a mistaken pragmatism. It would be incorrect, however, to identify all those who seemed at that time to be adapting, as really doing so. Many Jews, and amongst them those employed by the Soviet administration or in other work, continued quietly to conduct a Jewish way of life, to observe the Sabbath and holidays, circumcision and other Jewish customs, within the family circle which continued to preserve its character.

This was a broad, popular, unorganized underground, reflecting the desire to resist the consistent policies of the authorities, and essentially a desire to maintain a Jewish way of life.

The most difficult test of all was faced by the Zionist movement and all its local branches in the occupied areas. The ban that the Soviets placed upon any contact between the Jews of the occupied territories and Eretz Israel was both sharp and surprising. At one stroke they had cut the Jews' cultural life-stream and cast a death blow at all Jewish hopes. However, the form of the ties were indeed changed, but not the ties themselves. The longing for Eretz Israel among the Jews of the annexed territories grew and deepened. Jews continued to think and dream of the Holy Land and its future. Rumors were spread of the declaration of a Jewish state on both sides of the Jordan, of a Hebrew government and Jewish ministers, a Jewish army ... The rumors spread and many did not know how much truth or illusion they held.[43]

The group of persons who bore the burden of Zionist Party activity in the Western Bielorussian towns was small. The chief leaders of the Jewish parties, Zionist and non-Zionist, had been arrested. Some had fled and the few who remained lived in fear and preferred not to draw attention to themselves. The Soviet authorities called them in for questioning with the intention of breaking those they interrogated. Some held out. The organized underground in Western Bielorussia, as in Western Ukraine, was conducted by the Zionist pioneering youth movements. The cadres of these movements had gathered at the outbreak of the War in the territories annexed by the USSR, including Vilno, which became the most important center of all.

The idea that began to crystallize in these movements was that a section of the cadres would return to the area under German occupation and to Warsaw, in order to maintain the movements there; another section would work in the underground among the youth movements in the Soviet-occupied territories, and the final group would look for ways to immigrate to Palestine.

As early as the end of September 1939, a pioneer mission of "Hashomer Hatzair" and "Dror" members had gone to southern Poland in order to attempt to cross the Romanian border. Some of them were caught, questioned and tortured.[44]

In its session in Rowno at the outbreak of the war the Hashomer Hatzair *Hanhaga Rashit* (Supreme Council) had decided to put the maximal and swift transfer of the movement's older members to Vilno at the top of its priorities with a view to their possible immigration to Palestine. The movement's branches in the annexed territories had thus been abandoned by the best of their leaders who had gone to Vilno.

At the beginning of October 1939, the Supreme Council convened in Lvov and decided to organize the underground movement. This decision is of special interest because "Hashomer Hatzair", whose ideological program included a sympathetic attitude towards the Soviet regime, had decided to organize a Zionist underground within the regime towards which it had displayed and still continued to display a positive attitude. The resolution read as follows:

> We believe that the day will come when the Soviet Union will recognize that the Jewish people's road to national and social liberation is a special one and different from that of other peoples ... The decisive force in winning the recognition of this truth is first and foremost the Zionist enterprise in Palestine

... Until then we will unite in our groups, brother with brother, fill them with content ... We will deepen our Hebrew and social content, cultivate a sympathetic attitude towards the Soviet Union and when the day comes will arise and take the road to our homeland.[45]

At a meeting of the "Hashomer Hatzair" kibbutz in Vilno on 10 November 1939, Yitzhak Zalmanson, a member of the "Hashomer Hatzair" Supreme Council, declared:

The Soviet regime is destined to bring a bright life to all those dwelling within it, but for us it holds great mourning. It brings death and it makes no difference if it is death with a kiss. We cannot be partners to the joy. The Bielorussians and the Ukrainians have met their brothers and have been liberated in the full meaning of the word, and there is therefore reason for their joy. The Jews, too, have been happy.To the best of our knowledge the Jews have not been so happy in many generations ... However, I say, it is the joy of the individual, which can be understood and perhaps also justified, *but as a national grouping [we are] destined to annihilation if the development will be the same in the future too*.[45] (Italics author)

The emphasis lay in the fact that the underground activity was being directed not *against* the Soviet regime but *for* Jewish national existence. The central slogan was: "We shall continue under all conditions and all regimes." In November 1939, Yitzhak Zalmanson went to organize the movement's activities in the annexed territories.

On New Year's Eve of 1939/40, a movement meeting was held in Rowno. Among the resolutions adopted were: the establishment of a single organization with the name of "Hashomer Hatzair in Ukraine and Western Bielorussia"; the publication of an underground paper in Hebrew *From the Depths*; the formation of underground cells, each numbering five numbers from the age of 15 to 18; study of the Hebrew language; and close cooperation with the "Dror" movement. Soon after that New Year's Eve meeting the first issue of *From the Depths* appeared printed by an underground press in Rowno operated by Chaim Geller.

On 21 March 1940, a council meeting was held at the Tzizikov *Hachshara* training farm in the Lvov area. On Passover of 1940, regional meetings were held in Slonim and Bialystok. In October 1940, seven leading members of Hashomer Hatzair were arrested. After the arrests a new leadership was established. The trial of the seven was held in Lvov in

March 1941. Their conduct at the trial was courageous and proud. They admitted their socialist-Zionist loyalties, stressed their membership in "Hashomer Hatzair." Details of the trial quickly spread throughout the movement and the underground.

Loyal members organized on their own initiative in the cities and towns. In Dokszyce the movement hid the members' flag. In Kurzeniec educational activities were carried on and contact with Vilno maintained. During the first half of 1940, Yosef Kaplan, a member of the Supreme Council who was destined to be one of the organizers of the Warsaw Ghetto revolt, visited the underground branches in Dokszyce, Vilejka, Glebokie, Dolhinov, Stolpce and Kurzeniec and left instructions to avoid debate and useless demonstrations, to put the stress on comradely relations and, of all the symbols, to preserve only the local flag.

In the winter of 1940 there was a meeting in Slonim of 30 movement leaders from 20 cities and towns, where a debate was held on the underground's activities. It was decided to organize a nomadic summer camp. In reply to Yosef Kaplan's appeal, Lolik Abilevitz, Yaakov Harlap and Shalom Volochoviansky, senior members of the movement from Nieswiezh who had only recently returned from fighting the Germans, left to organize the smuggling to Vilno of *Shomrim* and other *chalutzim* who had come from other parts of Poland. They made their headquarters in Lida, Dziewieniszky and Sokoly; near the Bielorussian-Lithuanian border. Yaakov Harlap was arrested and deported.

In Nieswiez, younger members, together with some older ones, headed the underground. Most of the members were between the ages of 15 and 17. They published an underground paper, *Our Life*, organized meetings and parties, read poems by Bialik and Tchernichovsky, the articles of Ahad Ha'am, and also Halkin's "Bar Kochba." They raised money for the "Jewish National Fund" and transferred it to Vilno, established a mutual fund, read *From the Depths* and other publications coming from Vilno, spoke Hebrew amongst themselves, listened clandestinely to the Hebrew broadcasts from Palestine, and hid Hebrew books.[47] Similar activities were conducted in Pinsk and other places.

The "Dror" movement conducted a broad range of underground activities throughout the Soviet-annexed territories. In October 1939, Yitzhak Zuckerman, who was also to be one of the commanders of the Warsaw Ghetto revolt, came from Vilno to the annexed territories to organize the underground movement.

"Dror" activists met in Lvov on New Year's Eve of 1939–40, 20 members participated, and drew up a program to be carried out in the area of the Soviet occupation. Reports were given of the activities of the underground cells. On the subject of the movement's position towards Soviet Russia, one of the participants declared:

> Our movement is socialist in content. The new regime has brought new phenomena with it. An idea is not judged only by the twists and turns in its part of fulfillment. We must look at the content in its essential elements. What is the Soviet regime for us? What is the content and what the shell? What do we share and in what differ? In view of the changes, our movement requires at this time a clarification of concepts.

On the movement's path, the council heard:

The movement must cultivate an "narodnik" type (see footnote below) to fight for the soul of our people ... We must not allow superficial, demonstrative activity ... without the decision and ratification of the center. The fundamentals of our movement are:

1. The Hebrew language as a revolutionary element in our activity
2. education and attachment to the Histadrut in Palestine (Eretz Israel)
3. education for kibbutz and communal living
4. the obligation of every member to strive towards our homeland under all conditions and in every way
5. the obligation of every member to participate in raising movement's funds.[48]

Yudke Helman, a *shaliach* (emissary from Palestine) stressed the weight of the responsibility taken upon themselves by a handful of Hechalutz activists who, to the sound of the liberating Red Army's marching and the joy of the masses of Jews, concerned themselves with the problem of the great Jewish cause.

The council participants spoke of the three central tasks set before them:

1. Zionist influence among the Jews of Russia;
2. Influencing the Soviet authorities that the Zionist cause was just; and
3. The establishment of an underground socialist-Zionist movement.

---

*members of Navodnaya Volya, the late nineteenth century Russian movement to "go to the people".

While the first two tasks were mostly "good intentions" for the future, the establishment of a network of underground cells was immediate need. According to the reports at the council, 25 underground cells had been established, equipment for an underground press had been acquired and an underground poster had been issued ("We swear in the name of Eretz Israel ... we will be the last on the wall.")[50]

Zivia Lubetkin, also destined to be among the Warsaw ghetto commanders, spoke of the movement's character under clandestine conditions.

Chantshe and Frumka Plotnitzka worked in Pinsk moving children from the annexed territories to Vilno. In *Masuot Polin* (Poland's Flames), one of the activists wrote: "The Hechalutz Merkaz, our Executive (Hashomer Hatzair), and the leadership of Hanoar Hatzioni have held out and concerned themselves with constructive and planned activity ..."[51]

Hanoar Hatzioni organized its branches for underground activity. Yehoshua A. Gilboa came as a *shaliach* of the movement from Vilno to work in the annexed territories.

He related:

> "For about six weeks I moved about ... various cities and towns in the Soviet zone. We met comrades who organized holiday festivals, disseminated mimeographed programs, met to read a Hebrew book together, to sing a song of Eretz Israel ... and to find on their radios the Hebrew broadcasts from Jerusalem. One important activity was the "burial" of Hebrew and Zionist books ... Our boys and girls wrapped up the movement's symbols."[52]

In Yanov near Pinsk, in Wiszniewo and Lachwa, the Zionist youth conducted underground activities among young people. In Lachwa a "Bnei Yehuda" society was formed, whose members took an oath to speak Hebrew. Some of the young people left for Vilno. Hanoar Hatzioni also worked in the underground in other towns.

The Betar movement conducted underground activity in the annexed territories. In Pinsk, 25 Betar members left for Vilno. A second group was arrested and deported to Russia.[53] In Voronowo, members of Betar helped refugees across the border which was located near the town. Betar members also worked in the underground in other places.

Underground Activity in the Schools

In various localities there was spontaneous resistance, particularly by the students of the Hebrew schools, to the ban on the Hebrew language and the removal of Jewish content from the curriculum. These demonstrations of resistance were supported by the Zionist youth movements. On the first day of Hanukah, material printed in Hebrew was found in the pockets of the coats in the cloakroom of the Pinsk "Tarbut" Hebrew School to celebrate the holiday. When, in Stolin, the "Magen David" (Shield of David — the Jewish star) attached to the school wall was broken, second and third year students gathered the fragments and kissed them with tears in their eyes. The commissar, who was present, admitted that he had been moved by the sight.[54]

Students dared more than their teachers. In Bialystok the commissar visited the Hebrew high school and asked the principal in the presence of the students to what organization the students belonged. The principal replied: "to no organization". One girl student stood up and announced: "That is not correct. I belong to the Hashomer Hatzair organization". When the commissar left, the students reprimanded the principal for having denied the existence of the Zionist youth movements in the school. Teachers of the "Tarbut" school were considered suspect. During the elections to the local teachers' committee in Nieswiezh, the candidacy of the former principal of the "Tarbut" school, Saul Friedstein, was proposed. A teacher in the local Yiddish school moved to have his candidacy revoked because of his Zionist views. One "Tarbut" teacher stood up and declared:

> "If you mean to invalidate Saul Friedstein on the basis of his Zionist background, you must, consequently, declare most of the Jews here unfit, for they too, are Zionists. Hebrew is our living language, and the allegiance we have for Israel is sincere and unyielding. History will prove us right."[55]

Hebrew teachers who, after great soul-searching, went to work in the Yiddish or Russian-language schools, seemed in many cases, to have betrayed their Zionist past in the eyes of their students.

In the former "Tarbut" Hebrew school in Lida an underground was organized by young people from the Noar Hatzioni and Betar, who posted proclamations for teachers and students on the eve of Hanukah 1940: "Hebrew teacher, do not betray your people! Hebrew student, do not forget the heroism of the Maccabees!" As a result of this activity a number of Betar members were arrested. In one of the classes in the Soviet school in Lida, Jewish students stood up and sang the "Hatikva", and the teachers scolded them as "provocateurs".

The details mentioned above are only the tip of the iceberg of the various ways Jews employed to defend their way of life and their national attachments. The arrests, decrees, deportations and other measures adopted by the Soviets in response to the existence of forms of Jewish public life, deterred many and caused them to hide their feelings of Jewish sentiments. Relatively few, and mostly the inexperienced and innocent, dared to give expression, even hidden, to their national and Jewish identity. Some few took the risks and some paid the price.

Arrests

The arrests commenced immediately after the Red Army entered the annexed territories. The scope varied according to the population and circumstances. Sometimes there were widespread arrests among various circles, sometimes only isolated arrests, but they were always sudden as a blow, generally during the night hours. People were arrested and disappeared without leaving any traces.

In the language of the authorities, persons arrested were called "opponents of the revolution." They included Zionists, Bund members, Jewish delegates to municipal institutions, and traders. The arrests seriously harmed Jewish public life. There were also many arrests among the non-Jewish population.

In the course of time, arrests turned into an everyday matter. Any knock on the door might mean an arrest. The arrests and the fear of them became an integral part of the population's life under the Soviet regime and affected their feelings, conduct and attitudes towards the regime.

Deportations

The deportations were always mass operations and well-planned, and these too, were carried out by surprise. The deportees were taken at night, using harsh methods, and within a few hours were loaded in groups of 100–150 persons into trucks whose actual capacity was for 30 to 40 persons.

From the day they entered Poland and until the Germans invaded Russia, the Soviet authorities carried out four mass deportations:

1. The first wave began on 8 February 1940, and included civilian and government officials, judges, policemen, forest wardens, Polish settlers,

small leaseholders and farmers of various nationalities — altogether about 120,000 persons.
2. The second wave, in April 1940, included members of the families of those deported in February, members of the families of people who had gone abroad or were absent, the owners of nationalized land, traders, (especially Jews) and farmers of various nationalities, a total of 320,000 persons.
3. The third wave, in June-July 1940, included mainly Jewish refugees from western Poland, small traders, members of the free professions, intellectuals and teachers, 240,000 persons.
4. The fourth wave came in June 1941, on the eve of the German attack. The Russians completed the deportation of those who had escaped the previous three waves, 200,000 persons.[56]

In all, 880,000 persons were exiled in these mass deportations. According to the estimates of the Polish Delegation, the deportees fell into the following categories: 52 percent Poles, 30 percent Jews, 18 percent Ukranians and Bielorussians. The number of Jewish deportees therefore came to about 264,000. The deportees included refugees who had registered to return to the West, and also many who had not. The deportations continued up to the very onset of the war with Germany and even during the war's first days, despite the fact that the authorities needed every railroad car to evacuate their own people eastward.

The mass deportations may also be viewed as an attempt by the Soviets to affect an ethnic, political and social reconstruction of the areas that had been annexed to the Soviet state. It is estimated that some 120,000 Jewish refugees were deported from Western Bielorussia. At the outbreak of the German invasion there were, therefore, some 550,000 Jews in Western Bielorussia: 200,000 in the Bialystok district and 350,000 in the districts of Vilno, Novogrudok and Polesie.

There is some painful irony in the fact that the refugees from western Poland, Hitler's victims, were also the deportees of the Soviet regime. "It is ironic to note that these deportees provided the basis for the Soviet legend of having evacuated masses of Jews in order to save them from annihilation by Nazism.[57]

The mass deportations carried out in June 1941 almost coincided with the beginning of the Jewish flight eastward at the outset of the German attack, but the careful organization and implementation that the Soviet authorities displayed at the time of the mass deportations were not present at the time when Jews fled from the invasion. This fact is ignored by the Soviets.

In summing up, we must view the problem of the Jews of the annexed territories with reference to the background of the relations between the USSR and Nazi Germany, national relationships in the annexed territories, the processes of Sovietization, and the relationship between the Kremlin and the Jewish population. The latter was founded on the USSR's ideological position in denying the Jews any right to self-determination as a nation. The curve describing the attitude of the Jewish population towards the Soviet regime in Western Bielorussia during the 21 months of its existence, begins with the peak signified by the sight of relief at having been saved from the horrors of war. The advantages were evident: a feeling of security, an atmosphere of freedom, the feeling of equality, faith in the USSR's might and a belief in the fraternity among peoples that would persist in the time of trouble. Unfortunately, all these feelings later proved illusory. In addition, there were the relatively high positions of Jews in the Soviet administration, a more official status for the Yiddish language (at the beginning), a Yiddish theater, Yiddish literature, open doors to education for Jewish youth who had never known the like before, the possibilities of working on the railroads, in the postal service and heavy industry. On the part of the Soviet Jews there were expectations that the reunion with the Jews of the annexed territories would lead to a spiritual and cultural renaissance within Russian Jewry too. The assimilation prevalent among the Soviet Jews was mainly lingual and, for the most part, was not accompanied by a denial of their Jewishness.

The Jewish press in the USSR was superficial and limited and many Jews, despite their attachment to the Yiddish with its Hebrew print, did not like them because of their contents. Indeed, there was now a generation for whom Judaism and Zionism were very, very far away, but there were still people who maintained their love for Eretz Israel. There were also the faithful to Zion who had, out of their very enthusiasm for the October Revolution, tried to maintain a Zionist-chalutz underground with the USSR. The fires still burned. The Jews' adaptation to their environment was only partial and was accompanied by many expressions of the attempt to preserve their national individuality, values and contents.

During the 21 months of Soviet rule there were in Western Bielorussia adaptation and acceptance of Soviet ways of life, but there was also growing resistance. Almost from the beginning, with the Soviets' arrival, the feeling among the Jews of the annexed territories had begun to swing away from the Soviets.

Simultaneously with the sigh of relief came the awakening and with it the internalized disappointments, the accumulating fears, the feelings of silence and an inward closing, and the worry about "when would the world be opened?", the fear of arrest and deportation, whose heavy shadow swallowed up the real and illusory advantages in the eyes of the large majority of the Jewish population.

Internally, there were a number of crises/processes taking place at an astounding pace to shake the very foundations of Jewish existence in these regions:

1. The collapse of basic livelihoods: trades, crafts, free professions.
2. The dismantling of public life, with its institutions, political parties, and the erasure of any Jewish content from the educational system.
3. The liquidation — in the organizational sense of the term of the local Jewish leadership, who, with all their personal faults, had served the Jewish public, represented it, defended it and guided it according to the moral norms that had crystallized in the living experience of this section of Judaism.
4. The appearance of the Jewish refugees, who excelled in their levels of education and initiative and, many of them, in their difference from the local Jewish population. With the disappearance of the local leaders, these refugees were destined to play a special role.
5. The departure of the older members of the Zionist pioneering youth movements for Vilno where they now concentrated. This aspect is of great importance because of the special role the youth movements had played in the Jewish communities.
6. The Zionist underground, despite the very young age of its members and its relatively small size, symptomized an accelerating process of non-surrender, a will to continue Jewish existence under all conditions and the non-acceptance of outside decrees.

There were also external crises/processes:

1. In their press and spoken propaganda the Soviet authorities concealed the basic facts of Nazi policy towards the Jews in western Poland, although Soviet propaganda did speak of the political dangers of Nazi policies for the Jews in the region. It emphasized the danger of war on

the part of America and England, rather than on the part of Germany,[58] thereby diverting attention from the real and imminent danger from the Nazis.
2. Jewish trust in the USSR's military power was very strong. This power proved to be an illusion. Jewish reliance upon this power prevented them, in those very few days between the outbreak of war and the Germans' arrival, from taking the fateful decision to flee while there was still time, when there was still some hope of saving themselves.
3. The non-Jewish populations' hostility towards the Jews intensified during these years under Soviet rule, to a degree that was perhaps unprecedented. And all on the eve of the Nazi invasion.

Notes

1. Raymond J. Sontag & James S. Beddie (eds.), *Nazi-Soviet Relations* (New York, 1948), p. 78.
2. Molotov's speech at the fifth session of the Supreme Soviet, 1 November 1939, as reported in *Oktyabr*, Minsk, 2 November 1939.
3. Szymon Redlich, *The Jews Under Soviet Rule During World War II*, PhD Thesis, New York University, 1968, p. 10. At the same time in the Ukraine, 1.3 percent of the representatives were Jews, whereas the percentage of Jews in the area was over 10 percent.
4. *Oktyabr*, Minsk, 29 March 1940.
5. Benjamin Pinczuk, "Haglayat Hayehudim min Hashtachim shetzorfu leBrith Hamo'etzot ..." (The Deportation of Jews from Areas Annexed by the Soviet Union ...), *Shvut*, no. 2 (Tel Aviv University, 1974), pp.
6. David Yochvidowicz-Kahany, *Gilgul Mechilot* (Borrowing in Underground Passages) (Tel Aviv, 1973), pp. 11–14; cf. also YV 2866/210 (Yitzhak Arad), 1253/105 (Eliahu Kovanski) and many others, for the attitude of the Soviet Army.
7. YV 2866/210 (Yitzhak Arad).
8. Avraham & Moshe Kolakowsky, testimony in *Sefer Zikaron leKehillot Derczyn, Hulinka, Kutna, Siniesk* (Memorial Book of the Communities of Derczyn, Hulinka, Kutna, Siniesk) (Tel Aviv, 1972), p. 247. (Please correct spelling of Kutno).
9. YV 3000/218 (Zvi Olshansky).
10. Leah Lutzky, testimony in *Sefer Zholodok veOrlova* (Memorial Book of the Communities of Zholudok and Orlova) (Tel Aviv, 1967), p. 286.
11. Shalom Cholawsi, Ir Veya'ar Bematzor (A Town and A Forest under Siege) (Tel Aviv, 1973), p. 11.

12. YV 1299/36-J (Benzion Yavnowitz).
13. J. Lifshitz, testimony in *Sefer Zikaron David-Horodok* (David-Horodok Memorial Book) (Tel Aviv, 1957), p. 52.
14. Chaina Rabinowitz, testimony in *Wiszniewo kefi shehaita ve'einena od* (Wiszniewo, as she was and is no more) (Tel Aviv, 1972), p. 108.
15. YV 1-K (David Yochvidowicz-Kahany).
16. Dr. Aharon Machtiey, testimony in *Sefer Zikaron Stolpce-Swierżne veha'ayarot hasmuchot* (Memorial Book of Stolpce-Swierżne (note diff. spellings) and the Adjoining Townships) (Tel Aviv, 1965), p. 131.
17. Yossef Shapira, testimony in *Sefer Yizkor Dokszyce-Parafyanov* (Dokszyce-Parafyanov Memorial Book) (Tel Aviv, 1970).
18. Sontag & Bedie, op. cit., p. 106.
19. Shlomo Schwartz, *Die Yidn in Sovietn-Farband, 1939–1965* (Jews in the Soviet Union, 1939–1965) (New York, 1967), p. 25. Some 2,000 Jews from Chelm and 850 from Hrubieszow were brought to the Bug River by the Germans in December 1939. The Germans threatened to shoot them, while the Soviets declared that their government's instructions were not to let them cross. Many of them managed to cross the river to the Soviet side.
20. Bernard D. Weinryb, *The Jews in the Soviet Satellites* (Syracuse, 1953), p. 342. Estimates of the number of refugees range from 200,000 to 600,000. A reasonable basis for an estimate would seem to be the 180,000 refugees who returned from the USSR after the war (cf. Redlich, op. cit., p. 44). The death rate among the refugees in the wartime Soviet Union was about 30 percent, and the birth rate was very low, so that the number of refugees who escaped or were deported into the USSR from the newly occupied western territories was about 250,000. Most of them were refugees from German-occupied Poland. In addition, there were many more such refugees in Western Ukraine, so that their total number must have been larger than the 300,000 estimated by Weinryb.
21. Szymon Redlich, "Hayehudim bashtachim shesupchu liBrith Hamo'etzot" (The Jews in the Soviet-annexed Territories), *Behinot*, no. 1 (1970), p. 72.
22. Ivan S. Lubachko, *Bielorussia Under Soviet Rule, 1917–1957* (Lexington, 1972), p. 144.
23. Rabinowitz, loc. cit.
24. Uri Finkel, "A Briv a Heim" (A Letter to Home), *Oktyabr*, Minsk, 20 September 1939.
25. Pesach Piekacz, testimony in *Sefer Pinsk* (Pinsk Memorial Book), vol. 2 (Tel Aviv, 1967), p. 315.
26. Polish government-in-exile report, 1 November 1941–15 January 1942 (Szwarcbart Archive, Yad Vashem, M-2).
27. Lifshitz, loc. cit.

28. Shalom Cholawski, *Soldiers from the Ghetto* (New York, 1980), p. 17.
29. Out of 370 nationalized plants, 265 were owned by Jews. (In Lithuania, 1,320 of the 1,593 nationalized plants were Jewish-owned.) See Redlich, loc. cit.
30. Meir Sokolowsky, testimony in *Sefer Zikaron likehillat Rozhinoy vehasviva* (Memorial Book for the Community of Rozhinoy and Its Environs) (Tel Aviv, 1957), p. 151, and elsewhere.
31. *Bialystoker Shtern*, 2 February 1940; *Der Shtern* (Kiev), 22 April 1940; and Lifshitz, loc. cit.
32. Haim Rubinrath, testimony in *Yizkor Luninietz/Kozhorodok* (Memorial Book of the Communities of Luniniec/Kozhorodok) (Tel Aviv, 1952).
33. Lifshitz, loc. cit.
34. Piekacz, loc. cit.
35. E.g., *Bialystoker Shtern*, 6 April, 1941.
36. Cholawski, loc. cit.
37. Mendel Goldshmid, testimony in *Sefer Volozhin* (Volozhin Memorial Book) (Tel Aviv, 1970), p. 532.
38. Dr. Moshe Koritzky, testimony in *Sefer Zikaron Swiencian* (Memorial Book for 23 Communities in the Svienconys region) (Tel Aviv, 1965), p. 519.
39. Piekacz, loc. cit.
40. Redlich, loc. cit., p. 77; *Bialystoker Shtern*, 24 June 1940.
41. Dr. Margolin, testimony in *Sefer Pinsk* op. cit., p. 312.
42. Supra, note 31 above.
43. *Biyemei Shoah* (In the Days of the Catastrophe) (Kibbutz Meuhad, n.d. [1940]), p. 227.
44. Shlomo Kless, "Mahteret Zionist Chalutzit Bibrith Hamo'etzot" (A Pioneering Zionist Underground in the Soviet Union), *Yalkut Moreshet*, no. 12 (1970).
45. *Mima'amakim*, Hashomer Hatzair Archive (HHA) (Merhavia, 1939).
46. HHA File h-28.3 (2).
47. *Sefer Hashomer Hatzair* (The Hashomer Hatzair Book), vol. 1 (Merhavia, 1956),p. 458; Cholawski, op. cit., pp. 29–35.
48. *Biyemei Shoah*, op. cit., pp. 236, 241.
49. Yehuda Helman, testimony in *Sefer Pinsk*, op. cit., pp. 182–186.
50. *Biyemei Shoah*, op. cit., pp. 228–230.
51. *Al Massuot Polin* (On the Ruins of Poland) (Merhavia, 1940), p. 125.
52. Yehoshua A. Gilboa, *Leshamer Lanetzach* (To Remember Forever) (Tel Aviv, 1963), pp. 25–26.
53. M. Einbeinder, testimony in *Sefer Pinsk*, op. cit., p. 206.
54. *Al Massuot Polin*, op. cit., p. 128.

55. Cholawski, op. cit., p. 28.
56. Sikorski Institute (ed.), *Documents on Polish-Soviet Relations, 1939–1945*, vol. 1 (London, yr?), pp. 573–574.
57. Pinczuk, loc. cit.
58. In his speech of 31 October 1939, Molotov said that people can accept or reject Hitlerism as they can any ideology; or as *Izvestia* (9 October 1939) put it: "Hitlerism is a matter of taste."

CHAPTER 2

Operation Barbarossa: Nazi Preparations to Deal with the Jewish Population in the Occupied Territories to the East

Aims of the Barbarossa Campaign (Operation Barbarossa?)

The Non-Aggression Pact between Germany and the USSR, of 23 August 1939, had only postponed the date for fulfillment of German aspirations to expand eastward.

The aims of Operation Barbarossa, as the German attack against the USSR on 22 June 1941 was entitled, were anchored in the National Socialist program viewing the annexation of the territories in the east as providing *lebensraum* for the "Thousand-Year German Reich" and looking upon the Bolshevik state as a political power representing an outlook basically hostile to Germany. Hitler, who originally had favored a war on one front, did not cease, nonetheless, to think of a war on two fronts despite the opposition of the German generals.

On 9 August 1940, the German Army's General Staff (the Oberkommando der Wehrmacht (OKW)) issued orders to prepare to invade the Russians on the eastern front.

On 18 December 1940, a short time after Molotov's visit to Berlin, Hitler issued his *Weisung 21* (instruction 21) on Operation Barbarossa ordering the German armed forces to prepare to crush the Soviet Union in a swift campaign even before the end of the war against England. The preparations were to be completed 15 May 1941.

Admiral Raeder, the commander of the German Navy, argued that all the German forces should be mobilized to bring down Great Britain, that

Germany could not afford to fight on two fronts simultaneously, and therefore, the Barbarossa Campaign should be put off until Britain's defeat.[1]

Chief-of-Staff Halder had an ambivalent attitude towards the Barbarossa Campaign. General Guderian also voiced his surprise that Hitler, who had condemned the German leadership during World War I for permitting itself to be trapped into a war on two fronts, was himself taking the same risk.

Hitler, however, did not heed the views of these generals and was of the opinion that the last enemy on the continent had to be liquidated. He ordered preparations for an attack against the USSR.

The revolt that broke out in Yugoslavia on 26 March 1941 compelled Hitler to delay the Barbarossa plan for four weeks and to order, instead, that Yugoslavia and Greece be immediately invaded. Admiral Raeder argued once again that Germany should attack Egypt and the Suez Canal, and liquidate the British forces in the Middle East. Hitler was firm in his determination to attack the USSR on 22 June 1941. In a series of orders and speeches, Hitler defined the importance of the Barbarossa Campaign. On 3 March 1941, he declared: "... The battle that is about to begin is more than a battle of arms; it is a clash between world outlooks. In order to finish this war quickly it is not sufficient to strike at the enemy army in these areas. All that area must be divided into states with governments of their own ..."[2]

On 30 March, Hitler announced to the senior officers of all the German forces: "... The war in the east will be very different from the war in west ..." In an address to the Army leadership on 3 March 1941, he declared:

> The intellectuals who have developed these must be destroyed. The government machine of the Russian state must be crushed. Within the areas of greater Russia the use of the most total violence is necessary. The gang with the ideology had still not sufficiently united the Russian people. With the administration's liquidation it will fall apart ..."[3]

In a meeting with the heads of the Nazi Reich on 16 July 1941, Hitler said of the war against Russia: "Germany must take power, rule and exploit."[4] He also minimized the strength of the Soviet state and the Red Army, believing that a strong, swift blow would cause them to disintegrate. Alfred Rosenberg discussed the political aims of Germany's coming war against the USSR in an address on 20 June 1941: The enslavement of agrarian Russia and its attachment to industrial Germany were a traditional

German conception ... The war's aim was to provide Germany with the conditions with which to conduct its world policies and to defend the German empire. Field Marshal General Von Reichenau, commander of the Sixth Army, said in an order to his soldiers on 10 October 1941:

> The chief aim of the campaign against the Jewish-Bolshevik system is the total destruction of its state power and the merciless uprooting of the Asiatic influence on European culture ... Only so will we be able to fulfill the historic mission of freeing the German people forever of the Jewish and Asiatic danger."[5]

The heads of the German government planned the economic exploitation of the USSR and looked on the occupied territories to the east as colonies. Field Marshal Goering was chosen to implement the "Four Year Plan" (*Grüne Mappe* — the "Green File") for the reconstruction of the German economy for war needs, so as to provide German industry with raw materials from the occupied territories, to extract the maximum production from their inhabitants, and to provide Germany and the other European countries with this product.

In occupying the eastern areas, the Germans saw their goal to be the permanent weakening of the local populations. The Slavic peoples were an inferior race in German eyes. The treatment accorded them must uproot large sections of the population and thin it out.

Hitler said: "We are obliged to depopulate. We shall have to develop a technique of depopulation ... I shall simply take systematic measures to dam their great natural fertility."[6]

In keeping with the aims they had set for the Barbarossa Campaign, the Germans prepared for measures of harsh terror against the civilian population and prisoners-of-war of far greater severity than those employed in other occupied countries. "We must abandon any thought of soldierly ethics. Commissars and OGPU members are criminals and must be treated as such," Hitler declared.[7]

On 4 June 1941 the General Staff of the German Army issued the following orders to the forces which were to be used against Russia:

1. Bolshevism is the mortal enemy of the National-Socialist German people. Germany's war is directed against the destructive ideology and its bearers.

2. This war demands the adoption of harsh measures with full force against the Bolshevik propagandists, the guerilla fighters, the Jewish saboteurs, and the total liquidation of all resistance, both active and passive.

These, as well as other orders concerning the political commissars, held fatal implications for the Jews in the countries occupied by the Germans in Eastern Europe, since the Nazis, in their orders and doctrines, identified the Soviet political commissars with the Jews.[8] On 16 July 1941, Hitler invited his close circle of advisers to his headquarters in Prussia and spoke of Germany's aims in the war: "... The Russians have at this moment issued orders for partisan war against our rear. This partisan war holds its advantages: It provides us with the opportunity to annihilate all those arising against us ..." Continuing, he gave voice to the brutal terror he was about to conduct in the eastern countries: "The best solution of all will be to shoot anyone acting suspiciously ..."[9]

One order concerning the treatment of prisoners declared that: "... The Bolshevik soldier has hereby lost any right to be treated as a decent soldier according to the Geneva Pact ... Therefore, at the slightest signs of disobedience ... orders must be issued to act courageously, without pity and with full force ... The use of arms against Soviet prisoners-of-war is generally legal."

In an order of his own, Keitel declared: "Retribution for the life of one German soldier must generally be death for 50 to 100 Communists."[10] As for the civilian population, the method of rule would be terror without mercy: "fundamental measures to cast fear can only mean executions."

The Beginning of Operation Barbarossa

On the eve of the opening of Operation Barbarossa, Germany mobilized 190 divisions, 3,500 tanks, 50,000 cannon and mortars, and 3,900 combat planes on the USSR's western borders.[11] According to the plan, the German forces were divided into three "armies":

1. A northern group commanded by Field Marshal Wilhelm Ritter von Leeb, concentrated in East Prussia for an attack against the Baltic countries, and spearheaded towards Leningrad:
2. A central group commanded by Field Marshal von Bock, concentrated in the vicinity of Warsaw, with its task to crush the Red Army forces

massed in Bielorussia and, in coordination with the "northern" forces, to attack Moscow, whose conquest would be the turning point of the whole campaign; and,
3. A southern group commanded by Field Marshal Rundstedt, massed in the Lublin area and spearheaded towards Kiev.

The Germans assumed that within six to eight weeks of a powerful *blitzkrieg*, the Red Army would be defeated and destroyed and the Soviet state annihilated.

On 22 June 1941, a Sunday, at 3:15 in the morning, heavy German artillery fire was opened against Russia. The German Army crossed the border. The cities of Bialystok, Grodno, Lida, Brzesc, Volkovisk and Slonim were bombed that same night. In the first days of the campaign the German Army advanced with lightning speed. By the night of 25 June 1941 the German forces were 20 kilometers from Minsk. The Pripet marshes in Polesie served as a barrier to the attacking German land forces, and they therefore circumvented them, to the north and south.

The German forces' speedy advance into Russia intoxicated Hitler and his generals, some of whom had had reservations concerning Hitler's operational plans. Chief-of-staff Halder, wrote in his journal on 3 July 1941: "It will not be an exaggeration if I say that the military campaign against Russia will be crowned by our victory within 14 days ..." He, however, felt an obligation on to add: "... Of course, it will not be finished by that. These spaces ... will occupy us many weeks more."[12] Hitler announced on 4 July 1941: "... Actually, the Russian has already lost the war."[13] In an address on 31 July 1941, he added that the conquest of the territories alone was not sufficient and that his chief goal was the annihilation of the *lebendige Kräfte* (living forces) in Russia.

Einsatzgruppen (E.G.)

In the wake of the invading German army (the Wehrmacht) came units of the Einsatzgruppen. These were paramilitary forces that had been established by Heydrich and used for the first time in the 1938 occupation of Austria as a police force to combat elements opposing the Nazis. During the conquest of Czechoslovakia, the E.G. units came after the Army to maintain security. During the invasion of Poland in 1939, six E.G. units, notorious for their brutality, were deployed. The instructions concerning the concentration of the Polish Jews and the establishment of the Judenrate (Jewish councils) were issued by Heydrich on 21 September 1939, to the "E.G. commanders of the security police."

German Army head Keitel had, on 31 March 1941, issued guidelines for the relations between the Army and the security police in the areas of military activity and had declared that, in these areas of activity, S.S. Reichsfuehrer Himmler, under whose authority the Einsatzgruppen were subject, had received special functions.

The military authorities, who were aware of the key position in which Hitler had placed Himmler, were interested in formulating an agreement between the Army and the E.G. Thus on 4 April 1941 in an agreement concluded between General Wagner for the Army and Heydrich, the E.G. units were authorized, within their framework and on their own responsibility, to implement executions among the civilian population even in military areas close to the front.

The Einsatzgruppen commanders were Franz Stahlecker, head of E.G. A; Arthur Nebe — E.G. B; Otto Rasch — E.G. C; Otto Ohlendorf — E.G. D.

Heydrich had drawn the members of the E.G. command from the police forces and many were highly educated. Ohlendorf had studies in three universities, was a lawyer and had a degree in Economics. Biberstein, commander of E.K.*6 of E.G. C, was a Protestant minister; Weinman, who commanded E.K. 4, was a physician. Klinghofer, an opera singer, headed the *Vorkommando Moskau* and Steimle, head of E.K. 7a of E.G. B, was a student of history, Germanistics and French.[14] They all turned into efficient murderers.

The E.G. units numbered some 3,000 men. The units varied in size from 900 in E.G. A to 500 in E.G. D. In an address to the E.G. units Heydrich declared: "Judaism in the East is the source of Bolshevism and must therefore be wiped out in accordance with the Fuehrer's aims."[15]

E.G. A was attached to the northern group of armies and operated in Lithuania, Latvia, Estonia and east of these. E.G. B was transferred to the central group of armies in the Bielorussian area, in the direction of Moscow. E.G. C was moved to the southern group of armies in the Ukrainian area. E.G. D recruited for their operations members of the Waffen-SS and units of Lithuanians, Latvians, Estonians and the local police. The E.G. units' main tasks were the murder of Jews, the liquidation of Communist Party officials, commissars and elements dangerous to the Nazi regime. E.G. D commander, Ohlendorf, testified that: "Concerning Jews and Communists, the

E.G. and the officers of the EinsatzKommando [E.K.] were given verbal instructions on the eve of the operation. These instructions were that in the E.G.'s area of operations on Russian territory it was to do away with the Jews and also the Soviet political commissars. In saying 'do away' — I mean to kill."[16]

It was the E.G.'s task to "cleanse" the area of Jews, commissars and agents, both in the areas of military action and in the rear, and also to search out guerilla forces. Instructions in the tactical field were received from the command of the military sector to which it had been attached; the instructions concerning its "cleansing" goals it received from Heydrich himself.

The number of E.G. units was small; therefore they were very mobile. In many places, E.G. units repeated their "visits".

An important landmark in the formulation of the program for the murder of the Jews ("The Final Solution") was a letter from Goering, the "Reichsmarshal of the Great German Reich", who was responsible for the Four-Year Plan and chairman of the Ministers' Council for the Defense of the Reich, to Heydrich of 31 July 1941, in which he wrote:[17]

"In completion of the task which was entrusted to you in the Edict dated 24 January 1939, of solving the Jewish question by means of emigration or evacuation in the most convenient way possible, given the conditions at the time, I herewith charge you with making all the necessary preparations from the organizational, practical and material aspects for an overall solution (*Gesamtlösung*) of the Jewish question in the German sphere of influence in Europe."

The link between the "overall plan" demanded of Heydrich for the completion of the task of "solving" the Jewish question, and its timing, point to its wide scope and character.

The mass killing operation (*aktzias*) in which the Jewish population in the cities and towns of Bielorussia, Ukraine and the Baltic countries were annihilated by the E.G. units, are the essence of the "task" whose implementation was imposed Heydrich, with thousands of persons, men, women and children, led to graves dug in advance. Actually, it was here that the E.G. units began the total murder of Jewish populations. The fact that the E.G. left some part of the Jewish population in the cities and towns for some time does not alter the total character of the extermination. These Jews were left temporarily for utilitarian reasons, as a labor force for the military economy, following friction between the various German authorities into whose hands they had fallen. In his report of 15 October 1941, Commander Stahlecker of E.G. A wrote: "It was to be expected from the beginning that the Jewish problem ... could not be solved by pogroms alone. At the same time the security police had basic, general orders for cleansing operations aimed at a maximum elimination of Jews."[18]

In their extermination work the E.G. introduced into the eastern regions the mobile "gas-van" under the responsibility of a man named Backe. It had already been used at the beginning of 1942 by the R.S.H.A. in southern Ukraine, the Crimean Peninsula and the Caucasus. The van was filled with people and began to move when the doors were closed. During the ride carbon-monoxide gas was sent into the van. Within 10–15 minutes all the people inside died. The vans were ordered in Berlin and could hold from 15 to 30 people each. Later the gas vans were brought to Bielorussia. Ultimately, however, these vans were found to be "inefficient". There were also a number of E.G. commanders who refused to utilize them, not for humanistic reasons but because, in their opinion, death by shooting seemed to them to be more honorable.[19]

Wehrmacht and E.G.

The E.G. followed the Wehrmacht but, at times, as in Kowno, Riga, Kiev and other places came with it.

In his "Guidelines to Instructions 21," issued on 13 March 1941, German Army commander Keitel, practically empowered Himmler to impose a regime of terror in the areas occupied in the USSR in the name of the Reich. The mass murders carried out by the E.G. were implemented with the full cooperation of the military command. Keitel instructed his soldiers in this spirit, and in his order of September 1941, declared: "The struggle against Bolshevism demands merciless and energetic conduct first of all towards the Jews, the chief disseminators of Bolshevism."[20]

There were even cases where the Army urged the E.G. to carry out their *aktzias* more rapidly.

In his report of 15 October 1941, Stahlecker of E.G. A wrote that his relations with the armored corps commanded by Oberst-General Hoeppner were: "very close, frank, yes, almost friendly."

In the winter of 1941–42 the E.G. commanders reported on the total number of Jews murdered: E.G. A — 249,420; E.G. B — 45,467; E.G. C — 95,000; E.G. D — 92,000; altogether close to half a million. In the course of two years, 3,000 E.G. men murdered about 1 million persons an average of about 1,500 daily.[21]

The majority of the Soviet Jews were concentrated in the western part of Russia and were trapped by the German Army and the E.G. in the very first weeks of the war. As the E.G. moved eastward, the number of Jews steadily decreased: the Jewish population there had been smaller and some of the Jews in the internal areas of the USSR managed to flee.

With the establishment of the civil government, Himmler appointed his representatives who worked alongside the civilian regime and bore the title of HSSPF (*Höhere SS and Polizefuehrer*). In Riga, it was Pritzman; in Minsk, von dem Bach Zalevsky; in Kiev, Jaeckeln; and in the Caucasus, Koresman. Upon their appointment as HSSPF they were provided with police units and Waffen-SS units reinforced by "volunteers" recruited in the occupied territories, especially in the Baltic countries and the Ukraine. The HSSPF served as a form of reserve to the E.G.; whatever the latter failed to perform the HSSPF's units carried out.

Von dem Bach had been recruited to Himmler's staff in May 1941. With the outbreak of the German attack, he had, as HSSPF in the Bielorussian area responsible directly to Himmler, carried out bloody *aktzias* against the Jews and had even been elevated to the rank of general. After a time he had a nervous breakdown. Following his recovery von dem Bach volunteered to head the campaign against the partisans who had become very active in the Bielorussian forests. On 23 October 1941, Himmler appointed him "Reichsfuehrer-SS representative in the fight against the partisan bands." In keeping with this status, the SS leaders and the Bielorussian police were subject to his orders in their war against the partisans. At the end of 1941 the forces under von dem Bach numbered 14,953 Germans and 238,105 local "volunteers".[22]

The Civilian Regime

According to their prepared plans, the Germans divided the occupied areas in the east into two: the region of military government, subject to the Army and E.G.; and the area of civil government, where a German political administration was to be established.

On 24 April 1941, Hitler informed Rosenberg that at a later date he would be appointed Reichsminister for the occupied territories in the east. On 17 July 1941 an order signed by Hitler, Keitel and Lammers was issued dealing with civil government (*Zivilverwaltung*) in the eastern occupied areas to the following effect:

Clause 1. When the military activities in the occupied territories in the east come to an end, the government in these territories will pass from the military ...

Clause 2. Reichsleiter Alfred Rosenberg is appointed Reichsminister for the affairs of the occupied territories. His place of residence: Berlin.

Clause 5. Subject to the Reichsminister — the *reichskommissariats* are headed by *reichskommissars*, and these are divided into *hauptkomissariats* and *gebietskommissariats*."

On 17 July 1941 an order was issued transferring the Bialystok region to East Prussia, and Galicia to the General Government. On 20 August 1941 the territories were transferred to the civil administration and, on 1 September 1941, Rosenberg set this administration into motion. Its title was: *Reichsministerium für die besetzten Ostgebiete*. Under Alfred Rosenberg's control were *Reichskommisariat Ostland*, headed by Heinrich Lohse, to whom were subject the general-kommissariats of Estonia, Latvia, Lithuania and Bielorussia: the Reichskommissariat of the Ukraine was headed by Erich Koch. Lohse's headquarters were in Riga, Koch's in Kiev.

Alfred Rosenberg, the son of a German shoemaker, had been born in Tallin, the capital of Estonia. Though close to German traditions, he also knew Russia. He had joined the Nazi Party in 1921 and was the editor of the *Voelkischer Boebachter*. He became the Party's foreign spokesman and its ideologue. His book, *The Myth of the Twentieth Century*, is a defense of racism. Rosenberg was not too much appreciated by Hitler and his coterie. Hitler did not believe in his abilities as a man of action. Goebbels looked on him as a competitor in the field of propaganda and responsible for Germany's failure in the east. Both Himmler and Goering were interested in limiting Rosenberg's authority.

The differences between Rosenberg and the Nazi leadership were also reflected in their approaches to the problem of German policy in the east. Hitler looked upon Russia as one single hostile block. Policies of "self-government" seemed in his eyes to lead eventually to a battle for independence and he therefore was opposed to any autonomy at all for the eastern countries.

Rosenberg, on the other hand, distinguished between the Russians and the other peoples of the Soviet Union, arguing that one could not speak of Russia as a unity, but must differentiate between the various peoples within the occupied territories, establish a *cordon sanitaire* of the Ukraine, Bielorussia, the Baltic countries and the Caucasus against the Russians, and perpetuate and entrench Germany's domination upon this difference which he thought fundamental and lasting. The conflicts between Rosenberg and other German authorities, however, as we shall see further on, were reflected mainly in a number of practical areas in the field of civil administration. In summary, we may say: simultaneously with the preparations for Operation Barbarossa, preparations were also made to annihilate the Jewish population of the USSR and the areas annexed to it, in addition to severe policies towards the non-Jewish civilian population, and the liquidation of the USSR's political leadership and its apparatus.

In this war the Germans adopted merciless terror. Hitler and the Nazi leadership viewed the war as a mortal confrontation with the Soviet state that was, in their eyes, the fruit of two ideologies most hostile to Nazism: Judaism and Bolshevism; and it was their "Judeo-Bolshevik" combination, against which Nazism had decreed total war.

Up until Operation Barbarossa the Germans had carried out harsh measures against the civilian populations in the occupied countries, with the Jews being the first and the majority of those persecuted and murdered. With Operation Barbarossa and the utilization of the Einsatzgruppen and the HSSPF on the Russian front, the Germans went on to mass murder, to the "purification" of the eastern occupied territories and, in practice, the total annihilation of the Jewish population even before the Wannsee Conference of 20 January 1941 which discussed the implementation of the Final Solution.

Notes

1. Alexander Dallin, *German Rule in Russia, 1939–1945* (London, 1957), pp. 9–11.
2. Walter Warlimont, *Im Hauptquartier der destschen Wehrmacht* (trans (Frankfurt, 1962), p. 167.
3. Andreas Hillgruber, *Hitlers Strategie* (Hitler's Strategy) (Frankfurt, 1965), p. 526.
4. *Prestupniye tseli — prestupniye sredstwa. Dokumenty* (Criminal Aims — Criminal Means. Documents) (Moscow, 1968), p. 53.

5. Ibid., pp. 45, 67.
6. Hermann Rauschning, *Hitler Speaks* (Tel Aviv, 1941), p. 118.
7. Hans Hoehne, *The Order of the Death's Head* (London, 1970), p. 354.
8. Nuremberg Documents ((IMT) NOKW-1962.
9. *Prestupniye tseli* ..., op. cit., pp. 52–53.
10. Ibid., p. 90; Yad Vashem, *Mishpat Nurenberg* (The Nuremberg Trial) (Jerusalem, 1962), p. 194.
11. G.A. Rosanow, *Plan Barbarossa — Zamysly i final* (Plan Barbarossa — Intentions and Outcome) (Moscow, 1970), p. 62.
12. Werner Haupt, *Heeresgrupe Mitte, 1941–1945* (trans.) (Dornheim, 1968), p. 29.
13. Warlimont, op. cit., p. 194.
14. Raul Hilberg, *The Destruction of the European Jews* (Chicago, 1961), p. 187.
15. Hoehne, op. cit., p. 358.
16. Otto Ohlendorf, testimony in IMT, vol. 4, p. 319.
17. IMT, PS-170; Yitzhad Arad *et al.*, *Documents on the Holocaust* (Jerusalem, 1981), p. 233.
18. IMT, L-180; and Arad, op. cit., p. 390.
19. IMT, PS-2620.
20. IMT, NOKW-3294; translated in Arad, op. cit., p. 387. (Our translation differs slightly from that in Arad; it seems to be more accurate).
21. IMT, L-180; (NMT), (Should this be IMT?), Case 9, p. 35. Other estimates range from 1.2 to 2.2 million victims but these include Jews murdered by units other than the E.G.s.
22. Hoehne, op. cit., p. 369.
23. Otto Braeutigam, *Ueberblick ueber die besetzten Ostgebiete waerend des zweiten Welt rieges* (Survey of the Occupied Eastern Territories During World War II) (Tubingen, 1954), p. 2; also Dallin, op. cit., pp. 44–57.

CHAPTER 3
Nazi Policies in Western Bielorussia

The German Administration and Its Attitude Towards the Bielorussians

Considerable sections of the Bielorussian population had hoped that the arrival of the Germans would improve their economic situation and lead to the establishment of an independent Bielorussian state. Many were impressed by the overwhelming German power.

The S.S. commanders were eloquent in their reports about their reception by sections of the public.[1] The Germans' clear policy was to divide between the Bielorussians and the Russians, and to emphasize that division. They therefore called Bielorussia "White Ruthenia". *Reichskommissariat Ostland* embraced Estonia, Latvia, Lithuania and Bielorussia, each of which formed a *Generalbezirk*. The area of the Bielorussian Generalbezirk, according to the Germans' administrative partition, was some 225,000 square kilometers, with a population of some 9,850,000.[2]

In accord with their own needs, the Germans made changes in the previous administrative systems of the occupied territories. The southern part of Polesie, including Pinsk and Brzesc (Bresk), were included in the Ukrainian *Reichskommissariat*. The northern part of the Vilejka region was annexed to Lithuania. The Oriol and Smolensk districts in the east were annexed to Bielorussia. Minsk was the headquarters of the Bielorussian *generalkommissar*. The Beresina River was the border between the military area and the area of civil administration. On 1 September 1941, Wilhelm Kube took up his post as *generalkommissar* of Bielorussia. Upon entering into his new position, Kube defined the goals of his administration as follows: "We offer them our own goals: progress, culture, land and bread, the path of work, discipline and decency ..."[3]

Actually, however, the Germans looked upon the Bielorussians as an ethnic group that was inferior to the Lithuanians, Latvians and Estonians, The Bielorussians were viewed as a colonial hinterland, with all that implied for the population. They incited the Bielorussian elements against their Polish, Lithuanian and Ukrainian neighbors and attempted to profit from these conflicts. This policy was reflected in the diminished borders of the Bielorussian *Generalbezirke*. According to a Polish report, the Germans scorned the Bielorussians and put the Bielorussian language in third place after German and Polish.[4]

At the beginning of their rule, the Germans did not employ Bielorussians in their administration since these were lacking the required intellectual level. The Bielorussians' participation in the upper levels of administration was very limited. On the other hand, members of the Polish intellectual class living in this area were given a considerable role. Because of their knowledge of the German language and their diligence in work, they were, at the beginning, willingly hired by the Germans.

The hatred of the Bielorussians members of the Russian Orthodox faith towards the Poles intensified under the Germans. Bielorussians took part in the *aktzias* (actions) the Germans conducted against members of the Polish underground.

From the very outset of the occupation, the Germans adopted a harsh attitude towards the local population. One soldier of the German Wehrmacht, Emil Golz, describes the invasion of Bielorussia: "In the morning we went through Stolpce; we spoke to the civilian population in the language of machine guns." Keitel's instructions of 16 September 1941 had been: "... The fundamental means of imposing fear can only be execution."[5]

Dr. Wetzel, head of the colonization bureau in the occupied territories, spoke of a plan to transfer 75 percent of the Bielorussians to other places, especially to Siberia, and a remaining 25 percent — select Bielorussians of the Nordic type — would undergo the process of Germanization and be transferred as agricultural workers to Germany.

The *Ost* program planned to be carried out after the war was to settle some 4,500,000 Germans in the east.[6] Concerning the type of education the Germans intended to grant the population in the occupied territories, Himmler had said in May 1940:

For the non-German population of the East there must be no schools higher than the four grades of elementary school. The sole goal of this is to be simple arithmetic, at the most up to 500; writing of one's name; to learn the doctrine that it is a divine law to obey the Germans, and to be honest, industrious and good. I don't think that reading is necessary. Apart from this school, there are to be no schools at all in the East.[7]

The German authorities' attitude towards the civilian Bielorussian population became harsher as the Bielorussian partisan movement grew stronger. German policy of terror was a stimulus for the crystallization of an independent Bielorussian consciousness.

The Germans Establish "Independent" Bielorussia

There were two aims before the German civil administration in its attempts to establish a form of "self-government" in Bielorussia:

1. To establish a political and military force that would serve the Germans as an instrument in ruling or strengthening their rule; and
2. to establish an illusory entity in which many Bielorussians might find some expression for their hopes of national independence.

The Germans were also conscious of the fact that the Bielorussians' national consciousness was weaker that that of the Ukrainians. In their estimation, the establishment of "self-government" in Bielorussia did not involve any danger of a revolt on the part of the population in order to move from illusory independence to a true one.

In 1940, the Germans established a "Bielorussian Committee" in Warsaw, headed by Dr. Sczors, who represented a Bielorussian group with a pro-Nazi ideology. Dr. Sczors prepared a memorandum for the central authorities in Berlin in which he expressed his hope for the establishment of a Bielorussian state.[8] The Germans cultivated this illusion along with that of a possible Bielorussian army. After Minsk was occupied by the Germans, Dr. Sczors left Warsaw for Minsk in order to take up a position in the regime to be established.

However the Germans did not create an independent Bielorussian state, but instead partitioned Bielorussia and even curtailed its area. The establishment of *Ostland* destroyed the Bielorussians' hopes. Despite their disappointment, the members of the "Bielorussian Committee" continued their activities.

On 22 October 1941 Kommissar-general Kube ratified the formation of the "National Bielorussian Self-Aid" headed by Dr. Yermatzenko. In the middle of 1942, the Germans suggested to Yermatzenko the establishment of "Bielorussian Scientific Society" and promised to establish a Bielorussian university.

In July 1941, the "Bielorussian Defense Corps" was formed, eventually intended to number some 15,000 men under German command. An officers' course was held for Bielorussian officers who had served in the past in the Polish Army. The Germans began to give the Bielorussians preferment at the expense of the Poles who were consistently removed from their positions in the administration.

During the second half of 1942, as a result of the situation on the front, the continuing war and other setbacks, a growing number of Bielorussians began to nurture doubts about a German victory. The *aktzias* (see p. 70 in this book) against the Jews also raised second thoughts among many Bielorussians; soon too they also began to suspect German intentions. The widely disseminated slogan began to be: "Neither Russians nor Germans."[9]

The growth of the Bielorussian partisan movement at the end of 1942 and the beginning of 1943, and the Red Army's victories on the front (Stalingrad), led to a growing belief among the Bielorussian population in a Soviet victory. Anti-German forces within the population grew stronger.

In the spring of 1943 the "National Bielorussian Self-Aid" criticised the burning of villages and the murder of innocent persons. The Germans responded by executing Fabian Okienczyc, Kozlovsky, the editor of the semi-official *Belaruskaja Gazeta* and Ivanovsky, the mayor of Minsk.

At the beginning of September a German office was bombed in Minsk. In reprisal, the Germans arrested 300 persons and executed them. On 22 September 1943, General Kube was killed by a bomb thrown into his bedroom by the partisans. Kube was replaced by von Gottberg who after consultations in Berlin, established on 21 December 1943 a new committee, the "Central Bielorussian Council", with Radoslabel Ostrovsky as its president.

Ostrovsky asked that a general Bielorussian congress be convened which would decide on the administrative affairs of the Bielorussian people; the establishment of a Bielorussian defense force; and the employment of the Bielorussian force to be established against the Bolsheviks only within the limits of Bielorussia. The Germans agreed to fulfill all these requests.[10]

On 6 March 1944 the Central Bielorussian Council distributed posters calling on young men to enlist in the war against the Bolsheviks. In all, 60 battalions were mobilized in a military organization that was given the name of the "Bielorussian National Defense Forces" under German supervision.[11]

The "General Bielorussian Congress" convened in Minsk on 27 June 1944. The Congress ratified the principles of national independence, annulled the obligations of the USSR and of any other country concerning Bielorussian affairs, and proclaimed that the Central Bielorussian Council was the only legitimate body representing Bielorussia.

However, when the Red Army began its mass attack against Bielorussia the Congress delegates fled westward. The Bielorussian units that had been mobilized were also transferred to Germany and organized as combat divisions. Even before the attack the Germans had called for an evacuation of the population.

In sum, German policies in Bielorussia and the promises to grant independence that misled the Bielorussians, were intended to serve the interests of the Germans alone and led to divisions within the Bielorussian people; conflict between the Bielorussians and the neighboring people — the Poles and Lithuanians; and it led to that which was actually the Germans' main interest in this region, the formation of a militant political and military force against the Bielorussian partisan movement.

The German Regime and the Bielorussian Partisan Movement

Bielorussians served as a main reservoir of manpower for the Russian partisan movement that had begun its activities in the very first days of the German-Russian conflict. In the course of time this partisan warfare turned into a second front. The growth of the partisan movement may be explained by the following factors:

1. The Germans' murderous policies towards the civilian population drove many to guerrilla fighting; the more the partisan movement grew and expanded its activities, the harsher were the methods adopted by the Germans, intensifying the motive for greater partisan warfare.

The Germans' extermination policies towards the Jewish population aroused some fears among the non-Jewish population lest the same German brutality also be turned, in some form or other, against other portions of the population;
2. The Red Army's resistance in defending Moscow, the German Army's reverses because of the conditions of climate and terrain, and the entry of the USA into the war, all of which occurred in December 1941, aroused among the population the idea that sooner or later there might be the possibility of Nazi Germany's defeat.
3. The assistance in manpower, officers and equipment provided by the Soviet authorities through airdrops or breaks in the front;
4. The stream of prisoners-of-war who had escaped from the German prison camps, of Jews fleeing the ghettos, of peasants from the villages whose young people the Germans planned to send to work in Germany or which the Germans planned to burn in retaliation for the inhabitants' involvement in aid to the partisans, also swelled the partisan ranks.

By the winter of 1941–42 the weight of public opinion among a considerable portion of the Bielorussian population began to turn against the Germans. Characteristic of the mood of part of the population was the statement by one Bielorussian as recorded in a German report:

> If I am with the Germans I will be shot by the Bolsheviks when they come. If the Bolsheviks don't come, I will be shot sooner or later by the Germans. If I join the partisans, I may at least save my life.[12]

Starting from stranded groups of Red Army soldiers in the Bielorussian marshes, which provided vital natural conditions for partisan warfare, the partisans grew into a large force that, by 1943, covered about 60 percent of all Bielorussian territory.[13]

The partisans, in the course of time, developed from a tiresome situation into a real threat for the German occupation forces. Wilhelm Kube on 31 July 1942, asked the Reichskommissar for *Ostland*, Heinrich Lohse, to stop the flow of Jewish transports from the west to Minsk ..." at least until the time when the danger of partisan attacks will be completely removed. I require 100 percent of the S.D. soldiers for fighting against the partisans and the Polish movement of rebellion. The situation demanded the mobilization of all the S.D. forces, who in any event are not very numerous."[14] On that same day, the E.G. B reported that: "... The general situation in the area of the Central armies has greatly deteriorated in recent weeks due to the constant rise of partisan terror ..."[15]

The man responsible for the requisition of agricultural produce and manpower mobilization in the regions of Uzde, Kojdanow, Zaslawl and Minsk, complained in his report to the *Generalkomissariat* in Minsk that the local police could not be relied upon in the war against the "bands". He suggested reinforcing the local forces with German soldiers in order to impose order, or to send the police to Germany as a labor force.

The E.G.'s report of March 1942 says, among other things, that there was a growing cooperation between the partisans and the Red Army; that the partisans had heavy infantry arms at their disposal; that they were recruiting men into their units from the civilian population; and that they formed a disturbing force (*"Beunruhigungsfaktor"*) in Bielorussia.[16]

A Polish underground report of 30 April 1943, stated concerning Bielorussia:

> The Germans and the forces subservient to them rule in the cities and a radius of four to six kilometers about the city. Beyond that, the partisans rule. No German goes out of the city or town at night. All the factories, like the "Niemen" glass factory, the sawmills working for the army, the brick factory, are destroyed or under partisan control."[17]

The effect of the partisan movement on the state of mind in Bielorussia is laconically described in one E.G. report: "In German circles in Bielorussia the partisan question is the number one topic and all, without under estimating our own actions and propaganda, are concerned with a 'partisan hysteria' ("Partisanitis").[18]

Hitler was alive to the partisan danger from the beginning of the campaign. When the partisan movement grew stronger, Keitel, with Hilter's agreement, at the end of 1942, declared war against the partisans:

> Here, more than ever before it is a question of life and death. This war has no longer anything in common with soldierly chivalry or the rules of the Geneva pact. If in the war against the partisan bands in the east, as in the Balkans, the harshest measures are not adopted, in the not distant future we shall not have sufficient forces to challenge this plague. The military forces are therefore authorized and made responsible without any limitations to use all means in this war, against them, also against women and children, so that the results be successful.

... No German taking part in the war against the partisan bands must face disciplinary responsibility of a court-martial for his actions against the partisan bands and their helpers ...[19]

On 28 July 1941 Himmler sent von dem Bach an SS brigade for the systematic combing of the Pripet swamps. In August 1942, von dem Bach suggested himself to Himmler as the one to head the anti-partisan warfare, and he was appointed to that post.

Among the units at von dem Bach's disposal was Oskar Dirlewanger's brigade. In 1942–43 this brigade served under von dem Bach in anti-partisan warfare. The brigade was composed of criminals and was therefore called the "murder brigade" by the Germans. Von dem Bach was also assisted in his operations against the partisans by the Wehrmacht forces, since the SS units and the police forces were not sufficient.

According to German estimates, tens of thousands of German soldiers fell in the battles against the partisans, in addition to those wounded and the arms lost.[20]

P. Kalinin, the head of the partisan general staff in Bielorussia, estimated, in his report given at a summarizing session of the staff at the end of August 1944,[21] that 374,000 partisans had fought on Bielorussian territory; 283,000 as partisans and officers in the fighting units, and the remainder, 91,000, in family camps, who acted as couriers and attended to providing supplies. The number of partisan units came to 1,108, in 199 brigades. At the end of 1941, there had been 5,000 partisans and officers in Bielorussia; 73,000 in 1942; and 270,000 in 1943. A considerable growth in the partisan movement of Bielorussia, especially in the western part, took place in 1944.

According to Kalinin's estimates, the Germans had killed 1,500,000 peaceful citizens in Bielorussia, destroyed 209 cities and 9,200 villages. Soviet sources estimate that the partisans killed about 500,000 German soldiers in three years of war. The partisan losses: 26,000 men and women fell in battle and 11,797 disappeared without any traces.

Labor Evacuated to Germany as a Means Against the Partisan Movement

Two goals of equal importance motivated the Germans in sending laborers from the occupied territories to Germany:

1. To provide manpower for Germany's depleted labor force in the German economy, especially in agriculture, the need for which had grown after the large German losses on the battlefield; and
2. to prevent young men in the occupied areas who were fit for combat from joining the growing partisan movement.

At the beginning of 1943 the man responsible for labor, Fritz Sauckel turned with an urgent request to General Stapf, director of the *Ost* staff, to the effect that the Fuehrer's military plans demanded the mobilization of a manpower force of one million men and women from the occupied territories to work in agriculture for the coming four months. Of this quota, the Bielorussian *Generalkommissariat* was asked to provide 1,000 men and women workers every day. The mobilization of that labor force was necessary and must be carried out as quickly and efficiently as possible.

The fact that the Bielorussian civilian population served as a reservoir for the partisan combat forces worried the Germans during the summer of 1943, and the problem rose in their scale of priorities. On 1 December 1943, von dem Bach issued an order for the mobilization of manpower for Germany and defined the regions infected by the partisans as "zones of military action," declaring that men between the ages of 16 to 55 in these regions must be considered "prisoners who must be transferred to the Reich."

Germans Identify Bielorussian Jews as Potential Partisans

The Germans looked upon Jews as the main and fermenting force among the partisans and as a potential reservoir of manpower for them. Von Gottberg estimated that the Jews' role in the partisan movement was of major importance and that the Jews served as the spark for that movement. In a summary report von Gottberg wrote:[22] "The Jews in Poland [i.e. Western] Bielorussia, because of their intelligence and activeness, form a particularly dangerous element." And further on: "... It is estimated that until December 1941 there were 19,000 partisans and criminals, mostly Jews." Wilhelm Kube, in his report of 31 July 1942 to Reichskommissar Lohse, said:

> In all the battles with the partisans in Bielorussia it has been proven that the Jews in the former Polish area, as in the former Soviet area [i.e. Eastern Bielorussia] of the *Generalbezirk*, together with the Polish resistance movement

in the east and Moscow's Red Army in the east, form the main elements of the partisan movement ...[23]

According to the documents in our possession, the Jewish partisan movement was still in its first stages of envelopment at the end of July 1942. The spring and summer of 1942 were a period of growing flight from the ghettos to the forest and the formation of groups of Jewish partisans. At the end of July 1942, groups of Jews were still living in the Western Bielorussian ghettos and the flight had still not reached its peak.

Are the German estimates, as reflected in Kube's report, correct? From the standpoint of the static situation, the report did not reflect reality but it held a sharpened view of the partisan threat. It linked that threat with the Jews and provided an excuse (which the Germans themselves did not require, except perhaps to some measure for the local population and perhaps also from some other aspects) for their continued extermination of the Jews as a "necessity" connected with the war against the partisan movement. Kube's report proves that the Germans were quite aware of the measure of potential opposition to Nazism that was accumulating in the ghettos, especially after the first wave of *aktzias*, and that the ghettos were indeed the reservoir of fighting forces for the partisans and the Jews in the same breath, in many cases identifying the ones with the others.

The Germans' fears of Jews escaping to the partisans in the forests intensified with time. The SD commando in Baranowicze was not ready to implement the expulsion of 250 Jews from Novogrodok in 1943 without an *aktzia* first being carried out against 2,000 Jews in Lida, fearing that if the expulsion in Novogrodok indeed was carried out, about 1,000 Jews from Lida were likely to flee and join the partisans.[24]

Gebietskommissar for Hancevicz, Miller, reported that until the winter of 1942 one could not speak of partisan activity in the area; only at the end of the summer 1942, when the Jews fleeing the ghettos had gathered in the forests, was partisan activity felt to any considerable extent. At the opening of the *Gebietskommissariat* council in Minsk, on 8–10 April 1943, Kube reported that with the *aktzias* against the Jews, the partisan movement had begun to grow and to act with force. Edward Strauch of the SS, in his lecture to the same council in Minsk, said: "... The bands have better information services than we do. The Jews, and also part of the population, are prepared to transmit information to them."[25]

In reporting, on 31 July 1942, on the war against the partisans and the *aktzias* against the Bielorussian Jews in the course of the preceeding ten weeks, during which time 55,000 Jews had been murdered, Wilhelm Kube came to the conclusion that: "There is therefore no danger that in the future the partisans will be able to rely realistically on the Jews."[26] In their reports, the civil administration heads and the SS commanders sometimes made the Jews' partisan activities the excuse for murder and extermination, all in keeping with the Germans' covert and open propaganda goals. We should not forget, however, that the policies of Jewish extermination in the occupied territories in the east had been decreed on the eve of the German invasion (see Chapter 2).

The "Brown Book" and Instructions Concerning the Jews

On 3 September 1941, Alfred Rosenberg issued a document entitled the "Brown Book" (*Die Braune Mappe*) in which he outlined the activities for members of the civil administration under his command.

That "Brown Book" stated: "The Reichskommissar acts on behalf of the Fuehrer in the occupied territories." The Hague Accords, concerning an occupied country, the document said, do not apply to the USSR, and added: "Es sind daher aller Massnahmen zulässig. (All measures are permissible.)" On the Jewish question it went on to say:

"... The measures that will be adopted concerning the Jewish question in the occupied territories derive from the view that the Jewish question in all of Europe will be solved in a general form after the war. Here measures will be adopted in a partial form ... On the other hand, the experience in handling the Jewish question in the occupied territories can serve as a guide (*richtungsweisend sein*) for the solution of the general problem since the Jews in those areas, together with the Jews of the General Government, form the largest numbers of European Jews."

These operational instructions testify that those standing at the head of Nazi policy making had ordered the beginning of the implementation of the Final Solution within the area of the USSR at the very outset of the German onslaught, with the intention of applying the accumulated experience as a "guide" for the other European countries in implementing the Final Solution.

As for the Soviet Jews who had come to the western regions of Bielorussia from the Ukraine during the years 1939–41, the instructions state that "sharp measures" must be taken:

> ... The Soviet Jews in the central regions of the Soviet Union, since the Bolshevik Revolution, have consistently attempted to disguise themselves and to seize key positions. For that reason many have covered their Jewish names with a Russian character. We must therefore instruct them to restore their old names. This applies also to those who in the past had left their Jewish community (*Kultusgemeinschaft*) or changed their religion.[27]

The "Brown Book" contained instructions complementary to those issued in Kovno[28] concerning:

1. registering the Jews and imposing upon them the obligation to wear the yellow star;
2. preparing instructions concerning the movement of Jews;
3. the establishment of ghettos and the administrations within them;
4. transferring Jews from the villages and cities into the ghettos;
5. the establishment of a *Judenrat* and a Jewish police;
6. the transfer of Jewish property to the authorities;
7. displacing Jews from their occupations;
8. the introduction of forced labor.

As far as the economy was concerned, the "Brown Book" emphasized that in all the measures adopted against the Jews care must be taken that "economic needs should not be fundamentally damaged."

The instructions also spoke of the reorganization of the economy, especially in the fields of the free professions, banking, commerce, teaching, medicine, and pharmacy where the Jews played a large role. In these fields the Jews were to be eliminated. Only in cases of danger to public welfare might an exception be made for a Jewish physician to be employed. Jewish property must be confiscated. The Jews could continue to work in factories and crafts but only under intensified supervision.

Conflict Among the German Authorities

In addition to the troubled personal relationships within the Nazi leadership, and also in addition to the opinion of each of the German authorities operating in the occupied territories that it bore the Fuehrer's personal blessing, there were also direct instructions from Hitler and the Nazi leadership to each of the different authorities: the Army, the E.G., the HSSPF, and the civilian administration, that worked to intensify the conflicts inevitable created by all those operating in one geographical area.

"The first task of the civil administration in the occupied territories is to represent Germany's interests." This task, however, was not only that of the civil administration. Hitler's order of 25 June 1941 transferring full control over the occupied territories to the Wehrmacht commanders stated:[29]

> ... As the senior commanders of the Wehrmacht, they hold full control over the occupied territory, both from the military and the administrative standpoint ... In the area of civil administration, the implementation of the Wehrmacht's demands is placed upon the Reichskommissars. In circumstances in which delay cannot be permitted, the commanders of the Wehrmacht are authorized to intervene, if that is necessary, for the fulfillment of their military tasks.

Granting "full control" also "from the administrative standpoint" and the full right "to intervene ... in circumstances not permitting delay, if that is necessary," with the right to interpret those circumstances, once given to the Army, opened the door from the very outset for conflicts with the civil administration. The civil administration was alive to this situation. The "Brown Book" said: "... The Army commanders can, at the same time, on the authority of the order of June 25 [1941], take measures in urgent cases on the civilian level as well."

The HSSPF, Himmler's representative with the *Reichskommissar*, received his instructions directly from Berlin. Conflict with the civil administration, here too, was almost inevitable. Alfred Rosenberg complained in his letter to the Reich Chancellery head Heinrich Lammers that the SS was going "over his head."

According to Dr. Otto Bräutigam, there were also clashes between the administration and the E.G.; the E.G. units were supposed to operate only in the areas of the military administration, but not in areas subject to the civil administration where "normal" relations were supposed to prevail. E.G. units, however, carried out their *aktzias* against the Jews without informing the civil administration in advance. *Reichskommissar* Lohse himself complained of ignorance concerning the *aktzias*. The reasons given by the E.G. for the *aktzias* against the Jews, including the skilled workers, were "security", and no argument could stand against this.

The emissaries of Hermann Goering, in charge of the "Four Year Plan," also operated in the occupied territories and their powers did not always coincide with those of other bodies.

Differences over Anti-Partisan Warfare

There was however no difference of views among the various units of the German regime in the eastern occupied territories concerning the danger of the partisan activities and the need to stamp them out. There were though different views concerning the methods of doing this. The questions came, mainly, from the civil administration and the German bodies involved with the economy. One German official occupied in requisitioning cattle, argued against burning villages and the "Fritz" operation conducted in the Vilno region, and asked:

> "Why are these villages being set on fire at all … In the environs of Miadl in the Vilejka district, 20 villages were set afire during the recent operations. And now in the neighborhood of Miadl there are more partisans than before … If reinforcements do not come soon the lives of the Germans will be in danger."[30]

He went on to argue that burning the villages does not harm the partisans since they move to other areas where they can obtain their food provisions. On the other hand, the German soldier suffers when all the agricultural produce is taken out.

The staff of the civil administration were aware of the fact that the "scorched earth" policies diminished the Germans' own economic and agricultural resources in the occupied territories and, most important, reinforced the partisan movement with tens of thousands of villagers who joined the partisans.

Ehrenleiter, deputy *Gebietskommissar* of Slonim, in a report dated 21 March 1943, wrote:

> "There is sufficient proof that police actions alone will never solve the bandit problem. I am convinced at the bottom of my heart that the liquidation of the population of two villages not only does not harm the partisans but, on the contrary, forces large groups of the population into the partisans' arms."[31]

Kube and Lohse criticized the "scorched earth" policy adopted by the SS towards the civilian non-Jewish population. Lohse was concerned with what happened in the occupied territories as it would affect public opinion outside Germany. He argued that the SS behavior was unreasonable. When it did not distinguish between friend and foe, it damaged, he thought, Germany's prestige. A few months before his death, Kube declared that the problem of the east could not be solved by military measures alone and argued that such actions against women and children as were being taken were liable to do damage to Germany's prestige.

After Kube was killed, Himmler glowed: "Kube's death is a blessing for the homeland."[32] However, here too, the differences in views were essentially only pragmatic ones: differences in method, but not in aims and goals.

Jewish Labor Force as a Factor in the Disputes

The civil administration, by the very fact of its responsibility for administration and the economy of the occupied territories, and also because of its duty to provide aid to the Army, needed the Jewish labor force and especially that of the skilled workers who could not be replaced in the civilian population.

On 16 August 1941, Reichsminister Alfred Rosenberg issued an order[33] concerning Jewish labor in the eastern occupied territories, according to which men and women from the ages of 14 to 60 were subject to compulsory labor. For that purpose the Jews would be organized into "forced labor groups."

The Jews were employed by the German authorities in the occupied territories in the east as an unpaid labor force. With the wave of anti-Jewish *aktzias* the numbers of skilled Jewish workers decreased and the civil administration was interested in preserving a small Jewish labor force. We may assume, however, that in the eyes of the Nazi leadership and especially in Hitler's view, the matter of "solving the Jewish question" took priority over economic matters. To the civil administration's complaints that the anti-Jewish *aktzias* were being carried out without its knowledge, Heydrich replied that this matter was his sole responsibility. Alfred Rosenberg's arguments with Hitler's general staff for the coordination of the "Final Solution" with the needs of the civil administration did not impress the Fuehrer. Kube also argued that the too swift liquidation of the Jewish population was destroying the region's economy.

On 20 October 1941, the commissar of Slutzk, Carl, sent a secret letter[34] to Kube, telling him that on 27 October 1941 police battalion 22 had arrived in Slutzk. The battalion, mostly Lithuanian volunteers, had come to carry out an *aktzia* against the Jews. Carl had turned to the battalion commander and claimed that he had not been informed of any such *aktzia* which was horrible and "most brutal." Even Bielorussians who trusted the Germans had been shocked. Carl argued that such actions damaged the population's trust in Germany.

On the basis of this report, Kube demanded in his letter of 1 November to Reichskommissar Lohse, that the officers who had commanded the security police battalion be brought to trial. He argued that during the *aktzia* wounded people had been buried alive. "It is impossible to maintain order and quiet in Ruthenia by these methods." First of all, he thought, any action harming Germany's prestige in the eyes of the local population must be avoided.

There is in this document nothing of any reservations in principle with the Nazi policies of murdering Jews. Kube's demand that the Jewish skilled workers be left alive was not one of principle. He considered the existence of these Jews as merely a means to maintain the region's economy, albeit for a limited and undefined time.

Kube disagreed with burying people alive, but this too was not for reasons of principle. The main point of his disagreement was that these methods negatively affected other sections of the civilian population who feared for their own lives and thus intensified hostility towards the Germans. His condemnation of the robbing and looting was due to the fact that the property was taken by the local population. Holding an *aktzia* without previously informing the civilian administration was an insult to Kube's personal prestige, which he called "German prestige."

Reichskommissar Lohse, too, who had stopped the execution of the Libau Jews because of the methods employed, did not at all disagree with the murder of the Jews as such, and in his letter to Alfed Rosenberg he identified himself with it, only arguing for its coordination with the needs of the economy. "… It is self-understood that i.e. 'purifying' the Ostland of the Jews is a very urgent task, but its solution must go together with the vital needs of the war economy."

Reichskommissar Rosenberg replied in his letter to Lohse that on the question of the Jews he would receive verbal explanations; "essentially, economic considerations are not taken into account in settling the problem

... As for the questions that arise you are requested to settle them directly with the HSSPF."[35]

This answer from the Ostministerium headed by Rosenberg implied the acceptance of the Hitler-Himmler-Heydrich line stressing the dominance of the Final Solution policies over economic considerations, even including the needs of the Wehrmacht and the importance of the Jewish skilled workers.

The letter's recommendation that he apply to a lower level (the HSSPF) is testimony of the Ostministerium's own weakness and its desire to avoid a clash with Himmler, who enjoyed Hitler's support on this question. There is, however, also another point in the reply that deserves attention. The Germans preferred, for transparently tactical reasons i.e., in order to disguise their murderous actions from the local population as far as possible, and perhaps even because of as yet unconscious considerations of a "time to come", not to leave written legacies that would be filed away in the archives, but instead, to settle matters verbally.

Lohse was apparently not surprised by the Ostministerium's reply and perhaps even expected it, as even before he had received it he sent a letter to the *generalkommissars* in Riga, Reval, Kovno and Minsk to the effect that he had received complaints from the Wehrmacht authorities concerning the execution of skilled Jews vital for the war production factories; that he was attempting to hold up the execution of these Jews whose services were vital and who could not be substituted by others; and that he did not place much hope in appealing to the higher authorities and was therefore making an urgent suggestion: the training of non-Jewish skilled workers. Lohse's suggestion was implemented.

The *gebietskommissar* of Slonim, Gerhard Erren, worked for the Aryanization of the craft occupations at the time of the murder of 25,000 Jews in his region. The *gebietskommissar* of Baranowicze said that the number of irreplaceable skilled Jews employed by the Wehrmacht was not very large and that a large-scale operation was being implemented to train young Bielorussians for various jobs in the factories, but that the civil administration was not thinking of carrying out the Final Solution of Jews as long as there were no Aryan substitutes.

In the summer of 1942, at the peak of the second wave of the murder of Jews and of the intensifying activities of the Bielorussian partisan movement, Kube gave political considerations priority over the economic ones in an unequivocal manner: "I am of the opinion that in the matter of leaving the

Jewish skilled workers in their present numbers, this does not stand in any proportion to the damage caused by Jewish support of the partisans."[37] He suggested keeping the Jewish skilled workers under strict control, with separation between the sexes. He noted that he considered the existence of the Jewish skilled workers a temporary matter alone.

At a *gebietskommissars* council held in Minsk on 8–10 April 1942, Edward Strauch of the SS argued with the Wehrmacht that:

> When the civil administration arrived it already found economic enterprises operated by the Wehrmacht aided by Jews. At a time when the Bielorussians wanted to murder the Jews, the Wehrmacht cultivated them. In that way Jews reached key positions and it is difficult today to remove them completely, for then the enterprises are liable to be destroyed, something we cannot allow ourselves. I am of the opinion that we can confidently say that of the 150,000, 130,000 have already disappeared. 22,000 are still alive in the area of the *generalkommissariat* …"[38]

He suggested decreasing the number of Jews remaining to half (i.e. 11,000) "without causing economic difficulties."

Relations between Kube of the civil administration and Strauch of the SS had been tense in the past and that was a situation which continued in the summer of 1943, when the number of Jews in Bielorussia was very small. This may be testified to by an angry "dialogue" between them when Strauch arrested 70 Jews without Kube's knowledge.

In a report on 20 July 1943, Strauch related that he had arrested the Jews. Kube came to him angrily that same day: how had he dared to arrest working people subject to the authority of the civil administration? Strauch replied that he had received instructions on this matter. Kube asked to see the instructions in writing, Strauch replied that he had been given verbal instructions which satisfied him and he had to fulfill them just like written instructions. Kube argued that this was an illegal act against his jurisdiction and that Jews subject to him could not be arrested, neither by von dem Bach nor by the Reichsfuehrer. He announced that if he had no way of preventing the arrest by force, he would from then on not allow the security police to enter his office.

In the course of this "dialogue" the matter arose of valuables that had been taken and sent directly to Himmler's office and not to Kube. The subject was also raised of the extraction of gold teeth, by qualified dentists, from the mouths of murdered Jews. Kube argued that such methods were not fit for the Germans or the Germany of Kant and Goethe, that it was the Germans' own fault that Germany's prestige was being destroyed throughout the world, and that Strauch's men were satisfying their sexual urges by these acts. Strauch energetically protested against these charges and stressed that it was unfortunate that he and his men, who had to do a dirty job, served as the targets for mudslinging.[39]

Strauch blamed Kube before von dem Bach for being "at the root of his soul an opponent of the policies of *aktzias* against our Jews," and was only concealing this out of fear.[40]

Kube did not argue that the 70 Jews who had been arrested were vital for the economy, the Army, or the military production factories. His arguments were:

1. that 70 percent of "his" Jews had been arrested without his permission, though he was master in the area;
2. that the objects of value that had been stolen (mainly from Jews) had been sent to Himmler's office in Berlin, when, in his view, they should have come to him;
3. that dentists had extracted gold teeth from the mouths of murdered Jews and, again, this gold, almost certainly had not reached his office. We need not assume that Kube would have brought up the matter of Kant and Goethe if the gold had come to his office. Kube was known to be a consistent antisemite. Prestige of office and personal privilege apparently played a large, if not dominant, role in the tense relationships among the Nazi rulers.

Himmler complained of Kube to Rosenberg and the latter promised to send Kube a warning. Study of the documents at hand show that Kube did not argue with the aims of the Nazi policies. When the dominant line towards the "solution' of the Jewish Question in Bielorussia, as in the other eastern regions, was that of Hitler-Himmler-Eichmann, the competition between the various Nazi authorities was to the detriment of the Jewish population. It intensified, accelerated and made extreme the implementation of the policy of the Final Solution of the Jews.[41]

In summing up Nazi policy on the Jewish Question in the region, we might say that though the Germans had intended from the very start, on the eve of the Barbarossa operation, to act against the Jewish population with particular brutality as an "experiment" that would later be applied in the total "solution" of the Jewish Question, other local factors were added that increased the dimensions of the murder:

1. The Germans carried out their murderous actions against the Jews in the midst of what they considered the inferior Bielorussian people without any consideration for public opinion within it and its reactions to these murderous acts. It also found many collaborators among them to help in the work of annihilation.
2. The Germans appreciated the importance of the Jewish population to the tremendous partisan movement in the region, as a moving force, a potential reservoir of partisan fighters and as the fuel for anti-Nazi activities.
3. The competition, envy and the seeking of power and prestige was at the root of the clashes among the various German authorities in the region. This only accelerated the implementation of their policies.

These factors particularly affected the scope with which the Jewish population was murdered in the first wave of *aktzias*, which continued until the end of 1941 and the pace with which they carried out.

Notes

1. Werner Haupt, *Heeresgruppe Mitte, 1941–1945* (trans) (Dornheim, 1968), p. 33.
2. "Die Braune Mappe" (The Brown Folder — Instructions for Germany Administrators in the East by Rosenberg's "Ostministerium"), Yad Vashem (YV) 04/53/1.
3. Alexander Dallin, *German Rule in Russia, 1939–1945* (London, 1957), p. 204.
4. Report of May 1942 (Swarcbart Archive [SzA}, Yad Vashem, M_Z, folder 195.
5. *Prestupleniya Niemietsko-Fashystitskikh Okhupantow w Belorussi* (Crimes of the German-Fascist Occupiers of Belorussia) (Minsk, 1965), p. 28.
6. Ibid., pp. 34–35.
7. Yehuda Bauer, *A History of the Holocaust* (New York, 1982), p. 353.
8. SzA, YV M-2, folder 191, p. 56.
9. Ivan S. Lubachko, *Belorussia Under Soviet Rule, 1917–1957* (Lexington, 1972), pp. 161–162.
10. Ibid.; also P. Kalinin, *Partisanskaya Respublika* (The Republic of the Partisans) (Minsk, 1968), pp. 239–255.

11. Lubachko, op. cit., p. 163. A Polish report (SzA, YV, M-2, folder 229, 15/44) talks of 80 battalions, and of 100,000 volunteers, of whom the Germans took only 36,000 because they did not trust the others.
12. Dallin, op. cit., p. 219.
13. Lubachko, op. cit., pp. 157–158.
14. Nuremberg Documents (IMT), PS-3428.
15. YV DN. 54-4, Meldung (Report) 14.
16. Yad Vashem, Taetigkeits und Lagebericht der EG, der Sipo und des SD in der UdSSR (Report on Activities and the Situation by the Einsatzgruppen, the Security Police and the Security Service in USSR) no. 11, 1–31 March 1942.
17. SzA, YV M-2, folder 198, p. 129, 1/43.
18. YV DN/54-4, Meldung (Report), 7 October 1942.
19. *Prestupleniya ...*, op. cit., p. 65 for Keitel's order of 16 December 1942.
20. IMT, PS-3712.
21. Kalinin, op. cit., pp. 366–376.
22. YV 0-53/4, p. 537, von Gottberg (Report), 14 August 1943.
23. IMT, PS-3428. It is significant that this passage was simply omitted in the Soviet collection of documents, see *Prestupleniya ...*, op. cit., pp. 50–51.
24. YV 0-53/1, p. 247, 11 July 1943.
25. YV 04-53/2, p. 490; 0-53/1.
26. IMT, PS-3428.
27. YV TR-10/808, pp. 142, 145.
28. Ibid., p. 156.
29. YV 04-53/1, p. 88; *Prestupleniya ...*, op. cit., pp. 50–51.
30. *Prestupleniya ...*, op. cit., p. (no.?)
31. YV TR-10/808, p. 213.
32. Ibid., pp. 372–373.
33. YV 04-53/1, p. 54.
34. IMT, PS-1104.
35. YV 04-53/1, pp. 130–140.
36. YV 04-53/2, p. 241.
37. Ibid., p. 345.
38. YV TR-10/808, p. 191
39. IMT, NO-4317.
40. YV 04-53/2, p. 582.
41. Otto Braeutigam, *So Hat Es Sich Zugetragen* (Thus Did It Happen) (Wuerzburg, 1968), p. 418. Braeutigam says that some S.S. commanders reported the areas of their activities to be "Judenrein" before they had actually managed to murder all the Jews there, simply because they knew that this was what was expected of them and that their superior wanted to hear it.

CHAPTER 4
The Waves of Murder in Western Bielorussia

The First Wave

The Einsatzgruppen followed the German Army from the outset of the war; sometimes they moved together with it. In this way the Jews were trapped in their homes and were prevented from fleeing.

The German Army moved with lightning speed. The village of Svir in the Vilno district was reached by 24 June 1941; Eyszyszki, in the Novogrodok district, on 23 June; Dereczyn on 27 June; Iwieniec and Lachowicz on 28 June; Kleck, in the eastern part of the district, on 29 June. In the Polesie district, after cutting off the marshes from the north and south, the Germans moved more cautiously for fear of clashes with the Red Army forces stranded in the swamps. They entered the cities later: David-Horodok on 5 July, Lenin on 18 July. In the more easterly areas of the USSR relatively larger numbers of Jews managed to escape into central Russia.

In more than a few areas in Western Bielorussia the local population staged attacks and even pogroms against the local Jews. "The Germans were interested in showing the world that the local populations were carrying out the first actions as a natural reaction to their having been oppressed by the Jews for decades."[1]

Though the Germans were supposedly opposed to local forces in the area taking the law into their own hands, these pogroms were carried out under German influence, even when in certain cases they took place a few days before the Germans actually arrived.

The first series of *aktzias* that continued until the winter, were carried out by the following E.G. B units: Sonderkommando 7a and 7b,

Einsatzkommando 8 and 9, and a unit of the VKM (Vorkommando Moskau). Later, E.G. A units also participated.[2]

The German Army itself also took part in the slaughter, sometimes without any pre-coordination with the civil administration. Orders issued by the commanders of the armies explicitly stated that one of the goals of the military campaign was the annihilation of the Jewish population. What the E.G. units and the army did not finish was completed by the HSSPF units.[3]

An active role in the *aktzias* was taken by the local police and "volunteer" units from the local population. According to an E.G. B report of 14 November 1941, 45,500 Jews[4] were murdered throughout Bielorussia as a whole. According to a later report by Stahlecker, 229,502 Jews were killed.

The German reports in our possession are only partial ones and cannot provide the whole statistical picture of the annihilation of the Jews of Eastern and Western Bielorussia. In the regions of Vilno, Polesie and Novogrodok, there were approximately 350,000 Jews at the outbreak of the war. We may assume that about 10,000 managed to escape eastward into the USSR. In these districts, then, some 340,000 Jews had remained.

According to the details in our possession, in the 87 Western Bielorussian ghettos there were the following numbers of Jews:

District	Ghetto	Jews
Vilno	33	61,000
Polesie	21	139,000
Novogrodok	33	115,000
Total		315,000 Jews.

Some 25,000 Jews in the other ghettos in these districts.

During the first series of *aktzias*, more that 130,000 (some 38 percent of the ghetto population), were killed in the Vilno, Polesie and Novogrudok districts. The ghettos were liquidated in a second series begun in the spring of 1942. These then intensified during the summer and latter part of the year.

In some ghettos (mainly in Polesie) men were the first to be executed: in Brzesc — 5,000, in Pinsk 11,000 (on 13 August 1941), and the same in David-Horodok (16 August), Sernik (13 August 1942) and in Janow near Pinsk (5 August 1942). This murder of the Jewish males had a decisive effect upon the ghetto's future ability to resist. Though policies of annihilation had been decided in advance, the Germans, in their reports, gave "reasons" for the murders and the *aktzias*. In Pinsk, for example, the E.G.'s report stated that Jews had shot at a member of the municipal police force and therefore 4,500 Jews were executed.[5] In Rakov (35 kilometers west of Minsk) the Jews had begun to incite the population to rebellion and therefore an *aktzia* was carried out in that city.[6] In Iwieniec 50 Jews were killed because they did not comply with German orders.[7]

The Germans made all efforts for the *aktzias* to remain as secret as possible. The Germans believed that among the local population, and even among the remaining Jews, the impression was that the murdered Jews had been deported to elsewhere in the eastern regions.[8]

The truth is that the local gentile population, in part because some of them had participated in the *aktzias* themselves, knew much more than the Germans imagined, if not everything. Keeping the date and place of the *aktzias* secret was one weapon the Germans used in the attempt to deceive the Jews up until the last moment in order to prevent them escaping or resisting. The local population for the most part did not give over the information it had to forewarn the Jews in the ghettos. The Germans also took care that among the local gentile inhabitants fear should not arise for their own lives, since they thought this might accelerate the organisation of a Bielorussian partisan movement.

The first series of *aktzias* passed like a frightful storm and produced a bloody harvest. At the end of 1941, an E.G. report declared: "… The question of the Jews in 'Ostland' may be seen to be solved. Large *aktzias* have greatly reduced the Jewish population. The remainder have been gathered into ghettos."[9]

Among the reasons for leaving part of the Jewish population alive after the first wave of *aktzias* we may include the following:

1. The difficulties faced by the Germans on the eastern front compelled them to organize militarily and economically for a longer extended campaign and as a result they required the Jewish labor force, especially the skilled workers among them;
2. The destruction of all the Jews at one stroke would have done serious damage to the local Bielorussian economy;
3. Climatic conditions during winter hampered the implementation of the *aktzias* (digging graves in the frozen ground, etc.).[10]

The above E.G. report to the effect that the Jewish Question seemed to be "solved," did not refer to the statistical aspect but rather to the organizational-operational one — that a "proper method" had been found to "solve" the Jewish Question and that now it was only a matter of time.

Even in the course of the first wave of *aktzias* there were some Jewish communities that were completely destroyed or most of whose members were killed. The first community in Western Bielorussia to be annihilated, about a month after the Germans' arrival was Hancewicz, on 13–15 August 1941.

Those who remained alive after the first *aktzias* went through a "selection" process which sought skilled workers needed by the Germans. Sometimes only the workers alone were chosen, sometimes they were allowed to include members of their families.

"… The *aktzias*," said Slonim *gebietskommissar* Gerhard Erren, "freed me of unnecessary eaters. Seven thousand Jews in the city of Slonim are today harnessed to the work process, working willingly because of their constant fear of death."[11]

The Pause

During the period between the two waves of destruction, in the late fall and winter of 1941–2, the civil administration completed the following:

1. Ghettoization: concentrating the Jews behind barbed wire or walls, strict registration, severe supervision over the fulfilment of the instructions concerning mobility of ghetto inhabitants.
2. Exploitation of the Jewish labor force, organization of life within the ghetto, providing "security" in the stability of the ghetto's existence;
3. Expulsion of Jews from the smaller towns and their concentration in the larger ghettos, an act that dissipated the forces of the deported Jews and had its negative effect upon their resistance.
4. Preparations for the second wave of *aktzias*.

In the interim period many ghetto inhabitants tended to believe or to hope that they were "vital" to the German economy and that there was a German interest in their productivity, and therefore in their existence. They wanted to believe that the Jew's most important possession was his work certificate and that perhaps the stoppage in the *aktzias* presaged something for the future.

The resolutions of the Wannsee Conference of 20 January 1942, which took place in Berlin during this interim period, held nothing new as far as the annihilation of the Jews as practiced in the eastern occupied territories was concerned. Still, the unequivocal decision on implementing the Final Solution served to reinforce and legalize the German policies of murder towards the Jews in the region.

In the spring of 1942 the partisan movement gained momentum in its growth and began to bear the character of a mass resistance movement. From then on the Germans began to link the partisan danger to the destruction of the Jews in their propaganda and in their internal reports.

The Second Wave of *Aktzias*

The second series of *aktzias* began in Bielorussia in the spring of 1942 and continued until the annihilation of Western Bielorussian Jewry was completed in the fall of 1943. From the spring of 1942 until the end of that year about 170,000 Jews were killed: about 50 percent of the Jews of the districts of Vilno, Novogrudok and Polesie. On 21 March 1942, Lohse held a discussion with the *generalkommissars* of Riga and Minsk, in which he said: "... According to our general view the Jewish Question must be solved clearly and vigorously."[12] Edward Strauch spoke in February 1942 of "Ausrottung aller Juden." He published an order that in every place where there were Jewish partisan units, the Jewish ghettos were to be destroyed.[13] In his report to Lohse of 31 July 1942, Kube stated that the partisan movement relied upon help from the Jews, members of the Polish resistance and escaped Soviet prisoners-of-war. From the middle of May 1942 until the end of July, 55,000 Jews were murdered. He expressed his anger over transports of Jews from the west being sent to Bielorussia. "The Polish Jew, like the Russian Jew, is Germany's enemy. He forms an element of political danger greater than his value as a skilled worker."[14]

In the summer of 1942 the number of deaths was greater. In June 1942, the RSHA issued an order to Rasp, an S.D. commander, to kill the Jews of Pinsk and its environs.[15] Rasp's units carried out *aktzias* in the ghettos of Pinsk, Lachwa, Luniniec, David-Horodok, Visoky, Stolin, and Janow near Pinsk. The *gebietskommissar* took great care in digging the death pits. The Jews were brought in groups of 10 men each and were shot by the pits. At the time of the shootings and afterwards, the murderers received bottles of vodka. Towards the fall of 1942 the Jewish population of Bielorussia had decreased considerably.

On 27 October 1942, Himmler sent an order to HSSPF Hans Pritzmann to the following effect:

> The general staff of the Wehrmacht informs me that the Brzesc-Gomel area is being troubled more and more by the bandit attacks making it problematic to send reinforcements to the fighting forces.
>
> According to the information given me, the Pinsk ghetto must be viewed as the center of the general partisan movement in the Pripet marshes.
>
> I therefore order, despite the economic considerations, that the Pinsk ghetto be liquidated and destroyed. To the degree that the *aktzia* permits this, 1,000 male workers must be placed at the disposal of the Wehrmacht for the production of wooden barracks.
>
> The 1,000 workers must be kept in a closed and well-guarded camp. If the camp is insufficiently secure then the 1,000 must also be annihilated.[16]

The *aktzia* of the annihilation of the Jews of the Pinsk ghetto commenced on 29 October 1942 and took three days.

Annihilating the Last of the Western Bielorussian Jews

At the close of 1942 there remained in the area of the "Ostland" some 100,000 Jews, of whom about 30,000 were in Bielorussia[17] — half being within the borders of Western Bielorussia. In his report to Rosenberg of 23 November 1942, Lohse declared of Bielorussia: "All the small communities have been cleansed of Jews."[18]

In the spring of 1943 there were within the area of the *generalkommissariat* of Bielorussia, according to a German source, altogether 22,000 Jews[19] but the Jewish Question in Bielorussia still played an important part in the Germans' discussions.

At the Minsk *gebietskommissariat* council on 8–10 April, Wilhelm Kube, who opened the session, linked the growth of the partisan movement in Bielorussia with the German *aktzias* against the Jews. According to Kube, the Jews who had fled the ghettos had reinforced the partisan movement.

Vilejka *gebietskommissar* Hase, in whose area some 3,000 Jews were still located, reported that not one Jew was living in his former home and still "we must finally finish with the Jewish problem in my district soon."[20] Von Gottberg, who had headed the anti-partisan warfare in von dem Bach's place from 1943, said that the Jewish Question was the decisive one in these regions.[21] Edward Strauch said:

I therefore want to request of you that, at least, the Jew disappear from any place where he is superfluous. We cannot agree to Jewish women polishing shoes, to telephone operators ... They are found more than needed and they must disappear ... We will cut the number down to half without causing economic difficulties.[22]

The Judeophobia of those days, from the psychological viewpoint, perhaps lay in the fact that every living Jew reminded them of actions that could arouse their fears. Even murdered Jews cast their fears on some of them. Von dem Bach suffered, according to his doctor, from hallucinations resulting from his having personally killed Jews.[23]

The murdered Jews in the mass graves scattered throughout the occupied territories also aroused the Germans' concern from the point of view of the future. In June 1942, Müller gave Paul Blobel the task of burning the bodies hidden in the graves and of erasing all signs of the crimes committed by the Germans in the occupied territories of Russia. Blobel established "Unit 1005" to carry out that task.[24]

Himmler issued an order on 21 June 1943 to turn the existing ghettos into concentration camps. The date for this order's implementation was to be 1 August 1943.[25]

This change in the status of the Jews behind the barbed wire form a "ghetto" to a "concentration camp" marked a further deterioration of their situation.

Liquidation of the Western Bielorussian Ghettos

The year 1942 saw the annihilation of the large majority of the Western Bielorussian ghettos (83.5 percent). The last ghettos to be liquidated were Glebokie, (20 August 1943) and Lida (18 September 1943). The last of the Jews fled from Koldyczevo on 7 March 1944.

Liquidation of 74 Western Bielorussian Ghettos

Ghettos liquidated	Vilno	Polesie	Novogrudok	Total	%
Until end of 1941	3	1	2	6	8.0
First half 1942	10	8	–	18	24.0
Second half 1942	5	17	14	36	49.0
First half 1943	5	1	3	11	15.00
Second half 1943	2	1	–	3	4.00

The Ghettos in the Vilno District

The Jewish population in the Vilno district had numbered about 50,000 persons in 1939 (after the city of Vilno's annexation to Lithuania). We have examined 45 ghettos in this district (including one work camp) and other communities. In 33 ghettos there lived some 61,000 Jews. In 24 ghettos there were underground movements; in 13 ghettos and other communities, acts of revolt; from eight ghettos and communities the Jews were deported at the beginning of the Nazi invasion to larger ghettos.

The Ghettos in the Polesie District

In 1939 there were some 121,000 Jews living in the Polesie district. We have examined 28 ghettos (including one work camp) in this district. There were some 139,000 Jews in 21 ghettos: 16 ghettos had underground organizations; eight ghettos showed signs of revolt; from four ghettos the Jews were deported to larger ghettos at the beginning of the German invasion.

The Ghettos in the Novogrodok District

The Jewish population in the Novogrudok district numbered some 85,000 persons in 1939. We have examined 37 ghettos and other communities in this district (including two work camps). Some 15,000 Jews were living in 32 ghettos; 24 ghettos had underground organizations; nine showed signs of revolt and here too at the beginning of the German occupation the Jews were driven out of five ghettos to larger ones.

Notes

1. L-180.
2. E.G.A. sent her Units, among them Skib, SK_2, SK_3 to carry-out „akzias" against the Jews of Western Belorussia.
3. Eisenbach, pp. 273–274.
4. TR-10/593 YV.
5. NO-2846-EM. Ud SSR, N-58, 30.8.1941.
6. NO-4533.
7. Tätigkeits und Lagerbericht Nr.5.
8. NO-3279.
9. Tätigkeits und Lagerbericht Nr.7.
10. YV 04-53/1. Kube's letter to Lohse, 6.2.1942.
11. TR-10/808. Trial of G. Erren, p. 198.

12. Ibid., p. 183.
13. YV TR-10/582.
14. PS-3428.
15. YV TR-10/790.
16. YV TR-10/786.
17. YV TR-10-646.
18. YV TR-10/808.
19. Ibid., p. 191.
20. Ibid., p. 187.
21. YV TR-10/808.
22. Ibid., p. 191.
23. Bartoshewski, pp. 36–37.
24. Paul Blobel was Commander of S.K.4a (June 1941–January 1942).
25. NO-2403.

CHAPTER 5
The First Series of *Aktzias*

The German Army's lightning advance in its invasion of the USSR and the Red Army's hurried retreat left the Bielorussian Jews stunned, deeply disillusioned and with feelings of helplessness. Suddenly the Jews felt that they had been abandoned to their fate, a fate that no one yet knew. Dulled by fear, frightening thoughts troubled their hearts, though for the most part they did not voice them and attempted to repress them as far as possible. The great hopes they had pinned on the Red Army had been shattered at the beginning of the war when they saw the depressing picture of the Russian soldiers retreating. The sound of the hurried steps of the retreating Red Army beating in sorrowful monotony in their ears was like a death march on the narrow streets of Bielorussia's Jewish towns. The Jews sat locked up in their homes, avoided looking through the cracks in their closed windows at the soldiers, at their frightened and staring eyes, looking as if they already had months of retreat behind them. In the long files of retreating cars loaded with bits and pieces of salvaged material sat the death-weary generals and officials in their uniforms.

On the second morning of the war there was a wave of rumors in many Bielorussian towns that "Warsaw is already in our hands," but by the evening of that day the retreating cars began to move eastward. Fragments of information accumulated one after the other and the situation on the ground testified to the great collapse on the front. Molotov's declaration over the radio about Germany's treacherous attack, that "the enemy will be defeated and victory will be ours," could not alleviate the feeling of great defeat. Within two days people's state of mind changed from one extreme to the other.

Jews Flee Eastward

At the sight of the retreating Red Army, many Jews, mainly young people themselves, turned to flee eastward. Among them were Jewish Communists and others who had been active in the Soviet administration. Some refused to leave their aged parents and the members of their family. Those escaping fled, some by foot, some by bicycle, some on wagons hitched to horses, with their families and a few goods, moving without a preplanned destination through the forests and fields of Western Bielorussia. No one knew where the front was; the war was everywhere. None of those fleeing eastward could imagine that the Germans had already parachuted military units hundreds of kilometers in front of them. The Jewish wagon loaded with a Jewish family and its goods, moving over great distances almost without prospect of hope, and the tremendous German war machine brought home the terrible gap between the pace of German murder and the pace of salvation.

Many Jews, on finally arriving at the former Polish-Soviet border, were stopped by Red Army guards with the question: "What are you running away for? Why are you creating panic?" and were ordered to return to their towns and report at the mobilization offices. Many did so and when the young men appeared they found the offices closed and deserted. In the town of Disna the Jews were permitted to cross the Dwina River towards the USSR.[1] According to estimates, the number of those fleeing eastward who succeeded in filtering through the lines came to some 10,000. In the towns the streets were empty. German Military Police stood at the crossroads and sign in German showed the way: "Nach Moskau." In some towns all the Jews fled to the forests when the Germans appeared. When, for example, the rumor reached Michaliczki that the S.S. was about to come, the Jews fled to the forests and scattered. The non-Jewish population broke into their homes and plundered everything. When the Germans announced that no harm would be done to Jews returning to their homes before a specific time, whereas those who did not would lose all their "rights," the Jews returned. The question remains: why did Jews not flee in their thousands and tens of thousands in view of the Nazis' coming, when they undoubtedly knew something at least about their actions in occupied Poland? There are a number of answers to this question. Many Jews believed, and the Soviet propaganda organs had reinforced this belief, that the Red Army was the strongest in the world and that its retreat was only for a short period, and that it would ultimately triumph over the

Germans. Others, who remembered the days of World War I, thought that this war would be more or less like the first one.

A Jew from Raduszkowicze on the former Polish-Soviet border testifies as follows:

> Many people began to flee to Russia but they were not allowed to cross the border ... Our family did not at all think of crossing over. We had a house and my father could not imagine what was going to happen. He thought that this time it would be like it was in World War I. The town would pass from one hand to the other many times without anything happening to the non-combatant population. My father was attached to his house. We had many friends, gentiles and Jews. We decided to remain. Mother did suggest that we flee to Russia but father did not even want to listen: "Are we going to leave the house and property and run away?" From our town, altogether two families went to Russia ... Only young people, members of the Party and the Komsommol fled to Russia.[2]

The Jews' feelings of attachment to their homes and property, their deep fears of the pain of wandering that many had experienced during World War I, made many decide to stay where they were. In Kobylinik the Jews assembled in groups in the market on the very first day of the war and discussed what to do: to flee or to stay? The minority favored fleeing to wherever one could in order not to fall into German hands. Others argued:

> "Jews, where are you going to go? Here everyone has a house, a garden, a cow or goat and somehow we'll pass through the hard days. How can we abandon everything to the gentiles and go wandering to seek a piece of bread? If we have to die, better here than in Siberia or in the depths of Russia.[3]

Some attempted to rationalise their inability to flee: "We aren't Communists, so what will they do to us?" Others thought in their innocence that the Germans would not harm the aged or those who had no interest in politics and the like. So it happened that most of the Jews remained in their places and did not utilize the very limited possibilities of escape which were still open to them during the war's early days.

The First Days

Upon the Red Army's retreat, and even before the Germans' arrival, members of the non-Jewish population in the villages and towns began committing acts of plunder and murder against the Jewish population. That is what happened to Wasyliszky, Korelicz, Iwje, Novogrudok, Kamin-Koszyrsk, Stolin, Kurzeniec and some other towns. In Lubieszow, Szarkowszczyzna, Stolin and other places "Jewish self-defense" groups were organized. Armed with axes and iron rods, the Jews set out to defend their streets, families and property and physically attempted to stop the attacks.

Within six days the German Army had crossed Western Bielorussia (except for the Polesie region which was taken in a pincer movement) and stood at the gates of Minsk. Following the Army came the SS and the Einsatzgruppen. "German order" was immediately established everywhere. Judenräte were established, their members appointed directly by the Germans or sometimes elected by the ghetto's inhabitants against their will. In many cases the Judenrat members were refugees who did not know the people in the ghetto and were strangers to the local Jews, and who were placed in a tragic position between the hostile local Jewish population struggling to survive and the German authorities seeking to destroy them. The ghettos were erected partially before the first *aktzias* and, partially, after them. Decrees were imposed upon the Jews, one following upon the other: it was forbidden for Jews to walk on the sidewalks, to enter a Christian's house, to talk to a Christian, to buy produce from a peasant, and more. Against their wishes Jews were taken for forced labor; they were ordered to wear the yellow star; their dwelling space was curtailed and they were ordered from the main streets. Property confiscations followed, as well as "contributions."

With the decrees also came torture, and acts of humiliation increased from one day to the next, all forming a systematic method intended to reduce the Jew into a "subhuman" in others' eyes and into an impotent being in his own. In some towns (Iwje, Iwieniec) the Jews were assembled in the market place and ordered to sing *Hatikvah* before their gentile neighbors gleefully watching from the sidewalks. In one town, the Jews were ordered to kiss Stalin's picture: those refusing to do so received blows and those kissing it also received blows for doing so.[4] In many towns the Jews were called to appear in the market place to be counted. After the count they were returned to their homes. These counts were intended to turn these gatherings into habit and to dull the fear of meeting in the market place.[5]

In the early days of the German invasion, the Jews gathered surreptitiously in the courtyards and exchanged information on the serious setbacks that the Germans had suffered on the battlefront. Some Jews became very excited, and were powerfully influenced by their fertile imagination.

They analyzed the scanty information at hand from every angle, and tried to calculate when Hitler's death blow would come. They followed every aircraft that circled in the sky above, and they gave credence to their own predictions. Nobody was able to confirm or deny their "reports," which were colored strongly by their desire to believe in them. And even if the veracity of their interpretations was doubtful, their hopefulness and their expectations crowded out their doubts. But the passage of time increasingly confuted their predictions, although their hearts continued to refuse to accept what was threatening to happen.

Many of the Jews in the smaller towns believed that their towns were somehow "protected" by the blessings of their rabbis and holy men, or because of their factories or strategic railroad crossings. It seems as though some sort of internal, self-protective thought process lulled them into believing that the great evil would not reach them.

Neither was there a lack of voices saying, "I know the Germans from World War One. Whether it's work or workers — they will not kill without purpose."[6]

The First Shock Waves

The first waves of shock came when groups of Jews were taken out and murdered during the first two months of the German occupation, in almost all of the minor towns of Western Bielorussia. This was murder calculated to instill terror, to show the lack of any connection between the deeds of the Jews and the death punishment. At first, they chose to kill "Communist" Jews, using the non-Jewish citizens to walk through the line-ups and point out the so-called Communists among the Jews. In other cases, they murdered groups of Jews who had been falsely accused by local farmers of reporting German paratroopers to the Russians — paratroopers who were subsequently executed by the Russians. Or, the wealthy (as in the case of the town of Kobylnik.) Or, on the basis of membership in groups of Jewish intelligence. In Oszmiana, about 600 Jews were rounded up in the village square. Those who the local Polish townfolk pointed out as "Communists" were taken to an unrevealed location and never returned.[7]

On their entry into Swienciany, the Germans executed 150 Jewish "Communists," in Baranowicze 73, and so on for Swierzhen, Mir, Zholudok, Lubbieszow, Sernik, Wiszniewo and elsewhere. In the town Dakszyce there was a moving story of one family's sacrifice. A wagoner had two daughters: Chana and Chaya. The eldest, Chana, had been a member of the local council during the Soviet occupation. Meanwhile, she had given birth to a child and her father looked for some shelter for her in the villages, without success. When the Germans came to the father's house seeking Chana, her sister Chaya presented herself and declared: "I am Chana." The Germans bound her, tore her clothing and led her naked through the town streets. She continued to reply to them: "Murderers! Don't think that with my and my brothers' blood you are going to win the war. You will yet pay for this!" After harsh torture she was executed.[8]

In Rozhanka, the peasants told the Germans that during the war Jews had informed the Russians about German parachutists who had fallen in the neighborhood of the village; the Germans had been caught by the Russians and hung. Following this betrayal, 72 Jews were arrested and hung. A sign on their grave announced: "Here Jews killed our German soldiers."[9]

In other places, members of the local population found murder to be a way of getting rid of Jews who had entrusted their property to them. In Kobylnik, the mayor, Wanckovicz, tendered a list prepared by the town's Christians, of 48 property-owning Jews. All 48 were executed; the Germans labelled them "Communists."[10] In some places the Germans murdered Jewish intellectuals in order to deprive the Jewish population of a spiritual and intellectual leadership. The Nazi regime looked upon them as a potential threat. In Iwje, 224 Jews were killed, among them teachers of the Hebrew and Yiddish schools, the principal of the Hebrew school, Novoprocky, and the town rabbi, Perelman. In Zhetel, 120 of the town's intellectuals were murdered; in Szczuczyn 90 persons, mostly intellectuals. These acts of murder caused shock, anger and deep fear for what was to come.

Acts of Resistance

Even at this early stage, before the Jews could imagine what was in store for them and before the underground organizations had come into being in Western Bielorusssia, immediately after the Germans' arrival, signs of an underground could already be seen in some places, and we find cases of resistance by individuals and groups. These groups, mostly young people, formed without any guiding hand, certainly sensed and partly even knew what price they would have to pay for their actions. They resisted, fought, fled, challenged and promised vengeance against their murderers up to the last moments of their lives.

Yeshaya Plotnik, a 15-year-old from Pinsk, sought to smuggle a loaf of bread into the ghetto. He evaded the gate and went through the fence. A policeman ran after him and aimed his rifle. Yeshaya jumped, grabbed the rifle and began to wrestle with the policeman. He was overcome and killed.

Hershl Levin, also of Pinsk, was wounded by one of the Polish policemen. The wounded Hershl jumped over a nearby fence, tore out a board and struck at the policeman's hand. The policeman dropped the rifle, Levin jumped over the ghetto wall and escaped.[11]

Eliezer Ronkin of David-Horodok spat in a policeman's face when the latter attempted to pull a ring off his hand, and was killed. When Yosef Halib of Korelicze was ordered to bury two Jews who had been murdered by the Germans, he refused. When the policeman struck him, Yosef raised his hoe, hit the policeman on the head and shouted: "Your end will be like ours." He was shot on the spot.[12] A Jewish carpenter in the Dvorec work camp was slapped by his Polish supervisor. The Jew grabbed a hammer and hit the Pole on his head. The camp commander ordered his execution. Reuven Fort and Yehiel Segalowicz were arrested by the camp commander and beaten for having shown opposition.[13]

In Koldyczevo, a Jew refused to hand over his boots to the Germans and slashed them with a knife. The Germans chopped off his feet with an axe. When the Germans came to Riwa Stein in Lachowicz and demanded that she hand over two daughters, she refused and they murdered her.

Zelig Narocki of Kobylnik fled from the column in which 48 Jews were being led to their execution. He was shot while escaping.[14]

When the Germans murdered Jews in villages in the Stolpce neighborhood, they surrounded the house of Feivel, a tailor in the village of Krilovshzczyna. Feivel set his house on fire, jumped from the window and crushed a German's head with a bottle.

When Riwa Karp from Oszmiana was being led to her death she turned to the Germans with the following words: "Don't think you are going to rule the world. The day of vengeance will come and you will pay dearly for all your crimes and murder."[15] Doba Velitovska, a 19-year-old from Swierzhen, was among 30 young people being led to death. She called out to the Germans: "The revenging Jewish hand will yet find you. You will pay for our spilt blood, you contemptible German murderers!" Doba's last words were her testament for the underground that was to arise in that town.

There were also cases of group revolt. In Pruzhany the Germans ordered a roll call. The young people refused to appear. Members of the Judenrat attempted to convince them to report, arguing that by their refusal they were placing much responsibility upon themselves.

Deportations to Other Ghettos

After having carried out their murderous operations against the Jews of the smaller towns, communities and villages, the Germans began to concentrate them in the larger ghettos. In particular, they expelled the Jews from the towns near the forests. In addition to concentrating them, as part of Nazi policy, the Germans were also intent upon depriving the Jews of the time necessary to form any opposition. They also sought to force Jewish public life to disintegrate, weaken their will to live and diminish their powers of resistance.

About 1,000 Jews lived in the town of Iwieniec near the forest. On the day they entered the town 28 June 1941, the Germans murdered 34 Jews. Two weeks later, on 14 July another 14 were killed, and again, in September 1941, another group of Jews. On 16 May 1942 some of the Iwieniec Jews were deported to the Dworec work camp and, on 2 June 1942, to Novogrodok.

The Jews of Naliboky, also close to the forest and totalling some 300 persons, were transferred some months after the Germans' arrival to Rubzhewicze, where Jews from other nearby towns were concentrated. Before they had managed to accustom themselves to the place, the young and able were sent to work in the Dworec work camp. They were sent without food and water by a roundabout route on which many died.

The Jews of Svir, numbering some 500 persons, were deported at the end of 1942 to Michaliczky. Only some 60 skilled workers were allowed to remain. From Michaliczky they were taken to Vilno and to Kovno. In the same way, the Jews of Smorgon and Soly were driven to Oszmiana, from Ignalino and Lyntupy to Swienciany, from Iwacewicze to Slonim, from Sielec to Bereza-Kartuska, from Hermonowicz and Novy-Pohost to Szarkowszcyzna, from Woronowo to Lida, from Naliboky to Dworec and so on.

The First Wave of *Aktzias*

The Jews' greatest shock of all came with the first wave of bloody *aktzias* in which about 40 percent of the Western Bielorussian Jewish population and, in some of the towns, most of the Jewish population, were murdered.

The Jews were assembled in the market place and within a few minutes were surrounded by armed German forces and the local police forces, Bielorussian or Lithuanian. In the *selektzia* made on the spot, the Germans separated between vitally-needed skilled workers and others who were taken away in groups to be shot.

In Hancevicz in Polesie the entire Jewish population was murdered on 13 August 1941. In the towns of Polesie most of the Jewish men were killed as early as August 1941.

The first wave of *aktzia* continued until December of that year. In some places the *aktzias* were carried out in the summer of 1941, with almost all of the population killed, except for some dozens of skilled workers who were allowed to stay alive for a limited time (Lubieszow, Pohost, etc.)

Whole Jewish communities, in most cases numbering thousands of men, women and children, were assembled in the market places and carried off, accompanied by German forces and armed local policemen, to burial pits some kilometers away from the town that had been dug previously by members of the non-Jewish population, and sometimes even by Jews themselves. There, after having been ordered to undress, they were killed by machine guns. The Jews were led to their deaths in the light of day, before the eyes of the non-Jewish population. Despite all their fears most of them did not know during the first wave of where they were being taken. In some places, however, Jews attempted to flee even before the first *aktzia*.

When the Jews of Lachowicz were surrounded in the market place on 28 October 1941, many began to run across the nearby bridge over the river. The local police shot at those fleeing and close to 150 of them found their deaths by the river.

It is impossible to describe all the acts of murder known to us from those days. We will dwell only on the testimonies of a few witnesses.

The testimony of David Epstein, born in 1900, a shoemaker from the town of Lubieszow in the Polesie district tells the story of one small town in that district during the Holocaust. David Epstein went through the hell of the Lubieszow ghetto and upon the ghetto's liquidation obtained arms and left with his wife for the forest at the end of August 1942. His testimony is written in an old-fashioned Yiddish. "I, with only a little education, am going to write for you with a pen in a book what happened to the Jewish people in the World War." The "Jewish people" of this book are the Jews of his town, Lubieszow, and the feeling that impelled him to write was that of being the last chronicler of his "Jewish people" that had been annihilated. He stands face to face with Jewish history and he owes it his story.

He preserved a rare power of memory of the events and through chapter after chapter tells the story of the suffering and murder of the Jewish community in his town along with his own story. "... All this has been written by the only Jew who remained from the town and all this he lived and went through and saw with his own eyes ..."

"... On 26 June 1941 the Germans entered and on the following day the Ukrainians started a pogrom that lasted three days and took Jewish victims. Young Jews organized a Jewish self-defense group. Following that came the decrees that Hitler issued every day and every hour. On 1 August 1941, 32 Jews were executed and on 31 January 1942 — 12 women and 33 children ... Now, however, came the dark sad day that ended our Jewish lives forever. On 27 August 1942 ... at three in the afternoon, 30 members of the Gestapo came from the district city of Kamin-Koszyrsk with the death's heads on their hats, and 60 Ukrainian policemen, and the district kommissar to our black wedding.

At night the Hitlerite murderers surrounded the whole ghetto and stood on watchful guard so that nobody would escape from the ghetto, and we miserable Jews wept and cried that we had only a few hours to live.

And when the time came at four in the morning, the Hitlerite murderers began with their sticks to drive the Jews from the houses in the ghetto and concentrated them in one large square near the Judenrat. The murderers came into my house and with their rubber whips began to drive everybody to the Inquisition Square. My dear seven-year-old son was sleeping sweetly. With a breaking heart his mother went to his bed and woke him: "My son, my darling, get up from your sweet sleep, my beloved son. I'll help you put on your clothes." And my dear son got up all at once and said: "What's happened, mama? And she answered, "My darling son Velvele, dress fast, we are going, my son, to the slaughter!"

And my darling son, his young heart tightened and he was no longer able to say a word. We all went out of the house and went to the square where all the people were gathered.

First of all they read the names of some dozens of workers who were still needed and who were being kept back temporarily. It was my fate to remain for the time being. They also called my wife, Feige, because she worked sewing linen for the Germans. Our seven-year-old son, whom we loved and cherished more than anything, they took from us and we stood stunned. I ran with the child and threw myself on the ground, I cried and pleaded for them to leave my only son alive. I received terrible blows on the head from them."

In that way David Epstein led his only son, seven-year-old Velvele, to the sacrifice, and no angel of God appeared in the sky and no ram in the bushes.

"... The pits were dug. 2,000 Jews were taken in groups of 30. They were undressed in the synagogue and from there taken to the pits. Long boards were stretched over the pits; they made the Jews stand on them and shot them. The Hitlerite murderers threw the little children into the pits alive. 2,300 were buried in the 11 pits and the rest, elsewhere. The 80 Jews the Germans had left alive for work were surrounded on the night of 26 November 1942 and brought to the synagogue. They were undressed and the district kommissar began to read their sentence. A Jewish dentist, Machhandler, leapt out of the rows, fell on the kommissar and wounded him in his throat with a razor but did not succeed in killing him. The Germans caught him and trampled him with their feet ..."[16]

David Epstein and his wife, who had fled to a hiding place, wandered through villages and forests until they reached Fiodorov's partisan unit.

Rivka Yoslevska of Pohost near Pinsk relates the story of her fate and the fate of the Jews of her town on 15 August 1942:[17]

"The ghetto was full of Germans. The police surrounded the ghetto ... I held my daughter in my hands ... We ran all the way, anyone who fell — did not get up again ... We came to the place, all my family — we all came there. It was about three kilometers from the town. I already saw dozens of people who had been shot lying there. When I stood by the pit, my daughter said: "Why are we standing and waiting? Let's run." Other young people attempted to escape but succeeded in getting only a few steps away; they were immediately shot and killed. They pushed us towards the pit. We were already naked. My father did not want to undress completely and remained in his underclothes ... They hit him hard but he did not want to. They tore the clothes from him and shot him. I saw it ... Then came my mother's turn ... She was about 80. Then ... my father's sister; how much she had suffered in the ghetto and still she wanted to live — she stood there and begged for her life ... My sister and her friend ... both were shot. And another sister, and then my turn came ... He asked me: "Who shall I shoot first, your daughter or you?" I didn't answer anything. I felt how my daughter was torn from me, I felt her last cry and heard how she was shot ... He grabbed my hair and wanted to shoot. I heard a shot but remained standing. He began to load his pistol once again ... and shot and I fell. I fell into the pit and did not feel anything. I felt some weight, something heavy on me. I thought I was dead, and still — felt that I was suffocating because people had fallen on me. I was drowning. I began to move. I felt that I was able to move, that I was alive. I was choking. I heard shots. Another one fell but I was struggling not to suffocate. I didn't have any strength and then suddenly I felt that still I was lifting myself up over the others. I saw people pulling, biting, scratching and with the last of my strength I moved towards the top.

I got out and did not recognize anything ... Terrible sounds; children crying: "Father! Mother!" I couldn't stand on my feet ... I was naked and smeared with blood, dirty from all the broken bodies ... When I was shot I had received a wound in my head ... I thought, perhaps, despite everything, I might find by daughter among all the children. I began to call her name: "Markele," but there was no answer ... I walked; I sat among the trees and didn't move.

At night I went to the grave and wanted to die. Why had I remained? I thought the grave would open and I would fall into it. There was blood on everything ..."

Every ghetto in Bielorussia had its murder pits some three to five kilometers away. The forest groves and open pits absorbed the last sounds of the Jews and the terrible sights of what had taken place there. The covering earth moved after the massacre.

There were ghettos from which the large majority of the Jews were taken to the pits. The few who remained were left desolate. Yitzhak Aron, one of the Miory refugees, wrote in his diary after the *aktzia* in his town:

"A terrible slaughter. Only few were saved. I fled from the market place with a friend. They shot at us. Many fell in their escape and only few were saved. Until night I lay in Yitzhak Katzav's house and at night I left the town ... I thought of nothing except that I had lost my parents, my three sisters ... I stood among the bushes at night and said *Kaddish* [prayer for the dead]."

He goes on: "At night I went to look for a Jew. I so much wanted a Jew. I wanted to know who had remained alive. I didn't find anyone ..."[18]

The almost total blockade imposed on every ghetto and every Jewish community prevented the transmission of information of what was happening from one community to another. The German efficiency with which they carried out the mass murders concealed details about them and prevented communication between the Jewish towns. The dates of the *aktzias* were linked by the proximity of communities to each other; in Lachowicze on 28 October 1941, in Nieswiezh on 30 October and in Kleck on 31 October. These communities were from 15 to 20 kilometers apart. However, when some rumor did filter into a ghetto before the *aktzia* about what had occurred in some other ghetto, the very frightfulness of the information was so stunning that many people in the ghetto attempted to ignore it in disbelief in order to preserve the necessary measure of vitality and will to act needed to maintain themselves and their families. The few who remained alive began to grasp that what they were facing was not only murderers but a satanic plot for their extermination.

After the *Aktzias*

Of the days after the first *aktzia* we can read in the following testimony:[19]

> "Some 4,000 Jews from our city were executed on 30 October 1941. I don't have the strength to tell about that day. We left for a barracks. Piles of clothing. The people from the ghetto who were working at sorting the clothing, wept while they worked. Some recognized the garments of brothers and sisters. "Oh, this is Chaimke's!" "This is Sarah's!" And then they continued weeping in hiding so that the Germans would not notice.
>
> Only a few families had survived intact. Generally families were shattered ... Most terrible of all is the situation of those left all alone ... Where do they draw the psychological strength to continue living?
>
> There is one tree growing in the ghetto, alone in all the ghetto, near our house. More than anything else it reminds us of the life flowing in its channels, of the people living around us who are ready to come to terms with our death, to continue their joys on our graves, as if that were the most natural thing that they had the right to live — and we, to be killed ...
>
> In the morning we go out of the ghetto to work, cross the market, pass by the church with the chestnut trees, the palace's iron gate and the long avenue. Chinaberry trees, the chestnuts in flower ... The light morning breeze fluttering over the enchantingly beautiful lake ... The scene is so restful and still cuts like a knife. Not far from the palace are the pits with the murdered Jews. This is the path the Jews went ... Death walks in this wonderful landscape.

> The moods of the ghetto Jews change — who knows how many times a day. I go by my neighbor's house. Death haunts the house ... They have already "finished running" but after moments, hopes rise, they apparently do not desert one even in the scaffold's shadow. Maybe we will still "outlive them" and anything can happen."

Many in the ghetto did not believe the information about the mass murders even when it came from eyewitnesses. One such witness, Zowisky from Olkeniky, relates:[20]

> "Gershon from Dweig [a town 30 kilometers from Olkeniky] escaped from the *aktzia* conducted there at the end of June 1941. He arrived in Olkeniky and immediately came to my father ... Coming into our house, he said to all of us: "Sirs, I have escaped from Dweig. I only want to rest here a little. You must flee from here." He turned to my father and said to him: "You must know that all the Jewish inhabitants of Dweig have been annihilated, among them also your daughter Zippora, her husband and their children. The inhabitants of the nearby towns, Hanishak, Botrimanz, have not escaped that fate. They were trapped in the *aktzia* and killed. And you are sitting here quietly and do not sense the catastrophe hanging over your heads!"
>
> The people present stood petrified, stared at him in great pity, as if he had gone mad. Father broke the silence and said: "Brothers, this Jew has apparently gone through some shock that hurt his mental stability or he is shocked by fear and therefore exaggerates the danger. It is impossible for them to bring together people, among them women and children, and kill them for no reason. He saw when they were assembling them and his fear has overpowered him so he sees imagination as reality. They have surely moved the people to some ghetto or work camps.
>
> Gershon almost wanted to kill himself, but he was powerless. They did not believe him and he had nothing with which to convince the people that he was speaking the truth.
>
> Finally, my mother, Batya Zowisky, got up and said that she would put on peasant clothes and visit the villages to find out whether Gershon's words were true or not. The people in the house began to cry at mother's decision but father agreed. She left and returned only to verify Gershon's testimony."

The question of whether to believe or not involved tortuous soul searching that sometimes continued a long time. It was a psychological process replete with its nightmares and terrors.

The First Series of Aktzias

Together with the fear of death that haunted the ghetto, came isolation from the outside world, the hostility of the surrounding population and the alienation of Christian neighbors and friends. All these imposed a terrible isolation, intensified the fear and formed a dense cloud, a kind of lead beam weighing on the heads of the ghetto Jews.

Like dismembered limbs of a living body of community and family, the Jews sat in their few streets behind barbed wire, living-dead moving between the fences. The most astonishing thing is that together with the despair there also appeared a strong will to live, a spirit of revolt and revenge. Despair, the desire to live, and revolt dwelt together in the heart of the Jew, if not all at one time, then in turn. The deeper the despair became, the stronger the will to live. It is doubtful whether people ever had a will to live like that which appeared in the ghetto's most hopeless moments. This is the key to understanding the fighting Jewish response in the ghettos.

After the *aktzia* in Antopol, Dr. Czerniak, who had found a hiding place for his ten-month-old daughter, said:

> "Now it is clear to all that the end has come. Our first feeling at this moment is: good that the child isn't with us. Maybe she will stay alive ... a memorial for us ... After that comes a second feeling: no, no I will not give myself to death ..."

Dr. Czerniak and his wife founded a partisan unit. After he had found some hope for his little daughter, an additional personal motive had been created: "for whom" to fight and to continue the struggle.[21]

We are stirred in the following passage by the feeling of pride of belonging to the Jewish people in these times, combined with a strong longing for life in the last moments of a young Jewish woman in the ghetto. Fania Barbakov, aged 29, kept a diary and ended it with the following words:[22]

> "My hands tremble and it is hard for me to finish writing. I am proud that I am a Jewess, I am dying for my people. How much I want to live and to attain to a little good in life, but everything is already lost ... Be well; your relative, Fania, in the name of them all, father, mother, Sima, Sonia, Zosia, Rasia, Chanze and in the name of little Zeldele, who still does not understand anything ..."

Every generation has its own relationships to words and expressions. We must therefore go into the world of feelings of Fania Barbakov, the world in which she lived while writing these words in the dark, almost without any hope that the writings would survive, in a ghetto facing annihilation, in order to understand them as they deserve.

Ghetto reality and the longing to live led even a young person who believed in God to question the ways of the world. From prayers to the Creator to angry charges against Heaven and a curse against the human race, and to revolt.

Sarah Fishkin, a young girl from Rubzhewicze, left a diary opening a window to the thoughts of a young, God-believing person in the ghetto. She wrote:[23]

> "January 26, 1942
> God in Heaven have pity on us and save us from our troubles. Or let destruction and an end come to the whole world. Bring a flood again to wash away the human race from the face of the earth. Let this world be cursed forever.
> The sun's rays are going out! Why do they light and warm the murderers and only we do not enjoy their light? Our world is dark.
> My patience is at an end and I must write the truth that has overpowered all my thoughts ... But when I see all our difficult struggle for life in the great sea of blood and tears and when I see that there is no redeeming or saving hand then I can no longer be silent ..."

If we want to understand what was in the hearts of the ghetto inhabitants we must turn an attentive ear to the their voices. Sonie Czernia of Luzhky wrote: "I was so young, only 16 and had tasted so little of life's pleasures. Nobody wants to die in his youth ... The worse the situation becomes, the greater our appetite for life ..."

Rachel Reznik (Garbuz) of Yanow near Pinsk tells us:[25] "I always went with the thought that they would not succeed in exterminating me. That thought never left me. Truly, I don't know where I got that confidence. In the most difficult moments I was accompanied by the words: 'Me' they won't succeed in killing."

Even irrational belief has its effect on human life and gives it strength. The Germans would at times enter the ghetto and stroll about the streets. At such a time, the ghetto was seized by panic. Everybody fled and hid in their houses; the streets emptied completely. However, despite the bleakness and the mourning after the *aktzias*, the Jews and especially the younger people, revealed astonishing vitality. "In spite of the ban on going out of the houses in the dark hours, the young people used to gather in small groups and spend their time in telling jokes, reading novels and even courting ..."[26]

Pesya Mayevska tells about life in the ghetto:[27]

> There were those who turned their eyes towards Heaven. They were orthodox, put on *tefilin* [phylacteries] prayed three times a day and poured out the bitterness in their hearts before the Creator of the universe. Many looked for good literature. Franz Werfel's book, *The Forty Days of Musa Dagh*, passed from hand to hand, telling about the heroic revolt of a group of Armenians during the Turkish slaughters. Following that example the Jewish youth gathered arms, created an underground ...

On Sabbath eves Jewish mothers blessed candles using a potato or a piece of board, in place of the candlesticks that had been looted by the Germans.

Jewish children never seemed to have been so beautiful as they were in the ghetto, and how mature and wise they were. They knew it was forbidden to cry when the Germans were looking for Jews, that it was forbidden to run outside the ghetto.

The children used to play in the ghetto. Hershl Kaplinsky's daughter was playing with a cat by the fence. Suddenly the cat ran away from the ghetto. The child was excited and called out: "Cat, cat, do you have a permit to go out of the ghetto?"

No one went mad in the ghetto. The very ill and the invalids recuperated as a result of the shock they went through.

Moshe Mirsky had been blind all his life. He was lean and handsome. Together with his family of twelve he went to the burial pit and there, at the sound of the suffering and torture, his sight returned. He saw the sun only in order to say goodbye to it forever, in order to see the open grave.

Jews celebrated the holiday in the ghetto. The last Jews in Novogrudok roasted thin slices of bread over the fire and from potato peels made *kneidlach*. Old Gercowski arranged a *seder*. Some read the *Haggadah* but there were no children to ask the four questions. Graceful Linka Landau quietly sang:

> In a village not so far,
> In a house standing aside
> From a window not so big
> A Jewish child is looking out.

Mothers, whose children had been taken from them by force, sat at the *seder* and wept, and whispered: "Next year in Jerusalem."[28]

In the eyes of the ghetto Jews, Eretz Israel was a dream, a hope, the last Jewish bastion where the Jewish remnants would remain, where no harm could hurt, as if it were on some other planet. No wonder, then, that every discussion in the ghetto on the future after the war, about some "name and memorial to remain after us," was connected in some way with Eretz Israel, even among the former Jewish Communists. Those who had children or relatives in Palestine were the fortunate people in the ghetto. A witness from Żoludek relates:[29]

> "... At times of distress and despair we could hear father and mother attempting to comfort each other: "We are not sorry about ourselves, after all we have finished most of our lives. We are only sorry about the children, who have been sentenced to such an end. But we must not complain. Our lot is better than that of others; we have had the privilege of two of our daughters reaching the shores of safety in Eretz Israel. And most of the families in the town will leave no name or memory after them ..."

And in Nieswiezh ghetto:

> "Recently I have begun to interest a man by the name of Buzin, a Communist from Warsaw, to join our underground activity. It is interesting to see with how much love the man now speaks about Palestine. It is hard to believe that he once argued against Palestine.
>
> In the ghetto there is a young refugee woman who told me during a conversation: "How much I would like to be in Eretz Israel before my death." After a moment she added: "In any case I will be in Eretz Israel after my death." The tie to Eretz Israel was understood by her heart in transcendental terms.[30]

In strange ways echoes from Palestine sometimes reached the ghetto. A German newspaper happened to reach the Swierzhen work camp, with a caricature of a Jew dressed in a steel helmet and holding a machine gun, and under the picture, the caption: "A Jewish fighter in Palestine." From that picture the Jews in the camp drew encouragement because they had learned that there was indeed a Jewish fighting force in Palestine.

Despite the tremendous psychological tensions to which the ghetto Jews were subject, they did not lose their awareness of the need to preserve their ideas and testimonies for coming generations, so that what was happening would not be forgotten. Zirl Perlin of Kamen-Koszyrsk, before she fled from the ghetto, brought the manuscripts of her father — a rabbi — to her neighbors to be hidden in their homes. On her way to the forest she was killed by a policeman.

There was a natural, almost self-understood connection between the awareness and sense of history for the future and Eretz Israel. That connection implied that there was no place safe from the catastrophe except Eretz Israel, where the rules of political reality, interests and policies, war, strategy and geopolitics, did not apply.

When the last Jews of Lida were led to the railway cars that would take them to Maidanek, Yaakov Konskowolsky turned to his wife, Chana, who was walking with their infant: "Run away! Somebody must be saved. We have a large family in Eretz Israel and somebody must tell the world what they did to us!" Yaakov tore the yellow star off her garment. He himself feared to join her lest his Jewish looks endanger his baby's life. Chana came to the forest while the Germans searched it for Jews. She travelled 90 kilometers with her infant during the battles in forest. After the war she did reach Eretz Israel with her daughter.[31] A Jewish refugee from the Nieswiezh ghetto, by the name of Markovsky, said:

> "I would like there to be a monument over our grave, high until the skies, with letters of fire saying: "Here thousands of Jews were murdered at the hands of the Nazi Germans; so high that the writing would be seen by everyone travelling on the international railway from Moscow to Paris after the war."

The Zionist youth movements that had played an important role in Western Bielorussian public life before the war: Hashomer Hatzair, Hechalutz Hatzair, Gordonia, Betar, Hanoar Hatzioni, and who had established a *chalutz* Zionist underground at the time of Soviet rule, now adapted their activities to the new conditions and operated through personal guidance. After many of the movements' members were killed in the first *aktzias*, those remaining strengthened their ties based on shared beliefs and a joint past in the movement of their youth. The youth movements took a special place in the ghetto undergrounds. In some ghettos they also organized underground schools which were taught by the surviving teachers.

"Now I am teaching children in the ghetto. I have recruited a number of teachers who also teach general subjects — reading, writing, arithmetic, geography and history. I only talk with them. They come after work in small groups to a little room in our house and I tell them the legends of the Destruction of the Temple, the Scrolls of Fire, the decrees in the past, the Jews in Christian Spain, the stories of Jewish dreamers and fighters. The children follow every word. Their big black eyes glow and sometimes they are moist with tears. What I want to bring to their understanding is that all evil regimes seek our lives, that we fight for Jewish and human morality, and that is our special role … Sometimes, however, I read in their eyes a single question: "What are we to do? How are we going to save our lives?" Every meeting with the children is also an hour of great suffering …"[33]

The ghettos were full of people who needed help, treatment and care. The Judenrat provided food and medical care to a meager degree. The social aid institutions that had existed before the war were gone. In some places individuals appeared who excelled in their work for others and brought care and healing to the homes. These were admired by all the ghetto's inhabitants and turned into natural leaders. Dr. Olga Goldfein organized a hospital in the Pruzhany ghetto and was the living spirit within it. She was intelligent, energetic and had an aristocratic bearing. The Christian population also loved her. On the days the Jews of the Pruzhany ghetto were deported she stood by the gate and loudly and bitterly condemned the Germans. She succeeded in escaping, dressed as a nun.

In the Zoludek ghetto there was Devora Drewiansky.[34] Zholudok had long been known for its hospitable and charitable Jews. Devora (Devorele) Drewiansky was a talented woman blessed with a good heart and a pure character. She had married in the town and given birth to two children. Even before the war she had provided support for anyone in need, would go to the baker and pay with her own money and tell him to whom to send loaves of bread. The Christians in the town also respected her for her nobility; she was a leading figure in the ghetto. Judenrat members used to come to ask her advice and what she said they accepted. Every day she went from house to house, to bring one a loaf of bread, another some medicine, a garment to wear or just an encouraging word. In her actions, understanding and nobility she was a symbol for the whole ghetto. Devora wrote a letter to her husband, who had previously been exiled to Siberia, and her daughter Zippa also added her letter. The two letters were entrusted to a local Christian. Here are excerpts from the Yiddish:

"… It is superfluous to describe the times in which I am writing these words. That will be told by history. The living will only have to believe … Only this

I ask of God, that we all be privileged to read again these few words, that our pure souls be privileged to live in knowledge and awareness, and that we one day enjoy to the full the food of quiet days; to love our children and the Jewish people ... The time obliges me to say some words of farewell to you. We have united here together, the little blood that has remained, and in our hearts the prayer that it may be the will of our Father in Heaven that we will see you again ... But if, God forbid ... you will have to be strong in order to take part in the great privilege that is called — life.

For your honesty and gentleness, your diligence and untiring work, for your loving and pitying devotion to me and the children — we ask you to be strong, that you spare your health and continue to enjoy life. Try to find my father, my brother and their families. Be devoted to each other. Be strong and encouraged."

Zippa wrote to her father:

"Dear father, it is hard to me to write these words of farewell ... I won't describe what we are going through ... Our town is destroyed and burned. Hunger and poverty and helplessness — these are our lot. Everywhere, and for anything, and for nothing, the bitter end awaits us ... Even things that sound most imaginary — believe them! Every rumor is the bitter truth. Everything can be testified to by the piles of ashes and dust.

Dear father, how good it would be if we could meet and talk to you, but that sounds fantastic ..."

As we have said, the Germans adopted methods of deceit towards the Jews. After the first wave of *aktzias* they attempted to lull them by saying that those remaining alive were vital for the German economy and that therefore nothing bad would happen to them if they worked diligently. Indeed, in their primal will to live the Jews grasped a every spark of hope in seeking some security that the skilled workers were indeed vital for the German economy. The pause between the first wave of *aktzias* and the second also reinforced the hope that those who had remained would be allowed to live.

Despite the blockade, rumors filtered into the ghetto from various sources, from clandestine radio receivers and scraps of German newspapers, that the German offensive had been stopped at the beginning of the hard winter somewhere near Moscow because of the Red Army's massive defense. Even among those who had never been admirers of the Soviet Union there were feelings of gratitude and sometimes even admiration towards the fighting Red Army. Jews began to imagine that what had happened to Napoleon would occur again, especially after the United States entered the war and the German Army had not succeeded in its *blitzkrieg*. In the ghettos there were rumors from the peasants about long railway trains filled with wounded and dead moving westward, and that the German Army was sending new and younger forces to the front. Their hearts' desires added to these rumors.

All these together aroused hopes among many of the ghetto inhabitants that some change was possible on the front and that the Germans would retreat swiftly and not have time to deal with the Jews. Those who played with these ideas later formed the not-so-small camp that opposed the formation of the Jewish underground. On the other hand, the memory of the *aktzias* was too strong and aroused feelings that it was necessary to "do something," even if they still did not know how, and even more so, with what!

Sonia Czernia from Disna ghetto, expressed that feeling precisely:[35] "... We used to meet amongst ourselves, discussing and sensing that we had to escape, that in any case we had to do something ..." That feeling was shared by young people and adults alike.

Ben-Zion Gulkowicz of Korelicz relates:

> "The despair was great ... but the urge to live was strong in every one of us. We nursed the desire for revenge in our hearts. Many young men went about the ghetto with that idea. I talked to groups of young people to escape to the forest ..."

Leib Matusow, the owner of a charcoal factory in Kurzeniec, said:[36] "We are slaughtering ourselves ... We must go to the forest. Let us not wait with folded hands. I know the forests. There are deep forests which the Germans will be unable to penetrate ..."

The feeling that "something must be done" gave birth to the Jewish underground in the ghettos.

Notes

1. Yad Vashem (YV) 03/3017 (Ida Lekach).
2. Moreshet Archive (MA) A-517 (Berl Maneh).
3. YV 2381/174 (Yitzhak Gordon).
4. Shifra Solomiansky, testimony in *Sefer Lubcz-Delatycz* (Lubcz-Delatycz Memorial Book) (Tel Aviv, 1971), p. 384.

5. YV 2490/172 (Yaffa Abramowicz).
6. Dov Amit, testimony in *Sefer Zikoron likehillat Kamin-Koshirsk* (Memorial Book for the Community of Kamin-Koshirsk and Its Environs) (loc. date pub), p. 145.
7. YV 1160/1128 (Riva Machnitzka).
8. Zvi Markman, testimony in *Sefer Yizkor Dokszyce-Parafyanov* (Dokszyce-Parafyanov Memorial Book) (Tel Aviv, 1970), pp. 150–157.
9. Azriel Bezruczka, testimony in *Sefer Szczuczyn* (Szczuczyn Memorial Book) (Tel Aviv, 1967), pp. 443–446.
10. Yossef Blinder, testimony in *Sefer Kobylnik* (Kobylnik Memorial Book) (loc. date pub), p. 132.
11. Nachum Boneh, testimony in *Sefer Zikaron Pinsk* (Pinsk Memorial Book) (Tel Aviv, 1969), pp. 339–341.
12. (First name of initial) Meirowitz, testimony in *Sefer Korelicze* (Korelicze Memorial Book (n.p., n.d.), p. 241.
13. Yehiel Segalowitz, testimony in *Sefer Rubzhewicze* (Rubzhewicze Memorial Book) (Tel Aviv, 1965), p. 352.
14. Blinder, loc. cit.
15. Moshe Solc, testimony in *Sefer Oszmiane* (Oszmiane Memorial Book) (Tel Aviv, 1965), p. 352.
16. YV E/48 (David Epstein).
17. Rivka Yosselevska, in *Eduyot* (Testimonies — of the Eichmann Trial), vol. 1 (Jerusalem, 1963), pp. 416–422.
18. Yitzhak Aron, testimony in *Sefer Druya* (Druisk Memorial Book) (Tel Aviv, 1973), p. 101.
19. Shalom Cholawski, *Soldiers from the Ghetto* (New York, 1980), pp. 60–68. (Some passages have been retranslated.)
20. Chaim Zowisky, testimony in *Ha'ayara Bilhavot* (The Shtetl in Flames — Olkeniki) (Tel Aviv, 1962), p. 132.
21. YV 2910/44-3 (Pinchas Czerniak).
22. *Sefer Druya*, op. cit., p. 99.
23. *Yalkut Moreshet*, no. 4 (1965), pp. 21–35.
24. Sonia Czernia, testimony in *Sefer Zikaron Lekehilla* (Disna) (Memorial Book for a Town — Disna) (Tel Aviv, 1969), p. 162.
25. Rachel Reznik, testimony in *Sefer Zikaron* (A Memorial Book — Yanov) (Jerusalem 1969), p. 210.
26. Reuven Budownitz, testimony in *Sefer Druya*, op. cit., p. 160.
27. Pessia Mayevska, testimony in *Pinkas Zhetl* (Zhetl Diary) (Tel Aviv, 1957), p. 373.
28. Chaim Leibowitz, testimony in *Pinkas Nowogrodek* (Nowogrodek Diary) (Tel Aviv, 1963), p. 293.

29. Pessia Beirach, testimony in *Sefer Żoludok veOrlova* (Memorial Book of the Communities of Zoludok and Orlova) (Tel Aviv, 1967), p. 205.
30. Shalom Cholawski, *Ir Vaya'ar Bamatzor* (A Town and a Forest under Siege) (Tel Aviv, 1973), p. 70.
31. YV 2086/195 (Chana Berkowicz).
32. Cholawski, op. cit., p. 68.
33. Ibid., p. 67.
34. *Sefer Żoludok veOrlova*, op. cit., pp. 55–57, 296–297.
35. Czernia, loc. cit.
36. Zalman Gurvicz, testimony in *Megillat Kurnitz* (Kurzeniec) (engl trans. book) (Tel Aviv, 1956), p. 269.

CHAPTER 6
Beginnings of the Underground

The underground movements were a response to the inner imperative that "something must be done." There were even manifestations of revolt in ghettos where we have no information of any underground organization.

In some of the towns, including Kurzeniec, Nieswiezh, Swienciany, Lachwa, and Mir, there had been pioneering Zionist underground movements during the period of Soviet rule; the members of the youth movements continued their activities after the German invasion. In these towns the underground movements commenced their activities immediately upon the Germans' arrival or shortly after it. In other ghettos the underground organizations arose after the first wave of *aktzias* at the end of 1941 or after the murder of some Jews; in some ghettos this happened only at the time of the second wave of *aktzias* in the spring of 1942. Thus, 1942 was the peak year for underground activities.

Membership in the underground in the Western Bielorussian towns included persons from various sections of the population and of various ages. Two groups, however, were outstanding: an adult group from the working class and the youth movements. The working class were persons with a sharpened sense of reality, among them those who knew the region from all aspects, including geographical and demographical.

Younger members were from pioneering socialist Zionist youth movements, who had been educated towards a certain vision and values and towards their own self-fulfillment in Eretz Israel. This young element was dominant when the underground was formed, while the more adult workers joined later, especially during the flight to the forests. Originally, the underground organizations were composed of small groups, nuclei which were to expand and grow with time.

In Kurzeniec, during the Soviet era, there had been a pioneering Zionist underground of members of Hashomer Hatzair. Among its founders were Nachum Alperovicz, Shimon Cirulnik and Zalman Uri Gurvicz, all 17- and 18-year olds with Koppel Spector as their leader. They found rifles and ammunition and distributed them among those who knew how to use them. When the rumors spread that the neighborhood peasants were about to attack the Jews after the Red Army's retreat, the underground took up defense positions and the peasants were repelled.[1]

In Swienciany, on the day of the German attack (22 June 1941) five students of the Tarbut and the Yiddish schools, S. Gertman, D. Yohai Yoske Rudnicki, Moshe Szotan and Yitzhak Rudnicky (Arad) all 14 to 19 years of age, met to discuss the situation. They obtained a radio and looked for avenues of activity. However, only in February 1942 did an organized underground appear with Yerachmiel Maceikin teaching them the use of arms.[2]

In Nieswiezh, too, members of the former pioneering Zionist underground, the four Hashomer Hatzair members Lolik Abilevitz, Hedva Lachowiczky, Cila Gilerovits and Shalom Cholawsky met when the Germans entered, and decided to organize young people into groups and to lead them. They prepared a program for educational activity. Following the *aktzia* of 30 October 1941, those remaining met and discussed the situation in the ghetto. At this meeting they spoke of fighting, but still not about the way of fighting. The underground staff added members of Gordonia, Left Poalei Zion, the Communists, some local leaders and refugees, bringing its number to a total of 50 persons.[3]

In Lachwa the idea of an underground crystallized among the members of Betar, Hashomer Haleumi, Hechalutz, and Hashomer Hatzair. They, too, already had experience of a Zionist underground from the period of Soviet rule. The central figure in the underground here was Yitzhak Rochzin of Betar. The founders also included Asher and Moshe Leib Chefetz of Betar, Aharon Oszman of Hashomer Haleumi and David Feinberg of Hashomer Hatzair. Some members of the Jewish police also joined the underground.[4]

In Kazian the underground organized at the beginning of the winter of 1941 after the murder of twelve Jewish Communists and the arrival of refugees from "Polygon," a camp near Swienciany where some 8,000 Jews were prisoners. The underground was headed by Leib Voliak, who was about 30 years old and came from the village of Stojaciszok. He had been a member of Hechalutz and was a veteran of the Polish Army. He worked to help Jews escape to the forest.

Eight days after the Germans' entry, young people and adults of Olkeniky, among them Benjamin Farber and Eliezer Varman, met to discuss the organization of the youth, plans to escape to the forests and to other towns — Ejszyszki and Radun — that seemed to be more secure.[5]

In Swierzhen the underground was established after the *aktzia* on 9 November 1941, by 18-year old Benjamin Vielitovsky and 19-year old Monik Joselewsky, students of the Tarbut school and members of Hashomer Hatzair. Seven young people from the various youth movements participated in the first underground meeting, in which Vielitovsky declared: "... We must organize and accumulate weapons ... not only to save our lives ... We will fight and take vengeance!"[6]

In Rubzhewicze Josef Fishkin and Judel Garmiza went to the Mikulicz forest, some three kilometers from the town, gathered arms the Russians had abandoned in their retreat, and buried all of them in the forest. With the Germans' arrival, an underground of 25 members was organized that continued to accumulate weapons. Among its leaders were Shimon Shuster and Jacob Ribak.[7]

The underground was organized in Zhetel at the end of 1941, after the execution of six Jewish Communists and 120 of the town's intellectuals, and the deportation of 400 Jews to the Dvorec work camp. The underground activity centered about the personality and initiative of one man — Alter Dvorecky. He was a lawyer who had studied in Berlin and Vilno and had been active in Poalei Zion and the Freiheit movement. He had been one of the region's outstanding advocates during the Soviet period and had gained acquaintances throughout the neighborhood. Upon the Germans' arrival he was appointed vice-chairman of the Judenrat and later, chairman. One of his comrades in the underground described Dvorecky as "honest, acute, energetic and enthusiastic," and he served as a personal example for those about him.

When 200 Jews were called for to go to prepare wood for the winter, Dvorecky volunteered to go with them. When he received and order to establish a police force of 30 men who would be permitted to move about the ghetto during the night hours and outside the ghetto during the day, he called in the underground leaders and convinced them to join the police so that they could move about more freely. At the beginning some of his comrades disagreed with the proposal but finally 10 underground members were included among the ghetto police. The underground numbered some 60 persons operating in 20 cells of three members each. Among its founders were Moshe Pozdonsky, Chaim Shuster, Eliahu Kowiensky and Shalom Gerling.[8] The Mir underground was established after the first *aktzia* on 9 November 1941, as a continuation of the Zionist underground of Soviet days. Its nucleus was made up of young people, mostly Hashomer Hatzair members, and among its leaders were Shlomo Charchas and Berl Reznik, older movement members who at the outset of the German invasion had returned to the town from the *chalutz* center in Vilno. They were soon joined by members of other movements, among them the Bundist Hirsh Piernikow. The organization numbered some 80 young people and its aim was "to establish a Jewish defense in the ghetto." Its members armed themselves with iron rods, and bars and axes. About that time Mir was visited by Zorach Zilberberg and Gedalyahu Shayak, who had also left the Vilno center on their way westward (they were afterwards among the leaders of the revolt in Bialystok) and brought information about the activities of movement members in other ghettos.[9]

In the ghettos of Dokszyce, Vilejka, Glebokie, Dolhinov and Stolpce, too, underground organizations were established by the members of the former pioneering Zionist underground. In Molczad, after the second *aktzia* of 3 June 1941, a self-defense organization was set up mainly by men who had served in the Polish Army. They had a few rifles in their possession.[10]

The Communists took the lead in the Slonim underground organization. After the second *aktzia* of 14 November 1941 when some 10,000 Jews were murdered, an anti-fascist committee was established in the ghetto, with young people of various political leanings, both members of the Zionist movements and Communists. Among the leading personalities in this organization were Zorach Kremen, Munia Cerinsky, Aviezer Imber and Arik Stein.[11]

In some towns instead of one organization, several came into being, in most cases, however, they united in the course of time into a single underground organization.

After the 3 March 1941 *aktzia* three organizations arose in Baranowicze: an organization initiated by Eliezer Lidovsky of Poalei Zion that included among its members Dr. Abramovsky, Jewish police commander Warshavsky and Chaim Oshman; an organization headed by Moma Kopelowicz (Antek) of Hashomer Hatzair, with 24 members, among them Moshe Zalmanovicz, Aharon Gursky and Shalom Karyckevicz; and an organization of young people founded by Elyosha Zaryckevicz, that numbered some 40 members. The first organization, Lidovsky's, was also joined by 15 members of the Jewish police. At its founding meeting it decided to organize in cells of five and to accumulate money and arms. The members of this organization took an oath:

> "I swear in the name of the fallen and the living that I will exact vengeance of the fascist murderers, that I will loyally serve the goals of the fighting organization and obey its orders. If I betray, may I be judged by the punishing hand."

In April, 1942, Lidovsky's organization totalled 120 members. His attempts to unit the three organizations were rejected at first by Kopelowicz, who "had no great trust in adults," but after extended discussions the three groups united in the spring of 1942. Altogether they numbered some 200 members, among them 15 women; 60–70 percent were young people from 16 to 30 years of age. Lidovsky, Dr. Abramovsky, Kopelowicz and Zaryckiewicz were among the organization's commanders.

Two organizations appeared in Brzesc. One was the *Nekama* (Vengeance) organization of youths from the Tarbut schools, and the other an adult organization which maintained contacts with the Polish and Soviet undergrounds, and which included among its founders Aryeh Sheinman, Michael Omalinski, Shlomo Kandlik and Acksenbaum.[13]

In Pinsk, too, there were two organizations. One, headed by Lolik Slutzky, numbered some 50 members and was organized after the Lachwa ghetto revolt on 3 September 1942. Among its members were Hershl Levin, Shaike Kolodny, Noah Weiner, Aryeh Dolinko, Gleibman. The organization discussed setting the *gebietskommissariat* factories on fire and sending young people to the forest. The second was a young people's group headed by Dr. Prager, which also planned to flee to the forest.[14]

In the Nowogrudok ghetto underground activity began after the first *aktzia* on 8 December 1941. When the news reached them that Jews had been murdered in the nearby towns and the search for partisans began, a first group of 20 persons fled the ghetto, headed by Moma Czorny. A little while later it became known that all the members of the group had been killed on the roads and in the forest, apparently because the Russian partisans had refused to accept Jews into their ranks. The Jewish partisan group headed by Tuviya Bielsky, a member of a large village family from Stankevicz, aided the Jews fleeing from Novogrudok and the region. During the Soviet period Tuviya had been an official, his brother Asael, chairman of the village council, and another brother Zusya, councilman and treasurer. When the Germans came, the police began to look for them. Their aged parents were caught and killed. In the spring of 1942 the three brothers decided to organize a Jewish partisan unit. During the winter they hid in the neighboring villages. Tuvya was an outstanding leader and all the brothers were distinguished by their courage and fighting ability. At first the unit only numbered 17 persons but with time it grew into a large Jewish partisan fighting force. In its early days its members obtained their weapons from the neighboring peasants. They established contacts with the ghettos in the region and called on their inhabitants to come to the forest and fight the Germans.[15]

At that time, there were two other underground groups in the Novogrudok ghetto: Nachumovsky's group, with 30 members mostly from Betar, which decided to place its members in the Jewish police in order to replace undesirable elements in the existing police force;[16] and a group headed by Ostashinsky, former local Betar head and Judenrat chairman, with some 50 young people between 20 and 25. Some members of this latter group left the ghetto, were captured and killed. The remainder reached the A.K. unit (*Armia Krajowa* — the Polish underground organization) in the Naliboky neighborhood and fought as an autonomous unit. In the partisan attack on Naliboky, in which the Jewish unit was given the task of taking the police headquarters, all its members fell in battle because they received no assistance or support from the other units participating in the battle.

In September 1942 a revolt committee was established in the ghetto at the initiative of Dr. Kagan, a member of the Polish Poalei Zion's Central Committee. Hashomer Hatzair representatives Rakovsky and Niwichowicz, Betar representatives Ostashinsky and Burstein, Maccabee representative Berl Joselevicz, Poalei Zion representative Kantarowitz and the non-affiliated Moshe Leizerovsky participated in this committee. The revolt committee decided on an armed uprising and escape to the forest. A group of Polish Army veterans, about 15 men in all, also joined the committee. Candidates for membership in the organization swore their oaths of loyalty by candlelight.[17]

In Stolpce they also started with two organizations: one composed wholly of local people, and the second of refugees who had arrived from western Poland during the Soviet period. The Polish group defined its goal, from the outset, to be an escape to the forest. In the spring of 1942, after the two *aktzias*, the two organizations united. Now it included members of Hashomer Hatzair, Betar and Communists. The central figures in this organization were Josef Harkawy, Azriel Tunik, Jacob Spiegel and Hersh Posesorsky.

"Escape committees" were formed in the Vilejka, Dworec, Hancevicz and Koldiczevo work camps. People with some experience in underground activity had come to these camps which were close to the forest, particularly Dvorec and Hancevicz. In the Dworec work camp young people and former soldiers organized and attempted to establish contact with the partisans. Israel Kessler, a central figure in the underground and afterwards in the forest, roamed the region and brought arms to the camp.[18]

Three hundred men from Lenin, Lachwa, Mikashevicz, Pohost and Luniniec had been imprisoned in the Hancewicz camp in the spring of 1941. The camp's inmates established an escape committee, among whose members were Grinboim, Lipa Josselevsky and others. Its members were organized into cells of five. Their plans included an escape and a raid on the *gebietskommissariat*, the police and the post office. One of the men in the camp promised to secure a truck for the escape. The Germans warned that any Jew attempting to escape could expect to be executed, together with all the members of his family and 10 other camp inmates. In that way they were able to stop attempts of escape.[19]

The Koldyczevo farm, some 18 kilometers from Baranowicze, had formerly been a concentration camp and afterwards a work camp. In November 1942 a crematorium was built there in which 600 corpses from Baranowicze and Stolpce were burned. The underground group in the camp was headed by Shlomo Kushnir and Romek, amongst others. They obtained two pistols from one of the policemen and four grenades; the chemist Boria Neufeld prepared acid for defense.

The Germans conducted "partisan attack" exercises at night. By this method they hoped to determine the Jews' response to the partisans and to uncover partisan sympathizers.[20]

In Volozhin, Ejszyszki, Miory, Miadl, Michaliczki, Braslav, Druja, Raduszkowicze, Lubieszow, Wiszniewo and Byten the underground organizations were formed shortly before their members escaped.

The worker element was dominant in the underground of Ilja, Oszmiana, Dolhinov, Horodok, Lida, Wasyliszki, Janow, Pruzhany, Dvorec, Vilejka (the camp), Hancevicz (camp), Brzesc, Kobryn, Korelicze, Rubzhewicze, Koldyczewo, Glebokie, Volozhin, Ejszyszki, Miory, Krasna, Miadl, Michaliczki, Braslav, Druja, Raduszkowicze, Szarkowszczyzna, Radun, Kosov-Polesky, Lubieszow, Wiszniewo, Byten, Stolin and Pohost. Youth and movement elements were dominant in the underground organizations of Swienciany, Pinsk, Stolpce, Dereczyn, Zhetel, Bereza-Kartuska, Olkeniky, Nieswiezh, Postavy, Kamen-Koshirsk, Sernik, Lachwa, Zholudok, Mir, Novogrudok, Koziany, Disna, Kleck, Iwje, Molczad, Vidz, Kurzeniec, Swierien, Slonim, Baranowicze and Lachowicz.

Aims

In discussing the aims of the underground organisations we must, of course, differentiate between the aims the organisations set themselves at the outset and the actual tasks upon which they decided to concentrate and which they later faced as a result of changing circumstances. The first reaction to the *aktzias* had been: "No more *aktzias* in the ghetto! We shall not go to the selection! We shall resist!"

At the beginning these ideas were sufficient to satisfy the internal feelings of the ghetto's inhabitants. After a time, however, the underground organizations were compelled to face the practical question of "how?". Even those organizations which had spoken of fighting and of arms at their meetings had no more than vague or doubtful answers to the question of "how are we going to carry this out?"

Most of the underground organizations in Western Bielorussia viewed flight to the forest as the one and only program of activity and as yet had no other thought in mind. They were lead to this decision since, on the one hand, conditions of the small ghetto consisting of only some dozens of wooden houses in narrow streets, surrounded by a mostly hostile population, local police forces and Germans, with only slight prospects of obtaining the weapons for resistance were desperate. On the other hand, ghettos were located close to forests, sometimes only some few kilometers away. By joining up with the partisans in the forests there was hope of being saved.

At the beginning of their activities the members of the Swienciany underground had also considered the possibility of fighting within the ghetto before their escape, but there, too, they understood that the only hope of salvation lay in fleeing to the forest.

In the course of its deliberations the Zhetl underground had defined its central aim as that of preparing for an armed revolt in the event that the ghetto was surrounded and faced an *aktzia*. Dvorecky also prepared a detailed plan for such an uprising and made it the task of four of the cells to occupy the sawmill and flour mill and the local Gestapo commander's house. The plan's aim was to create confusion that would paralyze the *aktzia* and enable the Jews to flee to the forest.[21]

Dvorecky also had plans for action beyond the limits of the ghetto. He attempted to arouse anti-German feelings among the civilian population and to deter them from collaborating with the Germans, in his belief that such activity would also benefit the Jews. The underground published anti-German circulars and distributed them among the neighboring villagers. The circulars also warned that those collaborating with the Germans would be punished and that accounts would be settled with them. In the spring of 1942, groups of partisans began to appear in the Zhetl area. These were Russians, former soldiers who had escaped German captivity or had hidden in the villages until the spring. There was still no contact among these groups nor any overall command to bind them together. Their discipline, too, was weak.

Dvorecky established contacts with these groups. He also studied the map of the region carefully, gathered information about the German forces in the nieghborhood, and even looked for technicians to build a broadcasting station. He apparently nourished a dream of turning the region into a center of combat against the Nazi enemy, in which Jews from the ghetto and those saved in the forest would form the basic core. He attempted to transfer the idea of the struggle to other areas as well; to liberate the Jews from the Dvorec camp and to form a large Jewish partisan unit. He established contact with Beirach of the Dvorec camp who however refused to cooperate with him.

In the course of his activities, Dvorecky's plans underwent a basic change. He came to the conclusion that he would have to waive the idea of revolt in the ghetto and go to the forest to fight. There were a number of considerations that led to this change. On the one hand, there were only small prospects of succeeding in fighting and in saving Jews in a ghetto going up in flames and surrounded by enemy forces. On the other hand, the hopes that had been awakened in the ghetto with the appearance of the partisans in the spring of 1942 helped him crystallize his ideas of establishing a large Jewish partisan force with people from Zhetl and the nearby ghettos, and of forming a fighting alliance with the Russian partisan units. The non-Jewish partisan in the forest related to these ideas with indifference and alienation. The members of the Russian partisan groups roaming about Bielorussia had absorbed a great deal of antisemitic poison in the camps from which they had fled, in addition to the seeds of hatred towards the Jews that had already been present. These groups were not linked to Moscow and the partisan command, and many of them occupied themselves with robbery and the murder of innocent people.[22]

In Pinsk, Novogrudok, Baranowicze, and Sernik the undergrounds considered their aims to be to set the date for a breakout from the ghetto and thereby to surprise the Germans. The Pinsk underground discussed a plan to set fire to the factories and workshops all at one time and to exploit the ensuing confusion to liquidate the German command and to flee with the young fighters to the partisans. They also thought of setting fire to the city. However, since it was clear beyond any doubt that any signs of resistance on the part of Jews would lead to the extermination of the whole Jewish population, the underground ultimately decided that it would act at the final moment, and not before then. That concept was not given any operative definition and in the future this was to determine the fate of the action.

In Novogrudok, the underground planned to surprise the Germans by dressing in German uniforms and putting out the searchlight on the central building. The organization gave three groups the task of cutting the telephone wires and the wire fence, of throwing grenades at the German guard and liquidating them in order to open the way for a breakout. Dr. Kagan was chosen commander of the revolt that was set for 15 April 1943.[23]

In Baranowicze, views were divided concerning the underground's goals. Moma Kopelowicz and Alyosha Zaryckevicz, who headed a group of young people in the organization, argued that the battle against the Germans should be waged in the forest. If they remained in the ghetto the fighters would remain isolated against the enemy when the revolt broke out and the uprising would fail. Against this, the older Lidovsky and Dr. Abramovsky argued that the place for the revolt was the ghetto. In that way it would be possible to save thousands of Jews, who would flee to the forest while the Germans were kept back by the shooting.

There were also others who argued that no revolt should be initiated except when all hope had failed and the ghetto faced annihilation. This argument was similar to the reservation adopted by the Pinsk underground:

to wait "until the decisive moment." In the end it was decided that the revolt would be carried out according to the initiative of the Jews in the ghetto, that of the fighting organization.[24] In keeping with the detailed plan, arms, incendiary materials and explosives were distributed among all the workplaces; when a prearranged signal was given the action would begin in all the prearranged places. The date for the revolt was set for 19 July 1942. The Sernik underground organization planned to leave the ghetto before the *aktzia* and together with the peasant, Missura (a loyal Communist who promised to provide the underground with arms) to attack the Germans and free the Jews.

Two proposals were raised in Pruzhany: to set the ghetto afire so that in the course of the confusion and fighting the Jewish inhabitants could escape; or simply to escape to the forests without setting fire to the ghetto. Differences of opinion over these proposals persisted as long as the underground existed; meanwhile young people began to leave for the forest.

A special role in the underground organizations was played by refugees from western Poland. Their mutual ties were stronger than their ties to the local population. There were cases where they organized into separate underground groups and only afterwards united with the local organization. In most cases their position on the underground's goal was the same: immediate flight to the forest. Most of the refugees were dynamic individuals, with sharpened senses from their experience in Nazi-occupied western Poland. To a large extent they were unmarried and did not have the same family commitments as did the local Jews.

In Stolpce, from the very beginning two viewpoints existed in the underground. These were more or less in keeping with the two groups — the local people and the refugees. Each of the views reflected the situation and moods of the people from which it came. The local people's view was that they should act only when the enemy came to annihilate the ghetto; whereas the refugees' approach was to establish contact with the partisans in the forest and to escape there as soon as possible. The first asked how they who were native to the place and had grown up among their families and friends could be the factor leading to annihilation. The newcomers argued that the ground was burning and that any delay in escaping might be catastrophic. These two conflicting approaches existed in other localities as well and more than a little were the decisive factors in the underground's activities and failures. In May 1942 a group of refugees led by Jacob Spiegel left Stolpce; they never established any contact with the ghetto and apparently failed in their escape attempt. This debate within the ghettos and work camps went on at a later period, too.[25]

In the Swierzhen work camp information was received of the existence of the Zhukow Jewish partisan unit in the Kopyl forests in Eastern Bielorussia. A letter was also received from Hersh Posesorsky who had been one of the organizers of the Stolpce underground and was now a partisan in the Zhukov unit, to his family in the camp.

Dr. Offerman, a refugee from Poland argued: "We must not wait, we must leave for the forest immediately. Every one who can, should go. Every moment we delay may be fatal." It was the position of most underground members that individuals should not be allowed to escape on their own as the responsibility was too great. The organization had to prepare the conditions for a general escape of all the camp's inmates or, at least, of the large majority. Then those who remained would bear the consequences. It was intolerable, however, for people to liberate only themselves and their families, as if their lives alone were precious.[26] Dr. Offerman did not agree with the underground's view and decided to escape with his girl friend, Fella. The underground's opponents in the camp chased them in an attempt to bring them back. When Dr. Offerman and Fella returned to the camp after having failed to contact and join a partisan unit, many of the camp inhabitants wanted to beat them. The underground succeeded in rescuing them from the crowd and only reprimanded them for their attempted escape.

We find that there were hardly any ghettos in Western Bielorussia with organized groups of Communists. There were, of course, Jewish Communists in the ghettos, local people and refugees from western Poland, but after their experiences under the Soviet regime and within the ghetto they underwent spiritual and political changes, sometimes radical ones. On the question of the underground's role they mostly supported escaping to the forest, both because of their realistic analysis of the conditions of the ghetto and because of their feelings of solidarity towards the partisans in general and the Soviet ones in particular.

The Slonim underground was influenced by an organized group of Communists. When one of the leaders of the Bielorussian Communist Party, David Epstein, happened to come to Slonim, a discussion was held in his presence on the underground's aims. Anshel Delaticky, a Communist and active underground member, reported on this meeting. The participants decided to work within the ghetto, but not in the name of the Communist

Party, because they had not been authorized by it or its center. There were Jewish Communists who still feared their party's future reaction to their underground work in the ghetto because of the general-Jewish alliance which was, of course, not to their Party's liking. They did not want to make the Party responsible for this activity. On the question of the goals of the underground in the ghetto there were differences of opinion. According to Epstein, the underground organization should follow the example of the self-defense exercised by the leftist Jewish movements during the pogroms in Czarist days. The underground's goal must therefore be to defend the ghetto. His position in general was an independent and interesting one.

The analogy between the activities of the fighting organization in the ghetto and the self-defense units of the Jewish leftist movements of Czarist times was not only a misunderstanding (to use an understatement) of the situation of the ghetto Jews. This was after two *aktzias* in Slonim itself, and he certainly knew about the *aktzias* in other nearby ghettos. It testified to a clear intention to grant a certain measure of legality to the very existence of a Jewish underground by relying upon the fact that non-Jewish leftist forces in Czarist Russia, or at least some of them, had looked favorably upon the Jewish self-defense.

Anshel Delaticky, on the other hand, proposed that the underground organize and prepare for partisan warfare in the forests, arguing that defending the ghetto would not hurt the enemy seriously. This emphasis for fighting in the forest because "defending the ghetto would not hurt the enemy," again implied an evasion (again an understatement) of all the other Jewish aspects of the Jewish fighting.

The participants dispersed after the meeting without any clear decision, but in practice the underground followed Delaticky's suggestions, namely of escaping to the forest and conduction partisan warfare.[27]

Notes

1. Zalman Gurvicz, testimony in *Megillat Kurnitz* (Kurzeniec) (Eng. translation) (Tel Aviv, 1956), p. 269.
2. Moshe Shutan, *Getto un Wald* (Ghetto and Forest) (Tel Aviv, 1971), p. 16.
3. Shalom Cholawski, *Ir Vaya'ar Bamatzor* (A Town and A Forest under Siege) (Tel Aviv, 1973), pp. 50–56.
4. Yad Vashem (YV) 2368/157 (Yitzhak Lichtenberg).
5. *Ha'ayara Bilhavot* (The Shtetl in Flames-Olkeniki) (Tel Aviv, 1962), p. 117.

6. Moniek Yosselevsky, testimony in *Sefer Zikaron Stoiptz-Swier-ezhne Veha'ayarot Hasmuchot* (Memorial Book of Stolpce-Swerezhna and the Adjoining Townships) (Tel Aviv, 1965), p. 468.
7. *Sefer Rubzhewicze* (Rubzhewicze Memorial Book) (loc. date pub), p. 231.
8. Shalom Gerling, *Korot Lochem Yehudi* (The Story of a Jewish Fighter) (Lohamei Hagetaot, 1968), p. 47.
9. Central Zionist Archive (CZA) S26/1544 (Berl Reznik); Moreshet Archive (MA) A-99 (Shlomo Charchas).
10. Friedl Makresky, testimony in *Sefer Zikaron Likehillat Meiczet* (Memorial Book for the Community of Molczad) (loc. date), p. 303.
11. Anshel Deletitzky, testimony in *Pinkas Slonim* (Slonim Diary) (Tel Aviv, 1962), p. 280.
12. Eliezer Lidovsky, testimony in *Sefer Zikaron Baranowicz* (Baranowicze Memorial Book) (loc. date), p. 468.
13. YV 03/3657 (Moshe Smolar).
14. David Gleibman, testimony in *Sefer Pinsk* (Pinsk Memorial Book) (Tel Aviv, 1967), p. 341.
15. Tuvia & Zussia Belsky, *Yehudei Ya'ar* (Jews of the Forest) (Tel Aviv, 1946), p. 58.
16. YV 3139/78 (Herzl Nachumovsky).
17. Chaim Liebowitz, testimony in *Pinkas Nowogrudok* (Nowogrudok Diary) (sp?) (Tel Aviv, 1963), p. 287.
18. Yehiel Sgalowitz, testimony in *Sefer Rubzhewicze* (Rubzhewicze Memorial Book) (Tel Aviv, 1965), p. 352.
19. MA A/100 (Lipa Yosselevsky).
20. YV E/35 (Mieta Shimshonowicz).
21. Shalom Gerling, testimony in *Pinkas Zhetl* (Zhetl Diary) (Tel Aviv, 1957), p. 370.
22. YV 552 (Dr. Alpert).
23. Leibowitz, loc. cit.
24. Lidovsky, loc. cit.
25. YV 723/39 (Eliezer Melamed).
26. MA D.2.83 (Benyamin Velitovsky).
27. Delaticky, loc. cit.

CHAPTER 7
The Underground in Battle

The underground's activities from its formation and until the revolt's armed uprising and escape, mainly involved preparations towards that point obtaining weapons, expanding its ranks, seeking contacts with the partisans, preparing hiding places and ways of escape (bunkers and tunnels), but also aid for the most needy among the ghetto Jews, work with youth and sometimes educational work and underground schools. In addition to all these, the underground was compelled to struggle against its opponents within the Jewish ghetto public and the Judenrats until it won, in many ghettos, if not legal status, at least an accepted legitimacy or quasi-legitimacy. In more than a few cases it won the moral authority that enabled it to encourage Jews and to stand at the forefront in revolt, in war and in escape.

In order to describe these activities we shall have to survey a large number of ghettos.

Arms

The focus, and also the Achilles heel, of underground activity was arms. The tremendous difficulties in obtaining them, the dangers involved in doing so for those seeking them as well as for all the ghetto's inhabitants, the problems of transporting and hiding them, the bitter disputes with many Jews in the ghetto, the sharp confrontations with the Judenräte over the very attempt to obtain them, the problems of keeping them in the ghetto and of taking them when escaping — all these formed a complex web of problems that troubled and occupied the underground throughout its existence. All of the underground's hopes, no matter what its goals — Jewish defense in the ghetto or flight to the forests, depended upon one key factor: arms.

It was impossible to conceive of breaking out of an encircled ghetto without weapons and even more impossible to conceive of an uprising and revolt without weapons. All the plans for mass or group escape were based on armed units, even if small, of the underground serving as a rearguard covering the escape. In the forest itself, possession of weapons was a condition, if not the only one, for Jews being accepted into the Russian partisan units. Jews who did not succeed in being accepted into partisan units after their flight were abandoned to their fates in the forest. They were ambushed by Germans, police, peasants and even non-Jewish partisans. From this standpoint, there was one law for individuals and groups: they must possess weapons. At the very beginnings of the flight to the forest rumors about this situation had begun to filter into the ghettos. Sometimes a whole group of Jews lived because of one rifle.

The members of the underground were also not free of the fears involved in obtaining arms and smuggling them into the ghetto. Baruch Levin, one of the leaders of the Lida underground, and afterwards an active partisan, confesses:[1]

> As long as my family was alive I trembled even at the idea of keeping weapons. Among all the other horrors surrounding us, that might bring catastrophe not only on the person possessing the gun but also on others. The idea, however, remained with me and looked for some realization.

The problems were greater for the older people but the young were not immune:[2] "We could not imagine that the tremendous force that was moving here ... would be afraid of some dozens of boys who might have two and a half rifles and ten bullets ..."

The feeling that arms were a vital necessity became very apparent to individuals immediately upon the Red Army's retreat.

Eliahu Lidsky, later the organizer of the Horodok underground, changed his clothes when his Red Army unit was cut off and, in the event he might need them, hid his rifle and ammunition in the forest near his town. That rifle served as some support for the underground when Eliahu left for the forest on 15 March 1942. That was the Jewish unit's first weapon.

Moshe Tuchman of Bereza-Kartuska found a machine gun, some rifles and ammunition at the time of the Red Army's retreat. He hid the guns and ammunition in the forest and when he fled to the forest with a group of young people took the guns out of the cache.

Josef Fishkin and Judel Garmiza went out of Rubzhewicze to the Mikulicz forest immediately after the Red Army's retreat and gathered weapons that had been abandoned by the Russians: 2 machine guns, 8 rifles, 250 pistol bullets and 2 boxes of rifle shells. They hid it all in the forest.

Shortly after the Germans' arrival older men and women also began to recognize the need for arms. Beila Reichel, from Koziany, brought weapons to the ghetto. "Aunt Peshke" from Kurzeniec carried a sack of grass, in which she had hidden a rifle, into the ghetto. However, it was mostly the younger people who were aware of the need for arms. Berta Dimenstein, a member of Hashomer Hatzair and a village girl, obtained a pistol and acted as a courier between the Kurzeniec underground and a group of Red Army soldiers (the Volodya unit) who had escaped from German captivity. The Kurzeniec underground also obtained a few more pistols. Noah Dinerstein, a former sergeant in the Polish Army, taught the members how to use the weapons.[3] Yitzhak Percowiez, a 15-year-old whose family had been murdered in the *aktzia*, and young Benjamin Velitovsky smuggled a rifle and 60 bullets into the Swierzhen work camp. Natan Goldstein stuck a rifle into his trousers, acted as if he were limping because of a work accident, and in that manner brought a rifle into the camp. The youngsters also obtained a few more rifles. Benjamin relates: "We sat and touched every bullet and our fingers trembled. Even mother doesn't fondle her child in that way."

In most ghettos the organizations also prepared other weapons: pieces of iron, rods, axes, knives and wire-cutters. In the Lachwa ghetto the underground's members were armed only with such weapons until the day of the revolt on 3 September 1942. In many ghettos, bottles of acid were prepared for defense as, for example, in Nieswiezh (by the engineer Pordes), in Koldyczewo (by the chemist Boria Neufeld) and in other places.

The weapons smuggled into the ghettos came mainly from two sources: the German arsenals where young men and women from the ghetto worked, and purchases with money or valuables (watches, jewelry) from the peasants and the police. In many cases the weapons came from both sources.

Many and varied were the strategies adopted in order to smuggle weapons into the ghettos. In Baranowicze for example, the arms were brought in between the double walls of the garbage wagons that went in and out of the ghetto; in Lida they were smuggled in the long pipes of a stove; and in other places among logs brought in for firewood. In many cases the weapons were concealed on the bodies of the members of the underground. Sometimes parts were carried in and the guns were assembled with stocks made in the ghetto. Girls in particular ran risks in the smuggling, by wrapping their bodies with the bullets and carrying parts beneath their garments. In Nieswiezh, Leah Duckar and Rachel Kagan brought machine gun parts, grenades and ammunitions from the German arms stores in which they worked.

In Swienciany a large group of young men worked in the German arms stores. Yitzhak Rudnicky and Gershon Nadel brought the first two rifles into the ghetto. Other underground members stole four pistols and a haversack full of cartridges from a cellar in police headquarters.

In Kobryn young men and women brought gun parts and bullets from the German arsenals. A workshop was established in the ghetto to assemble weapons and repair them. Others bought guns from the Ukrainian policemen.

In Krasna weapons were brought into the ghetto from the German arsenals on wagons of wood by a group of 15- to 17-year-old girls. Devorah Kaplan was particularly adapt in smuggling pistols. Ex-soldiers taught the use of arms.

In Brzesc, Jews working in the famous fortress these stole arms. Others took guns and ammunition from the bombed-out airfield.

In Lida, the source of weapons was the barracks of the former Polish Army where Russian arms had been stored. There were also acquisitions from Christians in the neighborhood. Despite the risks involved, there was widespread commerce in weapons, as they had become the commodity most in demand. The price of guns rose in the spring of 1942 as word spread of the activities of Bielsky's unit and the *Iskra* units in the neighborhood. The price of a rifle varied between 25,000 and 30,000 rubles; and of a pistol between 10,000 and 15,000. Purchasing arms involved the risk of betrayal. Gershon Barchash offered a Polish woman a suit in exchange for a rifle. The woman informed on him to the Germans. Barchash was arrested. When the charges were being read out to him he burst his way outside but was killed in the course of his escape. A not insignificant number of arms were taken by Jews who worked in the German booty camps where captured Russian weapons were stored. The rifles were carried into the ghetto under piles of wood. One important center of underground activity was the workshops where some 600 Jews were employed.

Expert metalworkers working the shops secretly repaired guns. Yosef Kaplan headed one shop of 100 men; another shop was headed by Baruch Levin and Velvel Krupsky — both members of the underground and skilled machinists.[4] Yosef Kaplan himself obtained a pistol and 10 grenades for 150 dollars. Kaplan's shop repaired damaged guns; it also prepared cylinders for the printing press of the Lenin Brigade headquarters. The machinist Ozochovsky assembled rifles from parts. Immediately after the *aktzia* Baruch Levin prepared an axe and a knife, and later — together with Krupsky — 13 PPDs (Russian automatic rifles), 3 pistols and a machine gun. Along with his comrades, 16-year-old Yekutiel Boyarsky smuggled 20 rifles out of the German arsenals in a garbage can and hid them in the forest in preparation for their escape.[15]

In Baranowicze, individuals also acquired pistols as a personal weapon smuggled; in keeping with its goals, however, the underground required many kinds of weapons: rifles, grenades, pistols and explosives. These arms were obtained by underground members who worked in the German arsenals, where some 120 persons, including 40 women, were employed. Women members of the underground including Chilke Borishanska, Roza Swiecicka, Esther Volfovicz and Leah Rodes, who worked there, tied grenades and bullets around their bodies and in that way smuggled guns into the ghetto. The day the guns were to be carried in. Jewish policemen were stationed near the gate of the ghetto and they led the smugglers directly to the secret store.

Underground members established contact with Dutch soldiers who were serving in the German Army in Baranowicze and received grenades, pistols and ammunition from them. Arms exercises were carried out in one of the bunkers by underground members with military experience. Moshe Top and Chaim Stolovicky helped in repairing the guns. Aryeh Krulewicki, who worked in cleaning guns in a German Army unit, stuck rifle parts into his canvas boots and tied the stocks to his back under his clothing. In this way he smuggled 5 rifles into the ghetto. Sarah Gershuny obtained 2 pistols and 150 bullets from her place of work. By the fall of 1942 the Baranowicze underground had in its possession 70 rifles, 2 machine guns, 1,500 bullets, 500 grenades and some boxes of gunpowder. Approximately 40 pistols were in private hands. Part of the arms were concealed outside the ghetto.[6] The quantity of arms smuggled by members of the Baranowicze underground was very large in itself and also relative to all the other ghettos in Western Bielorussia and beyond.

Between 500 and 600 Jews worked in cleaning and storing Soviet arms in the German booty camps in Slonim. The Jewish workers stole guns, ammunition and grenades, sometimes in sacks of sawdust and carried them to the ghetto. The weapons were stored in the underground's arsenals and were also held by private individuals who were not underground members. In Shusterowicz's store there were 12 rifles, 15 pistols, 2 boxes of hand grenades and ammunition. Others found a hiding place in the booty storehouse and filled it with arms and ammunition. Rivka Moshkovsky carried weapons from the storehouse to a cache outside the ghetto. In Shelubsky's house arms were assembled from parts taken from the booty stores. Members of the underground carried out sabotage at their place of work: they damaged bullets, changed the markings on carloads of arms and equipment, rejected some 300 rifles as "unfit for use." Many machine guns were stolen from the booty stores for the partisans. Arik Stein carried out thousands of PPD bullets and Nagan pistols and smuggled them to the forest.[7] Rita Mukasey tells about one of the arms smugglers in the Slonim ghetto.[8]

> Zelig Milikovsky must be given a great deal of credit for organizing the underground movement in the ghetto. Before the war he had been a member of Freiheit and Poalei Zion. He was a carpenter by trade. He had married and had two beautiful children. His wife and children died in one of the *aktzias*, and Zelig remained alone. In his poor home on Hill Street (Oifn Barg) he dug a cellar with a hidden entrance. When the Jews were forbidden to live in this street he prepared an arms storehouse in his former home and members of the underground would, at great risk, smuggle arms into it from the arms stores on Zamoszcze Street.

Five pistols, grenades and ammunition.

In other ghettos the Jews bought weapons from the peasants and sometimes from the Bielorussian policemen. Pinchas Ormland of Kamin-Koshirsk wrote in his diary on 10 August 1942:[9] "... The acquisition of arms is becoming ever more expensive. For a rifle we already pay whatever they ask. There is no price. Sometimes you succeed, sometimes you go to buy arms and you don't return."

Buying arms with money or the equivalent of money was no less risky than smuggling them from the German arsenals. In this case, in addition to the dangers of hiding them and carrying them into the ghetto, there was also the fear of betrayal by the non-Jew after the transfer was made. The danger already existed at the very first stage, even before the sale, in sending out inquiries among the non-Jews about possible arms purchases. The civilian population was for the most part hostile to the Jews and many were tempted to inform on them because of the reward they would receive for this action. In most cases, before the Jews contacted the man possessing the gun, they had to turn to others, to estimate whether there was the possibility of purchasing weapons. From the viewpoint of the danger to the ghetto there was no difference between only trying to buy the weapon and actually carrying out the transaction. Sometimes the price was a very heavy one. That, for example, was the case of Gedalya Menches of Swierzhen.

Gedalya worked together with his father, Shmuel David, as a tailor for the Germans and the local police. Through a Ukrainian policeman he obtained a box of ammunition in return for a suit. The policeman informed on him and the ammunition was discovered. Gedalya was arrested, tortured, but did not reveal anything about the underground. His father feared that he would not have the strength to hold out in the tortures to be expected, should he be arrested and hanged himself. Three more Jews were murdered by the Germans following the discovery of the ammunition. Gedalya Menches' and his father's death had their effects upon the consolidation of the Swierzhen underground.

Four Mir Jews established contact with a Bielorussian peasant about obtaining weapons and joining the partisans. The peasant and his friends ambushed them and killed three of them. The fourth — Velvel Rabinowicz escaped wounded, but was later arrested. The efforts to save him were to no avail. Another Jew, Ben-Zion Shimonowicz, also from Mir, also made arrangements with a peasant to buy arms. He revealed to the peasant that 30 other young men from the ghetto were about to escape to the partisans. The peasant informed the police. Thanks to Oswald Rufeisen, the 30 were warned in time but Shimonowicz himself was not saved.

In Kamin-Koshirsk, too, a peasant informed to the police on someone who had bought a pistol from him. That was Shepsel Feldman, who was captured coming out of the peasant's house and executed together with his father.

Danger lurked for the smugglers, too. In Baranowicze, underground member Monik Mushinsky was caught carrying bullets into the ghetto. Thanks to bribes the incident ended with only a beating.

Even when the arms were already in the underground's hands serious accidents sometimes occurred. On 13 May 1942, three members of the Swienciany underground — Miadzolsky, Johaj and Gershon Beck — went up to an attic to sew leather holsters for their pistols. One of them, Miadzolsky, shot a stray bullet from his pistol and seriously wounded his comrade, Beck. The Jewish doctor for the Judenrat brought the incident to the Judenrat's knowledge; the Jewish police informed the Lithuanian police that boys had found a pistol in the attic and that was the reason for the accident. The two members, Miadzolsky and Beck, however, were arrested, severely tortured by the Gestapo and finally executed.[10]

In Zhetl, too, arms were decisive in deciding the underground's path. Its first action was to acquire weapons and to transport them into the ghetto. A fund was established in order to buy guns. On a frosty night in January 1942 Alter Dvorecky, Eliahu Kowiensky and Shalom Gerling went to the cemetery and there buried two rifles, a machine gun and a sack of bullets they had smuggled into the ghetto. Afterwards Dvorecky strove to establish contacts with people outside the ghetto. He established contact with three former Red Army officers who were hiding in one of the villages and received information from them about two automatic rifles and three pistols they had buried. After that he contacted another group of Soviets, advised them to leave for the forest and provided them with help and money. Dvorecky utilized Judenrat funds to buy weapons. Some of the Judenrat members knew of this but trusted him and, not only did not interfere, but even helped him. The underground conceived of a daring scheme to obtain arms. While moving furniture in the German command's building, Dvorecky discovered an arms closet. With the help of another underground member he copied the keys to the closet.

In Zhetl, the debate over where the arms were to be hidden was only a disguised reflection of the essential argument over the underground's operative goals: to fight within the ghetto or partisan fighting in the forest. Those who favored fighting in the forest argued; that the weapons should not be brought into the ghetto since it involved great risk for the smuggler and all the ghetto's inhabitants; guarding the weapons and taking them out at the time of escape were also dangerous. They also cast doubts as to whether so many would really be able to escape from the ghetto at the time of an *aktzia*.

Dvorecky, Gerling and others argued, on the other hand, that the attempt to escape was worthwhile no matter what the cost and that at the moment of an armed uprising many would be able to flee. There was no avoiding sacrifices but if those rebelling worked swiftly and suddenly they might surprise the Germans and many could escape. They therefore demanded that the weapons be kept within the ghetto itself.

The three Russians with whom Dvorecky had established contact also participated in the discussion over the location of the weapons and the plans for an uprising. This trust, in those days, in persons from the outside implied a great deal of naiveté and innocence, as well as a lack of caution. However, with the change in Dvorecky's plans about moving the scene of the battle from the ghetto to the forest, it was decided to take all the weapons in the ghetto to the Nakrishky forest that had been set as the meeting place for after the escape.[11] It was then that the Fiolun affair took place which greatly effected Zhetl underground's fate.

In April 1942 Vanya, the Russian group's contact, a former Red Army pilot, sent word that an automatic rifle and pistol could be obtained in the village of Hirocz. Shalom Fiolun had roamed the village as a "furrier" and looked for arms among the peasants. A young man who was daring and nimble, he had made friends among the peasants and with the group of Russians with whom he maintained contact. When the permit to work in the villages were cancelled, Fiolun returned to the ghetto and went to work in the Jewish police for the underground. On 19 April 1942 Fiolun set out for the agreed upon location in the Mirowszczyna forest in order to receive the promised weapons. Vanya handed him a damaged automatic rifle but the moment he passed over the gun, Fiolun was suddenly surrounded by Germans and police who had waited in ambush. It became evident that Vanya had been a provocateur. Fiolun was taken for interrogation and great terror fell on the ghetto. All the Judenrat members, except for Dvorecky, who was away from home, were arrested. Fiolun was tortured to death. A Jew found a note outside the prison that Fiolun had thrown through the bars: "Comrades, have no fear. I won't open my mouth. If you can, save yourselves." The words spread throughout the ghetto. It was clear that the Germans would look for Dvorecky first. The next day, on 20 April 1942, Dvorecky led to the forest with six other underground members. The members of the underground hid in their bunkers. The Germans declared a reward of 25,000 marks to anyone taking Dvorecky dead or alive.

On 30 April 1942 the ghetto was surrounded and the Germans killed 1,200 Jews in the Korfish forest. Dvorecky contacted a group of Russian partisans who numbered some 30 men and hurried with them to the forest in order to attack the Germans and save what he could. This action failed because of the refusal of the Russian partisans to take the risk of this battle.[12]

Shalom Gerling, who had fled to the forest after the Fiolun affair, returned to Zhetl with some other comrades in order to reorganize the underground activity. There were groups in the ghetto who received Gerling and his comrades with great anger; there were even those who wanted to turn him over to the German gendarmerie. However, the commander of the Jewish police, a member of the underground, soothed their anger.

The underground added new members to its ranks. However, after Dvorecky's departure for the forest the underground changed. Dvorecky, who was outstanding in his leadership and ability, aroused envy and hatred among the partisan groups in the forest and they were determined to eliminate him. Tension was created between the Russian group and the Jewish one. The Jewish group was invited by the Russians to a meeting to clarify matters. On 11 May 1942 Dvorecky and Pozdonsky arrived at the meeting place and on their return to their base they walked into an ambush and fell defending themselves. The detailed investigation conducted by Gerling and Rozovksy revealed that Dvorecky and Pozdonsky had fallen in an ambush by non-Jewish partisans.[13]

Dvorecky's short partisan experience from 20 April to 11 May and his sad end in the forest, left a bitterness in the Zhetl ghetto. There was a feeling of hopelessness after there had been a spark of hope. The underground did indeed continue to exist, but from then on with the feeling that its leader had been lost. New groups that had organized in the ghetto looked for contacts and continued to buy weapons in the villagers. The tragic arms affair had decided the fate of the underground in the Zhetl ghetto.

At times, weapons were moved from one ghetto to another or from the ghetto to the forest. Gershon Tennenbaum, who served as a courier between the ghetto and the outside, moved a few weapons from Brzesc to his own town, Kobryn. As members of the underground organizations left for the forest the quantity of arms in the ghetto itself decreased. Guns and ammunition were sometimes sent from the ghetto to the Jews in the forest. Jews who had escaped from the Vilejka work camp maintained contact with the camp through an old peasant. The camp inmates gathered bullets for those who had escaped to the forest. Before the aged courier's arrival Herzl Alperowicz would take thick wooden boards, open slits in their sides, hide the bullets in them, close the slits, plane them, dirty them with mud so that the glue would not be seen and throw them into the hospital courtyard bordering on the camp. The old man would come to the courtyard, look among the trash, put the boards with the bullets on his wagon and carry them to the Jews in the forest. The Jews called these boards the "boards of vengeance."

Before the Jews fled to the forest the underground from some ghettos sent medicines, clothing and weapons to non-Jewish partisans. In May 1942 Zorach Kremen, representing the anti-fascist committee, met Proniagin, a partisan commander, in the forest and agreed to send the partisans weapons, a doctor, a radio technician and a nurse. The Slonim underground also sent a radio set, batteries and clothing taken from the Judenrat, by means of the garbage wagons. Kremen used to go to the forest every Saturday, bring the partisans arms and ammunition, and return to the ghetto.[14]

The information reaching the ghettos from the Jews in the forest carried a serious warning. Even with arms in hand many dangers awaited the Jews from armed bands and collaborating peasants: without weapons the Jews were subject to the law of the forest: anarchy, robbery and murder. The permanent fear of another *aktzia* and the stories from the forest increased the pressure to obtain weapons, especially among the younger people who planned to escape. On the other hand, the difficulties of smuggling from the German arsenals increased as the Germans intensified their supervision.

According to a report of 26 September 1942 by *gebietskommissar* Gerhard Erren, the Jews were "active in supplying stolen weapons from the booty camp and in stealing medicines and instruments from the hospitals."[15]

Sometimes the underground organizations applied to the Judenrat for funds with which to buy arms. In Iwje the underground organization demanded of the Judenrat that it provide money for arms acquisition, but was refused. In Molczad, too, the underground asked the Judenrat to allot funds for arms purchase. When there was an opportunity in Swienciany to obtain additional weapons, the members of the underground demanded that the Judenrat finance the purchase; the Judenrat refused. At one of the Judenrat meetings 5 armed members of the underground appeared and asked for 100,000 rubles. With great reluctance, the Judenrat was compelled to give the money.[14] There were, however, also people in the Judenräte who had a favorable attitude towards the underground's arms acquisitions.

This story of arms acquisitions for the ghettos is a chapter of heroism, revealing the ghetto's special isolation and fate and the risks undertaken by those who took part in it. At times it was the main issue dividing the contesting groups within the ghetto, but without it neither resistance by the underground within the ghetto nor the establishment of Jewish partisan groups in the forest would have been possible.

Opposition to the Underground: The Question of Collective Responsibility

The underground had opponents, and in more than a few ghettos this included many of the Judenräte. The underground's opponents argued that its activities endangered the ghetto's inhabitants; that the prospects of the underground saving Jews were very small or even nil. Sometimes the dispute was bitter as death, because its subject was life itself. At the time which we are now examining, the Jews had already gone through one *aktzia* or even two, and knew about the murder and annihilation of Jews in the close vicinity. The central issue in their eyes was how to save their own and their families' lives. A.L. Poliak, one of the few survivors from the town of Motele, relates:[17]

> There were very, very many rumors that an extermination plot was being woven around us. From the nearby towns came rumors of killing and annihilation but we still did not want to believe. We deluded ourselves that the evil would not reach us. The will to live was very strong. We wanted to live. We believed that the enemy would be satisfied with our property and perhaps also enslave and torture us, but even in that event the strong would stay alive and everybody thought that he was strong. We clung with the last of our hopes to the narrow plank of life floating on the waves of hatred and torture. Only very few of us saw aright that there was no escape or refuge and that none would come out of this hell.
>
> These wiser people attempted to organize a defense movement by saying: "Our end is coming closer, our fate is sealed, and if we are to die, let us at least die with honor. Let the filthy murderers know that our blood won't be spilt readily. Let us buy arms with the last of our money and defend ourselves to our last breath. Let us not go like a flock of sheep." Most of the people in the town, however, fell upon them angrily: "What! You want to bring destruction on a whole community and on all the Jews? Some miracle can still happen and we can be saved in some way. We must not lose hope. What strength do we have against the masses surrounding us?" And in that way people divided in their views and dispersed without any decision or any plans.

The wiser, who saw "aright," were a small minority; the majority, despite all that had happened about them, still believed that "some miracle can still happen and they might be saved in some way." Many Jews, and especially the Judenrat members, pinned their hopes on the fact that were no replacements for the Jewish craftsmen. The chairman of the Swierzen Judenrat,

Czwiertak, used to say: "So long as the chimney in the sawmill smokes, there is some security for our lives."

In Lida, the Jews were divided into "optimists" and "pessimists." The latter did not believe the Germans' promises and had decided that they must escape to the forest because there were no hopes for life in the ghetto. Their leaders were the members of the underground. On the other side, the "optimists" believed that the Germans truly needed the Jewish labor force, that the local industrial plants were contributing to the German war effort, and that the Germans had their own interest in the existence of the Jewish skilled workers. In addition, the Jews were deterred by the difficult conditions of hunger, cold and disease in the forests, whose echoes had reached the ghetto. Perhaps a large part of the "optimists" understood that their claims could not stand up to facts but they continued to cling to them because of their deep attachment to their families, and they sought some justification for their inability to decide to escape.

The Germans also knew how to play on the strings of the Jews' deepest fears, and with smooth words and cynical hypocrisy deceived the ghetto's inhabitants. When the flights began from the Lida ghetto, *gebietskommissar* Hanveg came to the factories, assembled all the Jewish workers and addressed them. One of those present wrote his words down from memory:[18]

> Jews, you are bringing catastrophe upon yourselves. You want to suffer hunger, cold, when they are unnecessary. After all, you are a wise people. Do you think that with your rusty rifles you will be able to sabotage the German Army that has conquered all of Europe? I can promise you that in the city of Lida not a hair will fall from a Jew's head. Those who had to be liquidated have already been liquidated. I did it in a humanitarian fashion. Why anger the Jews a number of times by executing them one group after another? I carried out the program all at once and you who have remained can now live quietly. I will build a large kitchen. I will prepare a bath in the ghetto and set up a ritual bath for the religious Jews, so that you will be able to live hygienically. Only one thing I demand of you — work well and diligently. In order to prove how much I am your friend I am ready to pardon Jews who return from the forest.

That speech influenced some of the Jews and intensified the debate with the underground.

Altman, who was responsible for the workshops, met with Yosef Kaplan of the underground and urged him not to endanger the lives of hundreds of Jews in the ghetto. Alperstein, one of the workshop managers, assembled the workers and harshly condemned those going to the forest, who in their folly were endangering all the ghetto's inhabitants in order to save their own lives. He invited Baruch Levin of the underground to meet with him and turned to him with impassioned words: "You know that if any dream at all has been left to us, it is the dream that at least a few will remain alive. Believe me, that I myself do not hope to be among those few." Alperstein continued by charging Levin with damaging that small prospect by his war against the Germans with the "rusty rifle" in his hand. Levin replied strongly that it was a duty to fight but promised that he would avoid any action liable to endanger the Jewish lives. He still continued to encourage Jews to leave for the forest before it was too late.[19] When Mudrik and his brothers stole five rifles and two boxes of bullets from the German stores. Altman demanded of him that he return them. These weapons were returned but Mudrik and his comrades continued to smuggle out rifle parts.

In other locations the opponents of the underground used threats in an attempt to counter the underground's activities. In Raduszkowicze eight young men joined together, collected money to buy guns and planned to escape. The Judenrat members attempted to stop them from doing so by saying that their flight would lead to the killing of all the Jews, and threatened: "If you don't give up your plan we ourselves will inform the Germans." Actually, this debate also reflected the differences between the various age groups in the ghetto, between the younger men who wanted to go to the forest and the elder men and the women who could not do so. It should be pointed out that the Raduszkowicze Jews never had any contact with partisans in the neighborhood nor did they investigate the actual possibility of escape.[20]

Tensions rose especially when arms were being brought into the ghetto or a planned escape was close. In Vilejka there was a sharp dispute in the camp between unmarried men and those with families who were deterred from escaping. The unmarried argued: "We will escape; we won't die with the families." In Swierzhen the opponents of escape attempted to convince the underground to willingly hand their arms over to them and only after that was unsuccessful, threatened to betray them to the Germans. They watched the movements and actions of the members of the underground, set guards at night to prevent them from escaping from the camp and even attempted to break into the arms store by force. Underground member Benjamin Velitovsky stood in the cellar with drawn gun facing those attempting to break in and declared: "Anyone opening the cellar door is taking his life in his own hands."

Within the families the disputes continued, but even amidst the heated arguments the family unity was not affected due to the mutual concern that prevailed during that difficult period.

There were times when representatives of the two groups met facing each other, spoke from their hearts and understood each other though their views remained divided. Monik Joselewsky, one of the founders of the Swierzhen underground, relates:

> One evening ... one of our opponents' strong men was invited to the cellar of one of the houses in the damp and was told in unequivocal language and at gunpoint — to keep silent. How great the tragedy was: both of us burst into tears over our fate, without our being able to speak and convince each other of the justice of our actions, because both we and our opponents were acting out of despair, without knowing whose actions were more just and desirable at that time and in those circumstances. The poor Jew swore to keep his mouth shut and from then on his voice was heard no more in the camp.[21]

It is quite clear that each of the parties understood the other side's doubts. One direct confrontation in the Dvorec work camp broke down the divisions. One day representatives of the underground were called to the 75-year-old rabbi of Dvorec. Also present were members of the Judenrat. The rabbi opened by saying that the 2,500 Jews in the camp were being kept alive thanks to the 900 fit for work and that, if a flight to the forest began, all the Jews in the camp would be killed. To this the underground representatives replied that in any case all would be annihilated and that it was only a matter. The old rabbi burst into tears: "Look *kinderlach* (children) don't hasten the end!" Judenrat chairman Novik said, pointing to the representatives of the underground: "They're right, in this situation we can't sit with folded hands." It was decided, with the rabbi's agreement, that arms were to be acquired and that when the Germans came to kill the camp's Jews they would resist in the hope that some would escape. The rabbi also asked that anyone who had gold or valuables should bring them to him.[22] The rabbi did not reject the underground's arguments but only argued against "hastening the end." This was in keeping with the principle of the doctor not hastening his patient's end even when he knows he is incurable. There were, however, Jews who believed that by postponing the day of reckoning they might gain time in which something — a "something" they could not define — might happen. The underground saw this delay as a waste of time that might decide the fate of all the Jews in the ghetto.

Behind these disputes between the opposing views there was one fateful question of conscience of vital importance with personal and family implications that troubled the ghetto very much: this was the problem of collective responsibility imposed by the Germans which meant than one Jew's guilt would be placed upon all, and that all would bear the punishment. As we shall see below, this question became a very decisive factor in the activities and fate of the Jewish underground in the ghettos of Western Bielorussia. During a discussion among the young people in Janow near Pinsk concerning the flight from the ghetto. Judenrat chairman Alter Dubinsky suddenly appeared and warned:

> Remember well what you are about to do. You are going to bring catastrophe upon all of us. Perhaps a few of you will be saved, but you cannot forget that because of you, your parents, brothers and sisters, and the little children, will all die.

Dubinsky then told the meeting that Soviet planes had bombed the Brzesc fortress and expressed his hope that the suffering would swiftly pass; he therefore asked the participants in the meeting to disperse.

The question that troubled the young people was whether they would save their own lives at the cost of the lives of their parents and families.[23] The members of the underground were very well aware that the Germans intended to murder all the Jews in the ghettos, but that knowledge, no matter how correct it was, when it related to the lives and deaths of one's own family, always came with a train of doubts, second thoughts, hopes and expectations, no matter how irrational and irrelevant these might be.

The underground organizations had placed saving Jews at the very top of their aims and their members risked their own lives in order to attain these goals. That made the soul-searchings all the more difficult.

Pliskin, one-time chairman of the Jewish community in Dokszyce argued with Josef Shapira of the underground, who had prepared his comrades for escape:

> If you were going today to Eretz Israel with the fellows, and we stayed here as a sacrifice, so be it. You are going, however, 99 percent to death and 1 percent to life, and that will bring death for all for us. If you have a plan to take all of us and to blow up the ghetto — we'll go; if you don't, you must not do this.[24]

Abba Zakin, head of the Department for Social Affairs in the Baranowicze ghetto, argued that a group of 200 persons (the number of underground members in the ghetto) did not have the right to seek to escape and so endanger the 7,000 who remained. If the organization could succeed in saving 1,000 or 2,000 Jews on the day of the revolt and lead them to the forest, then perhaps its existence was justified. Otherwise, his conscience could not allow him to be a member of the organization. Despite this, however, he maintained contact with the fighting organization and collected money for it.[25] Pliskin had demanded that all of the ghetto's Jews be moved to the forest; only then would the escape be justified. Zakin saw in the prospect of saving one or two thousand Jews moral justification for endangering the remaining six thousand.

Within the underground organizations, that collective responsibility turned into an imperative to bear responsibility for the whole. The dilemma facing the underground members was a very difficult one. For many of them that imperative was an absolute.

Before the escape of Baruch Levin, who was on the list of "Communists' in his home town of Zoludok, his father, Shmuel Levin, chairman of the *kehilla* and a community notable, told him:

> My son, I know you and can guess your thoughts. Perhaps you are thinking of revenge against those who caused the murder ... and who also want to kill you ... I have no doubt that we must have thoughts of that kind; but you must know that something like that can bring an end to all of us. I wouldn't want that blame to be yours. If I knew, God forbid, that your vengeance was what caused the death of the many, I would not be able to rest in my grave ...[26]

Meir Yoffe of Byten writes:

> Can we conceive of there being a single Byten young man who will want to save his own life and bear on his conscience the lives of hundreds of other human beings?[27]

After the tragic case of Miadzolsky and Beck and their execution in the Swienciany ghetto, the underground determined to leave the ghetto for fear that the Germans would learn of its existence. However, when the underground's members gathered in order to leave, they found themselves facing people who argued:

> You are going and you'll save your lives and you'll leave us in danger of death. Tomorrow the Germans will ask where you are. You want to leave the ghetto when we are still depressed by what happened? Is that heroism?

The dilemma was, therefore, the personal security of the underground members who faced the immediate danger, or the risk of endangering the ghetto. After difficult deliberations the underground members decided to remain in the ghetto. That decision enhanced its prestige among the ghetto inhabitants.

> "In Korelicz we organized a small group and wanted to go to the partisans," related Meir Meirowicz. "We made all efforts to obtain arms. Leaving the ghetto would not have been difficult but it was clear to us that if we left the ghetto the Germans would murder all the Jews ... In May 1942 we were already organized. We had some guns, but every morning and evening the Germans counted the ghetto residents and if someone was missing there was danger of all being executed, and we therefore relinquished the idea of going to the forest lest all the Jews of the ghetto suffer because of us."[29]

In the Postavy ghetto a group of young people were organized for escape by Zaslavsky and Friedman. When the group was about to leave, a young man, Leibke, appeared with a gun and asked to be taken with them. The Judenrat protested the addition of that young man with the argument that he worked in the sawmill and if he didn't appear for work it would bring catastrophe on all ghetto's inhabitants. Zaslavsky weighed the matter, took the young man's gun and gave it to the members of his group, but did not take the young man with them.[30]

There were cases of extraordinary personal heroism in the matter of mutual responsibility. Josef Friedman of Antopol, a tailor's son and Communist, fled the city when the Germans entered. The Germans announced that if he did not return, they would execute his wife, child, parents and 10 community notables. After 48 hours of soul-searching Friedman appeared at the German headquarters and said: "Shoot me and free my family and the other prisoners."[31]

In another incident, two Jews had escaped from the town of Krivicz wanted to get to the home of Chanan Dimenstein in Kobylnik. They made a mistake, however, and knocked at the neighboring house, where a peasant collaborator was living. He informed on Dimenstein that he was maintaining contact with the partisans. Dimenstein and his wife fled to the marshes. The Germans took five Jews and announced that they were hostages and would be killed if Dimenstein and his wife did not turn themselves in. Jews found them in the marshes and tried to convince them to return. Dimenstein pleaded with them not to betray him, and the Jews left him. That night his wife came alone and appeared at the police headquarters. One of the hostages was freed, but the other hostages, Dimenstein's wife and two Jews from Krivicz were executed.[32] This served to deter Kobylnik Jews from fleeing.

Something different happened in Dolhinov. Sigalczyk and Mincel, who had organized young men for escape, left first for the Kulik forests in order to establish contacts with the peasants and partisans. They were caught by German guards, beaten severely and questioned under torture. With the help of a steel rod his brother-in-law brought him, Sigalczyk managed to break the bars and to escape from the prison together with Mincel, and to hide in a bunker. On 15 March 1942, the day after the escape, the Germans called the Judenrat chairman, Niomka Riyer, and informed him that if the two did not appear in their headquarters immediately, all the Dolhinov Jews would be put to death. The Judenrat chairman began to search, but without result. On 17 March 1540 Jews were assembled in the market place and killed. Sigalczyk and Mincel had gone to the forest in order to establish a base for the rescue of those who remained but after a while returned to Dolhinov. The *aktzia* carried out by the Germans had been planned; perhaps the Germans had advanced the date because of the two men, but the Jews interpreted it as a result of their escape. Sigalczyk, who secretly returned to the ghetto with Mincel after the *aktzia*, testifies:

> We were afraid of our neighbors because many of them hated us with a deathly hatred and we were pariahs among them. They looked upon us as being guilty for the catastrophe that had visited the town.[33]

Collective responsibility had a decisive influence on the conduct and reactions of the ghetto Jews. The Jews of a number of towns had faced pogroms at the hands of the non-Jewish population at the time of the Red Army's retreat in June 1941. There had been no question of collective responsibility and the Jews of those towns had organized self-defense, saving their lives and turning back the murderous rioters. However, when collective responsibility was imposed on them during German occupation, the

Jews of these same town acted otherwise. We might therefore conclude that collective responsibility was the chief restraint to Jewish resistance in the ghetto; it tied the hands of the underground with bonds of conscience and left them with hardly any room for action.

Contacts with the Outside: Looking for the Partisans

One of the difficult tasks of the underground was the search for partisan groups and the attempts to establish other links with the outside. A great deal of activity in this field was carried out by the Kurzeniec underground, whose nucleus was a group of Hashomer Hatzair members.

As early as July 1941, Nachum Alperovicz had established contact with a captive Russian major named Volodya, and helped him escape the prison camp. Volodya organised some former Communists and guided them in underground activity. Nachum was the link between Volodya's group and the ghetto underground. It was thanks to this contact that the underground received its first weapons — a short-handled-rifle and bullets — in exchange for salt and kerosene the underground secured from the municipal stores by forging the mayor's signature.

In January 1942 there was a meeting between the Kurzeniec underground and the nucleus of the non-Jewish underground in neighboring Vileyka. This was rare in the conditions existing in those days. Forty persons took in that meeting; among the Kurzeniec underground's representatives were Noah Dinerstein, Benjamin Shulman, Nachum Alperovicz and Zalman Uri Gurvicz. The policeman, Mackewicz, a member of the non-Jewish underground, led them to the meeting place.

A young man who had arrived from Moscow brought to the meeting the story of Russia's struggle against the German invader on the battlefield and in the partisan movement activities in the rear. He presented them with a concrete task; to leave for the forest in the spring. Volodya praised the activities of the Jewish underground, and the Jews' impressions were expressed by one of them; "I will not exaggerate if I say that we did not feel the darkness all about us. We were filled with light towards great deeds."[34]

After this meeting, members of the Kurzeniec underground, in coordination with Volodya's group, began to establish underground organizations in the neighboring towns: Neika, Krivicz, Dolhinov, Smorgon, Soly and Oszmiana. The task of these organizations was to prepare to leave for the forest in the spring and to establish a base for other groups that would follow them. The underground expanded its ranks, with, as they had been taught in their youth movements, the older members taking upon themselves the more difficult task first before imposing them upon the younger members. The underground also established contact with Jews who were working in Knianinina and provided them with food.

Berta Dimenstein, an underground member, a village girl and a courier between the ghetto underground and Volodya's group, brought the underground instructions to blow up two bridges — a railway bridge and the Lareczka bridge (five kilometers from Kurzeniec). She also brought four kilograms of explosives and technical instructions. The two explosions were carried out one night at the end of January 1942 by four members of the Jewish underground: Yitzhak Einbinder, Zalman Uri Gurvicz, Benjamin Shulman and Noah Dinerstein. This was one of the first acts of sabotage in the region against German transport.[35]

At the initiative of the Kurzeniec underground, one member, Joseph Norman, took founts, paper and ink from the Vilejka printshop in which he worked and the underground established a clandestine press and began to publish circulars which were distributed in the region. The first circular was disseminated among the neighborhood peasants in October 1941, and called upon them to: "Peasant, keep your bread. Not a grain for the enemy. Keep it for the partisans ... Everything for the war against the enemy!"

The text, including the word "partisans" was composed before there were any partisans in the region. In all, 150 copies of the circular were distributed by members of the Kurzeniec underground, pasted on posts and walls in the villages, and in one town was even put into the policemen's bags. A second circular directed at the police said: "Policeman, turn your gun at your true enemy ... Wake up while there is still time. Death to the German conqueror!"[36]

On 25 November 1941 two young men left the ghetto and joined the *Diadia Vasva* partisan group. On that same day, three other young men left, established a partisan base and maintained contact with the ghetto youth.[37]

The underground press later moved to the forest. At the recommendation of Norman, who had established it, Nachum and Rivka Alperovicz were taken to work in this press at writing the proclamations and printing them. "We began to feel that we belonged to some group and that someone would pay dearly for our lives."[38]

In Lida, three Jews prepared a small press, packed it into boxes and, hidden under bales of hay, smuggled it on a wagon to the forest. Eliahu Damesek was the printer.

The partisans published a paper *Za Rodinu* (For the Homeland), that was distributed in thousands of copies throughout the Baranowicze region. The Germans offered a prize of 100,000 marks for anyone revealing the whereabouts of the press.[39]

Underground members from the Ilja ghetto, some seven kilometers from the former Soviet-Polish border, looked for contacts with partisans in the Minsk and Pleszczenice forests. After the Vidz ghetto received not too encouraging news from the forest and after a wounded partisan, Leib Wolak, was brought to the ghetto because there was no doctor in the forest to treat him, two underground members — Noah Svirsky of Hechalutz Hatzair and Zalman Silber — went to the forest to examine the conditions there. They met a group of partisans and came to an agreement with them that Jews from the ghetto would be permitted to join the units of the partisans. On their way back to the ghetto, Svirsky and Silber acquired a rifle, killed collaborators and burned their houses.[40]

In many cases, however, young men left the ghettos and wandered for weeks throughout the area without finding any trace of partisan groups. That is what happened to some young men who left from Disna[41] and Postay. Two members of the underground — Aharon Kagan and Chaim Lifszyc who left Dokszyce in order to establish contacts among the peasants and the partisans. died in the course of their mission.[42] From Janow near Pinsk, two men also set out and returned after a week with the information that a group of partisans was prepared to come to the ghetto's aid when the ghetto's Jews attacked the police in the city. A vigorous debate ensued among the young people, some calling for revolt and others arguing that it was impossible to fight without arms, and that by the time the promised help came they would all be killed. Most of the young people apparently did not put too much faith in the partisans' promises and therefore did not see any possibility of rebelling against and attacking the Germans.

An attempt by two Jews from Stolin to reach the partisans also ended tragically. They were betrayed by a peasant who informed on them in return for two kilograms of salt and were hung, despite the Judenrat's efforts to save them. From Ilja and Novogrudok and other ghettos, too, members of the underground went to look for partisans. In Horodok and Korelicz the underground established contact with some former Soviet officers. In Korelicz this was brought to the attention of the Judenrat chairman.[43] In Pruzhany contact was established with a former member of the Soviet administration, Ostapczuk, who also visited the ghetto a number of times. The town of Brzesc's contacts with the forest were very unfortunate. The underground put its trust in a group of partisans headed by a man called "Sashka." A number of times, groups of ten men were sent to join the partisans with each man armed with a rifle, two grenades and ammunition. Only after a few groups had been sent to the forest and "disappeared" mysteriously, did suspicions awaken. It was found that the partisans had ambushed the groups, murdered them and taken their equipment.

In the Nowogrudok region there was a considerable and very patriotic Polish population and the region therefore had become an important center for the *Armia Krajowa* (A.K.) underground. In the middle of 1943 the region had eight A.K. units, Polesie — four, and the Vilno region — two.[44] A Polish A.K. unit took Iwieniec from the Germans, established contact with Soviet partisan groups in the area and planned joint military operations against the Germans. However, because of mutual suspicions and political events (the rupture in diplomatic relations between the USSR and the Sikorsky government in London on 26 April 1943), the relations between the two groups deteriorated and there was even growing hostility between them. At a certain stage, contacts were also established between some ghettos and the Polish underground. Such a link was formed in Wiszniewo. Members of the Polish underground sent information, received over the radio, to the ghetto; they also sent in underground newspapers and leaflets. There was talk of bringing explosives and arms into the ghetto, but there is no proof that this ever happened.

We have already told of the group from Novogrudok ghetto who had formed an autonomous unit in conjunction with the A.K. in the Naliboky region and which was completely destroyed when it was left without assistance in a battle against the German occupation forces.[45] The results of that battle led to growing tension between the partisan units and the A.K. units in the area and, also, to growing antisemitism. In December 1943 the Soviet partisan units received orders to disarm the Polish A.K. units. The A.K. resisted and relations deteriorated considerably. Many Jews in the forest were killed by the A.K. units.

The presence of partisan units in the vicinity of the ghettos created a tragic situation. On the one hand, the partisan activities encouraged the Jews and lit a spark of hope; on the other, however, the growing partisan activity aroused the Jews' fear for their very lives, since the Germans felt them to be maintaining underground links with the "forest bandits". An illustration of this situation was given by one of the inhabitants of the Byten ghetto:

> A tragic situation has been created. It appears that the Jews in the ghetto, starving and tortured, must pray to God that nothing bad happen to our torturers, that not even a single rusty bullet hit them, because then — 100 Jews will be killed for every dead German.[46]

The tragedy lay in the fact that the ghetto's Jews, who had prayed for the rise of a partisan movement, did not find any relief from that movement. The formation of the partisan movement only accelerated the annihilation of the ghetto's Jews.

Hiding Places

Looking for hiding places, *malines*, in ghetto language "resting places for the night," and building bunkers in the ghetto were a form of short-term defense, while hiding places outside the ghetto made it possible to stay alive longer and to exist with the help of food and clothing from Christian friends. Even after an *aktzia*, the ghetto remained under the searching eyes of the Germans, the police and the informing non-Jewish population. From the outset the ghetto hiding places were connected with escape from the ghetto, especially to the forest. After the first wave of *aktzias* Jews listened carefully for any rumors of further *aktzias* in which the remaining Jews would be killed. Their senses were attuned to any sound from within or without; and they especially watched the Germans' conduct carefully and fearfully.

One example of this was a small incident in the Byten ghetto. On 24 July 1942 the city's mayor, Anton Kuzmicz, came to a Jewish shoemaker, Yozhelewsky, from whom he had ordered a pair of shoes, and took the shoes away to be sewn by another shoemaker in the ghetto. Yozhelovsky, however, asked the other shoemaker and found that he had not received the shoes. The ghetto was immediately filled with rumors that something was about to happen.[47]

There was a similar incident in Nieswiezh, when information arrived on 17 July 1942 of the murder of the last Jews in nearby Horodzei. The next day some Germans came to the ghetto and asked for the return of clothing they had left to be laundered. Here too tension immediately spread throughout the ghetto.[48]

In this situation of tension and fear, Jews sought refuge in underground bunkers or other hiding places. In many ghettos the underground, too, built hiding places and bunkers and encouraged Jews to prepare some place in which to hide until the day of flight. When news reached Swienciany of a partisan attack against Lytupy and the murder of the last of the Jews there, the underground began to prepare shelters and to equip them with food. At the time of the second *aktzia* in Baranowicze on 22 September 1942, the members of the underground went down into the bunkers. This was true of the underground organizations in other ghettos as well.

The bunkers were mainly a form of self-defense for wide sections of the ghetto population who could not obtain weapons and were not ready to leave their families, even if they could have found a way to escape, when the Germans suddenly besieged the ghetto. In constructing these hiding places the Jews revealed maximal caution and unaccustomed ingenuity in finding suitable sites and in camouflaging them. Sometimes, however, these hiding places were the graves of those within them. During the third *aktzia* in Slonim, on 29 June 1942, some 1,000 Jews hid in the bunkers and many were burnt alive when the houses were set on fire.[49] Despite this, the digging of the hiding places continued in neighboring Byten, and in Horodok some 900 of the 1,700 Jews went into hiding on the eve of the *aktzia*.

Many Jews did not believe in the prospects of a successful revolt in the ghetto. Their natural realistic instincts led them firstly to do all they could to save themselves and their families. This they thought they might do with a little luck, and so they began by building a hiding place.

In May 1942, after the second *aktzia*, many Dokszyce Jews busied themselves in preparing such hiding places. There were then some 2,000 Jews in the ghetto. When the Germans arrived to carry out the *aktzia* on 31 May, all the Jews were in the bunkers. Only the Judenrat members appeared in the Judenrat building.[50]

Sometimes digging the hiding place was the last resort when all other paths of escape were sealed. Thus, for example, in the dark days in the Zhetl ghetto after Dvorecky's death, when all escape to the forest was closed, many of the ghetto's Jews invested all their energies in building hiding places and digging bunkers. When the Germans entered the ghetto on 6 August 1942, they found the streets completely empty. The ghetto's people were all in hiding. The Germans searched for them with the help of dogs.[51] Sometimes the people went down into their hiding places determined to defend themselves if they were discovered. In the Dereczyn ghetto, for example, the Jews went down armed with axes.[52]

In some places attempts were made to dig tunnels as a way of escaping from the ghetto. In Novogrudok an almost complete tunnel was dug and all the Jews were able to escape through it (see below). In Pruzhany they began to dig a tunnel but gave up the plan. In Dokszyce and Slonim, too, attempts were made to dig tunnels as a way of escape.

Intelligence and Sabotage

In many places the underground organizations set up night watches in order to follow the movements of the Germans, to try to discover their intentions and, as far as possible, to be able to escape before the *aktzia*. In Zholudok, for example, a number of men went out night after night, by turn, in order to warn the ghetto of any impending danger. On one of these nights three of these guard were shot to death. In Iwje, too, the underground set up watches to follow the Germans' movements.

The Germans knew very little about the activities of the underground, but there are reflections of these activities in German documents. A report by Slonim *gebietskommissar* Erren of 26 September 1942, declared:

> A large role in the acts of sabotage and destruction has been played by the Jews who not only serve as couriers and provide information, but are also active in providing weapons stolen from the booty stories and in stealing medicine and instruments from the hospitals. As armed "bandits" they provide considerable support for the Soviet commanders. One operation carried out by *Oberliutnant* Schroeder proves that of the 223 bandits killed. 80 were armed Jews. I am happy that of the 25,000 Jews who were here only 500 will remain, politically still a danger, but who, for reasons of the war economy, we cannot remove.[53]

Even if we question the German documentation about the central role played by Jews in the partisan movement, especially numerically, the facts concerning the arms smuggling from the German stores we have detailed above lend truth to the beginning of Erren's report. We do not have documentary proof to confirm or deny the number of Jews mentioned in the report as partisans who were killed. We can only point out that this regional report was written at the time when the Jewish flight from the ghettos was at its peak (September 1942). The number of those escaping from the ghettos in Western Bielorussia came to at least 25,000; while the numbers of all the Russian partisans through the whole region — Western and Eastern Bielorussia — came, in 1942, according to official Soviet documents, to 73,000 including the family camps. The proportion of Jews in the forests, in comparison with the non-Jewish partisans, was at that time at its highest for the whole war. As far as the acts of sabotage by Jews go, we should mention that the Germans gave the Jews credit for more sabotage than they actually carried out, for propaganda purposes among the non-Jewish population, in order to justify the *aktzias*.

The Jewish underground's activity in the field of sabotage was limited, especially because of the collective responsibility that cast its terror over the ghetto Jews. Despite this, Jews did carry out acts of sabotage on a limited scale in more than a few places. When the Germans in Kobryn attempted to separate the men from the women in a workshop of craftsmen, the Jews opposed this separation by force and organized a secret revolt. They broke machines and damaged materials. For this act the Germans executed 150 persons and imprisoned another 50.[54]

Confrontation with the Judenräte

The Judenräte's attitudes towards the underground were not always the same. In its main fields of activity the underground came into conflict with many of the Judenräte. We will examine one such conflict that took place in a number of ghettos. (For an inclusive evaluation see Chapter 13 on Underground and Judenräte.) In Swienciany there was conflict over the underground's very existence. The Judenräte decided to send the members of the underground to the "Todt" camps in the vicinity, with the transparent intention of disbanding the organization. Three underground members firmly replied to Judenrat member Mottel Gilinsky that they would not go those camps and warned him that if the Lithuanian police came to the ghetto to take the members of the underground they would resist with force. If, as a result, there were to be *aktzia* in the ghetto, the responsibility would lie with the Judenrat. The Judenrat retreated and the underground's prestige was enhanced.[55]

In many places, as we have noted, the Judenräte opposed the escape from the ghettos. In Pinsk, the Judenrat members warned the underground against endangering the physical existence of the ghetto's Jews by escaping. A group of young men who daily left the ghetto to work outside organized themselves for an escape. One day its members left for work but did not return. Judenrat members came to their families and warned them that they would have to turn them over to the Germans in place of the young men if the men were not brought back to the ghetto. Under the pressure of their families and the Judenrat they returned to the ghetto two days later.[56]

Arms, too, were a subject for conflict in many ghettos. In Pruzhany the Judenrat was opposed to the accumulation of arms, acts of resistance within the ghetto and the escape to the forests as endangering the lives of all the ghetto's inhabitants. When it became known to the Judenrat that Yitzhak Friedberg was bringing arms into the ghetto, he was waylaid by Judenrat men, beaten and prevented from continuing to work in the German arms stores. When Friedberg, in December 1942, brought to the Judenrat the partisans' proposal that the Judenrat supply them with clothing, arms and medicines, in return for which they would accept young Jews into their unit, the majority of the Judenrat rejected this proposal.[57]

In certain ghettos there were differences of opinion within the Judenräte themselves on the question of their attitude towards the underground. In Krasna two differing approaches crystallized. The chairman, Shabtai Arluk, "attempted with all his might to organize matters for the good of the population." Close to him in their views were Yitzhak and Moshe Kaplan. Arluk was careful to provide trustworthy information to the population. He argued that the underground should be given, more or less, a free hand provided it act with caution, taking due care not to be caught, to leave the ghetto in small numbers, to take care to find replacements for the workers leaving and to coordinate their escape with the Judenrat. The underground maintained contacts and discussions with him. In the course of time Arluk's influence declined and the underground's opponents grew stronger. A group of Jews who sought to escape one night were intercepted by policemen sent by the Judenrat. When the policemen did not succeed in preventing the young people from leaving, their parents were warned by the Judenrat that this would lead to the annihilation of the ghetto.[58]

In the Mir ghetto the underground had both contacts and conflicts with the Judenrat members. Most of the members of the first Judenrat were murdered in the first *aktzia* of 9 November 1941; the members of the second Judenrat, mostly local people, believed that gifts and bribes could annul the death sentence or forestall its implementation. When the underground learned of some prospective danger for the ghetto it transmitted this information to the

Judenrat. However, when the Judenrat wanted to know how many weapons the underground possessed, where they came from, and where they were hidden, the underground refused to reply to the Judenrat's representative. The later threatened to turn them all over to the gendarmerie if they did not disclose the source of the weapons.

A central member of the Mir underground termed the local Judenrat *nebechdike* (miserable creatures) who believed that in their way they could save the ghetto's Jews. In the ghetto's last days, when news came of fighting by the Jews of Nieswiezh and of *aktzias* in nearby areas, the Judenrat members recognized their mistake, but were still opposed to escape. The underground was also opposed to individuals escaping on their own account, but for a completely different reason. The underground believed that escape should be carried out together immediately upon receiving information of a pending *aktzia* from their contact, Oswald.[59]

In some ghettos the Judenrat members survived a long time; in others they were murdered even before the first *aktzia*. Generally the attitude towards the underground of the first Judenräte to be established, differed from that of those which were later established.

In Baranowicze, Izikson was Judenrat chairman until the first *aktzia* on 3 March 1942. At that time there really was no organized underground, but relations between potential underground members and the Judenrat existed. When the underground later came into being, some of the Jewish policemen joined it, but there were also cases during the first *aktzia* where policemen betrayed Jews to the Germans. The ghetto's inhabitants had great admiration for Izikson, for his behavior, his readiness to take risks and to help others. This is testified to by underground member Avraham Lidovsky, and the partisan Moshe Top. The latter even claimed that Izikson had saved his life. However it was Izikson's last act that gave him fame: his refusal to give the Germans a list of persons unfit for work. For this, he and his secretary were compelled for a whole day to watch the people of their city being murdered during the first *aktzia*, after which they too were executed. After Izikson, Jankelevicz was made Judenrat chairman. In his period in office the anti-underground forces grew stronger and this led to serious clashes between the Judenrat and the underground. The partisan Sarah Rubinowicz (Schiff) said of Jankelevicz: "An honest and just man, but very tragic."[60]

In Stolpce the relations between Judenrat and underground were complex: in some cases they cooperated with each other, as for example when the Judenrat chairman refused to obey the Germans' order to hand over young girls in August 1941. In other matters there was friction, as for example over the issue of collecting money, clothing and other articles for the Germans and registering refugees from other ghettos.[61]

In Slonim, on the other hand, the Judenrat openly worked to aid the underground. After the first *aktzia* in November 1942, the decisive figure in the Judenrat was Gershon Kwint, with Max Rabinowicz as his loyal assistant. The underground enjoyed the Judenrat's cooperation in finding leather with which to sew shoes and boots for the partisans. They were warned to flee to the forest when the Gestapo was looking for them. Members of the Judenrat even bribed Germans to liberate partisans who had been caught.[62]

In many ghettos the harsh disputes with the Judenräte which opposed their activities, hampered the underground and slowed them down.

Personalities and Actions

This book does not include the unorganized resistance displayed by Jews in the region, which deserves a separate study. This unorganized Jewish resistance has not been summed up quantitatively (and it is doubtful that it could), but it took many and varied forms. We should not divorce the organized underground from this unorganized resistance since both these phenomena took place in the same valley of the shadow of death and inevitably influenced each other.

Resistance is not to be measured only in terms of arms and battles, but also of conduct according to elementary moral values and of defending one's life in keeping with them; of people's capacity to yield and even to endanger themselves for others. It began with the piece of bread in the ghetto and sometimes with even less than that. It is difficult to describe the hunger that prevailed in the ghetto and the camps and its accumulating effect on those tortured by it for weeks, months and years.

P'nina Schlossberg of Naliboky, who was moved together with her mother to the Dworec work camp, relates that she used to sneak secretly into her mother's barrack to bring her own bread ration. In Dworec they received 125 grams of bread daily.[63] To give that single piece of bread, even to one's mother, required great moral force and devotion. Generally, difficult conditions tend to make people more self-centered, to care first of all for one's own self and one's own family, but one witness testifies:

There was in Dvorec in those hard days a Jew who helped others. Josef Dasky was his name, who had been brought to the camp with his daughters and his older sister's infant. He was an ordinary Jew but with a warm heart and a pure soul. He actually looked for hungry people to help secretly, so as not to embarrass the recipient. Every Saturday he used to come into our room quietly with a large radish under his arm. Very swiftly he would prepare the radish with an onion on a large plate, put it on the table in the middle of the room; all the dozens of people who lived in the room ate of his radish and bread and he was happy. That precious man died together with all the members of his family.[64]

The story of the Jewish doctors of Brzesc also belongs here. In February the Germans issued an order in Brzesc permitting some of the Jewish physicians to live outside the ghetto walls. The order's intentions were evident: there were only a few physicians on the Aryan side, Jewish intellectuals were not desired in the ghetto, the health of the ghetto's inhabitants would be impaired and, in addition to all these — it would confuse the Jews. Indeed, as a result of this order, the optimists became firmer in their belief that the Germans did not intent to murder all the Jews. However, none of the doctors agreed to work on the Aryan side of the city. Dr. Yaffe was slapped by a German because of his refusal to move out of the ghetto; Dr. Zelikson was forcibly moved to the Aryan side, and Dr. Kiwielecky who worked on the other side, aided the ghetto with money and food.[65]

The concern for one's own and one's family's life, with unending effort and personal risk, is an inseparable part of the story of the Jewish resistance and is the main theme of the broad gray background of ghetto life. That story had many paths, one of which was the story of Yehoshua Swidler from Kobylnik.

On 5 October 1941 there was an *aktzia* in the town. Yehoshua hid and was saved from this *aktzia*. It was rumored that the ghettos of Miadel and Kobylnik were shortly to be liquidated. On 19 December 1942 the Jews were aroused once more — the Jews of Miadel fled to the forest while Kobylnik was surrounded by Bielorussian police and the Gestapo. Yehoshua Swidler succeeded in escaping together with three other Jews to Svir. Afterwards his wife and two daughters came to join him. On 21 September 1942, there was an *aktzia* in Svir. Yehoshua and his family fled to Michaliczky. On 7 November the Judenrat demanded that Yehoshua and his family leave Michaliszky since German orders barred the absorption of refugees from other towns. Meanwhile Yehoshua was among those sent to Vilno and there, in Vilno, the battle for survival continued.[66]

Yosef Beder from Chomsk was a soldier in the Red Army when the war broke out. At the beginning of the war he returned to Chomsk. During the *aktzia* there he hid and escaped to Drohyczyn. When the Germans issued an order that the Chomsk Jews who had fled must return, Beder fled to Antopol, from there to Bereza-Karbuska, and from there back to Drohyczyn. Here he heard that there were still Jews living in Chomsk. He returned to his city by day, sleeping in the fields at night and continued that way until he left for the forest.[67]

Then there is the story of Max Chenczynsky of Lyntupy in the Vilno district. The town's Jews were deported to Swienciany, with only 100 Jews being left behind, among them Chenczynsky and his family. In December 1942 the partisans staged an attack against the Germans and police in the area near Lyntupy. Chenczynsky feared that the German would blame the Jews for the partisans' actions and decided to flee the ghetto. He took his 13-year-old daughter through the fence, showed her the way to Swienciany and promised to follow her. His wife, however, would not agree to separate from the other children and Chenczynsky therefore remained with his family. The ghetto was surrounded and the *aktzia* began. Chenczynsky succeeded in escaping to Swienciany. There he related to the Judenrat chairman what had happened in his town and demanded of him that he organize the young people's escape to the forest. When the end came to Swienciany, Chenczynsky escaped with five other Jews and his struggle for survival continued.[68]

Unorganized resistance was a sequence of innumerable events that reflected the ghetto Jews' fears for their own and their families' lives, their despair and hopes — a story which might be entitled: one day in the life of the ghetto Jews. This unorganized Jewish resistance was marked by the fact that it embraced not only young people, but also older men and women, people from all walks of life.

Such, for instance, was "Aunt Peshke," the aunt of underground member Zalman Uri Gurvicz of Kurzeniec. It was in her house that the meetings between the young underground members and Volodya took place. Aunt Peshke heard that the boys "were going to do something and that a rifle had been hidden by Chaim Suckever by the river, under the roots of a high tree." No male could get to that spot. In general, women were less suspect, Aunt Peshke was 50-years-old or more but overflowed with energy, and her slogan was: "We must do something!" She went out with Yitzhak Einbinder and Zalman Uri Gurvicz. The two remained in the courtyard of one of the houses and she went down by herself to the trees, found the rifle and concealed it in a sack full of grass she had brought with her. The rifle was too long for the sack and extruded from it. The sack was wet and heavy. She walked hurriedly with her heavy and dangerous burden and arrived at the courtyard, to the astonishment of the two men shivering there with excitement and fear.[69]

Grandmother Beila Reichel from the Koziany ghetto in the Vilno district was 62 when the Germans entered Koziany. She did not put on the yellow star, but dressed herself in peasant clothing and went to the neighboring villages to obtain food for her family. Even before the partisans had reached the neighborhood, the grandmother had been bringing the ghetto food, arms and information. Many Jews fled from Koziany and the neighboring area to the forests. Beila tendered aid to these Jews and brought information about relatives she had discovered in the forests and villages. She also extricated Jews from Szarkowszczyzna and Glebokie and led them to partisan territory. After her husband and son were taken to Glebokie she entered the ghetto, appeared before the Judenrat and asked that they be freed. When she did not succeed, she returned to the forest. From there she went to work as a (Christian) dishwasher in the Polygon camp in order to rescue her daughter Malka, her son-in-law Meir and her four grandchildren. Malka was ill. Beila wanted to take out the son-in-law and grandchildren but her daughter did not want to remain alone. Before her eyes, her daughter, son-in-law and grandchildren were, after a short time, taken to the pits. She returned to the forest and found one of her grandchildren in a partisan unit. She served in that unit until liberation. She was privileged to reach Eretz Israel and join her son Avraham Reichel, who had arrived there in the 1920s and her daughter Rivka, who had come from the USSR.[70]

The ghetto of Janow near Pinsk was surrounded on 25 September 1942. The Jews were led to the Borowica forest some four kilometers from the town. One young woman who was carrying an infant was heard murmuring to herself in Yiddish: "Mir hart nisht der toit, nur die cherpa! (I don't mind death but only the shame!)"

The Germans caught Chana Gorodecka with her four sons, aged 10 to 17, and made them run to the market and from there to the forest towards the pits. Chana arranged with her sons that she would fall upon the guard walking at their side and then they would escape. Those lagging behind were beaten with the rifle butts. Chana saw to it that her sons stayed close to her all the way. One of the guards struck her son Chaim. Chana leaped out of the file like a tiger, flung her hands around the policeman's throat and threw him to the ground with the weight of her body. She seized the policeman's rifle and shouted to her boys: "Kinder, antloift! (Children, run!)" People began to run, the murderers opened fire, Chana and three of her sons, Chaim, Avraham and Yehuda, were riddled with bullets, but her other son Israel escaped and survived.[71]

Unarmed, the Jewish mother sought to defend her children. Peshka, Beila Reichel and Chana Gorodecka — great figures of our people, their heroism emerging out of their pain.

The Second Wave of *Aktzias* — Jews at the Pits

The second wave of *aktzias* began in May 1942 and continued until the liquidation of the last of the Western Bielorussian ghettos: Glebokie, on 20 August 1943, Lida on 18 September 1943, and Koldyczevo — on 7 March 1944.

During the first half of 1942 about 24 percent of the Western Bielorussian ghettos were liquidated, in the second half of that same year — about half (49 percent); from the spring of 1942 to the end of that year, about 180,000 Jews were murdered in the Vilno, Novogrudok and Polesie districts. In this second wave many ghettos were completely liquidated, in others there were two *aktzias*, with a small number of "vital" workers being allowed to remain alive at first.

The second wave began when the German Army was stalled on the eastern front and had even been repulsed, with heavy losses in men and equipment. The Nazi leadership's confidence in a speedy victory over the Red Army was shaken; a large partisan movement had developed in their rear and public opinion among the non-Jewish population had begun to veer more and more against the Nazi regime.

All these held out hopes which could have matured in the course of time. It was precisely then, however, that the second wave of annihilation began and showed that Nazi policy would not tolerate Jews living in the ghettos at the side of an expanding partisan movement.

As in the first wave, the murder sites were close to the forests (except for Oszmiana, Swienciany, Lida and Pruzhany, from which the Jews were deported to other places). In this wave, too, the Germans maintained the element of surprise.

In most cases the pits were prepared by the local population and in great secrecy. In Motele (and in other places) there was a table at the murder site with vodka, and the murderers drank before shooting. First, 800 Jewish men and children were brought. The children were photographed, as well as the pit. While the children were still turned towards the cameras, machine guns opened fire.[72]

In this wave many Jews already knew what was in store for them. In many ghettos, many people went down into the bunkers and hiding places when they heard the order to come to the market place. The Jews were led to the murder site surrounded by Germans and local policemen.

During this second wave of annihilation there were cases of Jewish self-defense in many of the ghettos. These were acts of resistance, revolt, battles, of groups breaking out of the burning ghetto, of flight by masses and of groups and also of unsuccessful attempts at revolt. We shall discuss these in the following chapters.

Concerning Jewish resistance on the day of the *aktzias* in the market place or at the pits we shall mention here only a little of what has reached us from refugees or non-Jewish witnesses.

> On the day that the Jews in Lida were assembled in the square on 8 May 1942, one man went among the crowd and muttered: "Jews, you see what the Germans are doing to us; there is only one way out: pick up rocks, throw them in the murderers' faces and scatter in the fields. They'll shoot? Let them; in any case they're going to shoot us. At least we'll die with honor." He went on talking but many were sunk into their own thoughts at these moments. The Jew continued walking about and murmuring without tiring.[73]

The rabbi of Lida, Aharon Rabinowicz, who went to the slaughter with his flock, turned to the Jews: "Jews, don't cry, don't weep; don't give pleasure to the murderers in their hearing us crying!"[74]

Individual Jews attacked armed Germans. The commander, Saurer, wrote an operational report of the mass murder of the Pinsk Jews on 19 October 1942, and said, amongst other things:

> One Jew turned to a German and told him that he had hidden a lot of gold. The German accompanied the Jew to the hiding place. Since the Jew moved very slowly and wanted his guard to accompany him to the attic, the German brought him back to the gathering point. The Jew refused to sit on the ground like the rest and suddenly leaped on one of the cavalrymen, seized his rifle and began to strike at the German soldier. Only thanks to the intervention of the soldiers was the attack ended. Since it was forbidden to use firearms at this place they hit the Jew with an axe and in that way he fell …[75]

Small children also fought for their lives. In the course of their searches in the cellars and bunkers of Raduszkowicze after the 7 March 1943 *aktzia*, the Germans found three women and four children between six and ten years of age. The children fought with their "hands and feet." The policemen shot them on the way and hung their bodies on the ghetto's barbed wire.[76]

Chaim Suckever attacked a policeman on the day of the *aktzia* on 9 September 1942, and began to strangle him, but the police killed him on the spot.[77]

Sturdy Dov Banszczyk from Kleck fought with the Germans in order to save his son. Luba Kacelenbogen from Slonim fell upon a German by the pit and hit him with her fists.[78] Leah Benkin of Wasyliszky grabbed a policeman's rifle and was immediately shot. Baruch Shalom Gendel of Swienciany refused to go to the pit; Morashkin, also of Swienciany, called upon the Jews to resist. Both were shot.[79]

Calls for revenge were hurled at the Germans. On the day of the *aktzia* in Baranowicze (3 March 1942), when the Jews leapt off the trucks carrying them to the pits, Dr. Nachumovsky's sister-in-law shouted at the Germans: "Leprous dogs, you, your wives and children will pay in blood for our spilt blood and the blood of our children!" On another truck the Jews sang: *Am Yisrael Chai* (The Jewish People Lives)[80] Dr. Olga Goldfein, who had organized the hospital in the Pruzhany ghetto, stood up on the day of the deportation (28 January 1943), and shouted imprecations at the Germans.[81] Standing by the pit with his wife and five children, Rabbi Milstein of Lenin shouted at the Germans: "Now you are shedding our blood; but the day will come and vengeance will be taken on you for your actions!"[82] When the *selektzia* began in Kamen-Koshirsk on 10 August 1942, Mottel Stryjer's wife spat in the face of the German standing near her and told him: "Your fall is going to come!"[83] Cila Jokton of Disna also spat in the face of a German officer. Alter Dubinsky, the chairman of the Judenrat of Janow near Pinsk, was brought to the council courtyard on the day of the *aktzia*. He opened with a speech against the Germans and was shot before the eyes of the Jews present.[84]

There were Jews who did not want to fall at the Germans' hands and preferred to chose their own death. On the day of the *aktzia* in Kurzeniec (9 September 1942), Zusia Benes and his wife set their house on fire and committed suicide. Jews wrapped in their *talitot* (prayer shawls) leaped into the flames.[85] Witnesses to the Kurzeniec *aktzia* related that the Germans wanted to spare Dania Sosensky, who worked for the police, but she mocked them and said that the fate of her people would be hers too. She cursed the Germans and reminded them that their day would come, and then they murdered her. Zalman Krawiec of Wasyliszky was in a bunker on the day of the *aktzia*. On hearing the shooting he burst out of his hiding place and shouted: "I can't stay here. I must go to them. What happens to them will happen to me!" The pleas of the other Jews in the bunker were of no avail and he went out.[86]

The family tie was so strong that, even when they stood at the pit, parents were unable to abandon their children and gamble on some prospect of saving themselves. Shlomo Kaganowicz of Kamen-Koshirsk tells about the *aktzia* on 10 August 1942 when all the Jews were brought to the cemetery:

> I went from one group to the next and asked what they thought we should do. People, however, were so depressed that they couldn't reply. I attempted to convince them to fall upon the S.S. men, to grab their guns: "we'll kill some of them and anyone able to do so will run for the forest." Some were prepared for such a revolt, but the others said: "What will we do with the infants? In any case we can't run away!"[87]

People worried about their families even at their very last moments. Henya Dolinsky grabbed her daughter's baby and shouted: "Run, get away with your husband and brothers!" Mirel Einstein shouted to her son, near the cemetery: "Run, avenge our blood!" Chana Popko called to her father: "Father, run and save yourself!" Mina Schwartz pleaded with her son: "Yehuda, I adjure you — run! Don't go to the pit!"[88]

We are witness to a phenomenon of tremendous power that marked the Jews on their tragic road: even more than they were concerned for their own lives, they worried about the members of their families and dear ones, that someone of the family survive. Not fear of ... but worry for ...

The will to save others was strong; often they paid for it with their lives. Monish Fein of Olkeniky was left alive with the other skilled workers in his town. Since he had lost his family, he adopted, just before the *aktzia*, another family and attempted to save it. He was caught in the attempt and executed.

A.L. Poliak of Motele tells of the last moments of one Jewish woman:

> ... The pit had not yet been covered when the policeman brought the wife of Shmuel Grajewer from the village of Zamosz. The blood-thirsty animals received her with wild shouts of glee. Every one of them attempted to make her tell where her husband had fled, but she approached the still only partly

covered pit. They tried all kinds of temptations to make her tell where her husband was and where they had hidden their property. She, however, repulsed them with contempt and declared that she would not reply. Their patience gave out and one of the soldiers ordered her to undress. She did not take off her dress fast enough and they threatened to kill her immediately. She, however, continued to reply: "Robbers, you have already stolen all our property, what else is there left to hide?" Then the first rifle blow hit her and a vulgar curse. They ordered her to stand with her face to the pit but she insisted on looking at them and seeing who shot her, saying: "You can shoot me; I will look in your faces and see who the murderer is." Two shots reverberated in the air and brought an end to the life of this courageous woman."[89]

Notes

1. Baruch Levin, *Beya'arot Hanakam* (In the Forests of Revenge) (Lohamei Hagetaot, 1968), p. 50.
2. Yad Vashem (YV) S2987/258 (Arieh Shevach).
3. Zalman Gurvicz, testimony in *Megillat Kurnitz* (Kurzeniec) (Eng. trans.) (Tel Aviv, 1956), p. 268.
4. Yossef & Ida Kaplan, *Ad Yom Kippurim Ze* (Until This Day of Atonement) (Lohamei Hagetaot, 1976), p. 49.
5. Yekutiel Boyarsky, testimony in *Sefer Zikaron Likdoshei Voronovo* (Memorial Book of the Martyrs of Voronovo) (Tel Aviv, 1971), p. 120.
6. Eliezer Lidovsky, testimony in *Sefer Zikaron Baranowicz* (Memorial Book for the Community of Baranowicz) (loc. date pub), p. 486.
7. Central Zionist Archive (CZA) S26/1544 (Zorach Kremen).
8. Rita Mukasej, testimony in *Pinkas Slonim* (Slonim Diary), vol. 2 (Tel Aviv, 1962), p. 354.
9. Pinchas Ormland, testimony in *Sefer Zikaron likehillat Kamin-Koshirsk* (Memorial Book for the Community of Kamin-Koshirsk and Its Environs) (loc. date). pp. 565–568.
10. YV E/486.
11. Shalom Gerling, testimony in *Pinkas Zhetl* (Zhetl Diary) (Tel Aviv, 1957), p. 47.
12. YV 552 (Dr. Alpert).
13. Gerling, op. cit., pp. 60–63.
14. CZA S26/1544 (Zerach Kerman).
15. YV TR-10/808, p. 209.
16. Moshe Shutan, *Getto un Wald* (Ghetto and Forest) (Tel Aviv, 1971), pp. 40–41.
17. A.L. Poliak, testimony in *Churban Motele* (The Destruction of Motele) (Jerusalem, 1957), pp. 14–15.

18. YV M-1 E 981/855 (Filon Freund).
19. Baruch Levin, testimony in *Sefer Zholudok veOrlova* (Memorial Book of the Communities of Zhulodok and Orlova) (Tel Aviv, 1967), p. 177.
20. YV 1436/133-S (Baruch Shub).
21. Moniek Yosselevsky, testimony in *Sefer Zikaron Stovvetz — Swierezhne veha'yaarot hasmuchot* (Memorial Book of Stolpce — Swerezhna and the Adjoining Townships) (Tel Aviv, 1965), p. 470.
22. Yehiel Segalowitz, testimony in *Sefer Rubzewicz* (Rubzewicz Memorial Book) (Tel Aviv, 1965), p. 352.
23. Eliezer Portnoy, testimony in *Sefer Zikaron* (A Memorial Book — Yanov) (Jerusalem, 1969), p. 345.
24. YV 2085/189-S (Yossef Shapira).
25. Lidovsky, loc. cit.
26. Levin, op. cit., p. 171.
27. Meir Yaffe, testimony in *Pinkas Bytan* (Bytan Diary) (Buenos Aires, 1954), p. 443.
28. YV M-1 E 2519/2653 (Yitzhak Parush).
29. Mordechai Meirowicz, testimony in *Shaveha Vechurbana shel Kehilat Korelicz* (The Life and Destruction of the Community of Korelicz) (n. p., n. d.), p. 240.
30. YV 03/3498 (Shmuel Zaslavsky).
31. YV 2910/44-Z (Pinchas Czerniak).
32. YV 2381/174 (Yitzhak Gordon).
33. Moreshet Archive (MA) A-331 (Ya'akov Sigalczyk).
34. Gurvicz, loc. cit.
35. Ibid.
36. YV E/262 (Magress).
37. YV E/591.
38. Yossef Norman, testimony in *Sefer Zikaron Kehilat Vilejka Hamechozit* (Memorial Book for the Community of the Regional Center of Vilejka) (Tel Aviv, 1972), p. 98.
39. CZA S26/1544 (Eliahu Damesek).
40. YV 2846/99-S (Noah Svirsky).
41. YV 03/2017 (Ida Lekach).
42. Yossef Shapira, testimony in *Sefer Yizkor Dokszvce-Parafyanow* (Dokszyce-Parafyanov Memorial Book) (Tel Aviv, 1970), pp. 212–217.
43. Meirowicz, op. cit., p. 241.
44. Stefan Korbonsky, *Polskie Panstwa Podziemne* (The Polish Underground States) (Paris, 1975), p. 97; *Polskie Sily Zbrojne* (The Polish Armed Forces — in World War II), vol. 3 (London, 1951), p. 524.
45. Shmuel Amarant, testimony in *Ayaratenu Naliboky* (Our Shtetl Naliboky) (Tel Aviv, 1967). pp. 138–139.

46. Yaffe, loc. cit.
47. Yosselevsky, op. cit., p. 431.
48. Shalom Cholawski, *Soldiers from the Ghetto* (New York, 1980), p. 67.
49. Noah Kaplinski, testimony in *Pinkas Slonim*, op. cit., p. 38.
50. Mordechai Worfman, testimony in *Sefer Yizkor Dokszvce-Parafyanow*, op. cit., p. 217.
51. MA D2105/15 (Shmaryahu Furmanski).
52. Yekutiel Chmielnicki, testimony in *Sefer Zikaron leKehillot Dereczyn, Hulinka, Kutna, Siniesk* (Memorial Book of the Communities of Dereczyn, Hulinka, Kutno, Siniesk) (Tel Aviv, 1972), p. 306.
53. YV TR-10/808, p. 209.
54. G. Bill, testimony in *Meqilat Chavim Vechurban* (The Scroll of Life and Destruction — Kobryn) (Tel Aviv, 1951), p. 309.
55. YV 2866/210-A (Yitzhak Arad).
56. David Gleibman, testimony in *Sefer Edut Vezikaron Li Kehillat Pinsk-Karlin* (Memorial and Testimonial Book for the Community of Pinsk-Karlin). vol. 2 (Tel Aviv, 1967), p. 341.
57. Berl Kirshner, testimony in *Pinkas Pruzhane,* etc ... (Diary of Pruzhany, etc ...) (Buenos Aires, 1958), p. 640. (See also Zalman Urievitch. ibid., p. 599).
58. YV 2987/258-S (Arieh Shevach).
59. CZA S26/1544 (Berl Reznik); MA A-99 (Shlomo Charchas).
60. Avraham Lidovsky, *Ba'yaarot* (In the Forests) (Kibbutz Meuchad, 1946), p. 34.
61. YV 1292/111-K (Eliezer Melamed).
62. Kremen, loc. cit.
63. Pnina Schlossberg, testimony in *Avaratenu Naliboky*, op. cit., p. 146.
64. Rachel Itzkowitz, testimony in *Pinkas Belice* (Belice Diary) (Tel Aviv, 1968), p. 301.
65. L. Gluzman, testimony in *Sefer Brisk* (Brzesc Memorial Book) (Tel Aviv, 1954), p. 488.
66. Yehoshua Swidler, testimony in *Sefer Kobylnik* (Kobylnik Memorial Book) (loc. date), p. 151.
67. YV 03/2285 (Yossef Beder).
68. YV M-1/E 2166/1944 (Rosa Ichanowicz).
69. Gurvicz, op. cit., p. 274.
70. Michael Z. Rayak, testimony in *Churban Glubok, etc* ... (The Destruction of Glebokie, etc ...) (Buenos Aires, 1956), pp. 400–404.
71. YV M-1/E 2166/1944 (Rosa Ichanowicz).
72. Poliak, op. cit., p. 26.
73. Leizer Engelshtern, *In Gettos un Welder* (In Ghettos and Forests) (Lohamei HaGetaot, 1972), p. 59.

74. Menachem Reznik, testimony in *Sefer Lida* (Lida Memorial Book) (Tel Aviv, 1970), p. 320.
75. *Prestupleniva Niemietsko-Fashvstitskikh Okhupantow w Belorussi* (Crimes of the German-Fascist Occupiers of Belorussia) (Minsk, 1965), p. 57.
76. Baruch Schepsenboll, testimony in *Sefer Zikaron Raduszkovicz* (Raduszkovicz Memorial Book) (Tel Aviv, 1953).
77. Natan Alperovicz, testimony in *Meqilat Kurnitz*, op. cit., p. 234.
78. Chava Feldman, testimony in *Pinkas Slonim*, op. cit., p. 126.
79. YV M-1/E 319/207 (Yerachmiel Korb).
80. J. Levinbok, testimony in *Sefer Zikaron Baranowicz*, op. cit., p. 546; MA A-166 (Chaim Oshman).
81. (first name or init.) Altshuld, testimony in *Pinkas Pruzhane*, etc ... p. 693.
82. YV M-1/E 318/204 (Dvora Schuster).
83. Dov Amit, testimony in *Sefer Zikaron likehillat Kamin-Koshirsk*, op. cit., p. 146.
84. Isser Apfelboim, testimony in *Sefer Zikaron* (Yanov), op. cit., p. 328.
85. Alperovicz, loc. cit.
86. Chaya Alpert-Kravietz, testimony in *Sefer Szczuczyn* (Szczuczyn Memorial Book) (Tel Aviv, 1967), p. 255.
87. Shlomo Kaganowicz, testimony in *Sefer Zikaron Likehillat Kamin-Koshirsk*, op. cit., p. 605.
88. Alpert-Kravietz, loc. cit.
89. Poliak, op. cit., p. 67.

CHAPTER 8
The Resistance

In the previous chapters we have described the terror cast upon the Jewish community, its suffocating isolation, the lack of means and the inner restraints — all the factors that prevented the Jewish underground from conducting resistance, rebellion or self-defense within the ghettos. We should emphasize that the story of Jewish self-defense in the ghettos does not in reality fully reflect the strength of the desire and impulse to revolt and exact revenge that filled the hearts of many Jews, especially the youth.

Eyewitnesses testifying about the Holocaust in their towns and amongst their families are very naturally under the impression of the mass murders they saw with their own eyes and that impression turns into the dominant motive of their testimony. Under the impression of the reawakened experiences of the abominations and killings their minds are diverted from the spirit of revolt that prevailed in the ghettos. Still, that spirit does find reflection in their testimony. One reflection of what was in the hearts of many ghetto Jews was can find in the words of G. Bill of Kobryn: "God Almighty! If only the ghetto had been organized then; if only we had had at least the weapons in order to give the sign for revolt!"[1]

The question of whether to revolt in the ghetto or to fight from the forest was certainly discussed in many of the underground organizations. However, in many places it was not decided in advance but only in the course of time and as a result of the changing situation. Still, we can affirm that the flight to the forest was included *a priori* and not only *post factum* by the Jewish resistance movement in all the ghettos and other communities, even in those which had no underground organizations.

It is possible to classify the Western Bielorussian ghettos according to the criterion of the resistance they displayed, as follows: ghettos where there were calls for resistance; ghettos where there was local self-defense; ghettos where there were preparations for revolt that ended in flight; ghettos where there were local revolts; ghettos where there were revolts but no underground organization; and ghettos from which there were mass escapes.

Calls for Resistance

We have echoes of a call for revolt from more than a few ghettos. In Janow, near Pinsk, young people called for a revolt but their appeal was rejected by their opponents. In Wiszniewo the members of the underground had proposed setting houses on fire on the day ghetto was surrounded, and after that to escape to the forest. However, after much deliberation, the suggestion was rejected.[2] In Radun ghetto, after it was surrounded on 10 May 1942, Jews proposed setting the ghetto on fire and escaping during ensuing confusion, but the proposal was not accepted because of the lack of any prospects of escaping from the besieged ghetto.

In the Vilno district where the bloody *aktzias* started early in comparison to Western Bielorussia, ideas of a revolt had already been raised a few months after the Germans' arrival. On 21 September 1941, the men of Olkeniky near Vilno were ordered to assemble in the market square preparatory to their deportation to Ejszyszky. Some young people proposed attacking the guards and fleeing to the forests. Others argued, however, that the Germans would take their revenge on the women and children remaining in the town and "so long as there are no proofs that they are taking as to slaughter we must not take any hasty actions." The suggestion of revolt was therefore rejected.[3]

Rumors began to reach Ejszyszky, near Vilno, that "whole towns are being emptied of their Jews. "The community rabbi, Shimon Rosovsky, called on the Jews not to hand over their jewelry and money in trust to the Christian peasants since the latter would than want to get rid of the Jews and to enjoy their spoils. When rumors of Jews being annihilated increased, the rabbi assembled the community heads once again and said: "Jews, you see that our end is nearing with speedy steps ... God does not desire our salvation. Our fate is sealed and we must accept it, but if we die, let us die with honor ... With the money we have left let us buy arms. In any case our money has no value. Let use defend ourselves to our last breath." The rabbi's words aroused some of those present to opposition. Josef Wicenberg angrily asked: "Do you want war? To bring an end to a whole Jewish community and all its Jews?" Opinions were divided and the community leaders dispersed without any decision or any preparations. However, on September 24, 1941, many hundreds of Jews escaped from Ejszyszky and fled to the forest.[4]

Rabbi Rosovsky's sensing, only a few months after the Germans' arrival, that the Jews of the ghetto were facing extinction and his belief in the necessity to fight back "to our last breath" for an honorable death deserves to be noted. Most of the opponents of revolt did not argue against the revolt in itself but claimed that: 1). the revolt might bring an end to the whole ghetto; and 2). that the revolt should be carried out only when no other path of salvation remained.

Self-defense in the Ghetto

In several ghettos Jews revolted on the eve of the impending *aktzias*. In Volozhin, the Germans brought 800 Jews into a smithy on 10 May 1942. Among them Rabbi Reuven Chadash from Olszany. The rabbi called on the Jews to break up the smithy stove, to attack the S.S. men with irons, bricks and stones, and to escape. Judenrat member Israel Lunin argued in reply that "a moment's life is also life". After a German fired at one Jew, Kamieniecki and the others began to flee. The Germans fired at them and only a few succeeded in escaping.[5]

One Jew, Kusze, encouraged the members of his group, who were being led to the murder site and who had stopped for a moment to fill their pockets with sand. When the Germans approached them, they threw the sand into Germans' eyes and escaped.

In Bereza-Kartuska the Germans surrounded Ghetto A on 15 October 1942 in order to send the Jews "to work in Russia." The young men of the underground defended themselves with arms and set the ghetto afire. Jews begin to flee and, though some were killed on the roads, others managed to reach Pruzhany. The members of the Judenrat committed suicide in their meeting room. On that day the last Jews of the community were killed.[6]

The Kobryn ghetto was surrounded on 14 October 1942. The Jews resisted. Underground member Gershon Tennenbaum fought a group of Germans on Kindler Street and 20-year-old Rachel Goldin threw a grenade at the Germans. Others set the ghetto houses on fire. Dr. Chaim Goldberg, one-time head of the Hashomer Hatzair branch, shot at the Germans and with his last bullet killed himself. Among the fighters in the ghetto were Hershl Zkubacky, Dr. Yaakov Angelowiez, Mottel Breznick and Abrasha Herman.[7]

In Wiszniewo the Jews were gathered into the square on 30 August 1942, when they were loaded onto trucks. Batya Podberezky leapt of and shouted: "Jews, save yourselves!" A German bullet hit her but in reply to her call, Jews began to leap off the cars and to run into the fields of grain in the direction of the forest. Most, however, were shot. Their bodies covered the road from the square to the forest. A few were caught by mounted policemen. However, a group of 15 Jews succeeded in reaching the forest.[8]

In Meiczet the Germans cut off the ghetto on the night of 15 July 1942. The members of the self-defense group attempted to break through the siege but were met by strong German fire. The defenders had three rifles held by ex-soldiers: Noah Mordokovsky, Yaakov Margolin and Chaim Szelubsky. Some 20 young men fell in this defense action. A group of 25 men reached the Zolotov unit and organized into an autonomous partisan unit.[9]

The Germans surrounded the Lachowicz ghetto on 10 June 1942. A resistance group of some 60 men, among Josef Pecker, Mottel Chwediuk and Michael Bussel gathered at the gate with the intention of blocking the Germans' entry into the ghetto. When the clash began the Germans began to shoot and to throw grenades and bombs. Some 1,200 Jews were murdered in that *aktzia*. Some of the Jews hid in the bunkers. On 25 June 1942 the houses of the last 300 Jews were surrounded. The Jews set their homes on fire. Yeshaya David Yelin stabbed a German who entered his bunker with a razor. Here too, a handful of Jews succeeded in escaping to the forest.[10]

The Germans conducted a third *aktzia* in Slonim from 29 June to 15 July 1942, during which time they murdered some 10,000 Jews; only 800 were left alive. About 1,000 Jews hid in bunkers. The Germans set fire to the houses in some of the ghetto streets and many Jews were burned alive in their hiding places. A spirit of resistance to the Germans prevailed among the ghetto youth. At the time of the *aktzia* only part of the underground arms were found in the ghetto; as we have mentioned previously, the Slonim ghetto was organized for flight to the forest and the partisans, and had hid part of its weapons outside the ghetto. When the first truckload of Jews was taken out, some jumped off the moving vehicle. Young people escaped from the burning houses into the river in the hope of escaping by swimming but the river water turned red from the blood of the escaping Jews. The Germans sought to separate the craftsmen left alive from their families, who were to be sent away, but the Jews resisted that separation. The Germans desired to leave a refugee engineer alive but he accompanied his wife to death. One Jew killed with his axe the German who had shot his child in its cradle.[11]

The Braslaw ghetto was surrounded on 3 June 1942. Germans and local police began to drive the Jews out of their homes. Young people resisted with whatever they had in their hands. There was also an organized group that possessed firearms, among them Fisher and Lubawicz; some of them escaped to the partisans. Another source in our possession described the self-defense of groups of Braslav Jews in March 1943. The Jews entrenched themselves in one of the houses and defended themselves with pistols and rifles. When their ammunition ran out the Germans broke into the house. One of the Jews grabbed an automatic rifle from on the Germans and continued shooting until he too was killed.[12]

In June 1942 terrifying news from the region began to reach the Disna ghetto. The Jews sensed the impending *aktzia* and gasoline was prepared in every house. On June 15 German gendarmes attacked the ghetto with gunfire from all sides. The Jews threw everything that came to hand at the attackers: stones, pieces of iron, bricks and bottles; others began to flee. The gendarmes threw grenades and bombs. At the same time, some Jews (among them the Judenrat members), set the ghetto houses on fire so that they would not fall into the Germans' hands. Many Jews succeeded in hiding that night but the peasants found them in their hiding places and betrayed them to the Germans. A few group escaped to the forest.[13]

Glebokie served as a refuge for the neighboring Jews and its ghetto was one of the last in Western Bielorussia. Thousands of Jews fled to the forest. Sick, swollen by hunger and ragged they were persecuted in the forest, too, by peasant informers, Germans and police. The Germans learned that it was "inefficient" to chase after the Jews in the forests and marshes and offered a "pardon" to those returning to the Glebokie ghetto. Instructions were also given to peasants who met Jews returning to Glebokie to bring them to the ghettos in their wagons. In that way, Jews who had fled from dozens of other communities, including Vilno, and the Jews who had remained in the ghetto all the time, saw the fate of those escaping. The Germans achieved two goals: the capture of Jews who had fled from other locations and the discouragement of other potential flights from the ghetto. The ghetto population grew to 7,000 Jews.[15] When German authorities announced the "right" to return to the Glebokie ghetto, Jews were given special permits to move about and Judenrat chairman Lederman was sent to the fields and forests in order to bring escaped Jews back to the ghetto. Ultimately, Jews from the towns of Harmonowicz, Luszky, Hajduciszki, Verapajewo, Parafianowo, Dolhinov, Druisk, Braslav, Bildugy, Swienciany, Podbrodzh, Szkonciky, etc. came to Glebokie.

Jews who returned to Glebokie did so out of naiveté, delusion and weakness but, above all, because of the forest and its terrors, the murder of Jews in the forests, fields and villages, the hunger and the extremely difficult conditions, that seemed in their eyes even more difficult than life in the ghetto.

Some military events took place in the Glebokie area that affected the ghetto's existence. The Chief-of-Staff of the 229th Red Army division, Gil Radyonov, who had been cut off with his units by the Germans' during their invasion of Bielorussia, had moved over to the German's side and engaged in battles against the partisans in the Biegomel area. In the spring of 1943 his units were cut off by the partisans and, after negotiations were conducted with the permission of the Communist Party, Radyonov and his forces went over to the partisans on 18 August 1943. His force then received the name of the "First Anti-Fascist Brigade." The force worked behind the German rear and also attached Bokszycze. Many Jews joined it.[16]

The Germans looked upon the Glebokie ghetto, with its thousands of Jews, as a manpower reservoir for the Radyanov and other partisan units in the vicinity. These fears hastened the implementation of their plans to liquidate the Glebokie ghetto. According to the testimonies of Michael and Ziv Rayak, the "Suworow" partisan brigade had intend to give the Kaganovics Jewish partisan unit and its commander, David Pinczov, the task of liberating the Glebokie Jews.[17] Baruch Zimmer, who was sent to Glebokie by Pinczov, returned to the forest with a group of 20 men and reported that there were another 300 young men in the ghetto who could be organized for an armed uprising but that they had only a few weapons and needed the time to organize and prepare. In the end, the military confrontation between the Germans and the Gil Radyonov forces came too early.

On 20 August 1943 the Germans announced that the Glebokie Jews would be moved to Lublin. The Judenrat members assured the ghetto Jews that they were being moved for work. The ghetto was surrounded by forces of Germans and the police. Young people with pistols and other weapons broke through the barbed wire fences and escaped. Others hurried to their hiding places.

When the Germans entered the ghetto they were met with gunfire and grenades. They began to search for Jews, who resisted. In the course of the battle the Jews set their houses on fire and fled on all sides. Some hiding places were discovered because of children crying. In one hiding place there were 84 Jews with 3 pistols and 1 rifle. Mothers urged their children to run. Jews broke out of the burning ghetto; some of them armed.[18] The Germans went from one place to the next — attics, stables, latrines — and searched everywhere — in the stoves, closets and chimneys. The gunfire did not cease that whole day. The murder of the Glebokie Jews went on for many days and the streets were piled with bodies. The Germans and their lackeys went among the corpses and pulled out gold teeth and took off rings and other jewelry. Peasants were brought from the villages to collect the bodies.[19]

Planes hovered over the ghetto, coming down low and strafing. They sprayed incendiary material on the houses and the ghetto — some hundreds of houses — went up in flames. Hundreds of people and children in the bunkers, pits and cellars were suffocated or burned alive. Those fleeing from the fire and smoke were felled by German bullets. When the conflagration increased, German and police guards were set by the houses to look for Jews escaping from the burning buildings. Those escaping from one shelter hurried to another and thus brought catastrophe upon those already hiding there because the Germans had followed the movements of those fleeing. Some ran with their scorched bodies from the fire to the well ...

On 28 December 1942 the Dworec work camp was surrounded, with the explanation that the Jews were going to be taken to work in Bobruisk. The reactions of the Jews in the camp were divided. Some of the inmates had fled from the ghettos where they had lost their families and did not believe they would live to see the end of the war: "Mir vellen sei vi nit iberleben (We won't live so long) and "I'm going to face my fourth *aktzia*, to hell with this life." Some of the Jews displayed resistance and encouraged others to do the same. Benjamin Rudicky, with some young men from Rubzhewicze hurried to the gate with grenades in their pockets and shouted to the Jews. "Don't go to the trucks, they're taking you to death!" Judenrat chairman Novik, who was negotiating with the German commander, pleaded with Benjamin, who was about to throw a grenade at the German officers: "Child, a little patience, we still have hope, maybe there will be a miracle, so long as I haven't finished talking!" A few minutes later Novik arrived stunned and turned to the Jews with a broken voice: "Dear ones, there is no more hope. Shmah Israel!

(Hear O Israel!)" and climbed onto the truck with his daughter. Benjamin Rudicky, Isser Beckman and Moshe Funt decided to break through the wire fence, and with others who joined them, were successful. The Germans replied with machine gun fire. Some fell on the fence and others retreated to the bunker but, despite the German shooting, some Jews cut through the wire and escaped from the camp.

> "… I met Baruch Rubzhevsky who had escaped from the camp. In one hand he held a pistol, in the other a knife. His face was sooty from the fire. His hair waved in the wind and his eyes flames. He seemed to us at that moment to be angel of vengeance."[20]

Many Jews hid in the bunkers. In one bunker some 160 men were packed. In small groups they stole out of the bunkers to the nearby forest.[21]

From these stories of the uprisings in the ghettos we learn that the Jews revolted only when they stood before the actual threat of an *aktzia* or the "deportation to work" that meant annihilation. Jews in the ghetto, including members of the organizations, refrained from endangering the ghetto in "ordinary times" lest, perhaps there was some hope … When they stood facing the danger, the rebels used whatever weapons came to hand: stones, brick, pieces of iron, cold steel or firearms. They set fire to their homes and property so as not to leave them to the murderous enemy. Sometimes they attacked the armed Germans and policemen with their bare hands. Those calling for revolt were the young and the old alike — sometimes individuals, sometimes an organized group which, at the end, convinced the rest of the population to join them. Those ready to revolt faced the opposition of many Jews who had despaired of any salvation or who, at the other extreme, believed up to the very last minute that the evil decree might be annulled. Following the resistance in the ghettos came flight to the forest in an attempt to escape.

Preparations for Revolt which Ended in Escape

Many of the Jews were of the opinion that any decision on an immediate uprising seemed to herald the "beginning of the end." It appeared to them to be preferable to gain time, even if it did not hold many prospects, rather than to decide on resistance. After the wave of annihilation, some of the ghetto Jews argued that those remaining were vital for the Germans and therefore: "Let us walk, perhaps we shall be saved." Most, however did not heed these pacifying words. There was, however, a growing demand not to hasten the end; perhaps time and circumstances would bring some salvation, and any resistance that did not promise salvation was tantamount to suicide. On the other hand, there were more than a few who called for action, for resistance, intuitively they felt that time was against them. This is the background for the many deliberations within the underground organizations when they were about to decide on an uprising.

There was a plan in the Stolin ghetto to set the ghetto on fire and to break out if the ghetto faced annihilation. Barrels of kerosene were made ready and arrangements were made to ignite them.[22] I have been unable to ascertain why the plan was not implemented at the last moment.

One of the two underground organizations in the Brzesc ghetto planned an uprising that was supposed to receive aid from outside the ghetto by the Polish and Soviet underground units. The plan was that when the Germans began shooting, underground groups would set the ghetto on fire. The escaping Jews would be directed through Kobryn and via Jagielony Streets to the forest. Michael Omalinski was given the task of covering the escape. According to Omalinski's testimony, the ghetto was prepared to revolt. The underground groups were ready. On 14 October 1942 the ghetto still did not know what was going to happen. The following day the ghetto was sealed off by the Germans but the expected uprising did not come about. We can only speculate as to the reasons preventing the revolt.[23]

The Pruzhany ghetto was surrounded on 28 January 1943 and the deportation began on that day. Some 2,500 Jews were taken out of the ghetto to the railway to Auschwitz. The following day the Judenrat chairman, Yitzhak Yanovicz, appeared on the council balcony and announced that he was convinced that the Germans were deceiving them, that the Jews were not being taken to work and that everyone there should act as he thought best. In the course of four days some 10,000 Pruzhany Jews were sent to Auschwitz. The youth deliberated whether to go with their parents, to revolt in the ghetto or to escape to the partisans. In the end most of the young people decided to go with their parents. Only a few Jews succeeded in escaping from the ghetto during those four days and in reaching the forest. In some streets the Jews broke out; but many fell by the ghetto gate and only some succeeded in getting through. Some 2,000 hid in the bunkers.[24]

The Stolpce underground organization had planned an uprising in the event of an *aktzia*. The signal for the uprising was to be the burning of the German headquarters by underground members who worked there and the burning of one of the ghetto houses. Isik Berkowicz who worked in the electric power station, was given the task of setting the plant on fire. In addition, Jews who worked outside the ghetto were to set fire to their places of work. The underground prepared sets of German uniforms and the armbands of the German police which the members of the underground would wear on the day of the uprising when they cut the wire fences and caused the uproar that would facilitate the escape. The workers in the headquarters prepared gasoline. Underground members linked the city's electricity to that of the ghetto's so that it would be possible to black out the city from inside the ghetto. Those working for the Germans were to take weapons from their places of work and use them against the murderers.

Rumors of the Nieswiezh revolt reached Stolpce on 21 July 1942 and of Kleck on 22 July. The Stolpce underground became tense with expectation when, after a few days, a German order came to send 500 Jews to work in Baranowicze. A group of German officers and NCOs arrived at the ghetto's gates. Emotions became high in the underground organization. Some members argued that the taking of the 500 was only a tactic designed to weaken their power of resistance and therefore they should act at once. Others, however, wondered whether perhaps the Germans really did need more workers. It was forbidden to hasten the end and endanger the whole ghetto. The latter's arguments did not convince the former but were sufficient to weaken them and prevent from organizing the revolt on their own. One member of the underground tells of that day:

> We met at the gate. Every moment we expected the order for the uprising. Under my coat my hands fondled the sharp axe and in my pocket — a bottle of acid. Some dozens of Germans and policemen stood near the gate without suspecting anything or that anything was about to happen. And indeed, nothing happened. The order did not come. Today, I wonder — why? Was it because the right man was missing at the right spot, who would not pity the women and children? One man could have ignited the revolt, and then — who knows? Disappointed and depressed, we returned our weapons to their hiding places and began to gather in order to go to work.[25]

"The right man in the right spot" was of prime importance in critical situations, especially in the ghetto. Perhaps, some focal figure of influence could have united the organization for revolt. On 23 September 1942 the ghetto was surrounded for an *aktzia* that lasted eight days and left 500 "vital" Jews in the town. Elyakim Milcenson set his house on fire. The underground, that had organized cells and had a few arms, remained with the same dilemma as at the time of the *selektzia* of workers for Baranowicze. Group of the remaining Jews who survived began to organize for flight to the forest.

The Pinsk underground had also planned to set the city on fire. The decision had been taken with one reservation: to act only at the decisive moment and not before then. On 22 October 1942, a rumor spread in the ghetto that long and deep ditches were being dug in the Dobrowelia airfield. A few days later the German commander, Ebner, met with Judenrat chairman Minsky, and informed him that the ditches at the airfield were to store fuel tanks and warned the ghetto's inhabitants against escaping or attempts at resistance, saying: "I promise you by my German word of honor that nothing bad will happen to the Jews of Pinsk since they are working for the German war effort."[26]

Ebner was apparently very well aware of the relaxing effects of his words "working for the war effort" on the Jews. Minsky reported Ebner's words at a meeting of the ghetto's inhabitants. The underground organization met for consultations and opinions were divided. Some argued that the German could not be trusted and that resistance action should be commenced at once. Most of those present, however, argued that the decision should be put off a few days until the situation became clear.

The next day there was a rumor, apparently from a German source, that only 3,000–4,000 Jews, who did not work, would be taken from the ghetto while the rest would remain. This "good" news also made it even more difficult to come to any decision and reinforced the majority in the underground who was unprepared to take upon itself the responsibility for the annihilation of all Pinsk's Jews when there was a prospect of most remaining alive. The majority decided, therefore, to prepare for action but to carefully follow the measures taken by the Germans. So too they were to make attempts to obtain secret information about German activity well in advance.

On 27 October 1942 Himmler sent an order to annihilate the inhabitants of the Pinsk ghetto. The *aktzia* began the next day. The Germans mobilized a large army force, a police battalion, as well as a police cavalry unit and an armored police unit for the task. At least 16,200 Jews were murdered, of these 1,200 were within the ghetto. Only about 100 succeeded in escaping. According to a report, about 150 had attempted to escape but were caught, some of them some kilometers from the city. The surviving 143 persons were housed in 11 buildings (the "little ghetto") Despite the warning of the German commander, Ebner, these Jews nevertheless attempted to escape.[27]

Baranowicze

The plan of Baranowicze's fighting organization was that the uprising would be carried out at the ghetto's residents' initiative. This innovation would provide the fighters with the considerable advantage of surprise and enhance the prospects of escape from the ghetto.

The organization distributed incendiary materials and weapons at specific places. A guard of 30 men was set up to alarm the ghetto in the even of a surprise German attack. Should such an attack take place, five members of the guard were to attack the Gestapo building and the Bielorussian police headquarters. One member was to set fire to the ghetto's houses. Wire-cutters were also prepared. The date of the uprising was fixed for 19 July 1942. It was decided that the flight after the uprising would be in the direction of the Kalibav forest, some seven kilometers from the city, and that there would be guides to lead the escapers. A woman who worked in the German headquarters was to poison the German guards' food before the escape. The sector commanders were: Monik Mushinsky, Chaim Oshman, Moshe Himmelfarb, Shlomo Rev, Monik Dubkovsky, Chaim Stolowicky and Zigelbaum were in charge of the arms caches.

At the beginning of July the leaders of the underground decided by a majority vote to put off the date of the uprising for the following reasons: 1). It was not possible to call for a revolt on the date fixed if one was to act with consideration for the residents of the ghetto; 2). The ghetto Jews who would be in the bunkers and cellars when the ghetto was set on fire would be asphyxiated by the smoke; 3). The ghetto was still unprepared for an uprising; and 4). Contacts with the partisans had begun to be established giving better hopes of escape to the forest.[28]

After the date of the uprising was postponed, some members of the underground leadership, among them Kopelowicz and Zaryckevicz, asked to take 40 young people, mostly Hashomer Hatzair members, to the forest. One member vigorously opposed this and threatened that if this were done he and other members of the fighting organization would open fire on the Germans and the whole ghetto would go up in flames. Judenrat members Bialoskurnik and Sapczyc declared that if the fighting organization did not disband and hand over its arms they would turn them over to the Gestapo. They also sent police to arrest Zaryckevicz and Lidovsky. The two imprisoned members of the underground declared that from then on they did not recognize the Judenrat as the representative of the ghetto Jews and that any attempt at betrayal would be punished by death. Bialoskurnik and Sapczyc retreated. Zaryckevicz returned to the bunker and convinced the group of 40 that they could not leave for the forest in the current circumstances. The group yielded and did not leave. Lidovsky summed up the clash with the Judenrat thus: "They want to make us responsible for the 9,000 Jews in the ghetto."[29]

In June 1942 a train brought 3,000 Czech Jews to the Baranowicze railroad station. They were taken out of the cars for "lunch" and murdered at a nearby site. The Jews who had been sent from Koldyczewo to bury the dead and the Czech police who had accompanied the train were also killed. Rumors of this reached the ghetto and heightened the tension among the Jews.

On 29 August 1942, 700 young Jews were chosen and sent to work in Moldevezna. The Germans hoped in this way to weaken the ghetto's power of resistance. During the kidnapping, Jews hid in the bunkers.

Since the majority of the underground staff were opposed to an organized flight to the forest and the idea of the uprising had for all practical purposes been put off without any date being set, the plan of an initiated revolt no longer existed. However, the instructions concerning the fighting in the ghetto were still in force. On 22 September 1942 the ghetto was attacked by German and police forces and an *aktzia* began. There were then close to 8,000 Jews in the ghetto. Gestapo men dressed in Todt uniforms came to the ghetto supposedly to take people for work. Some members of the underground saw through the disguise. When Yitzhak, an underground member of the Jewish police, came out with a bottle of gasoline and a grenade in order to blow up the ghetto police building and thereby give the signal for the uprising to begin, Warshavsky grabbed his hand and said: "Yitzhak, don't throw it! It's not an *aktzia*!" Yitzhak did not throw the grenade. The signal was not given.[30]

The kidnapping began. The underground members also went down into their bunkers. Members of the command were scattered in different places. One girl courier was killed while running to Warshavsky. Another courier, Hilka Boryszansky, arrived at Dr. Abramovsky's bunker and informed him of the *aktzia* in the ghetto. Abramovsky said that according to the Judenrat sources these were "Todt" men coming to take people for labor details. Moshe Zalmanovicz, Zeitlin and Aharon Gorsky demanded that they set the ghetto on fire and escape to the forest. Abramovsky rejected the demand and most of those in the bunker agreed with him.

Eliezer Lidovsky was in a second bunker where there were many families with children. The families did not allow the underground members to leave the bunker. The underground men estimated that, in the given situation, isolated shooting or one house going up in flames would not serve as an alarm and would only mean suicide. The women and children wailed and pleaded that they not open fire. "That was the most miserable day in the life of the ghetto underground," Lidovsky later said.[31] In Moshe Top's and Chaim Oshman's bunker there were some 25 men armed with rifles, a machine gun, grenades and explosive material.

A consultation that night among the underground members in the two bunkers had to decide on the question of whether to open fire in the ghetto or to leave for the forest. Most of the people who took part in this meeting did not want to take upon themselves the responsibility for the lives of those people in the ghetto that the Germans might perhaps permit to live. On the other hand, fighting in the forest held the prospect of revenge and even some hope of being saved. It was decided to send a number of people at night to the wire fence in order to prepare an opening towards the forest. Dr. Abramovsky, as the only doctor in the ghetto, went to the ghetto hospital.

The *aktzia* continued about ten days and all that time the debates continued in the underground between Dr. Abramovsky, who opposed the flight and Moshe Zalmanovicz and his comrades, who demanded an escape to the forest.

A critical clash took place during those same days between the underground headquarters staff and the Judenrat members who demanded that the underground's arms be turned over to them or else they would turn the underground over to the Germans. A compromise was reached: the arms would remain hidden in the ghetto and not turned over to the Judenrat, but there would also be no departure for the forest.[32]

A bunker in which 55 Jews were hidden was discovered by a Bielorussian policeman. A Jew slashed the policeman's head with a razor and he fell wallowing in blood. The Bielorussian policemen who arrived at the site blew up the bunker and all its occupants with hand grenades. On Sadova Street, a Jewish young man attacked a Lithuanian officer and put a knife into his head. In one of the trucks carrying Jews to the pits, the barber Zubak fell upon a Bielorussian policeman and wounded him in the throat. Jews jumped off the trucks and ran. In the second *aktzia* some 3,000 Jews were murdered. Immediately afterwards, Zalmanovicz and Zeitlin, armed with Russian automatics, escaped to the forest. It was also decided to take out of the ghetto the weapons that underground members had previously paid with their lives in order to bring in. These had been concealed by them close to their places of work. A plan for a revolt in the ghetto was no longer on the underground agenda and flight to the forest increased.

On 17 December 1942, the Germans carried out a third *aktzia* in which 3,000 Jews were killed. In one of the trucks carrying the Jews to the pits, 18-year-old Mirka Vigdorczyk shouted: "Jews, why are you so quiet? Don't you know where they are taking us?" When the trucks left the city the Jews broke down the door and jumped into the snow.[33]

Underground activities continued among the 700 Jews who remained in the Baranowicze work camp after the third *aktzia* and the ghetto's liquidation.

To sum up the events at Baranowicze, we can say that by postponing the original date for the uprising — 19 July 1942 without setting any new date, the underground actually put an end to any initiated uprising. The second *aktzia* put the underground to the test and its plans for defense proved faulty. The decision to raise the alarm and give the signal for battle was not placed in authoritative hands. The members of the command were not in one place but in separate bunkers and therefore could not make joint decisions. In some of the bunkers (Lidovsky's) the fighters had no weapons. The fact that fighter and the non-fighting population were in the same bunkers prevented the fighter from opening fire. Every one of these essentially operational faults made its contribution to the course of events and together frustrated the fighters' aims, thereby serving as an explanation for what happened.

In addition, there were more essential reasons:

1. There was no support among the people in the ghetto for underground fighting within the ghetto. On the eve of the first *aktzia* when the underground was prepared to fight, 70 percent of the Jewish population was still there. In their hearts many Jews still nurtured the illusory hope that there could be or perhaps might be some small salvation for the ghetto's Jews; that all hope had not disappeared. By the nature of things every one of these Jews saw himself as one of those who might be saved. The ghetto Jews were not convinced that the underground's plans for leaving the ghetto, and even less its plans for fighting in the ghetto, would open a door to salvation even for some considerable

number of Jews. The tragic paradox was that this will to live — even if only for the moment — clashed with the preparations of those who wanted, because of that same will to live, to defend their lives with their own bodies.

2. However, not even all the members of the underground were wholly in agreement with the decision for an uprising in the ghetto. The debates that took place within the underground on the eve of the second *aktzia* over who would decide on a zero hour — the underground or the Germans and during the *aktzia* itself, over whether to open fire on the Germans, testify that the underground's central figures (like Dr. Abramovsky) considered an uprising to be taking responsibility for the lives of all the ghetto's inhabitants; it was that responsibility that deterred them from deciding to fight. These were generally the views of the older men in the underground organization, while the younger men demanded going to the forest or resisting.

> One thing is clear: it was not a lack of ideals or courage among three members of the fighting organization. Perhaps they were stopped by their feeling of responsibility for the Jewish population and the few thousands of Jewish workers who still had prospects of remaining alive.[34]

The debate raged within the bunkers throughout the *aktzia*. Outside, thousands of Jews were being killed. In their hearts, many underground members had come to the view that in the end the Germans would annihilate all the Jews in the ghetto and that if it were still possible to save something it was only by escaping and fighting in the forest.

In the Mir ghetto the underground, together with Oswald, had planned an uprising but after some time abandoned the plan. Oswald was not inclined to the idea of resistance within the ghetto since he did not believe that anyone would remain alive after it. He drew up a plan for escape, believing that he would know the date of the *aktzia* some days in advance and would be able to inform the underground in time, thus enabling the Jews to escape.

In Zhetl too the plan for a revolt was changed to one of escaping to the forest, both because of the limitations of fighting and escaping within the confines of a small ghetto and because of the prospects aroused with the appearance of partisans in the region.[35]

Novogrudok

In Novogrudok the uprising had been set for 15 April 1943 (see previous chapter). Dr. Kagan was elected to head the uprising. The organization estimated that about half the population would be able to escape to the forests. During the winter of 1942–43 news came to the Novogrudok work camp of the Germans' defeat at Stalingrad and of the activities of Jewish partisans. These two pieces of news encouraged the people in the camp. The regime within the camp, however, became even more severe. The information had increased the Germans' caution and they conducted a roll call twice daily. They introduced a Jewish informer into the camp. The underground sentenced him to death and carried the sentence out within the camp. In response, the Germans arrested Moshe Burstein, who was a member of the Judenrat and also an underground member, and Reuven Shevkovsky. They were questioned and tortured, and when they refused to talk, were murdered. The plans for an uprising became known to many in the work camp. A considerable number, especially the older people, opposed the underground's plan, arguing that: "An uprising holds no prospect of salvation. Revolt and escape — are suicide. Why commit suicide? If we are going to commit suicide — there is time!"

On the day set for the uprising the members of the underground were deterred for carrying it out, despite the fact that the groups were already on the alert. One indirect reason was the fact that the wife of Dr. Jakobowicz, who lay wounded in the camp, demanded that the date for the revolt be postponed until her husband recuperated. Otherwise, she threatened, she would tell the Germans about it.[36]

Though an individual can disrupt the plans of an entire campaign, we may assume that it would have been possible to overcome this one problem; the real reason for delaying the uprising lay in the sharp opposition of a large part, perhaps the majority, of the camp's Jews to it. The uprising's supporters were labeled by its opponents as "the fine death people."

The Germans prepared lists of the specialized craftsmen and granted them an additional bread ration in order to strengthen their illusions of survival. On 7 May 1943, in the fourth *aktzia*, the Germans killed 399 Jews in the vicinity of the camp and the murderous activity could be seen from the higher floors of the "court building." People were aroused and wanted to break out of the camp. At the end of the *aktzia* it was decided to break through the fence and that anyone who could and wanted to do so would escape, even if he thereby endangered the others. In the evening the Germans reinforced the guards and the breakout was put off from one day to the next.

At that time news reached the camp (via the radio in the underground's possession) of the revolt in the Warsaw ghetto and the bombing of German cities. The direct implications for the Jews in the camp was a new awakening; hopes for the war's conclusions and a higher premium on life. Opponents of the uprising in the camp met and decided to remain in the camp as long as possible. Among the rest, it was said at the meeting that the Americans would almost certainly attempt to exchange Jews for Germans. The plans for the uprising were laid aside.

The Tunnel

A suggestion had been raised in the camp to dig a tunnel through which all the occupants could escape. This idea was a kind of "golden mean" holding both risks and prospects. The suggestion's progenitors were Dr. Kagan, Berl Joselevicz, Dvorecky and Natan Sucharsky, together with some other men of operational ability.[37] There were, indeed, persons in the camp who doubted the idea, but they did not oppose it. Some members of the underground feared that "it might be too late" by the time the tunnel was completed. However, the opponents of the uprising also sent a delegation to the underground staff and recommended that the tunnel be dug. The work was directed by Berl Josselevicz and it began at the end of April 1943. All of the camp's inhabitants knew of the plan and the risks it involved, but they all maintained secrecy. All were to participate in the digging and received supplementary food rations on the days they worked on the tunnel. Those freed for reasons of health had to fill other functions involved in the project. The tunnel was to be 250 meters long, 50 centimeters high, 60 centimeters wide and 1.5 meters beneath the surface. The digging was done lying down and only during the day so that the noise would not be noticed. The tools — drills, shovels and other equipment, were prepared in the camp workshops. The diggers poured the soil into sacks which were pulled out of the tunnel with ropes made of cloth. The dirt was scattered in the attics of the houses and in the latrines. The carpenters and Dvorecky built a wooden rail with a car pulled by a rope, with which the earth was pulled out of the tunnel. Electric lighting was also installed in the tunnel with a lamp every 20 meters. At fixed distances air vents were dug and pipes installed. Work progressed at a rate of two to three meters daily. The carpenters prepared wooden supports to reinforce the wall that began to disintegrate when it rained. The camp electricians "prepared" the guards by causing a short circuit every two weeks, like the one they planned to put into operation to black out the searchlights, on the night of the escape.

According to the plan, the digging was to be completed by August. It was to open in a wheat field, with the high grain serving as shelter for those leaving. When the digging was finished a poll was conducted among the 233 people in the camp and 165 (71 percent) voted to leave through the tunnel.[38]

A German report tells of a meeting between the commander of the Baranowicze work camp and commander Traub of Novogrudok on 11 July 1943. At this meeting Traub asked his superior in Baranowicze to agree to the deportation of the 250 Novogrodok Jews. The commander replied that he would not agree to this deportation without carrying out an *aktzia* against 2,000 Jews in Lida, because if the Novogrudok Jews were deported, 1,000 Lida Jews were liable to flee the next day to the "bandits." Traub apparently wanted to move the occupants of the Novogrodok camp since he feared that they might soon break out. Traub's alternate suggestion, to move the Novogrudok Jews to the Baranowicze camp also met the Baranowicze commander's refusal since there was no room in Baranowicze to absorb more Jews; and any transfer of Jews from Novogrudok would be seen by the Lida Jews as a liquidation.[39]

What is interesting in this report is the Germans' speculations about the Jews' intentions of escaping to the forest. The Germans reinforced their guards in the work camps and gave the better workers additional rations in order to tempt them and have them abandon that thought of escaping. In view of all this, we can imagine the cautionary methods the occupants of the work camp had to adopt in order to carry out the tunnel digging under the Germans' watchful eyes.

The Escape

The date for the escape was set finally for 26 September 1943. The underground's leaders selected an armed guard and authorized it to punish anyone attempting to prevent the escape. It also established priorities for the order of exit: the sick and wounded and the recuperating Dr. Jakobowicz were to go first. In preparation for the escape people were equipped with warm clothing and two-day's supply of food. An operation order was prepared which dealt with discipline and a letter to the camp commander telling him that the Jews were leaving to avenge the spilt blood.

Every man received a number for his place in the line of escape. The arms at the disposal of the escapers were some pistols, rifles, grenades and some "weapons" made of wood, with which to obtain food from the peasant. Tin cans were tied to the house roofs so that the wind moving them would hide the noise of the departure.

The operation was carried out almost perfectly in keeping with the set rules. The autumn was windy (making it easier) and dark (making it harder). Crawling through the tunnel took two hours; the last to come out were the members of the fighting organization, some or them armed. Unfortunately, a large group erred because of the dark and the excitement and ran right back into the camp's fence ...

The German guards sensed the people running towards the fence and imagined that they were partisans coming to liberate the Jews and opened fire. About 120 men fell that night, among them the men behind the uprising and the tunnel — Dr. Kagan, Berl Joselevicz and Yaakov Nivichowicz. About 100 reached the partisans. There had been no advance coordination with the partisans — apparently for security reasons — about the plan to dig the tunnel and the date of the escape. Eight members of the underground Kozhuchovsky, Tchernichovsky, and Orliansky among them — who reached a partisan unit on the third day of their escape were ordered to hand over their weapons (the unit's commander was Victor). When they refused, they were attacked by the partisans and murdered.

The few Jews who had remained in hiding in the camp were discovered by the Germans on the next day and murdered. Most of the others who escaped and reached the forest joined partisan units and fought in their ranks.

Some conclusions may be drawn from the Novogrudok incident. First, the Novogrudok Jews' will to live had not been broken despite all they had gone through. We face a very special phenomenon: after the despair and impotence following the first *aktzia* on 8 December 1941, a second on 8 August 1942, a third on 4 February 1943 and a fourth on 7 May when they stood face-to-face with death, there was an even stronger will to live that was reflected in the digging of the tunnel and the escape.

Second, though there were bitter debates within the camp over the method of response, when a joint plan was found for most of the camp's inmates the Jews revealed unity in action and in maintaining secrecy, even when there was no full agreement on that joint way of response.

Third, and a central point, there is the similarity between the uprising that was never carried out, as compared with the completion of the tunnel. Both were planned by the same group of people in almost the same set of circumstances. The incidents at Novogrudok raises a problem that has more than local significance. Most of the Jews in the Novogrudok work camp did not believe that an uprising and breakout would provide any salvation or any hope of saving their lives. They considered it a total risk with almost no hope of anybody coming out alive. They said that the uprising's protagonists sought a "fine death." On the other hand, they found in the idea of the tunnel and escape some prospect of life despite the not inconsiderable risk they assumed and faced as a collective. We should also add that the proximity of Jewish partisans in Naliboky reinforced their hopes.

This plan of the digging of the tunnel, the unity and discipline, the collective responsibility in carrying it out, the coordination, ingenuity and craftsmanship, the infinite thought and energy invested in the operation under the conditions of the Jews in a work camp, surrounded by Germans who were attentive to every sound, is astonishing from many standpoints and especially from that of the spiritual strength it revealed. Perhaps it can tell us something about the much larger Jewish community which did not have the same possibilities as the Jews of the Novogrudok camp.

"Novogrudok Calls" in the Warsaw Ghetto

Jutrznia, Hashomer Hatzair's underground paper in the Warsaw ghetto, published an article on 28 March 1942, headed "The Heroes of Novogrudok" which included the following:

> ... Among all the flood of dark news of the slaughter of the masses of the Jewish population, news coming from all parts of the Hitlerite occupation, we have received one piece of news that must arouse a completely different echo:
>
> There were in the city of Novogrudok 200 young Jews who refused to go to the murder site like beasts led to the slaughter. They found the courage in themselves to arise with arms in hand against Hitler's butchers. True, they all fell in the unequal battle, but before they died they left 20 corpses.
>
> ... Novogrudok has redeemed the honor of the murdered Jewish masses ... It has become an example of proud and honorable resistance ... The heroic

action of the 200 young people will be in vain if their self-sacrifice does not serve as a call to all Jewish youth ...
  ... There is no doubt about it that Hitler ... wants to drown the Jews in a sea of blood. In view of these difficult days the Jewish youth must prepare. It must begin to mobilize all the vital forces in the Jewish street. Despite the murders, there are still many such forces. For centuries we have been weighed down by the burden of passivity, but the pages of our people's history also holds beautiful and glorious pages of heroism and struggle ... To that we are commanded by the heroic death of the 200 Jews in Novogrudok ...[41]

In his book on the Warsaw ghetto,[42] Berl Mark related that a new slogan appeared in the Warsaw ghetto: "Novogrudok is calling!", like the PPA's slogan in Vilno: "Liza is calling!" (in the name of underground member Liza Magun who was killed in Ponar). Eliezer Geller, one of the leaders of the Warsaw ghetto revolt, said:[43]

  Only in Novogrudok did the Jews know how to die with honor and to avenge their shed blood by the blood of their enemies. Only there, together with the innocent victims, local gendarmes were killed while carrying out their murderous work. The city of Novogrudok has turned into a symbol for the Jews languishing in the hands of the Hitlerite murderers and a symbol of heroism for our generation and generations to come ...[43]

It impossible to exaggerate the importance of such "news" for the youth in the Warsaw ghetto of March 1942.

We might add that the events that actually took place within the underground of the Novogrudok ghetto, with all their importance, were actually different than the contents of the article on the "Heroes of Novogrudok" and took place much later.

However, this story, as it was published, was a powerful legend influencing the underground and shaping the psychological mood in the Warsaw ghetto, in Zaglembia, and in other ghettos maintaining underground links with the Warsaw ghetto. Where did it come from? Who was interested in disseminating it? The assumption is, and there are grounds for this contention, that the information about Novogrudok was brought by members of the Polish *Armia Krajowa*, who had an interest in disseminating it.

Novogrudok was the home of Adam Mickiewicz, the Polish national poet, whose poetry proudly expressed his people's strong desire for independence. It became one of the symbolic site of Polish national consciousness and it was also one of the A.K.'s battle zones. The largest A.K. force in Poland was situated in the Novogrudok region. It is reasonable, therefore, to assume that the A.K. was very much interested in bringing to the Polish masses in the heart of Poland and the capital, Warsaw, the message of "Fighting Novogrudok Calls!" Where even the Jews, under their terrible ghetto conditions, were fighting against the Nazi conqueror, while you Poles ... What are you waiting for ...?

This assumption is reinforced by the fact that young Jews from Novogrudok did indeed meet with A.K. members, their onetime schoolmates in the former Adam Mickiewicz Polish gymnasium in Novogrudok, and told them of their sufferings, and their desire for revenge and their need for arms.[44] This desire to fight, so strongly present among the young people in the ghetto, was transmitted by the A.K. as reality in the form of the newspaper article. A.K. members in Warsaw almost certainly passed the news on to the ghetto.

The message of Jews fighting in Novogrudok was, then, a myth that fulfilled its task in the Warsaw ghetto no less than any news based on reality.

Notes

1. G. Bill, testimony in *Megillat Chavim Vechurban* (The Scroll of Life and Destruction — Kobryn) (Tel Aviv, 1951), p. 309.
2. *Wiszniewo kefi shehaita ve'einena od* (Wiszniewo, as she was and is no more) (Tel Aviv, 1972), p. 115.
3. Chaim Zowisky, testimony in *Haa'yara Bilhavot* (The Shtetl in Flames — Olkeniki) (Tel Aviv, 1962), p. 134.
4. Ribak Ben-Shemesh (Shalom Sonnensohn), testimony in *Ejszyszok, Koroteha Vechurbana* (Eiszyszky, Its History and Its Destruction) (Jerusalem, 1950), p. 63.
5. Yossef Schwarzberg, testimony in *Sefer Volozhin* (Volozhin Memorial Book) (Tel Aviv, 1970), p. 537.
6. Eliahu M. Bockstein, testimony in *Pinkas Pruzhane, etc ...* (Diary of Pruzhany, etc ...) (Buenos Aires, 1958), p. 690.
7. Bill, loc. cit.; Aharon Herman, ibid., p. 332.
8. Gdalia Dudman, testimony in *Wiszniewo kefi ...,* op. cit., p. 125; Chaina Rabinowicz, ibid., pp. 117–125.
9. Chanan Shlomowitz, testimony in *Sefer Zikaron LiKehillat Meiczet* (Memorial Book for the Community of Molczad) (place date, pub), p. 320.
10. Yossef Pecker and Zalman Rabinowicz, testimonies in *Sefer Zikaron Lachowicz* (Lachowicz Memorial Book) (Tel Aviv, 1969), p. 320.

11. Noah Kaplinski, testimony in *Pinkas Slonim* (Slonim Diary) (Tel Aviv, 1962). p. 38.
12. Yad Vashem (YV) 1631/98-R (Yitzhak Reichel); YV M-1/E 2129/1908 Shmuel Kopelowicz).
13. Nina Samushkin, testimony in *Sefer Zikaron LeKehillah* (Disna) (Tel Aviv, 1969), p. 168; Raphael, Max Zalman Elkind, ibid., p. 180; Leah Kacenelenbgen, ibid., p. 134.
14. Michael Z. Rayak, testimony in *Churban Glubok, etc* ... (The Destruction of Glebokie, etc ...) (Buenos Aires, 1956), p. 127.
15. Dov Katzowicz, testimony in *Sefer Yizkor Dokszyce-Parafyanov* (Dokszyce-Parafyanov Memorial Book) (Tel Aviv, 1970), p. 282.
16. Ibid., pp. 183–185.
17. YV E/587 (Shlomo Mushin).
18. Samushkin, op. cit., pp. 170–172.
19. Rayak, op. cit., p. 184.
20. Moshe Gurion, testimony in *Sefer Rubiewicze* (Rubiewicze Memorial Book), p. 258.
21. Ibid.; Yehiel Segalowitz, ibid., p. 352.
22. Esther Gissin-Blizovsky, testimony in *Sefer Zikaron Likehillat Stolin Vehasviva* (Memorial Book for the Community of Stolin and Its Environs) (Tel Aviv, 1952), p. 213; Moshe Gal, ibid., p. 215.
23. YV 1348/162-A (Michael Umalinsky). Umalinsky believes that the Germans had prior knowledge of the Jewish underground.
24. Zalman Urievitch, testimony in *Pinkas Pruzhane, etc ...,* op. cit., p. 599.
25. Izik Berkowicz, testimony in *Sefer Zikaron Stovvetz-Swierezhne veha'ayarot hasmuchot* (Memorial Book of Stolpce-Swerezhna and the Adjoining Townships) (Tel Aviv, 1965), p. 140.
26. David Gleibman, testimony in *Sefer Pinsk* (Pinsk Memorial Book) (Tel Aviv, 1967), p. 341.
27. Ibid.
28. Eliezer Lidovsky, testimony in *Sefer Zikaron Baranowicz* (Baranowicze Memorial Book) (place, date pub), p. 476.
29. Avraham Lidovsky, *Baýaarot* (In the Forests) (HaKibbutz Hameuchad, 1946), p. 59.
30. Moreshet Archive (MA) A-166 (Chaim Oszman).
31. E. Lidovsky, op. cit., p. 493.
32. A. Lidovsky, op. cit., p. 74.
33. J. Lewenbuk, testimony in *Sefer Zikaron Baranowicz*, op. cit., p. 563.
34. Shmuel Jankelewicz, testimony in *Sefer Zikaron Baranowicz*, op. cit., p. 499.
35. Shalom Gerling, testimony in *Pinkas Zhetl* (Zhetl Diary) (Tel Aviv, 1957), p. 57.

36. Chaim Leibowitz, testimony in *Pinkas Nawaredok* (Nowogrudek Diary) (Tel Aviv, 1963), p. 287.
37. YV 3095/230-G (Shaul Gorodinsky).
38. Ibid.; Leibowitz, loc. cit.
39. YV 0-53/1, p. 27159.
40. Shaul Gorodinsky, loc. cit.
41. *Sefer Milhamot Hagetaot* (The Book of the Ghetto Uprisings) (Lohamei Hagetaot, 1956), p. 63.
42. Ber Mark, *Der Oifshtand in Warshever Getto* (The Warsaw Ghetto Uprising) (Warsaw, 1955), p. 76.
43. Melech Neustadt, *Churban Vemered shel Yehudei Warsha* (The Destruction and Rebellion of the Jews of Warsaw) (Tel Aviv, 1947), p. 406.
44. YV 3539/250-A (Yitzhak Alperowicz).

CHAPTER 9
Revolt in the Ghetto

Nieswiezh

When the Russians evacuated the city of Nieswiezh some few days after the German invasion they promised to return within two or three weeks. However, before the last Russian left, most of the Jews also had departed the city. Everyone who could flee, and especially the younger people, did so. However, the Soviet soldiers blocked off the escape routes and many returned to their homes.

On 27 June 1941 the Germans entered the city. Three days after that the members of the Jewish *kehilla* were called to the German headquarters and by German order a Judenrat was established. Its members, appointed by the Germans, were headed by Magalif, an advocate and refugee from Warsaw, and was composed mainly of refugees and some of the city's notables including Leibl Koifman and S. Grinwald. It was the refugees who made the decisions in the Judenrat, and the members of the Jewish police that was established were also for the most part refugees who also did not know the local Jewish population.[1]

Fear of German terror prevailed in the ghetto but Jews had as yet not grasped the truth concerning rumors of the German plans of mass murder.

In September 1941, Lolik Aboilevitz, Siomka Farfel, Hedva Lachowiczky, Zila Gilerevicz and Shalom Cholawsky, all leaders of Hashomer Hatzair, met secretly in order to discuss what should be done to help the youth and schoolchildren who felt abandoned and confused. They decided to organize the children who were 14 years of age and older into educational groups. A program of activities was prepared for them and the

16- and 17-year olds of the former Zionist underground groups from the Soviet era assisted in the activities. In general, the underground that began operations under the Germans was a carryover of the Zionist pioneering underground that existed during the Soviet regime. At this time, some people from the Hashomer Hatzair and Hechalutz center in Vilno reached the town and met with the local underground members.[2]

From October 1941 German decrees began to be issued in greater frequency and numbers. On 20 October, Reb Aharon Levin, a community notable who had gone to Horodzei, some 14 kilometers away, in order to circumcize an infant, was executed. This murder shook the whole city. On 22 October, three Jews were sentenced to death for buying potatoes from a peasant.

On 30 October 1941 the Jews of the town were ordered to assemble in the marketplace for a "document examination." A *selektzia* was conducted, 585 Jews were separated from the rest and 4,000 were taken out of the city and killed alongside the ditches that had been dug by members of the local population some few days earlier. A whole Jewish city was murdered and buried in one day. A ghetto was established for the remainder. Some Judenrat members, among them Magalif, survived. Of the 585 remaining Jews about two-thirds were refugees.[3]

In December 1941 the underground members Siomka Farfel, Hedva Lachowiczky and Shalom Cholawsky who had survived the *aktzia* met and discussed the situation in the ghetto. Armed resistance was mentioned at the meeting, but methods were not taken up. Additional members were selected for the underground leadership — Yerachmiel Shklar, formerly of Gordonia, Borenstein of Left Poalei Zion (a refugee), Natan Messer of Hashomer Hatzair (a refugee), Buzin and Rechtman, Communist refugees.

The central issues were the question of arms and contacts with the outside. These two matters were interconnected. Part of the local Bielorussian population had collaborated with the murderers during the *aktzia* and only isolated individuals maintained their contracts with the Jews. Most of the Polish population was hostile to the Jews because of the deportations during the Soviet occupation era for which they considered the Jews partly responsible.

The underground prepared weapons — knives and iron rods — and looked for some link to young Poles. A second underground group arose in the ghetto, headed by Moshe Damesek and Berl Alperoviez, but after a while the two organizations merged.[4]

Underground members Leah Duckar, and Rachel Kagan, who worked in the German arms stores, brought machine gun parts, grenades and ammunition to the ghetto. The underground possessed a few pistols. Eliahu Polaczek of the underground devoted himself to preparing chemical weapons — acids and explosives. The ranks of the underground now embraced the best of the ghetto youth, most of them members of the pioneering Zionist youth movements. The dominant motive behind the underground's formation was the slogan: "The 30th of November [day of the *aktzia*] will not happen again!" A Russian poem written in the ghetto by Michael Ordiansky, declared: "The day will come, it is coming closer/ when the tides of our people will storm and rise/vengeance for the split blood to take."[5]

Shalom Cholawsky organized an underground school. The children came to the teachers' homes and learned reading, writing, arithmetic, geography and history. The teachers were Eliahu Polaczek, Rechtman, Litwakova and Cholawsky.

No *aktzias* were carried out by the Germans during the ghetto's existence: with the exception of two cases of murder — of Jehoshua Kraviecz and Mesita, who were killed for having gone to Christian homes. The flood of decrees and victims before the *aktzia* had been intended to cast terror and paralyze the will to live and the ability for resistance; the lull after the *aktzia* was intended to delude and encourage optimism.

The Judenrat chairman ruled the ghetto almost alone. He was the only one who spoke on behalf of the ghetto before the German command; within the ghetto, however, and especially among the local Jews, he did not enjoy much confidence.

The underground thought that an uprising in a small ghetto — even if only a few weapons were obtained — would be possible only if resistance was carried out by the ghetto as a whole and especially by all the younger people. In order to strengthen its own status in the ghetto and to create a base to organize the entire ghetto's resistance — the underground decided to undermine Magalif's status, but without harming the ghetto. So too they wished to introduce practical reforms in the ghetto's way of life, as for example in food distribution, and other procedural matters. Since the ghetto was mainly composed of craftsmen and their families, the underground conceived the idea of electing an independent representative group of the skilled workers within the ghetto as an additional authority that could exert its own influence on ghetto life.

The underground members organized trade unions, elections were held and an executive committee of the trade unions was elected, composed almost exclusively of underground members. Among its members were Natan Mosser, Siomka Farfel, Chedva Lachowcizka, Borenstein, Goldberg, Yerachmiel Shklar and Cholawsky. In that way a public body was established within the ghetto that was intended to limit Magalif's rule and which the Judenrat would have to consult in its deliberations and decisions. The underground's influence within the ghetto became stronger.

In reply to the unions' executive committee's demand, Magalif appeared before it. He was questioned about events on the day of the *aktzia* and about the information the Judenrat had concerning the Germans' intentions. Magalif presented proof that he had not known anything about German intentions on that day. The very fact of Magalif's appearance before the executive committee added much to the underground's moral authority.[6]

With the approach of the summer of 1942 the underground began to look for the partisans about whom rumors had reached the ghetto. The underground's view was that if contact could be established with the partisans, the underground would then organize the ghetto for an escape to the forest. However, if before that contact was established another *aktzia* was attempted then the ghetto would revolt.

Under the union executive committee's pressure, elections were held for a new Judenrat. Magalif was re-elected. The other members were mostly persons known to the public, among them Drs. Kessel and Kiwielewiez, both local people.

On 17 July 1942 the Germans murdered the Jews of nearby Horodzei to the very last person. The frightening news struck the Nieswiezh ghetto like lightning, tore away the illusions and were a turning point for the underground. That same day the ghetto's Jews assembled in the synagogue for a memorial service for the Jews of Horodzei. The congregations said the *kaddish* memorial prayer. Magalif described the critical situation, but added that in his estimation the pogrom would bypass the Nieswiezh ghetto. Shklar spoke about the end of all illusions. Cholawsky declared at the time:[7]

> Jews! We are cut off and isolated from all the other Jews and the world. Perhaps not even an echo of our call will reach them. Perhaps we are among the last of the ghettos and the last of the Jews. Only these silent walls will tell what they have absorbed.

> Let us resist, defend the ghetto — the suffering land. Let us fight the way the last of the Jews on the land of Eretz Israel did. Let us be ready for it. It may come upon us at any moment.

That memorial meeting was a turning point in the ghetto's life. Resistance became the avowed cause of the whole ghetto and the underground became the authoritative leadership.

In the days following the destruction of the Horodzei ghetto desperate efforts were made by the Nieswiezh underground to establish contacts with the partisans but they failed. Through lack of choice, it became necessary to resist within the ghetto. The underground accelerated its activities in preparing weapons and in digging bunkers. The ghetto was about 400 meters long and 250 meters wide. The houses were built of wood, except for some synagogues, which were of brick.

On 19 July 1942 Cholawsky divided the young and those fit for combat into units and marked out each group's positions.[8] These combat units numbered 46 men. The underground's plan for the uprising was that when the ghetto was surrounded, a pile of straw within the ghetto would be ignited. The combat units would then set fire to the houses and, in the course of battle, would break out of the burning ghetto to the forest along with all the ghetto's Jews. The chemists Pordess and Goldberg were to prepare small bottles of acid and to distribute them among the ghetto residents.

On 20 July information was received that a Lithuanian unit had come to the town. Towards evening Jokow, Israel Schusterman and Yosef Langman distributed kerosene and gasoline to the houses. As darkness fell the ghetto was suddenly surrounded by Bielorussian police from the town and the immediate neighborhood. The Jewish policemen were removed from the gate and replaced by Bielorussians. Magalif still pacified the Jews though his own self-confidence had been shaken. In the evening the Jews gathered in the synagogue. The debate centered mainly around the question of whether to escape before the uprising or after it. One of the witnesses has written:

> ... I don't know who first raised the revolt. It seems to have come out of the depths of our souls at the right moment.
>
> The moment the ghetto was surrounded we knew that the next morning the end would come. The murderers opened fire with light arms in order to paralyze the ghetto and prevent any movement or attempts to escape.

... The ghetto prepared that night for a final battle and the end. The combat units ... were stationed in their positions. The central battle station was the "Cold Synagogue" that had been built like a fortress and stood in a very strategic location: facing the ghetto gate and the city. The fighters had in their possession two machine guns, a few rifles and grenades. There was another important task — to ignite the ghetto, to send everything up in flames.[9]

All night long the underground command received information about what was happening with the ghetto. After midnight a machine gun was placed in the large synagogue, facing the ghetto gate. Aharon Gach, Polaczek, Israel Schusterman and Leah Duckar were stationed by the gun. Their instructions were not to begin battle before the Germans opened fire. Tracer bullets flew over the ghetto all night.

At dawn on 21 July 1942, the combat groups took their positions. The Jews gathered in groups in the center and near the ghetto gate. The German commander appeared at the gate with his company, called Magalif and informed him that a selection would be thirty, vital professionals, including textile workers, will remain alive without the families.

When Magalif brought the German commander's demand before the Jews massed by the gate, their reply was, "No! No selection! If we are to be given life — then the entire ghetto — and if not, we will defend ourselves!" Magalif brought the Jews' answer to his commander. The Germans immediately opened fire. The fighting group in the great synagogue returned fire. The Germans passed the Ghetto gate. The Jews ignited the houses. Among the first to light the fires were Yukov, Shmuel Nissboim and Yosef Langman.

"Before our very eyes, through the opening next to the gate entered an S.D. member in a helmet, a tall, blond murderer, accompanied by two police officers. His face had the expression of cold-blooded murder, and his eyes were like spears, entering the hearts of those gathered around ... the murderer holds a paper, a list ... who will live, who will die.

"... the chairman of the Judenrat was pale, but calm ... suddenly someone in the first row shouted: Jews, follow me! We will break through the gate! ... At that moment the hand-grenades that were thrown from the other side of the ghetto exploded. In a moment, the area turned into a mass of earth, stones and people. Those in the first rows bursting through the gates and those close by fell killed or wounded.

"The mass of people began to retreat, but the bullets also wounded those in the back, from the fences surrounding them.

"... the ammunition of revenge in the ghetto was fire. The houses, built of dry wood, were doused with benzine ... The murderers, surrounded by the blazing fire were at a loss. The first flames burst into the "alley of the dead" (toiteh gessel) ... when I moved away from the gate I saw Yoscf Langman, the courageous youth, running out of breath, excited, between the houses, and behind him the columns of smoke and fire growing ...

"... the entire ghetto is going up in flames. Through the windows, looking out across the Polish Street, we can see the Christians carrying their household articles to the fields, while the flames are already licking their houses ...
... The young men held knives and iron bars in their hands as they faced the enemy ..."[10]

The Germans wanted to move the Jews from the ghetto by force. The Jews resisted with iron bars, rocks, knives and every sort of homemade weapon that they had prepared. Jokow, with a group of Jews who stood near him fell on a German and killed him. Klaczko and Israel Schusterman attacked a Bielorussian policeman and threw him down dead. The Germans intensified their fire. By the houses there were hand-to-hand battles between Jews defending themselves with cold steel and the Germans and local police. The Jews of the ghetto had become a fighting community. There were dead and wounded Germans. The area was filled with bodies. The ghetto was fighting. The fire spread to most of the ghetto's houses. The flames ignited the other nearby streets and reached the city's center. Surrounding the ghetto there was a large crowd of local inhabitants and neighboring peasants who were looting Jewish houses that had not yet gone up in flames and pointing out any child or woman attempting to flee from the burning ghetto.

The fire spread from the "Toite Gessel" towards the ghetto's northeast sector placing the Jews who had hidden in the bunkers beneath their houses in danger. On the southeast side some houses remained unburnt.

Mottel Farfel died attempting to break through the wire fence. In Yishai Mazin's house there were some 30 men in the darkness with iron rods and knives who left their hiding place, some of them moving towards the cemetery.

Cholawsky's group left at dawn heading for the partisan unit headed by Kapusta in the Kopyl forest, and was one of the first groups that organized the Zhukov partisan unit. Moshe Damesek left for the forest with his family and joined Marhvinsky's unit. Moshe Lachowicky and his men reached the same unit. David Farfel stayed in the synagogue cellar with a group of

Jews five whole days and then left for the forest. Many Jews, as individuals and groups, broke out of the ghetto, some to be killed while escaping, some to be betrayed by the local population and some to reach the partisan units in the forest.

The Nieswiezh revolt was the first ghetto uprising. The neighboring peasants told of dozens of police and Germans who had been killed in it. Echoes of the uprising reached the neighboring ghettos of Mir and Stolpce and influenced the resistance of the Jews there.

The "Bund's" report of 31 August 1942 to London on the situation of the Jews in the area of Poland stated: "... There were here and there phenomena of active resistance; barricades were set up in the houses. In some towns as for example in Nieswiezh, there was armed resistance."[11]

Kleck

The Germans entered Kleck on 26 June 1941. "In the second week of the occupation the Jewish population was psychologically ready for the worst ... We were depressed and without hope ..."[12]

On 31 October 1941 came the first *aktzia*, in which about 4,000 Jews were executed. Dov Banszczyk who was physically very strong, fought fiercely with the murderers and refused to give them his child. Apparently there were active groups of young people, perhaps without any contract among them, who organized with the coming of summer 1942 for an escape to the forest.

On 21 July 1942 ominous rumors reached the ghetto. Some 200 young people met in order to leave the ghetto. Judenrat chairman Cerkowicz came and asked them not to carry out their plan, since it would lead to all being killed, but he concluded in tears with the following words: "Perhaps it is too early and perhaps it is too late; do as you understand."[13] All those assembled dispersed. A few hours later towards the dawn of July 22, the ghetto was surrounded by Germans and policemen. The Jews (including some members of the Judenrat) poured kerosene on their homes and set them a fire. Jews took up positions and threw rocks at the Germans. The latter opened fire. According to reports, Yitzhak Finkel and Avraham Pozharik threw grenades at the Germans.[14]

Many Jews were killed and wounded. Others broke through the fences, cut the barbed wire and escaped in various directions, but many fell in their flight. Some attempted to find refuge in the cellars and bunkers. Many were burned in their homes or asphyxiated by the smoke and some committed suicide by swallowing poison.

Mejerowicz fled with a group of 23 men. Most were shot on their way and only five were able to escape. A few Jews escaped to the nearby forests, most of them to Kopyl forest to the Jewish Zhukov partisan unit, and were among its first members. A total of 16 men eventually returned alive after serving with the partisans.[15]

Lachwa

After the Russians retreated at the end of June 1941, groups of hooligans had broken into the streets shouting "Death to the Jews!" "Hitler the savior is coming!" and "We'll make you pay." A group of Jews fled eastward but were not allowed to cross the former Polish-Russian border. On 8 July 1941 the Germans entered Lachwa.

Dov Lopatin, former chairman of the local Zionist organization, was chosen Judenrat chairman. His colleagues included Yosef Guzewicz, Manis Brodes and Eliahu Shechtman (all General Zionists), Yaakov Master and Israel Drabsky (both Revisionists) and Nachum Milman. Zalman Chefetz and the rabbis Avraham Chaim Zalman and Leizerke were Judenrat advisors. Yitzhak Lichtenberg commanded the Jewish police.

When some Jewish Red Army soldiers succeeded in escaping from German captivity and reached Lachwa, Lopatin added them to the ghetto's Jewish population and found them forged documents even though he knew the great danger in providing refuge to escaped prisoners-of-war.

On 16 and 18 August 1941, Jews were mobilized to dig ditches and there were rumors of an impending slaughter. The Judenrat succeeded in putting off the danger by paying bribes in gold. The Jews looked upon this as "proof" that the German decrees could be averted. The Judenrat claimed the credit for having averted the slaughter and the ghetto's Jews looked at it in the same light.

The ghetto was established on 1 April 1942, with 45 houses.

The idea of an underground began to crystallize among the youth who had grown up in the Zionist youth movements: Betar, Hashomer Hale'umi, Hechalutz and Hashomer Hatzair. Some had experience from the Zionist underground during the Soviet era.

Rumors reached Lachwa that the Jews of Hancewicz and David-Horodok had been taken away to some unknown destination. Young men who had been taken to accompany a shipment of horses and gone as far as Kiev, reported that they had not met any Jews throughout Ukraine and had found signs which read: *Judenrein* (Free of Jews.)

Some of the Lachwa Jews did not believe these rumors; others while fearing that they were true chose to ignore them. Despite the growing stress and fear still there were young people who married in the ghetto at that time. It was a kind of demonstration of a will to live rebelling against the winds of despair and depression.

The underground apparently began in January 1942, with its founders including Yitzhak Rochczyn, Asher Chefetz and Moshe Leib Chefetz, all three from Betar, David Feinberg from Hashomer Hatzair, Aharon Oshman from Hashomer Hale'umi, and Moshe Kolpanicky, Yehuda Guzewicz, Shimon Chefetz, Yitzhak Slucky, Mendelovicz and Yitzhak Lichtenberg.

On its establishment the underground numbered 30 members. The central figure was Yitzhak Rochczyn, an athlete active in local education and culture, who together with Asher Chefetz had participated in a Revisionist course for combat training in 1939 in Ivaniky near Pinsk. During the Soviet regime he had attempted twice, without success, to reach Vilno with his comrades but had been caught and returned home.

Rochczyn's right-hand man, David Feinberg, had been in the Polish Army and had fallen into German captivity in 1939. He was later mobilized into the Russian Army and again fell into German captivity, jumped from the train and finally reached Lachwa.

Three of the underground's members belonged to the local Jewish police: Asher Chefetz, Moshe Koplinsky and Aharon Oszman. In Lachwa a spirit of cooperation prevailed between the underground, the Judenrat and the police. Shechtman, a member of the Judenrat, agreed that the youth be organized within the underground and promised that the Judenrat would provide means for the purchase of arms. David Feinberg maintained contact with two Russians in order to obtain four pistols in exchange for flour and suits of clothing. However, the Russians took the payment but did not supply the guns. In January 1942 a partisan commander, Poliakov, agreed to provide two pistols. Again, the Russian took the money but did not supply the weapons.

The underground remained on the alert and posted guards at night to report every unusual movement. Lopatin was ordered by the Gestapo to send 100 Jews but he did not respond to the demand and was beaten. The ghetto attached importance to this act and Lopatin considered it an achievement that throughout the ghetto's existence Jews were never executed.

In the summer of 1942 news of partisan activity in the region reached the ghetto and this excited the imagination of the ghetto residents. The real change in their thinking and, as a result, also in their psychological preparation, came at the end of July 1942 when the Germans caught seven Jewish girls in Prinovo and put them to death for having wandered to the villages in search of a little food for their families in the ghetto. This act of murder was close and very real and aroused the ghetto's Jews to the real danger to their lives. In the middle of August there was also news of the murder of the Jews in nearby Mikaszewicze. Ditches were dug in Lachwa on 27 August and on 2 September Rochczyn and Lopatin learned of these pits. At first both attempted to calm the ghetto residents to prevent any ill-considered actions. However, towards evening the ghetto was surrounded by 150 Germans and some 200 policemen. Before the *aktzia* the S.D. men received strong drink. Heavy machine guns were placed on the ghetto's border on the other side of the river. Most of the Germans were armed with automatic weapons.

Investigations made at Rochczyn's order showed that close to the ghetto fence there were 22 policemen at a distance of 50 meters apart. Rochczyn's plan was that at midnight the underground's 22 groups would attack the policemen at the fence and in the course of the battle, the Jews would break out in the direction of the Hryczyn area and the forests.

Rochczyn presented his plan to Dov Lopatin and Yaakov Master of the Judenrat, but they rejected it. They suggested waiting until the next morning at five, when the Germans would come to take Jewish workers outside the city. In their opinion, it would only then be possible to know what the Germans' intentions were.[16] Lopatin and the other Judenrat members still believed and hoped that it was only a German exercise and their coming to take the workers to work would serve to verify this belief. They also hoped to perhaps avert the decree by bribery. Rochczyn bowed to Lopatin's opinion and put off the decision until five in the morning. At the same time, he ordered bottles of kerosene to be distributed among the combat units who would remain on the alert, to set the houses on fire if the signal was given. Members of the underground gathered axes, pickaxes, hammers and pitchforks.

Spirits were stormy in the ghetto on the night of 2 September. Some people demanded that the fence be breached in the course of a battle with the Germans. Others asked that bribery be used to put off the danger.

David Feinberg wanted to attack a policeman with his axe but the Judenrat members stopped him. One man from Lachwa describes that night:[17]

> After the act it is not difficult to judge who were in the right, but on that night, when old mothers were asking their sons not to leave them alone in the murderers' hands, to be burned alive after the young people escaped, not one could be found among those preaching escape to be the first to break through the fence.
>
> The worry for the fate of those left behind and the hope of putting off the sentence moved the Lachwa Jews to remain ... True, we had decided that if all the requests and bribes were of no avail — we would not go to the pits prepared for us but would be killed on ghetto territory, in battle.

During the night Lopatin did not give his consent to attack and break through the fence. Only in the morning, when the Germans did not come to gather the workers and a Bielorussian policeman asked one of the Jews to give him his boots since "you're not going to take them to the grave, anyway," were the Jews finally convinced of the Germans' intentions.

In the morning, five truckloads of armed Germans arrived and the German commander announced that he was going to liquidate the ghetto and spare only 30 persons, mainly craftsmen, as well as a number of Judenrat members, including Dov Lopatin. Lopatin replied to the Germans: " You are not going to kill us by degrees. "Either we all stay alive or we all die together."[18] To the Jews he said that all hopes had ended and that they had to break through the gate.

The Germans entered the ghetto and the Judenrat members gave instruction for all the ghetto's buildings to be burned. Dov Lopatin set one house on fire. Judenrat member Israel Drabsky lit a second but was shot by a German. That first shot was the signal for battle. Yitzhak Rochczyn leaped, axe in hand, and split open one German's head and immediately afterwards jumped into the river near the ghetto, where German and police bullets killed him. Asher ben Zalman Chefetz fell upon a second German and split his head with his axe but he too was killed by the Germans. His brother, Moshe Leib, fell upon the German who had killed Asher, took his rifle away from him and rained fire in the direction of the Germans and policemen near the fence. Nineteen-year-old Chaim Chefetz attacked a German by the gate and killed him. Sixteen-year-old Tuviya Migdalovicz attacked a German and ran for the river but was killed. Lopatin, who attacked a German, was wounded in both hands. Dr. Igalnik was shot when he refused to bandage up a wounded German. Berl Gittelman attacked a German and killed him. One witness reported:[19]

> ... I saw how they were taking positions in the full military sense. Across the river that was the ghetto's border, they had placed three heavy machine guns ... Around the ghetto walls ... light Spandau machine guns ... After the first round of shooting by our fellows with the guns they had taken from the Germans who had been in the ghetto — the Germans began to retreat in confusion from the ghetto in the direction of the market or to take defensive positions in the houses. From Zelig D.'s house, which had been ignited after fire had been set to Zalman Chefetz' house, there came a lot of smoke that covered the whole street and made a kind of screen against the machine-gunners across the river.
>
> We did not have any operational command. Everyone acted on his own ... Our aim was the one and single one: not to go like sheep to the slaughter, to destroy, to break through the fences and ghetto gates and get beyond the range of the murderers' bullets ... Instinctively, we looked for shelter in houses that had not yet caught fire and advanced through the courtyards between the houses ... We moved through them towards the gate that had in the meantime already been broken down, went through it to the market and outside the town. The Nazis shot unceasingly and without any aim ... They shot standing up and killed many. It was mostly the young men and children from five to twenty, who succeeded in getting away by running ... To the grave pits they did not go ...

The ghetto fence was broken down and a large mass of Jews broke through to the market and fled for their lives. The Germans and police rained murderous fire from the porches and roofs on those fleeing. The streets, alleys and the market through which the Jews were fleeing were strewn with bodies. According to one witness' estimate, six Germans and eight policemen were killed. Pnina Drabsky-Levin, who was ten at the time of the flight from the ghetto, relates:[20]

> ... In the morning whole families moved about holding hands, in order to die together. The street was filled with people, weeping, praying, and begging for mercy, for some miracle to happen from heaven. No miracle happened. The Germans were already among us ... I saw Basha-Leah Chefetz jump into the river ... The Jews began to fight the Germans. They shot mostly girls and children. I saw one gentile, his name was Polin, as I learned, standing on a haystack with a dog and a machine gun and he began to shoot at the group. I jumped into

a deep pit and sat there until the shooting stopped ... We gathered together some 30 persons.

A large number fled, at least about 1,000 persons. About 600 of them succeeded in breaking though the Germans' and the police's fire to the Hryczyn marshes on the Pripet.

Many were killed in the ghetto. Some 500 elderly people and women were led to the pits. Many of those who escaped were caught by the local people and betrayed to the Germans in return for half a kilogram of salt for every Jew they caught.

After the killing on the roads, the betrayals and the informing, some 120 persons from Lachwa gathered in the forest:[21] 25 of them, with two rifles, were accepted into a partisan unit. Dov Lopatin reached the "Stalinsky" unit, but on 1 February 1944 stepped on a mine and was killed. Moshe Leib Chefetz also served in that unit and fell as a machine-gunner on 30 April 1944.

Revolt in the ghetto was an act of last resort after the underground had exhausted all other means to escape to the forest and perhaps join a partisan unit. It was that way in Nieswiezh, in Kleck and in Lachwa. As long as the people of the underground thought there was some prospect of remaining alive they avoided an uprising. Even when the ghetto had been surrounded and the fighters were in their positions, the order was: not to open fire first.

Despite all the differences in their movement affiliations, the leading force in the revolts was the national-minded, pioneering Zionist youth.

It should be noted that where revolts took place the underground was relatively small in proportion to the actual numbers of the ghetto population. It was only when the underground had succeeded in bringing home to the inhabitants of these places that there was no other road and that all the other possibilities of saving their lives had been exhausted, and when the underground had won authoritative status for itself within the ghetto, particularly among the youth, only then did the Jewish population become a fighting community.

Between the underground and Judenrat in Nieswiezh there had been tension and sharp differences on the question of an uprising in the ghetto. In Lachwa there was cooperation between underground and Judenrat and on the day of the revolt the two became one fighting body. In other places individual members of the Judenrat were swept into the uprising together with the fighting population.

Revolt was not the answer to the question of "how to save lives?", and we should not delude ourselves that anyone believed that. However, even if the underground was careful not to promise the Jews salvation, in their hearts more than one person nurtured the hope that by fighting in the ghetto and breaking out, some part of the population might be saved. In rebelling, those fighting were saved the distress of separation from their families. Those that fled to the forest had to face this most heart-breaking dilemma.

In the circumstances of the ghettos, revolt had Jewish and human value, than which there is perhaps none higher; however, the measure of salvation that it brought was very small.

Notes

1. Moshe Lachowicky, *Churban Nieswiezh* (The Destruction of Neswiezh) (Tel Aviv, 1948), p. 2.
2. Shalom Cholawski, *Soldiers from the Ghetto* (New York, 1980), pp. 29–32.
3. David Farfel, testimony in *Sefer Nieswiezh* (Nieswiezh Memorial Book) (Tel Aviv, 1976), p. 392.
4. Yad Vashem (YV) 03/2746 (Moshe Damesek).
5. Cholawski, op. cit., p. 67.
6. Ibid., p. 60.
7. Ibid., p. 68.
8. Ibid.
9. Ishai Mazin, testimony in *Sefer Nieswiezh*, op. cit., p. 419.
10. Ibid.
11. Based on testimonies as in notes 2–10 above, and Moreshet Archive (MA) D.2.105/26 (Shmuel Nissenboim). Also YV 0–25, folder 97 for an underground letter from Dr. Feiner in Warsaw of 12 August 1942, in which the Nieswiezh rebellion is mentioned. The Palestinian newspaper *Hatzofe* of 11 November 1942, probably from the same source, mentions the rebellion as well.
12. *Pinkas Kleck* (Kleck Diary) (Tel Aviv, 1960), p. 155.
13. YV 2214/24-P (Yitzhak Preiss).
14. MA D.2.105 (Rachel Jucha-Diencielska).
15. Yeshayahu Kashecki, testimony in *Sefer Kleck* (Kleck Memorial Book), (loc. date), p. 156; Alter Meirowitz; ibid., p. 162.

16. The Lachwa story is based primarily on: *Rishonim Lamered — Lachwa* (The First to Rebel — Lachwa) (Tel Aviv, 1957), testimonies of Yehoshua Lichtentstein, Koppel Kolpanicky, Shimon Chefetz, Aryeh Slutzky, Ch. A. Michaeli; also on Central Zionist Archive (CZA) S26/1544 (Aharon Swaryn), YV 2368/157 (Yitzhak Lichtenberg), YV E/452 (Eizik Olomoucky).
17. Y. Millman, testimony in *Rishonim Lamered — Lachwa*, op. cit., p. 109. According to Kolpancky (ibid.), Lopatin was summoned to the underground command post on 3 September 1942 at 6 am, and did not yet give his approval to start the rebellion.
18. Michaeli, ibid., p. 109.
19. YV E/460 (Berl Gittelman); also Lichtentstein, Michaeli and Milmann, *Rishonim Lamered — Lachwa*, op. cit.
20. Pnina Drabsky, *Rishonim Lamered — Lachwa*, op. cit.; YV 2368/157 (Yitzhak Lichtenberg).
21. YV TR-10/786, pp. 94–96; YV M-1/E 522/462 (Chaim Szklar, Avraham Feinberg).

CHAPTER 10

Revolt in the Ghettos without Undergrounds

In the chapter we shall survey the activities of those ghettos and communities in which there were apparently no underground organizations and yet there were cases of revolt.

In dealing with the documentary material we sometimes have the impression that the events which unfolded and the actions which were carried out must have demanded the guiding and organizing hand of some individual or organized group, that is — an underground organization. In our opinion, there is hardly any doubt that in some of these ghettos there certainly must have been underground organizations which left no direct evidence of their existence or of the names of the people who worked in them and operated them.

For the most part, these were small communities, ranging from small towns to villages as in the case of the town of Donilovicz in the Vilno district, some 120 kilometers from Vilno. One long street there was occupied by the non-Jewish population — some 500 persons, while the Jews, some 900 persons, lived in the center of town. There was a white church in the town's center that cast some measure of fear on the Jewish inhabitants. Every Tuesday was "market day" in the town. The peasants from the nearby villages streamed in to sell their produce and with the money obtained purchased their needs (salt, sugar, kerosene, salted fish etc.) in Jewish shops. It was the income from this day's sales that the shopkeepers and grain dealers earned their weeklong living.

There were no very wealthy persons in the town, though the situation of the cloth and iron dealers was a little better that average. The pharmacist was a Jew. There were many poor people. There were too many wagoners for the town's small size and if a wagoner's horse died, the Sabbath Torah-reading was delayed until the synagogue elders promised to buy him a new one. There was also a considerable number of tailors and shoemakers who worked from dawn to sunset and lived in poverty. The situation of the glaziers, who went to the villages, was better.

There were three synagogues in the town: the "Mitnagdim's" (non-Hassidic), the poor people's and an "aristocratic" synagogue. There were also three *heders* (traditional schools) and, between the world wars, a Hebrew Tarbut school, a Yiddish school and a branch of Hashomer Hatzair had been established.[1]

While conditions in every town were slightly different, still they shared a great many thing in common.

At the war's outbreak Jews began to flee eastward towards the Soviet Union, even from the smallest towns. Many Jews fled from Olshany but the roads were blocked and they were compelled to return to their homes. Some of the youth of Luniniec, close to the former Polish-Soviet border, fled eastward, but Red Army guards sealed the route close to the border and many were compelled to return. Only a very small part of those fleeing succeeded in filtering through and escaping eastward. From Svir about 50 persons fled to the USSR.

The Polesie district saw the systematic extermination of the Jewish men in even the smallest towns. In Luniniec, all the Jewish men aged 12 and above were executed in August 1941, with the exception of a number of tailors and shoemakers. In David-Horodok all the Jewish men were killed on 16 August 1941.

A short time after their arrival, the Germans began to drive the Jews out of many of the smaller towns and to concentrate them in other places, generally leaving behind only some craftsmen needed by the Germans and local populace. This perpetual wandering inflicted much hardship and suffering on the deportees and the ghettos in which they were temporarily lodged. In actuality, this method was also an element in the extermination policy.

The Svir Jews were moved to Michaliczky (some 60 craftsmen were left in the town) and from there on to Vilno and Kovno. Some 150 Olszany Jews were moved to Volozhin and 100 — to a camp in Zezmary. Some of the Bielica Jews were deported to Lida and some to Zhetel and Szczuczyn. Around 500 Szczuczyn Jews were deported to Lida, 500 to Vilejka, Krasna, Oszmiana and Borisov, and so on.

There was resistance in these smaller Jewish communities as well. On his final journey, Dr. Rabinowicz from Lubcz-Delaticz shouted at the Germans that their day of punishment would come and that they and their leaders would pay dearly for their crimes.[2] Chana Milsztein of Rakov succeeded in escaping from the ghetto to peasant acquaintances in a village but the latter informed on her and she was brought to Rakov on the day of the *aktzia*, 2 February 1942. Before she was thrown into the flames of the burning ghetto she shouted at the Germans: "Remember, villains, today you are burning us, tomorrow you will be burned!"[3] When the Jews of the Kimieliszky ghetto were killed, on 22 October 1942, Karol, the father of eight children resisted and was murdered. His five-year-old son succeeded in running away and years later was privileged to see the liberation. In Zholudok, Dr. Konarsky turned to the Germans during the *aktzia* on 8 May 1942 saying: "Murderers, you will pay dearly for your crimes," and was shot on the spot.

Esther Leah Seger resisted a policeman who wanted to rape her and was shot. The members of the Grazhevsky family set their house on fire and escaped.[4] During the *aktzia* in Donilovicz, Bielorussian and Lithuanian policemen broke into Boris Friedman's house. Josef Hanger, their neighbor, burst into the flat, hit a policeman with an axe and grabbed his rifle, he shouted to Friedman: "Run as fast as you can!" Josef, too, began to run towards the forest but was shot. Friedman reached the forest wounded.

As we have said, although we do not know of any underground organizations in these areas we do know that in some of these ghettos there were preparations for resistance.

In Zholudok every night a number of men went out in turns to keep watch and to warn the ghetto people of any approaching danger. One night the three guards on watch were shot. Many people in the ghetto began to prepare hiding places. Pesya Beirach (Levit), formerly secretary of Hechalutz Hatzair, related: "We began to think of escaping to the forest but unfortunately there was no one to organize the youth."[5] There was then also no contact between the ghetto and the partisans.

Tuviya Groll, who came to the Visoky ghetto in Polesie in October 1942, related: "The youth were prepared for battle activity, organized and ready at any moment to leave for battle activity organized and ready at any moment to leave for forest."[6] The *aktzia* in Visoky took place on 2 November 1942 but we have no information about what happened after October 1942.

Jews of the Donilovicz ghetto bought weapons and even travelled to Glebockie to buy weapons from the local police. "All the ghetto prepared for self-defense."[7]

The attitude of the local non-Jewish population to the Jews in our region will be discussed separately (see Chapter 14), but we should mention here that even though the relationships between Jews and non-Jews prior to the war had been more even that in larger communities, the measure of hatred towards them by the local population, encouraged no doubt by the Nazis, was no less.

When in the fall of 1942 the women of the David-Horodok ghetto were being led to the pits, their non-Jewish neighbors ran after them for some kilometers, shouting: "Go, we don't need you." [8] It was much the same in other places.

In the Vilno district the Lithuanians' hatred was so marked that many Jews fled from the Lithuanian towns to Bielorussia. Some 40 Lithuanians participated in the murder of the Jews of Niemenczyn. Of the 24 local Lithuanian officials, 22 took part in the murder.[9]

Most of the *aktzias* in these ghettos and communities took place during 1942 as in the whole region. The first of the ghettos in this group was Rakov in the Vilno district. Early in the morning of 2 February 1942 the ghetto was surrounded by Germans and all Rakow's Jews — 950 in number — men, women and children, were assembled in the synagogue. The building was set on fire and every one of them perished in the flames.[10]

In many ghettos Jews sought refuge in hiding places but these did not always provide safe shelter. During the *aktzia* in Donilovicz, many Jews went into hiding. In one bunker alone there were 60 persons; a child's crying betrayed all of them. In another, where there were about 20 Jews, only seven survived.[11]

Jews fled both before the onset of the *aktzias* and while they were going on. A Hashomer Hatzair member, Ruchama Oliker, from the village of Berezov in Polesie, which had 18 Jewish families, related that two days before Rosh Hashana of 1941 the S.S. arrived in the village and broke into their homes:

> At that moment I decided that they would not take me alive; they would not lead me to the grave. I saw my father holding the hands of my two brothers and my sister and mother standing by them. I tried to get out of the kitchen and I received a rifle blow from the policeman. I ran forward, broke out and

began to run the whole length of the porch. I jumped over the fence and began to run. I had decided: "If they are going to kill me it will be while running" ... I saw that some other people were beginning to run after us. When I was already near the forest I saw my sister, who said ..."I saw you run and I got the courage from you to run after you." The last words I head from father were "*Shmah Israel*" and I didn't see him any more.[12]

A considerable number of the villages' Jews escaped. Ruchama Oliker joined the Kovpak partisan division and crossed all of Bielorussia while serving with it. She was a combatant and also served as a nurse in one of the partisan units.

A large German unit appeared in Rozhanka on 21 September 1941. Many Jews fled from the town and some were shot while fleeing.[13] In the fall of 1942 rumors reached the Ostryn ghetto that the Germans intended to deport the ghetto's Jews. A group of 12 young men fled to the forest.

In Jody, the Germans mobilized peasants from the neighboring villages on 15 December 1941 to dig pits, supposedly for artillery emplacements: 260 men and women fled to the nearby forest. The next day the remaining Jews were brought to the pits. Some succeeded in fleeing to nearby towns: Braslaw, Miory, Szarkowszczyzna and Glubok. Some wandered in the forest, hid in bunkers and found shelter among the peasants. There were cases where when they no longer had money to pay the peasants betrayed them to the Germans.

Jews fled from Niemenczyn: some to the Bielorussian forests, others wandered about the neighboring villages. More than a few of the latter were betrayed to the German authorities by the local people. In Parafianowo the Germans carried out an *aktzia* on 30 May 1942. On their way to the pits the Jews began to flee. The Germans shot at them and many were hit. Some of the wounded reached the forest. Some 25 families fled Svir for the forest. When news reached Kimieliszky of the liquidation of the Bielorussian ghettos, many Jews fled to the forest. Religious peasants living in the area provided shelter for Jews and partisans. Jews from Dukszty Zhetto fled for the Karona forests.[14] Before the *aktzia* on 9 September 1942, 20 Jews headed by Zev Shapir (Shtopper), fled the Visoky ghetto and reached the Zhukov partisan unit. Jews from Drohyczyn in Polesie fled to the Pinsk and Pruzhany ghettos and the nearby Radostov work camp after the second *aktzia* on 15 October 1942, as well as to the partisans. Fifteen Jews escaped to the Lachowicz forests.

Forty Jews escaped from the Radostov work camp on 4 November 1941. Some were murdered by peasants; others died of hunger and cold but 15 reached the forest. Forty Jews escaped from the Petrovicz work camp, also near Drohiczyn, but were murdered by members of the Dzankovsky partisan unit.[15]

Only a few escaped from the Motele ghetto. A.L. Poliak, who hid together with a fellow townsman, related:

> ... We lay and covered ourselves with straw ... I took out the *siddur* [prayer book] I had with me and began to pray ... "So long as my soul is within me I thank you ... Blessed are Thou who did not make me a gentile." ... and I thought, we are a curious people, we Jews. Here lie two members, without any tomorrow and they have no present, without a slice of bread and without hope. Any slight movement is liable to betray us to death, and still ... Blessed are Thou ... who did not make me a gentile, because a gentile means a beast of prey ...[16]

When the Germans arrived, the Jewish inhabitants of Dugaliszky village, in the Vilno district, who were engaged mostly in farming, were ordered to concentrate in Radun. Almost all the Jews fled to the forest or hid among the peasants. Some of them later joined groups of Jewish families and some managed to reach the "Leninsky Komsomol" partisan unit, whose fighters and officers were, to a large extent, Jews who had escaped from the nearby towns. There were families in which in the course of their escape, sons separated from parents, according to the rule set by the patriarch Jacob so that the "camp remaining will escape," and also that, if the peasants betrayed the parents, the sons could exact revenge, and vice versa.[17]

Twenty Jews fled from Dukadowo, a village in the Novogrudok vicinity, to the forest, when the Germans and police arrived in July 1942. Another twenty men and women cut the barbed wire fence and armed with submachine guns and pistols, fled the Antopol ghetto during a snowstorm in the winter of 1942. Once in the forest they joined Ostapczuk's partisan unit.[18]

When on 19 September 1942, the last Jews from the work camp in the Lida vicinity were being transported by train to Majdanek, Moshe Schneider, Melech Vitovsky and Yerachmiel Lidsky tore the iron net from the car's only window, jumped from the train and later joined a partisan unit.[19]

On 16 June 1942, the Germans sent some 100 young Jews from Ostryn to the Ignatka camp. In November 1942 they sent a train to the camp to take away all of the people. One of the Ostryn men, Jazersky, learned from a railroad worker that the train was going to Treblinka. All of the men, who were in one car, decided to jump off the train. Shaike Goldberg climbed up to the window in the door, broke the iron bars, put his hand out and opened the latch from the outside. Although the train was going at great speed Jews began to jump off. They gathered in a grove and divided into groups. The groups dispersed, apparently for reasons of security, in different direction. Jazersky's group went towards the Oszmiana district. On the way they obtained two rifles, a pistol and medicine. After a time they were accepted into a partisan unit.[20]

Jews who fled from these ghettos and communities and reached the partisan units later fulfilled missions of rescue and revenge. Josef Kalmanovicz, a partisan from Nei-Pohost, in the Vilno district, established contact with a number of families in his town in order to take young people to the forest. Six young men fled to the forest. Shmuel Markman, Chanoch and Mottel Begun, who had fled the Parafiyanowo ghetto for the forest, obtained three grenades and returned to their town to exact vengeance on the German commander Benz, who had sent the town's Jews to their death. They reached Benz' house and threw two grenades into it. Benz was not at home but an S.S. man who was there was wounded.

Jews fled to the partisans from Svir, Rakov, David-Horodok, Antopol, Luszky, Timolovicz, Shkonczyki (near Glubok) and other communities where there were no underground organizations.

Notes

1. Michael Z. Rayak, testimony in *Churban Glubok, etc ...* (The Destruction of Glubok, etc ...) (Buenos Aires, 1956), p. 323.
2. Yisrael Slonimsky, testimony in *Sefer Lubcz-Delatycz* (Lubcz and Delatycz Memorial Book) (Tel Aviv, 1971), p. 368.
3. *Sefer Zikaron Likehillat Rakow* (Memorial Book of the Rakov Community) (loc. date), p. 147.
4. Moshe Beirach, testimony in *Sefer Zholodok verOrlova* (Memorial Book of the Communities of Zhulodok and Orlova) (Tel Aviv, 1967), p. 243; Yad Vashem (YV) 3467/314 (Pessia Beirach).
5. Ibid.
6. YV 03/1162 (Tuviya Groll).

7. YV 1900/181 (Boris Friedman).
8. Batsheva Kushnir and Grunem Filon, testimonies in *Sefer Zikaron David-Horodok* (David-Horodok Memorial Book) (Tel Aviv, 1957).
9. YV M-1/E 378/336 (Deitz).
10. *Sefer Zikaron Likehillat Rakow*, op. cit., p. 175.
11. Yitzhak Mushkat, testimony in *Churban Glubok, etc* ..., op. cit., p. 339.
12. YV 2977/217-A (Berl Reznik).
13. Azriel Bezruczka, testimony in *Sefer Szczuczyn* (Szczuczyn Memorial Book) (Tel Aviv, 1967), p. 81.
14. YV M-1/E 319/208 (Yerachmiel Karb).
15. *Drohiczyn* (Chicago, 1958), pp. 300–304; Zvi B. Wolf, ibid., p. 334.
16. A.L. Poliak, testimony in *Churban Motele* (The Destruction of Motele) (Jerusalem, 1957), pp. 72–73.
17. YV 3-2/A (Avraham Aviel-Lipkansky).
18. Shoshana Katz, testimony in *Sefer Yizkor Antopol* (Antopol Memorial Book) (loc date), p. 386.
19. Lash Liber, testimony in *Sefer Szczuczyn*, op. cit., p. 81.
20. Ibid., p. 351.

CHAPTER 11
Escape from the Ghetto

Flight from the ghettos was an integral part of any plan of salvation made by the ghetto Jews, no matter whether it was as an aftermath of an uprising within the ghetto or preparations for partisan fighting or individual attempts for survival. In the reality of the frightful *aktzias*, degradation to subhuman status, with the unending fear of death weighing like lead upon their heads and destroying the very soul of life — the conditions in the forest, free of the ghetto, and the *aktzias* and German orders, seemed like a paradise. What is more, escaping to the forest seemed to be the proper course of action for every Jew in order to fight the Germans to the death and to avenge the blood of families and relatives that had been shed. The physical distance between these two conditions was often only a step — from the ghetto to the forest that was sometimes to be seen on the horizon from the cracks in the ghetto walls, a dark-green mass concealing in some mysterious fashion the very antithesis of the ghetto. That "step" however, sometimes turned out to be an infinite distance and the forest — an unattainable goal.

Most of the Western Bielorussia is abundant with dense woods stretching over hundreds of square kilometers and sometimes forming a continuity of deep forest (called "Puszcza"). The forest's presence beckoned to the ghetto Jew.

The partisan is crowned in glory in the eyes of the Russian population of today. That is the way he has been pictured in literature, cinema and in all the Soviet artistic media. In the eyes of the ghetto Jew, he seemed a freedom fighter and the vanguard of the Soviet people in their fierce and bloody battle against Nazi Germany. Among the partisans there were also members of the local population who were hostile towards the Jews, and even though this was certainly known in the ghetto, it seems that when the partisans first appeared in the region, the Jews believed that they shared a common ground with them through their enmity to the Germans and that the enemies of my enemies are either my friends or at least comrades in arms.

Locating the partisans and their bases was one of the central problems facing the underground organizations in the ghetto when organizing groups for escape. Partisans are, as we know, by nature nomadic, and any information possessed by an underground organization concerning some partisan base was of prime importance since it could help avoid losses among those fleeing until they attained their goal of fighting and saving themselves. Very many, sometimes whole groups, fell even before they reached the forest.

From mid to late 1942, the partisans entered into a new stage. At the outset the partisans were formed of loose groups with no central command. There were small units of escaped prisoners-of-war who had hidden in the villages during the winter of 1941–42, or small groups of Soviet paratroopers who had dropped behind the lines on behalf of Red Army intelligence, committing acts of sabotage, or very small units, sometimes made up of bandits, occupied mainly in robbery and in killing Jews fleeing from the ghetto. But in the second half of 1942 the partisans were transformed into an organic movement, all of whose parts were linked in a quasi-military organization, in a hierarchy of squads, regiments, brigades and divisions. It became an organized military force maintaining inter-regional cooperation and subordinated to a supreme Soviet partisan command. During this time the Bielorussian partisan movement reached its peak from the organizational standpoint, though not from the numerical one.

This qualitative and quantitative transformation by the partisans was a serious consideration in establishing German policy in the area as a whole and also accelerated the implementation of the annihilation of the Jews in the ghettos. The Germans saw great danger in the simultaneous existence of a strong partisan movement and ghettos filled with Jews, and of the cooperation liable to be effected between the two. However, except in only a few cases, such cooperation did not exist because of the partisan's unwillingness to appear, in the eyes of the Germans or of the local populace, to be defending the Jews, and also because they were unprepared to accept the burden that Jews fleeing annihilation would necessarily impose upon them. In the large majority of the partisan units there prevailed an atmosphere of intense antisemitism during the initial period. This was considerable from the end of 1942, but continued to prevail in a moderate and disguised form throughout the war, even though official orders from the partisan headquarters did not permit any discrimination among Soviet citizens.

Still, we should mention that there were also partisan commanders and rank and file fighters who revealed sympathy for the Jewish refugees, did not harm them and even helped them. This attitude, however, was based on local customs and individual background. Partisan units sometimes attacked towns where there were Jews trapped in ghettos, not with any intention of liberating the Jews but for military reasons. In those cases where the Jews of certain ghettos or work camps were liberated, this was done at the initiative of Jewish partisans applying pressure upon their unit's command, and with a mind to those Jews' combat potentialities. If the non-Jewish partisans had encouraged the Jews in the ghettos to join them, the dimensions of flight would have been immeasurably greater than they were. One witness from the Stolpce ghetto related:

> The rumors about the partisans were scattered and conflicting ... Was it possible to exist in the forest? Did the partisans sympathize with us? All these were riddles for us ... At that time [the close of 1942] all the ghettos and camps in the neighborhood had been liquidated and everybody understood that the end was near, but in his subconscious everybody hoped for some last minute miracle.
> ... If any sign, even the slightest, had been given by the partisans, perhaps a mass escape might have been organized ... The Christian partisans hardly lifted a finger to save Jews from the ghettos and camps. More than once, when they came upon a solitary Jew or a small group in the forest, they disarmed them of their weapons and robbed and killed them. If not for that hostile attitude, thousands more would have fled to the forest and saved their lives.[1]

There are numerous accounts of the non-Jewish partisans' attitude towards Jews escaping to the forest. Rumors of this attitude reached the ghettos by various ways and very seriously affected the Jews' willingness to attempt to escape. The activities of the partisan units in their area only enhanced the sense of danger of the ghetto residents.

The first *aktzia* in Ilja on 17 March 1942, in which about 900 Jews were murdered, was carried out shortly after a partisan operation in the region. The second *aktzia*, on 7 July 1942, in which some 300 Jews were killed also came after another partisan attack.[2] The second half of 1942, during which the pace of annihilation was greatly accelerated, was also a peak period of Jewish flight to the forests.

The main factors interfering with escape — the collective responsibility and the lack of arms — have already been discussed in Chapter 6. Here we can add some additional factors. The Jew fleeing from the ghetto did so with the feeling that the whole world was against him and that he was an animal being hunted by all. His life was free for the taking by anyone he met on his way. There were also psychological and emotional restraints, as reflected by Pinchas Ormland of Kamen-Koshirsk in an excerpt from his diary entry for 13 August 1941:[3]

> ... There is only one way out — arms and the forest. The young people were thinking of escaping. I was very helpless. I did not want to listen to what they were saying. Many asked me to go with them. I didn't promise anybody. It was also forbidden to mention to my wife that they wanted me to go. The children were lying there and rotting — and we would save our own lives?

More than a few in the ghetto were torn between their very deep attachments to their children who would be murdered and their knowledge that the only way out was "arms and the forest".

Except for some few individuals — timber dealers and peddlars who in the past used to roam the fields, forests and villages throughout the week, the Jew was not at home in the forest. He did not know the forest and it cast its terrors on him, he who was far from nature. Added to that was the new "law of the jungle" of the forest to cast new fears onto him. Certainly, too, the Jew did not put his trust in the villagers who lived close to the forest and whose kind grace he would need in order to survive, to wander unarmed among the peasant homes to beg for a piece of bread. He had already managed to learn these people during the *aktzias* when some stood at the ghetto gates, eager for blood and spoils. For example, the Jews of Druja and Michaliczky, who lived close to the forest, had fled to it at the beginning of the German invasion, but only spent two or three days there before returning to their towns.

In the course of time terrifying rumors reached the ghettos of how the forest "welcomed" the refugees. These rumors, brought by those returning after fearful adventures and suffering, dissuaded others from attempting to escape. That is what happened, for instance, in the Lida ghetto and with some of those who had fled the Volozhin ghetto, after the first *aktzia* in May 1942, and who returned home because of the difficult conditions in the forest. Jews who had wandered the fields and forests, escaped to other ghettos and told the inhabitants there of what they had seen and thus dissuaded others from fleeing.

Above all, as mentioned previously, there were the family ties that formed the most powerful restraint against escaping. In the distresses and catastrophes that befell the inhabitants, the individual found solace only in his family. After the first wave of *aktzias*, most families were left like dismembered bodies, having lost children, parents, sometimes with only isolated remnants remaining. This led to even greater attachment among those still living. Jews who had previously encouraged their children to flee were in many cases unwilling to desert their other children or mates who could not join them. David Rubin of Ilja, who was about to escape from the ghetto before its liquidation, held the following conversation with his father:[4]

> If life is precious to us then we must escape very fast. This time there is no one to save us from them ..." [I said]. My late father turned to me with his constant smile ... and said: "Dear son, if you want to save your life, do so. Don't pay any attention to me, maybe the good God will help you. I cannot join you; what will happen to the family? I will go with them ... Can I allow my family to be destroyed and I escape and live without them? ..." I looked about. The trees were in blossom ... The noise of motors, German orders ... I will resist my fate this time and rebel against it. I want to live ... I hid and saw everything ... How they led my dear and beloved father, standing in the court and looking at some invisible point ... How they led my dear mother ... We were 13 souls in our family ...

Zirl Kamieniecka of Derezyn called on her father at the time of the *aktzia* on 24 July 1942, to escape with her and her children, but he shouted to them: "Children, run and get away! I won't go with you. I have lived with your mother 54 years and now too we must be together."[5]

The members of the underground, who were aware of the need to escape, also faced the same pangs of conscience as the others on leaving their families. The Kamen-Koshirsk underground instructed Stryjer, who had "Aryan" features, spoke Ukrainian and knew the neighborhood, to leave the ghetto with Dov Drug. Dov Drug came to Stryjer's home at midnight to call for him.

I knocked quietly at Stryjer's door. On my back I had a bag with food and in one of my boots a little pistol ... He opened the door. I asked if he was ready. "Yes." he replied, "I must only say goodbye to my family" (he had a wife and two children). Suddenly there was lightning and heavy rain began to fall. The children awoke from the noise of the rolling thunder and began to cry, and also his wife. I went up to him and said: " Now is the best time to get out of the ghetto, with the rain and thunder covering us they won't notice us." He sat, looked at me with a blank look, without replying. Then his eyes turned to one side and looked at a picture of the family hanging on the wall. I understood, nothing would help this time. I got up and left his house.[6]

On the day when 20 members of the Swienciany underground were prepared to escape from the ghetto before the deportation on 5 April 1943, two members, Kosha Ligumsky and Gershon Nadel returned their weapons and stayed with their widowed mothers. On 9 August 1943 the members of the underground and many other Jews in the town of Mir were about to flee to the forest; the town was empty of Germans and policemen. Berl Reznik, one of the founders of the underground, got up and said: "You want to go? Go! I won't leave my mother and my sisters, and I can't go with them."[7]

Baruch Levin, one of the founders of the Lida underground, related that when three Jewish partisans arrived there in order to take Jews to the forest, he went to the ghetto to recruit other comrades for immediate escape. He met Yitzhak Mansky, who agreed to his proposal and said: "I'm certainly ready, but first I have to go to my house; I have to say goodbye to my family." "You want to say goodbye?" Levin asked him. "You should know that anybody going in to say goodbye says goodbye to the idea of going to the forest." Levin added: "We already had a great deal of experience."[8]

These pangs of conscience also troubled many of those who had left their families behind in the ghetto. It seemed to them that they had not done enough to convince others to flee, especially when they discovered that despite all the difficulties it was possible to survive in the forest, something they had not thought possible when they had first fled there. Reuven Budownic of Druisk confessed that after his flight "we immediately began to wonder whether we had done right in leaving our families in the ghetto and not calling on more young people to join us".[9] There were also some who returned to their families in order to march the last road together with them. Moshe Levin from Olkienik roamed the forest for two days with other townsmen and even though he knew where they taking the people of his town on their way Ejszyszky, he appeared in the horse market in order to go with his family.[10]

Mass Escapes

Except for some few individuals, most of the Jews who participated in the mass flights had no weapons. Such flights sometimes took place between the *aktzias*, but usually they occurred during the *aktzia* in the face of death. In many cases people did not know and had not planned in advance the goal of their escape, because in most cases these flights were spontaneous in nature; an escape from the murder site — a real danger — to some place unknown, to some refuge. It was also an escape from the people who represented the danger from which the refugees were fleeing. At the moment of immediate danger, flight, at least in the short term, meant safety. So it was in the town of Lachowicz, which was surrounded by the Germans, Lithuanians and Bielorussians in October 1941, when the Jews ran from the market place en masse.[11] Something similar occurred in the town of Miory, where the Jews had been assembled in the market place on 2 June 1942 after a deep pit had been prepared in a nearby grove. When the Jews were sitting there packed together in the square, surrounded by local policemen and German soldiers, some young people managed to converse in whispers and gestures, until one of them got up and said: "Shmah Yisrael …!" and then many Jews got up and broke through the circle of armed guards. Many succeeded in running in the direction of the river on whose side lay the forest. The guards opened fire and very many were hit, including some who had already gained the forest, but a small number succeeded in escaping.

The remaining Jews were divided into two groups. One group was imprisoned in the shops and the second remained in the market. Its members were ordered to lie facing the ground and the Germans photographed them in that position. Then they were ordered to get up and were led to a site in the forest some two kilometers from the town. When they came to the pits, the Germans ordered Judenrat chairman Sosnovik to undress and stand by the pit. When the Jews saw this they began to fall upon the Germans, strangling them with their bare hands and hitting them, and began to run away. One Jew, Shkolnik, succeeded in taking a pistol out of a German's hands. Some 200 Jews fled to the forest.

The second group, numbering some 400 Jews, was also ordered to lie on the ground and was photographed. "When we saw that we were being led to death, we shouted 'hurrah' and fell upon the Germans.[12] Some 50 Jews succeeded in escaping, the rest were shot and killed. About 100 Jews escaped to the Kaziany forest and there conceived the idea of establishing a Jewish partisan unit.[13]

The underground in Szarkowszczyzna numbered some 40 men and women. On 17 July 1942 Judenrat chairman Hirsh Birkan was called before the German commander, Heit, who ordered him to bring furs and gold and, while doing so, told him pacifyingly that the next day there would be army exercises in the town. A Jewish girl, Zimmer, who worked in the *Kommandatura*, heard information about police preparations for the ghetto's annihilation. When this information reached the ghetto, the Judenrat instructed the Jews to flee. On the next day, 19 July, the ghetto was surrounded by Germans and policemen. The underground members sounded the alarm: anybody who could escape should do so. Before fleeing they set their houses on fire, broke through the barbed wire fences and began to flee en masse from the ghetto. About 1,200 Jews escaped. Those who remained in the ghetto were murdered on that same day. Hundreds of Jews were killed when they met a German force coming to the aid of their comrades in Szarkowszczyzna. A considerable number were killed by the local population. The danger, hunger, disease and lack of any weapons impelled many of the refugees to be tempted by the call of the *gebietskommissar* and Glubok Judenrat chairman Lederman to come to the Glubok ghetto and so went there. Some, however, fled once again from Glubok to the partisans.[14]

The Jews were taken out of Olkeniky on 21 September 1941, and moved to Ejszyszky. On 24 September 1941, the Jews of Ejszyszky, Olkenik and the neighboring area were assembled in the horse market square. The Germans divided the Jews into large groups. When the third group's turn came the Jews fell on the Lithuanian soldiers guarding them, catching them by surprise and fled from the city through the courtyards and alleyways. Some 500 Jews escaped from Ejszyszky. Hundreds of Jews fled to Radun, but most were killed by the Germans, the Lithuanians, the neighboring peasants and the Polish members of the *Armia Krajowa* operating in the region.[15]

We have the written testimony of Moshe Michalowski for the description of the flight from the Radun ghetto. The flight began spontaneously when 180 Jews were ordered to dig pits and one of the Germans was heard to say "kaput." The Jews understood from this that the pits were intended for themselves. One of the Jews cried out: "Chevra, did you hear it? Don't wait! Run away immediately! Michalowski wrote:

> Everybody threw their spades at the Germans and scattered in all directions. The Germans began to shoot. I ran. After a minute I received a bullet in

my hand. I fell and got up and continued to run. I was hit in my leg. Dead were already lying all around. Those who could — reached the forest. The Germans continued shooting.

A Jew who was running alongside me was hit in his stomach and his intestines poured out. He cried and shouted for them to shoot him. The German came near. I put my hand in the blood and smeared my face. The German shot the Jew. I lay without moving, held my breath. The German kicked me and said "kaput" and continued to run after the others. When it was quiet in the neighborhood I crawled on my stomach. After every minute I stopped for lack of strength. I was like a half-slaughtered chicken running and falling and then trying to escape again. I don't know how long I crawled until I fell into a puddle of water. It seemed to me then that the water was a miracle from heaven. I lay in the water and my strength returned. I saw a house ... I entered a peasant's house. The peasant's wife was frightened and said: "Oh, Jesus, Satan has come!" and fainted. The peasant called out to me: "Who are you?" I asked him: "Did you hear shooting? The Germans are chasing me." The peasant began to revive his wife: "It's nothing, they're only killing Jews." He gave me water to wash and I bandaged my wounds.

I began to miss my family. "God," I said, "why didn't they kill me together with my family?" It was a terrible night and if I am alive after that night I must be as strong as iron.[16]

Six persons left the Sernik ghetto for the forest in September 1942, among them central figures in the underground: Feivel Glazer, Ephraim Bakalczuk and Nachman Zilberfarb. Together with the Communist peasant Misiura they established a partisan cell. News reached the ghetto that the partisans were waiting in the Botwa forest and would defend the ghetto Jews. Young people prepared to escape from the ghetto. On 27 September 1942 the ghetto was surrounded by the Germans and the police and at nightfall the Jews began a mass flight towards the forests during which 272 Jews escaped. We have details of the age distribution of those who fled:[17]

Ages of Those Who Fled

	8–18	18–40	40 and over	total
Men	19	127	20	166
Women	12	74 + 5 infants	15	106
Total				272

Some of the refugees were shot while crossing the Stobla River. All those who had remained in the ghetto were murdered the next day. Leib Fialkow was the only one to emerge from the death pit and reach the forest.

The Sernik Jews who escaped the ghetto, together with the Glazer-Misiura partisan cell, afterwards established the Voroshilov Jewish partisan unit that became known as the Misiura unit in southern Polesie. The unit later numbered some 300 members, with Jews comprising 80 percent of the total and was part of the Biegma Brigade.[18]

There were two escapes from the Miadziol ghetto with the aid of Jewish partisans: the first escape included 140 Jews who were taken out of the ghetto to the forest; and the second, the remaining 86. Despite the orders of the partisan command to take only those who were "vital" to the cause (e.g., doctors and the like), Sigalczyk, a Jewish partisan, acted on his own initiative and took all the Jews who remained in the ghetto.[19]

In other locations where Jewish partisans did not have so great an influence, the situation was completely different.

On 3 August 1942 a partisan force attacked Kosov-Polesky. The battle lasted four hours and five partisans fell, among them Danny Berkowicz. After the Germans and the local guards fled, the partisans gathered all the Jews outside the city; and from there they took with them only a group of some dozens of young people, and sent the older Jews and women back to the ghetto. There is no doubt that they were very well aware of what awaited the Jews who were sent back. The next day these were all killed.[20]

Some 600 Jews fled from the Zhetl ghetto. Most of them broke out of the ghetto during the second *aktzia*, which continued for three days, 6–8 August 1942. Among those who escaped was Hirsh Kaplinsky, the future commander of a Jewish partisan unit in the Lipiczansk forest. A local Hashomer Hatzair leader, he left with a group of 50 persons he had organized at the last moment and continued to lead in the forest. During the breakout, Shlomo Bussel and Shalom Krashinsky, who had defended themselves with arms, were killed, as were three partisans who had come from the forest to take Jews. Alpert escaped with a group of 30. The Zhetl Jews and the members of the Zhetl underground helped establish the "Atlas" unit, the Hirsh Kaplinsky unit, the "Pobieda" and "Borba" units in the Lipiczansk forest, the Bielsky and other units (among them — the "Kovalov" parachutists unit). Partisans who were distinguished for their activities as saboteurs and platoon commanders came from Zhetl: Eliahu Kowiensky, Shalom Gerling, Yechiel Joselevicz and others, and also

Aharon Hajdukowsky — a young boy who later smuggled Jews out of the Novogrudok ghetto, and Shlomo Shifmanovicz — a youngster who turned into an outstanding scout in the forest.[21]

Some 500 Jews fled from the Kobryn ghetto, the majority in a mass escape at the time of the *aktzia* on 14 October 1942. Most were betrayed by Polish and Ukrainian peasants. More than 100 succeeded in reaching the forest. Many fell while being hunted. A group later fought as partisans.[22]

Some 500 also fled from the Dvorec camp, most of them during a breakout on 28 December 1942.[23] There were large-scale escapes from most of the Western Bielorussian work camps. This may perhaps be explained by the fact that the Jews in these camps already possessed underground experience from the ghettos and the problem of family ties was not so painful here. In addition, most of the work camps were adjacent to the forests.

Some 300 skilled workers from Lenin and other ghettos had been concentrated in the Hancewicz work camp in the spring of 1942. The Germans warned the camp's inmates that the family of anyone escaping would be killed. In the middle of August 1942, when news reached the camp that the Lenin Jews had all been executed, Jews began to escape from the camp. People began to run in the direction of the forest, tearing off the yellow patches from their clothing as they ran. In all, 320 fled. The Germans opened fire on those escaping but most were already in the forest when the shooting began. The escape of the 320 left its impression on the neighborhood as a whole. The Germans offered prizes for the capture of the escaped Jews. Some were indeed deceived by peasants who pretended they were going to give them food but instead turned them over to the Germans. Some of the escapees reached partisan units, among them 102 refugees from Lenin.[24] A courier between the camp and the forest was arrested in Vilejka work camp on 13 March 1942. His arrest frightened the Jews and on the same day 40 men fled to the forest.[25]

The 100 Jews who were still alive in the Koldyczewo camp came to the conclusion that they had to escape at all cost. Members of the underground began to prepare an opening in the wall of the stable, through which the camp's inmates were to escape. The carpenters among them made the hole and concealed it; machinists prepared wirecutters. They also plotted to poison the watch dogs at the time of the escape. During these preparations, two Jews escaped of their own accord and their comrades considered this a betrayal of solidarity. Because of this escape Jews were beaten and tortured. The escape's date was also postponed, because of the escape of the two.

The camp's Jews trained incessantly for the escape; they learned to walk silently, to crawl on hand and feet, sewed cloth patches to the soles of their shoes and cast lots for the order of escape. They also prepared knives for self-defense. Shlomo Kushnir was elected commander of the escape operation and the date was set for 7 March 1944. The night was a stormy one and all the camp's inmates, except for one who had fallen asleep, fled and scattered in the forest. When the Germans approached the ditch where 26 of them were hiding, one of the locals shouted: "Flee!" but all were caught except for two. Shlomo Kushnir shot himself. Some 75 of the Koldyczewo inmates reached the forest and joined partisan units. This escape was a less complicated one than the flight from Novogrudok but it was unique because of the solidarity of the camp's Jews in decision, precision in implementation and dedication to the goal.[26]

In the Swiezhen camp there was cooperation between the camp underground and Jewish partisans who had come to free the inmates. The underground conducted intensive secret discussions in order to win over the camp's majority to the idea of the general escape. It also observed closely the camp's security measures that were maintained by 32 armed guards at the fence and on the watchtower. At the beginning of the winter of 1942–43, Hersh Posesorsky, a partisan in the Zhukov unit, applied to the commander of the Molotov Brigade and received permission to liberate Swiezhen camp. In January 1943 he sent his brother-in-law in the camp a letter carried by a peasant, calling on the Jews to escape to the forest. On 28 January he entered the work camp disguised as a peasant and armed with a pistol. He met the underground staff secretly and set the time for the escape at nine o'clock at night. At the appointed time the escape began: the boards of the camp's fence were easily broken through since they had been attached to the posts with only a "quarter of a nail" when they had been put up by the camp's inmates with thought to some future escape. Members of the underground who possessed weapons marched at the head of those escaping. About 200 Jews left on that stormy night — the temperature was minus 33 degrees Centigrade — who broke up into two groups: one moving eastward to the Kopyl region (130 men) and the other towards the Naliboky forest. Both groups reached partisan units due to the fact that they knew in advance where they were headed and the location of the partisan units which they were going to join. According to a report by the commander of the Stolpce gendarmerie of 15 February 1943, the Germans had planned to carry out an *aktzia* in the camp on 1 February.[27]

The Mir ghetto's story is a special one. Oswald Rufeisen promised the members of the Mir underground that when news of an impending *aktzia* reached him, he would transmit it immediately. On 6 August 1942 Oswald learned from his superior, Eichhorn, that an *aktzia* would be carried out in Mir in the coming week. He transmitted the information immediately to the underground and included an escape plan of his own: he would "plant" information about a partisan penetration into the nearby neighborhood on the night of 9 August and accompany the police forces on an "anti-partisan operation".[28] The town would be empty of German and police forces, thus enabling the Jews to carry out a mass escape. The underground transmitted the information about the date of the *aktzia* to the Judenrat and the ghetto Jews. A delegation of two Judenrat members expressed their fears to the German commander following reports of an impending *aktzia* and asked that it be put off. The latter replied categorically that this was impossible and, despite his misgivings, Judenrat chairman Shulman reported to a general meeting on what the German commander had said. The Jews of the ghetto knew of the planned escape "but at that time no one could imagine that those leaving would come out alive. They were all of one opinion: that all would be killed," one member of the underground has since written. The misgivings concerning the escape were shared by all the ghetto's Jews, including some of the members of the underground, especially because of the problem of the families. Berl Reznik of the underground, testified:

> Our aim was to oppose the Germans when they attacked ... We knew that we could not go to the forest ... Where were we to go? Here everyone had a family and how could he abandon it? We thought of falling upon the police, of setting fires, and these were out chief aims ...[29]

A few days before the *aktzia* a group of refugees from Nieswiez arrived worn out and ragged in Mir after difficult experiences in the forest. They reported that the partisans chased after the Jews in order to kill them and that the forest only had leaves for food. Understandably, this did not encourage the desire to escape very much. Despite this, the underground decided on its members escaping and granted the possibility of escaping to all the ghetto's Jews. Reznik, too, who at the beginning had refused to leave his family, decided to go along. Shlomo Charchas announced in the name of the organization: "Jews, the *aktzia* is imminent. Flee wherever you can. Everyone must save his own life. Anyone staying here will be killed by the Nazis." The Judenrat, too, did not oppose the escape and even encouraged it. In keeping with his plan, Oswald left on 8 August with the Germans on the "anti-partisan operation" and Mir was emptied of Germans and police. That night the path to escape was open to all the ghetto's inhabitants, but of the 850, only 300 left for the forest. One of those who fled described his impressions of the flight:

> Michael Pupok stood with his meager bundle ready to leave and, by him, his wife and child. He wanted to go but he heard his wife ask: 'With whom are you leaving me and the child?' He threw down his bundle and remained with them. He could not conceive of taking them to the forest.
>
> Chaim Yurshan also stood there with his bundle, looking at his wife and child. He wanted to say goodbye but could not. His wife said to him quietly: 'If we are going to die — let us die together,' and he too threw away the bundle and remained with them.
>
> Busel from Baranowicze handed his boots to Solly Charny and said: 'I'll go to my wife (who had been killed in the first *aktzia*).'
>
> There was wailing ... Religious Jews stood and waited for a miracle. The rabbi from Ostrolenko said: 'A miracle? It isn't coming. It is the way of miracles not to appear.'
>
> The group wended its way through the fields ... They all meet for the first time in the Tatar graveyard ... A whole day they sat there, holding their heads ... The silence shouted at the top of its lungs ... Some demanded that they return. 'Where were we going?' The group marched forward.
>
> There were complaints: 'Why did we leave?'[30]

The escaping community broke up into small groups and dispersed in the nearby forests. Some groups came afterwards to the Bielsky partisan unit; others continued to the family camps and forest clearings.

On 13 August, the date fixed, the Germans carried out the *aktzia* against the remaining Jews. They arrested Oswald on suspicion of having transmitted to the Jews information about the date of the *aktzia*, of having armed them and actively assisted in their escape. He was interrogated by the commander, Schultz:

> Oswald, you are charged with treason. Is it true that you revealed to the Jews the date of the *aktzia*?
> Yes, sir.
> Why did you do this?
> Because of my pain for their fate. They are innocent.
> I have thought about this and reached the conclusion that there was another

reason other than pain for their fate. Very simply, you wanted, as a patriotic Pole, to take revenge for the arrest of Poles and to increase our enemies in the forests.
  No, sir.
  Then what?
  I will tell you, on condition I receive a pistol for suicide.
  So, good, tell me.
  Sir, I am not a Pole, I am a Jew.
  What?
  Yes!
  Now I understand; this is a tragedy.[31]

Oswald managed to escape and after three days of wandering and pursuit, found refuge in a monastery where he remained for 16 months. When the searches for him intensified, he fled to the forest. The partisans charged him with being a German spy. Through the intervention of Jewish partisans and especially of Shlomo Charchas of Mir, he was saved from the death sentence and attached to one of the battalions.

After the war, Oswald was active in capturing and bringing to trial people who had collaborated with the Germans in the Mir region. Following that he left for Krakow, was baptized a Christian and received the name of Daniel, the son of Miriam, and went to Israel.

The Mir Jews who fought with the partisans provided food for and also defended the family camps in their region.[32]

The essential question in the Mir story that troubles us is why did not all the 850 Mir Jews flee on 9 August rather than just 300. Here there were at least two factors that were not present in the same form in other places. First, they had trustworthy information from Oswald concerning the date of the *aktzia*, information that was trusted not only by the underground, but also by the other ghetto inhabitants. Second, there was an almost danger-free opportunity to leave the ghetto for the forest while the city was empty of Germans and police forces and even more, the certain knowledge that all those who did not flee would be liquidated in the *aktzia*.

The case of Mir makes it possible for us to see how the Jews responded when they faced the decision of fleeing or remaining. We can also examine the motives behind that decision. Such an examination will make it easier for us to understand what took place in other ghettos.

It would seem that most Jews did not have the feeling that they were escaping to life or even to some measure of certainty of remaining alive. It seemed to them that they were escaping from the danger of dying together with their beloved families — a fate which would be shared by the whole community, to death alone, isolated and separated from all these. In view of so small a prospect of living, their direct emotional attachments to their families and to their Jewish environment weighed the scales in favor of remaining.

In many cases women with infants prevailed upon their husbands not to leave them. On the other hand, mothers, even when they had decided to stay, accepted their sons' desire to escape and even encouraged this with all their hearts. Many of those who did escape looked upon the members of their families — parents, brothers, sisters, wives and children — as having been betrayed. Though not all considered themselves traitors, they were troubled by deep feelings of guilt (I could have taken mother along, and also sister) when they discovered that there were conditions for an existence of some kind, even if only a temporary one, within the forest, although at the time of their escape they had not seen any possibility for women and children to exist in the forest.

The news that came from the forest, about the dangers lurking for the gun-bearing Jew, and even more so for the unarmed Jew, from peasants and non-Jewish partisans, deterred many from escaping.

Moreover, quite a few of the ghetto's residents were already totally apathetic to what was going on about them. Deep shock arouses different and even opposite responses among different individuals. Some of the Jews were aroused after the *aktzia* to an even stronger desire to live; while others — saw only their devastation. These became apathetic to events. This polarization in responses under exceptional situations was a common phenomenon in the ghetto.

The Mir ghetto was distinguished first of all by a pioneering Zionist youth movement (Hashomer Hatzair), whose young members formed both the foundation and the large majority of the underground. It was also unique by the fact of the very rare case of cooperation between the underground and Oswald, who worked courageously in the face of danger to save the Jews of Mir.

From time to time, the underground organizations, after internal discussions concerning the goals of their activities, sent groups to the forest to establish contact with the partisans, to locate their bases and negotiate with them to accept into their ranks Jews from the ghetto.

There were, however, individuals and groups who had fled earlier on their own initiative and did not succeed in maintaining any contact with the ghettos from which they had come. Some were murdered on their way or wandered too far from their own region; some, despite their desire to do so, did not succeed in establishing such contact. Some 30 men had escaped from Olkeniky to the forest only a few months after the German occupation; in Janow near Pinsk, some groups escaped on their own initiative when the ghetto was established in the months of August-September 1941. Three young men left Iwje in the early months of the occupation.

Individuals, too, went to the forest. M. Borecky, a Hashomer Hatzair leader from Meiczet, went to the forest on 5 April 1942. Since he knew the neighborhood, he became a guide for a partisan unit that was then formed in the region. Other young people, too, who had escaped from Meiczet, went to the forest and were guides for partisan units in the area.[33] The first to flee to the forest from Korelicz was Hashomer Hatzair member David Lifszyc who joined the partisans. Dr. Levinbuk, from the Koldyczewo camp, established contacts with the partisan commander Jarockin and smuggled a great deal of medicine to the forest. At the end of October 1942 he escaped from the camp together with his wife and child, and even left a letter for the camp commander:

> Honorable commander,
> You will forgive us for our swinish act towards you. No one is to be blamed for our escape. We, too, are not to be blamed for being Jews. We are still young and capable of serving humanity. Forgive us for wanting to live.[34]

Groups and individuals also escaped from other ghettos. Though there were no contacts between the refugees and the camps from which they had fled, their very act of escaping served to encourage others to flee and "to do something" to save themselves and fight in the depressing conditions prevailing in the ghettos.

Fleeing and Returning

There were, however, also groups which fled to the forest and then returned to the ghetto, sometimes only in part. Fifteen Jews fled from the Dvorec camp and returned after a little while when they discovered that it was impossible to exist in the forest without weapons. In that same summer of 1942, Israel Kessler, one of the heads of the Dvorec underground, organized a group of nine young men to escape to the forest. They left, but a peasant who had promised them guns betrayed them to the Germans. They escaped by a miracle and returned to Dvorec.[35]

Three men left Lida for the forest. They met Polish partisans, who murdered two of them. The third succeeded in returning to the ghetto. After the great *aktzia* in Pinsk (at the end of October 1942), 20 Jewish young men escaped to the forest and came up against a group of armed horsemen who robbed them of their weapons and valuables, and they were compelled to return to Pinsk. Following a partisan attack in the Raduszkowicze area in the spring of 1942, five young men and a young woman escaped to the forest. They returned to the ghetto after they were rejected by the partisans. They were caught in the ghetto and executed.[36]

Murdered in the Forest

Many groups that escaped to the forest were murdered by roaming bandits or by peasants, especially when they did not succeed in reaching the partisan bases. Sometimes, however, Jews were murdered on their way to the partisans even when they knew where the nearby bases were located. During the Kobryn *aktzia*, Palevsky and Fuksman escaped with a group of ten others, but even before they reached the partisans they were all killed by local peasants.

Organized Groups

The underground organizations attempted to establish partisan bases or ties with existing partisan units, especially those which had Jewish partisans. As far as possible, they provided the Jews with weapons and other equipment and maintained contact with them so that they would absorb additional groups.

Some of the underground organizations maintained almost continuous contact with the partisans in their area, and this contact was reflected in the number of organized escapes, the fate of those escaping and in the cooperation between the ghetto and the Jews in the forest. Among these were the underground organizations of Lida, Novogrudok, Baranowicze, Slonim, Kamin-Koshirsk, Dereczyn and Zhetl.

From the fall of 1942 and until the ghetto's liquidation on 17 September 1943, at least 20 groups of Jews left the Lida, ghetto for the nearby forests: Naliboky, Lipczany and Nacza. In keeping with circumstances, the groups varied in size, sometimes, numbering 30 and even 45 members. One group, of eleven members, had a rifle for every man. The groups escaping to the forest included physicians, who were vital for existence in the forest. There were also elderly persons in these groups, like 70-year-old Shmuel Pupko and his wife.[37]

Many groups also escaped from Novogrudok. The first group, which numbered 20 young men and was headed by Moma Czorny, had a tragic fate: all its members were killed on the roads and in the forest. We do not know the date of its flight precisely, but it was almost certainly at the end of the winter of 1941–42.

In the spring of 1942 the contacts between Bielsky's units and the Novogrudok ghetto were strengthened. In addition to the Jewish partisans who came from the forest to take Jews from the ghetto, Bielsky also sent in a Bielorussian to encourage Jews to escape. At least 25 groups fled Novogrudok, most of them between the second *aktzia* of 8 August 1942 and the fourth on 7 May 1943. Sometimes these escapes involved hand-to-hand fighting. Welwke Janson, who cut the wire fence near the watchpost and left with his group, came up against an Estonian guard:[38]

> I stood face-to-face with the Estonian. There was no other way out and before he began to shoot or to shout I showed him my knife. He threw away his gun in fright. I hit him on the head with pistol I had taken with me from the ghetto and dragged him to the place we had fixed to meet. There we met, left the Estonian unconscious and hurried to the forest before daylight ...

The pressure for escape grew stronger. Sometimes the partisan guide who had come to the ghetto made a list of people and prepared them for the escape. At the last moment other persons who lurked in wait for them appeared and hoped to join the group in its departure. However, these persons' unplanned inclusion would have endangered the escape itself. The next time the guide would arrange to leave with his group secretly, so that it would not become known to others.

Though Bielsky's unit had few weapons and found it hard to provide food and security to the Jews, it complied with its commander, Tuviya Bielsky's, principle of accepting all Jews who reached the forest, even in the most difficult conditions.

Within the Baranowicze underground there had been one group of young people who had argued from the very outset that the battle against the Germans must be waged from the forest. They yielded to the underground's authority during the second *aktzia* of September 1942 not willingly but only under the threat of an ultimatum of the other members of the staff. After the second *aktzia*, when the plan for the revolt was not implemented, an intensive flight of organized groups began. During the three months between the second and third *aktzias*, from September to December 1942, at least 200 Jews fled from the Baranowicze ghetto. However, these organized groups also faced ambushes and very serious dangers. One group of nine was surrounded by the Germans and only two escaped to reach the Zhukov unit. Another group of 12 lost half of its members on its way. Sarah Rubinowicz reached a parachutist unit that carried out special missions.[38] Flight also continued from the Baranowicze camp and some 250 Jews fled from there.

In Slonim, after the third *aktzia* in June 1942, there began an accelerated flight of young people to the forests and of the older people to the territory of the Third Reich — the Bialystok region. In the course of five months, until the end of 1942 when the ghetto was liquidated, 400 Jews fled from Slonim. In July 1942 two partly armed groups left, headed by Zorach Kremen and Aharon Band. They established the basis for the "Szczors 51" Jewish partisan unit. Its members won renown as skilled saboteurs. Fifty-seven-year-old Josef Rachmilevicz, who had secured arms and explosives, left with a group of 15 young people, including his four sons, for the Derzhinsky partisan unit, where he was made a platoon commander. Among those who escaped from Slonim were persons who were to become famous for their activities for example, Heniek Mal'ach, who had come as a refugee from Warsaw and derailed 31 German trains. He was killed while serving with the Red Army near Koenigsberg. Among those escaping were also Arik Stein, Nionia Cirynsky, Natan Liker, Yehudit Graf, Zehava Rawic, and many others.[39]

Of the 300 Jews who fled from the Kamin-Koshirsk ghetto, about 120 did so in organized groups. Here, too, some of these escapes involved hand-to-hand combat with the Ukrainians. The main danger to the escaping groups lay in the unorganized groups roaming the forest.

In the summer of 1942 a number of groups escaped from Dereczyn to the "Atlas" unit. A group of 37 persons left Zhetl for the Naliboky forests. A number of small groups had left Kurzeniec for the forest as early as November 1941, after the execution of 54 so-called Soviet "kommissars." Yaakov Alperovitz and Ida Gelberstein left on 10 November 1941 and joined a partisan unit. Two weeks later they were followed by three other 17-year olds who established a partisan base and maintained contact with the youth in the ghetto.⁴⁰ These were the first groups to flee to the forests from this region. In April 1942, Josef Fishkin and his 62-year-old father, Shabtai armed with pistols, from Rubzhewicze left at the head of a group. They were the pioneers of the partisan movement in their area. Afterwards they were joined by escaped Russian prisoners-of-war and together attacked three police stations. Garmiza and Reuven Port had worked as machinists for the German commander. When the rumors reached Rubzhewicz of pits being dug near the town, the two put on German uniforms they had taken from the commander's house, and crossed the town, full of soldiers and policemen, on a motorcycle they had also taken from the Germans, in the direction of the forest, and went to a partisan group.

The pressures for flight intensified in Stolpce after the second *aktzia* in September 1942 and, immediately following it, a number of organized groups left. In the fall of 1942 a group of 21 members of Hashomer Hatzair and Betar headed by Josef Harkawy left for the Kopyl forests with seven rifles. When they reached the partisan area they were robbed of their guns by non-Jewish partisans. It was only afterwards that they were accepted into the Jewish unit. A group of 25 young men escaped from Meiczet and organized as an autonomous Jewish force alongside the "Zolotov" partisan unit. Zimmel Stolowicky organized a group of 60 from Meiczet who were armed with eight rifles, 12 pistols, a submachine gun and grenades.⁴¹

At the beginning of June 1942, before the second *aktzia*, a group of 20 fled Glubok for the marshes in the Luszky area. The members of their families were threatened with execution and those suspected of desiring to escape were arrested by the Judenrat. The police, and also many ghetto Jews, watched each other so they would not escape. Despite this, young people in the ghetto both as individuals and groups sought to obtain weapons and to escape to the forest. A group of 30 men who had left the ghetto and gathered in the Jewish graveyard were discovered by the Jewish police and returned to the ghetto. After the second *aktzia*, one group left for the forest headed by Avner Feigelman. This group included Yitzhak Blatt, who was to become known for his daring as the commander of a commando group in the "Czapajew" regiment of Markov's brigade.⁴² The groups that followed were to some extent armed and managed to reach the partisan units, but the members of the Milikyn and Feigelson families — 18 persons in all — were executed because two of their number had escaped to the forest. A group of 18 persons escaped in November 1942, among whom were the two sons of Judenrat chairman Lederman. There was great fear among the ghetto's inhabitants. Lederman turned to the *gebietskommissar* and told him of his "trouble," and the latter agreed that people should be sent to the forest to bring Lederman's sons back. The two were indeed returned after two weeks, but Lederman was arrested and removed from the Judenrat, and his sons were shot.[43] At the time of the August 1943 *aktzia*, more than 200 Jews succeeded in breaking out by force and escaping to the forest. A group of 40 reached the fourth Bielorussian brigade in the Koziany forests. In all, some 300 Jews escaped from the Glubok ghetto: about 150 in organized groups, and at least 100 of the total reached the partisans.

In Pruzhany members of the underground established ties with Ostapchuk, a one-time member of the former Soviet administration. The latter organized people for escape to the forest, visited the ghetto a number of times and encouraged its residents to flee. Starting from June 1942 the Pruzhany underground sent a number of organized groups to Ostapchuk's partisan base. One of these groups attacked the home of the German commander and even disarmed a German guard unit in the town. The second underground organization in the town, the "anti-fascist committee", established contacts with the Bielorussian anti-fascist organization and sent organized groups of seven to eight persons to the forest. Escape from the ghetto during the winter was limited because of the difficulties in finding hiding places and the danger of footprints being found in the snow. However in January 1943 a group of twelve persons, headed by Yosef Untershul, left for the forest. They were well-equipped: in addition to rifles and a machine gun, pistols, grenades and a radio, they also had heavy coats, canvas and leather boots, hoes, axes and pickaxes with which to build earth huts in the Samec forest where they established a partisan base.[44]

At least five organized groups escaped from the Janow ghetto near Pinsk; the first after the initial *aktzia*. In Lenin, a young woman, Chaya Gurvicz, organized a group of girls on the day of the *aktzia* in August 1942 and fled with them to the forest. Organized groups also escaped from the ghettos of Vilejka (with Norman as the group's guide), Horodok (Eliahu Lidsky), Krasna (Chanan Rogovin), Vidz (Svirsky), Postavy (S.H. Zaslavsky), Kobylnik (M. Chadash), Sernik (Sh. Galecky), Pinsk (S.H. Zaslavsky), Bereza-Kartuska (M. Tuchman), Kosov-Polesky (S. Ragutner), Wiszniewo (N. Podboresky), etc. Most of these groups fled in the second half of 1942.

Oszmiana and Swienciany

In September 1942 Oszmiana and Swienciany together with other small ghettos in the Vilno district, were annexed to the area of the administration and responsibility of the Vilno ghetto. Vilno Judenrat chairman Gens was appointed the official representative of the Lithuanian ghettos and of those annexed to them. He sent officials and police to these ghettos to inaugurate procedures similar to those in the Vilno ghetto. On the eve of these ghettos' liquidation, escape groups were organized with the assistance of emissaries from the Vilno underground, the F.P.O. (the United Partisan Organization): Liza Magun and Auerbach. In October 1942 the Germans decided to limit the Jewish population in Oszmiana and to execute the elderly persons. Gens and the Vilno ghetto police assisted in carrying out the killing operation in which 700 aged Jews were murdered. Explaining the horrifying action to Jewish public figures at the end of October 1942 Gens in declared that "Jews dirty their hands with blood," and that if it were not for the Jewish police the number of victims would have been much larger; and, he continued, if in the future the Jewish police would have to take part once again in such an operation, they would do so.

In May 1943 the Oszmiana ghetto, then numbering 2,830 persons, was liquidated. Five hundred wagons carried the Jews to the railroad station, joined on the way by more Jews from Soly, Michaliczky, Oshmianka, Gudagei and Ostrowiec — in all, some 5,000 Jews. The train was supposed to be going to Kovno, but the Jews were carried to the Ponar murder site.

There was an underground organization in the Oszmiana ghetto. When the news reached the Vilno ghetto that the ghetto police were about to leave on a "special mission," the F.P.O. instructed Liza Magun, one of its central figures and a member of Hashomer Hatzair, who looked like an Aryan, to go to Oszmiana and warn the Jews of the impending *aktzia* and, more importantly, to organize the young people for an escape to the forests. She was also to call for resistance when the Germans came to lead them to the slaughter. A few groups of young people with whom Liza had established contact previously, fled on the night of the *aktzia*. A group of 50, armed with two rifles and two grenades, left for the Volozhin forest during the ghetto's liquidation. Although 10 of them returned to the ghetto and were shot, 40 reached a partisan unit. Two other groups escaped from this ghetto: one was abandoned by its guide and its members returned to the ghetto even though they had weapons. They were added to the "transport" to Kovno and killed.

Members of the Vilno Jewish police came to the Swienciany ghetto in March 1943 and made two lists: one, of members of the Judenrat, the police and craftsmen, to be removed to the Vilno ghetto, and the other of the remainder, who were to be sent to the Kovno ghetto. Gens appeared in the synagogue and declared that only Jewish policemen would be present at the time of the move. In order to indicate how much trust the Germans had in him, he displayed to the congregation his pistol and declared:

> In our ghetto we don't go about with lowered heads. We must drive out the sadness. We must have hope. The youth must not be depressed and impotent but encouraged and capable of work. We have in Vilno enough places of work, entertainment and cultural institutions ... We must arm ourselves with a great deal of courage and patience. We must live courageously in order to come through these days ...

The audience stood there in silence. Many did not believe him. One member of the audience asked: "Why are you sure that those listed for Kovno will really get there?"

Gens replied: "Brother Jews! The Germans have decided to move the Jews from the frontier towns situated in the partisan area to the larger cities. I am prepared to share your fate, to go with you to the Kovno ghetto. I call upon you to accept discipline, to fulfill the Germans' orders, don't make the moving difficult. Help us!"

Concerning the youths' intentions, Gens said: "... I have heard that the youth want to go on 'vacation' [i.e., to the forest]. I advise them not to do so. I have spoken to the *gebietskommissar* and he has promised me that what happened will not happen again. He will not deceive me again. All are going to live. When I know of something evil I myself will tell you when to go on vacation ..."

More than a few believed him.

Auerbach, a member of the Vilna F.P.O., assembled some 150 young men and women in the schoolhouse a few days before the deportation and warned them that the deportation to Kovno was a voyage to death. Anyone who could, should save himself; flee to the forest, hide somewhere or attempt to reach the F.P.O. organization in Vilno. On 5 April 1943 the Swienciany Jews were loaded onto railway carriages that carried them to

Ponar. Meanwhile 20 members of the fighting organization and another 40 unorganized individuals fled to the forest.[45]

The Escape from Raduszkovicze

On 7 March 1943 two young people fled from the Raduszkowicze ghetto. The ghetto's Jews, some 350 persons, were filled with the fear of death because of the Germans' previous warnings. On that same day the Germans conducted a roll call, discovered who were missing and, within a few hours, 290 Jews were executed. Another 35 succeeded in escaping to the forest, and 22 were left alive by the Germans.[46]

Escapes During the Last *Aktzias*

Thousands of Jews, individuals and groups, some of whom had organized previously and some who had joined spontaneously at the last moment, fled at the time of the last *aktzias* to liquidate the ghettos of western Bielorussia. So too, many of those who during the previous *aktzias* had hidden in bunkers, now fled from the ghettos, either in search of a more secure shelter, or because of the critical lack of food or the fear of ultimately being discovered by the Germans. Now all illusions were shattered, including the remaining one that the Germans still needed Jews who possessed vital skills. Even in ghettos where only some dozens (or less) craftsmen remained, the Jews were annihilated to the last person.

In most cases the Jews fled without arms. Anyone who succeeded in reaching the forest and in meeting a partisan unit, asked to join. Jewish partisan units accepted other Jews under certain conditions: to obtain arms or to join without any members of one's family. Some Soviet groups did not accept them all. There were some that were indifferent and some, mainly the unorganized bands, who were openly hostile. They robbed the Jews of their few weapons and meager bundles and sometimes killed them.

Hundreds of Jews escaped from the Kurzeniec ghetto to the forest on the day of the *aktzia* on 9 September 1942, among them the members of the underground. Some of the refugees turned towards the Rosaky forest in the Narocz region, some crowded the family camps in the Kurzeniec region and moved afterwards, under partisan guides, to behind the eastern front. Some underground members remained with their families who had escaped to the forest since the partisan units refused to accept elderly persons and children. The members of the Kurzeniec underground were outstanding in the partisan war and won many decorations. Some fell in battle. Kurzeniec Jews fought in the Melinkov, Voroshilov, Dombrowsky and other partisan brigades.[47]

Some 200 Jews fled from Horodok to Krasna on the night of the *aktzia* on 22 June 1942; eight made it to the partisans. The Germans left 12 craftsmen in Horodok. Some of the Michaliczky Jews fled to the forest when the Jews of that town were sent to Vilno and Kovno together with the Jews of Oszmiana and the neighboring towns in March 1943. Some 200 Jews fled the Druja ghetto on the day of the *aktzia* on 16 June 1942, and some 200 hid. It is almost certain that some of those who had hidden later escaped from their hiding places. One of those who escaped from Druja was the teacher Shlomo Moshin, who later established the Kaganowicz partisan unit. Jews also succeeded in escaping to the forest from the Postavy ghetto on the night it was annihilated, on 25 December 1942.

Dokszyce Jews attempted to escaped from the pits on 31 May 1942, but the Germans killed many of them. Josef Shapira, organizer of the Dokszyce underground, who had been deterred from escaping with his comrades as long as the ghetto existed, because of the collective responsibility, now fled to the forest with a group of twelve. Some 30 boys fled the pits on 16 August 1942, the day the Pohost ghetto was annihilated, but they were captured and shot.

A tumult broke out in Janow near Pinsk during the 25 September 1942 *aktzia*, when Chana Gorodecka attacked one of the policemen. People broke out of the lines and ran in all directions. The Germans opened fire. Individuals and groups burst through the encirclement and got to the fields. Among them was the Hebrew poet Berl Pomerantz, who later fell in the forest. Stolin Jews attempted to escape on the night of the *aktzia* on 10 September 1942, but found the way blocked by German guards. On the following morning, when the Jews were surrounded, some escaped from the square. Jewish families who had been sitting in the bunkers for many weeks were compelled to leave their hiding places because of lack of food and to attempt to flee, but were caught. On the day of the Kamin-Koshirsk annihilation many Jews escaped to the forest. Some reached partisan units. In the course of the four days of the deportation of the Pruzhany Jews 28–31 January, hundreds fled to the forest.

On the day of the annihilation of the Brzesc Jews (15 October 1942), 13 persons fled, among them members of the underground, armed with three machine guns, three rifles, grenades and ammunition. A second group, headed by Omalinski, also escaped with arms. The group met Sashka's group of murderers and two of its members were killed. Five members returned to Brzesc and hid in the synagogue cellar throughout the winter. In March 1943 they left for the forest once again. Shlomo Kandlik fled the ghetto, shooting two Germans with his pistol on the way. Few Brzesc Jews reached partisan unit.

Lida Jews fled to the forest on the day of the deportation (17 September 1943) and some 50 reached Bielsky's unit.

Almost 200 Jews fled to the forest on the day of Iwje's liquidation 16 January 1943. Among them were the brothers Mordechai and Bezalel Ginsburg, who were to be among the outstanding fighters of the "Iskra" partisan unit, and Fruma Tanpel, who won distinction in partisan battles. At least 25 Iwje Jews who had been moved to Lida and had worked in the underground, fled to Bielsky's "Iskra" unit. Jews from the Volozhin ghetto fled after the second *aktzia* on 10 May 1942. Some 200 Jews fled from Byten at the time of the *aktzia* on 25 July 1942.

When the Dereczyn ghetto was surrounded by Germans and police on 24 July 1942, almost 3,000 Jews fled to the forests, some to the Borelom forest. A number of those who escaped were in time to become famous partisans: Eliahu Lipshovicz, a platoon commander in Dr. Atlas' unit and afterwards platoon commander in the Pobieda unit; his brothers, Chaim Yehoshua and Gershon, and his sister, Taibe, who were among the founders of the Atlas unit and the best of the partisan fighters in the Lipczany forests. There were also the brothers Benjamin and David Dombrowsky and others, who won distinction for their fighting as daring partisans. Young people from Dereczyn joined Dr. Atlas' unit. Approximately 300 Jews, among them refugees from Dereczyn, were organized with the help of the commander, Bulak, into a family camp.

Notes

1. Izik Berkowicz, testimony in *Sefer Zikaron Stoipc-Swierzhne veha'ayarot hasmuchot* (Memorial Book of Stolpce-Swerezhna and the Adjoining Townships) (Tel Aviv, 1965), pp. 142–145.
2. Yad Vashem (YV) 03/1289 (David Rubin).
3. Pinchas Ormland, testimony in *Sefer Zikaron likehillat Kamin-Koshirsk* (Memorial Book for the Community of Kamin-Koshirsk and Its Environs) (loc. date), p. 557.

4. David Rubin, testimony in *Sefer Ilja, Yizkov-Bukh* (Memorial Book of Ilja (Tel Aviv, 1962), p. 323.
5. Zirl Kamiencka, testimony in *Sefer Zikaron leKehillot Dereczyn, Hulinka, Kutna, Siniesk* (Memorial Book of the Communities of Dereczyn, Hulinka, Kutno, Siniesk) (Tel Aviv, 1972), p. 290.
6. Dov Amit, testimony in *Sefer Zikaron likehillat Kamin-Koshirsk*, op. cit., p. 146.
7. YV 2447/149-R (Berl Reznik).
8. Baruch Levin, testimony in *Sefer Zholudok veOrlova* (Memorial Book of the Communities of Zhulodok and Orlova) (Tel Aviv, 1967), p. 179.
9. Reuven Budownic, testimony in *Sefer Druya* (Druisk Memorial Book) (Tel Aviv, 1973), p. 169.
10. R. P-R., testimony in *Ha'ayara Bilhavot* (The Shtetl in Flames — Olkeniki) (Tel Aviv, 1962), p. 125.
11. Yossef Pecker & Zalman Rabinowicz, testimonies in *Sefer Zikaron Lachowicz* (Lachowicz Memorial Book) (Tel Aviv, 1969), p. 320.
12. Ilja Bunkowiec, in L. Speismann, *Chalutzim in Poilen* (Chalutzim in Poland) (New York, 1961), p. 559.
13. Gitta Aron-Simkin, testimony in *Sefer Druya*, op. cit., p. 217.
14. Michael Z. Rayak, testimony in *Churban Globak, etc ...* (The Destruction of Glubok, etc ...) (Buenos Aires, 1956), p. 295; Bielka Chadash, ibid., p. 316; YV 103/1779 (Eliahu Kalmanowicz).
15. P.-R., op. cit., p. 127; also Ribak Ben-Shemesh, ibid., p. 240; Shalom Sonnensohn, testimony in *Ejszyszok, Koroteha Vechurbana* (Eiszyszky, Its History and Its Destruction) (Jerusalem, 1950), p. 63.
16. YV 03/2815 (Moshe Michalowski).
17. Melech Bakalczuk-Fellin, *Zikhroines fun a Yiddishn Partizan* (Memoirs of a Jewish Partisan) (Buenos Aires, 1958).
18. YV M-1/E 518/457 (Ascher Teitelboim).
19. Moreshet Archive (MA) A-331 (Ya'akov Sigalczyk).
20. YV 2938/63-T (Moshe Tuchman); YV 980/850 (David Liebowicz).
21. YV E/583; E/457 (Shmariahu Furmaski); Shalom Gerling, testimony in *Pinkas Zhetl* (Zhetl Diary) (Tel Aviv, 1957), pp. 189–190.
22. Aharon Herman, testimony in *Sefer Kobryn* (Kobryn Memorial Book) (loc. date), p. 332.
23. Chaim Schlossberg testimony in *Sefer Hapartizanim Hayehudi'im* (The Book of Jewish Partisans) vol. 1 (Merhavia, 1959), p. 423.
24. Zaichik, testimony in *Sefer Zikaron Kehilat Lenin* (The Lenin Community Memorial Book) (Tel Aviv, 1957), pp. 45–65; Yehuda Ziklik, ibid., p. 104.
25. YV 2235/2212 (Hillel Shapiro).
26. YV E/35 (Mieta Shimshonowitz).

27. *Prestupleniya Niemietsko-Fashystitskikh Okkupantow w Belorussi* (Crimes of the German-Fascist Occupieres of Belorussia) (Minsk, 1965), p. 72.
28. Moniek Yosselevsky, testimony in *Sefer Zikaron Stoipc-Swierezhne ...*, op. cit., p. 472; YV 2104/96 (Aharon Harkavy); YV 2084/74 (Avraham Slutzky).
29. Dov Reznik, testimony in *Sefer Mir* (Mir Memorial Book) (Jerusalem, 1963), p. 350.
30. Ibid.
31. Shalom Cholawski, "Mahteret Ba'ir" (An Underground in Town), *Hedim: A Journal for Kibbutz Problems*, no. 53 (April 1957).
32. YV M-1/E 761/624 (Yisrael Piernikow); D. Reznik, op. cit., p. 367.
33. YV E/550 (Mordechai L. Shlomowicz).
34. J. Levinbuk, testimony in *Sefer Zikaron Baranowicz* (Baranowicze Memorial Book) (loc. date), p. 625.
35. Eliezer Gurion, testimony in *Sefer Rubżhewicze* (Rubżhewicze Memorial Book) (loc. date), p. 625.
36. YV 1436/133 (Baruch Shub).
37. Levin, op. cit., pp. 72–74; Yossef and Ida Kaplan, *Ad Yom Kippurim Ze* (Until This Day of Atonement) (Lohamei Hagetaot, 1976), p. 54.
38. Welwke Janson, testimony in *Sefer Lubcz-Delatycz* (Lubecz-Delatycz Memorial Book) (Tel Aviv, 1971), p. 348.
39. Luba Rudnicka, testimony in *Sefer Noworudek* (Nowgrudek Memorial Book) (loc. date), Tuvia & Zussia Belsky, *Yehudei Ya'ar* (Jews of the Forest) (Tel Aviv, 1946), pp. 60–62; YV 3107/173-M (Leizer Malbin); Avraham Lid, *Bayearot e* (In the Forests) (Kibbutz Meuchad, 1946), p. 80; MA D.2. 105/6 (Shalom Kaczanowsky); MA D.2.105/76 (Moshe Topp).
40. Central Zionist Archive (CZA) 826/1544 (Zorach Kremen); MA A-200 (Zehava Ravitz).
41. Testimonies of Dov Amit, Avraham Rofe, T. Berliner and Kalman Roitenstein in *Sefer Zikaron likehillat Kamin-Koshirsk*. op. cit.; YV E/687; YV E/591. Ida Gelberstein was active in the "Mstitiel" (Avenger) sapper unit of the "Diadia Wasia" Brigade, fell in battle on 3 September 1943 and posthumously received a high military decoration.
42. MA D.2.105/79 (Yossef Fishkin); YV 723/39 (Eliezer Melamed); Reuven Port, testimony in *Sefer Rubzhewicze*, op. cit., p. 213; Shmuel L. Aginsky, testimony in *Sefer Zikaron Stoipc-Swierezhne ...*, op. cit., p. 325; Hanan Shlomowitz & Abrasha Chaneles, testimonies in *Sefer Zikaron Likehillat Meiczet* (Memorial Book for the Community of Mochadzh) (loc. date), pp. 307, 328.
43. Yitshak Blat was born in Glubok in 1921. After he had taken his mother, sister and her husband, and their two children out of the ghetto, he fought until

he was fatally wounded in an attack on a German position on a railroad in January 1944. He was recommended by his unit for a posthumous award as a Hero of the Soviet Union. (Did he get it?).
44. YV E/512 (Tanchum Gordon).
45. YV 03/727 (Yitzhak Friedberg), Yossef Elman & ?. Shaieck testimonies in *Sefer Pruzhane* (Pruzhany Memorial Book) (loc. date), pp. 659, 725; Ruzhka Korczak, *Lehavot Ba'efer* (Flames in Ash) (Tel Aviv, 1965), pp. 121–127; MA D.2.8. (Hinda Deial).
46. Moshe Shutan, *Getto un Wald* (Ghetto and Forest) (Tel Aviv, 1971), pp. 44–45; YV 1905/129 (Leizer Levitan); YV M-1/E 1278/1243 (Max Chenczynski); also Shmerke Katcherginski, *Partizaner Geien* (Partisans are Maching) (Munich, 1948).
47. Baruch Shepsenbol, testimony in *Sefer Zikaron Radushkovicz* (Radoshkovicze Memorial Book) (Tel Aviv, 1953); MA A-517 (Berl Maneh).
48. *Megillat Kurnitz* (Kurzeniec) (trans title) (Tel Aviv, 1956), pp. 268–269; MA A-7 (Rivka Gewint). (The Scroll of Kurnitz) (Kurzeniec).

CHAPTER 12

On a Mission of Rescue and Revenge

As long as the ghettos still existed the Jews who had fled to the forest, and especially the members of the underground who had left the ghettos, considered it their first obligation to their conscience to attempt to bring other ghetto Jews to the forest. They did this regardless of whether they had already been accepted into partisan units or had still not established their own existential base. Jewish partisans visited the ghettos and sent letters via non-Jewish couriers to encourage the Jews to escape and even more important, to inform the members of the underground of the location of the partisan bases. The Jewish partisan units looked upon this activity of rescue as self-evident. Particularly outstanding in rescuing Jews from the ghettos was Bielsky's unit, which operated in accordance with the principle that Bielsky himself had set down: any Jew reaching the forest would be accepted: rescuing Jews came before everything else.

In mixed units, where the command was in most cases non-Jewish, the Jewish partisans attempted to convince their officers to agree to these rescue operations. Unfortunately however, only rarely was consent given for such actions. In many cases the Jewish partisans attempted to produce reasons to justify their Jewish mission, such as the need to bring arms from the ghetto, to bring physicians and their instruments, clothing, medicines and the like. In many cases, however, they carried out their mission secretly and against the command's instructions, despite the risk that this breach of discipline implied. When Jewish partisans sought to influence the command to attack a town where there was a Jewish ghetto, they were compelled to find purely military arguments. The decision on whether to accept or not accept Jews escaping from the ghetto into the partisan unit was generally taken according to the views of the local commanders.

Immediately after having fled to the forest, the members of the Swienciany underground carried out a number of missions to the Vilno ghetto. On returning to their town they had discovered that all its Jews had been moved to Vilno. They established contact with a Vilno Jewish policeman, Auerbach, who was also a F.P.O. member, and, as a result, Shaike Gertman and Yitzhak Rudnicky (Arad) left for Vilno by train, armed with a pistol and a grenade, and met the F.P.O. command. In the discussions which took place between them and the F.P.O., differing approaches came to light. The Swiencany young people wanted to join the F.P.O. in order to organize an escape to the forest, while the F.P.O. command wanted them to join the organization and to accept the principle of fighting within the ghetto. No compromise between the approaches was found. Gertman and Rudnicky were arrested by the ghetto police, almost certainly because of an informer, but they were liberated with the help of the F.P.O. and left Vilno. They reported to their partisan unit's command on the Vilno organization. After a time, two other young people from Swienciany, Moshe Shutan and Porush, also went to Vilno, where they met Itzik Vittenberg, the F.P.O. commander, and he promised to consider the possibilities of escaping to the forest.

Shaike Gertman and Israel Wolfson came to Vilno once more. They came in the name of the commander of the partisan brigade, Markov, and brought a letter calling upon the ghetto youth to come to the forest, but with arms in hand. The F.P.O. command deliberated the problem. Arms in ghetto were few, and if the young people took them to the forest, what would happen to all the other Jews, namely the older men and women who formed the major part of the ghetto and whom nobody was inviting to leave? In the meantime Shutan was arrested in a raid conducted within the ghetto and brought before Gens, but succeeded in escaping and in returning to the forest.

Shutan and Gertman returned on a mission to Vilno once again in July 1943. The F.P.O. held to its view that they must remain in the ghetto despite everything, but views were already crystallizing within the organization that fighters from the ghetto should be sent to Markov's partisan units. As a result, two groups left Vilno, the first on 24, July 1943 numbered 21 men headed by Yosef Glazman, with Gertman serving as guide; and the second on 13 August numbered 19 persons, with Shutan as guide.[1]

A short time after Harkawy's group came to Stolpce to join the Zhukov partisan unit, a 17-year old Moshe Zarecky left the group for the ghetto in order to recruit additional Jews. To his misfortune he encountered in the ghetto persons who were opposed to the escape and they drove him outside the fence. He was caught by Bielorussian policemen and killed. Elimelech Machtey left for Stolpce to bring more Jews and did not return. In September 1942 Siomka Farfel, and Shalom Cholawsky who were partisans in the Zhukov unit, sent letters via a courier to the members of the movement in Stolpce. The following is an extract from Cholawsky's letter:

> ... We have remained alone of all the cities; murderous fascism has raised its bloody sword first of all against the Jews. [You must] be the vanguard of the youth. Prepare in groups. The tasks of every man are twofold: revenge and victory! Don't sell your lives cheaply ... The partisan movement is a tremendous force and is becoming stronger every day. Don't delay [lest] ... you come too late ... It is your duty to be among the fighters. Prepare and act, of course with caution, but vigorously, as best you can. [This is] the only path. Remember this!
>
> P.S. Pass this letter on to trustworthy comrades ... In the matter of arms prepare every possible weapon: grenades, rifles, bullets — everything is important. Go to the Kopyl region, that is where we are.

Farfel wrote:

> ... Your young lives are precious and must not, God forbid, be destroyed ... Prepare arms for they are the main thing. They will save you. Your lives are worth even greater expenditures. Pay no attention to the old generation. By your death you will not save them. I speak from experience. Prepare and organize the best of the youth for partisan life.
>
> ... Fascism is crumbling; it is throwing in its last forces ... Victory is on our side ... I speak to you from my heart: Our past was a common one, let our future, too, be one. Remember my words.[2]

Hersh Posesorsky left afterwards with a group of partisans from the Zhukov unit to liberate Jews of Swierzhen.

Tuviya Bielsky sent emissaries to the Lida ghetto to bring Jews to his unit. These emissaries came three times. The first time they took 50 Jews with them. Binyamin Baran went to the Lida ghetto twice. The first time, he came up against a German, threw a grenade at him and killed him. The second time he took six young men to the forest. Yaakov Druk, Velvel Krupsky and others also went to the ghetto and brought out Jews. There were also similar ties between the Bielsky unit and the Novogrudok ghetto. Bielsky sent people to the ghetto and brought out a number of groups.

Partisans from the Baranowicze ghetto also carried out rescue missions. Five days after his escape from the ghetto Zalmanovicz returned with the message that his partisan commander, Czorny, agreed to accept armed Jews in the forest. Zalmanovicz organized a group of 11 men and took them to the forest. After that another group of 17 left. In December 1942, Moshe Top, Noah Rotman and Sevek Ravic went to Baranowicze to take out a group of Jews. As they left they met Bielorussian policemen. Top shot and hit two of them with his pistol but was wounded in the exchange of fire. He was brought to the ghetto's hospital and after he recuperated two comrades came and rescued him together with another 15 Jews. Sarah Rubinowicz (Schiff), a Betar member, came a number of times from the forest to Baranowicze to fulfil missions. Members of the Baranowicze underground established ties with a Pole, Edward Chacia, from western Poland whose home became a shelter for people escaping from the ghetto and for Jewish partisans coming from the forest on missions to the city.

Jewish partisans from Glubok maintained continuous contacts with the ghetto's inhabitants and were even assisted by couriers. Two Jewish partisans arrived at the beginning of July 1942 to take young people to the forest. As a result, 32 men escaped in small groups in March 1943. In addition, dozens of Jews who had relatives in the forest also fled, both in groups and as individuals. Even some Judenrat members assisted them in their flight.[3] The fourth time, the courier, Vujca, was caught together with Zalman Cimmer, his contact in the ghetto, and both were executed.

The Germans had left only 28 Jews alive in Lenin after the August 1942 *aktzia*. After a time the city was attacked by partisans at the initiative of Yehuda Ciklik, who had escaped from Hancevicz. The 28 Jews were liberated and with the agreement of the unit's commander were brought to the forest.[4] The partisan Chanan Alterman came to Krasna with his commander's permission in order to take out a group of armed Jews. In the ghetto he played sick and spent some time there until he succeeded in organizing a group that smuggled guns out of the German arsenals. One night he fled with a group of 30 men.[5] The Horodok, Wasyliszky and Zhetl ghettos were also visited by Jewish partisans coming to take people out of the ghetto.

Some partisan commanders based their accepting Jews from the ghetto on the condition that they would bring arms and other equipment with them; sometimes the commanders were interested only in obtaining the arms and equipment. Bakaler and Appelbaum went to Bereza-Kartuska, brought arms and a radio receiver to their unit and also brought a group of armed Jews with them. In Pruzhany there was a very serious incident:

In the evening of 26 January 1943 the engineer Berl Segal came suddenly to the Judenrat chairman with two armed partisans. They demanded money with which to purchase arms, medicine and food, clothes and shoes. Suddenly, the head of the Gestapo arrived at the Judenrat building. The partisans immediately escaped from the building and the ghetto. The Gestapo commander began to shoot at them, killing a Jewish policeman standing in front of the building and wounding two Judenrat members. He demanded of the Judenrat that they turn over the armed partisans. Two days later, 10,000 Pruzhany Jews began to be sent to Auschwitz.[6] The deportation plan had already been prepared but the Germans now linked it with the shooting incident.

The partisan Josef Segal from Kamin-Koshirsk, who maintained close links with the ghetto, prepared a plan according to which his comrades in the partisan unit would attack the town on the day it was surrounded and thereby enable the 600 Jews to escape to the forest. The plan, however, was never implemented. Benzion Malik was brought out of this ghetto, also Dr. Hotnick, an excellent surgeon, together with his instruments. Ten days after Dov Drug and Josef Segal's group had left Kamen-Koshirsk, the partisans decided to send Drug back to the ghetto in order to bring more men and arms. They obtained two grenades and a short-barrelled rifle, 50 bullets and a radio receiver. Drug entered the ghetto again to take people out, but while he was there the ghetto was surrounded by German forces. Drug came out of hiding, hit the German in his way in the face, and leaped over the fence to the forest. Drug and his comrades asked their commander to be allowed to return to the ghetto once more in order to bring back weapons. They also asked that a non-Jewish partisan go with them so that the people in the ghetto would believe them. Segal, Kupperszhmit and a Russian partisan, Mustafa, left for the ghetto. When the three did not return the Jews were charged with the responsibility for the Russian partisan, Mustafa's death. There was strong antisemitic feeling in the unit and the Jewish partisans were asked to return their arms to headquarters. They moved swiftly, however, and secretly left to join other units.[7]

In the Postavy ghetto there was a sharp confrontation between partisan emissaries and the Judenrat. Shmuel Zaslavsky and Avraham Friedman were allowed to go to the ghetto to bring out people and weapons. Their commander added 14 additional partisans to the operation. Zaslavsky and Avraham Friedman entered the ghetto and demanded of the Judenrat chairman that those fit for combat be sent to the forest. The Judenrat refused and argued that either all the ghetto's inhabitants leave or none. When the two partisans were about to leave the ghetto, and with them a group of 15 men they had organized, Judenrat chairman Rubinstein arrived and threatened to turn them over to the Germans if they escaped. The two decided to put Rubinstein under "house arrest" until all the group's members had left the ghetto. The commander of the Jewish police, Zaslavsky's boyhood friend, arrived and promised not to interfere with the group's departure. On their way to the forest the members of the group attacked six Lithuanian policemen and took their guns and uniforms. A second attempt in that same ghetto did not succeed. Reuven Vant came to the ghetto to organize a group of young people for escape. A large crowd, among them Judenrat member Hirsh Gendel, surrounded the group, accused them and warned that if they left the whole ghetto would be annihilated. Gendel threatened to call the Lithuanian police. Vant did not succeed in extricating the group, only his wife. Despite the failure of Vant's mission, Friedman sent a Christian courier with a letter to the ghetto's young people and, as a result of the letter, another group left for the forest. Friedman sent the courier a second time with the warning that the ghetto faced imminent annihilation. That same day a large group set out for the forest. This took place a few days before the ghetto's liquidation on 25 December 1942.[8]

Leib Voliak and Lifszyc returned to Koziany from the forest in order to organize groups of Jews for escape. They gathered together a group of ten young people, but the Judenrat members noticed them and demanded that they leave the ghetto. On leaving, they met a group of Germans and police. The Germans captured Voliak and were leading him to execution but he was powerfully built and struck at the Germans by the site; though he was hit by four bullets, he escaped and was concealed by his comrades. The latter also smuggled him to Vidz when the Germans demanded his surrender.

On 29 August 1942 a group of 70 partisans reached the Koziany forest in order to organize a partisan movement in the region. The unit grew and within two months had become the "Spartak" brigade, with 500 men. On its arrival in the forest the unit had found two Jewish family groups, numbering 50 persons each. The "Spartak" command promised to accept the Jews into its ranks on condition that they come with arms. After recuperating in Vidz, Leib Voliak organized a group of 30 Jewish fighters who formed a Jewish battalion under the Spartak command, Voliak and his comrades knew the region well, also the paths in the forest and also had established relationships with the village inhabitants. This helped the brigade establish itself in the region.

Voliak, a member of the Hechalutz movement, came from a family of Jewish farmers from Stoyaciszek, and became known as one of the region's most daring commanders. He established ties with the neighboring ghettos in order to enlist young people for the formation of a large Jewish unit. He fell in an attack on the town of Opsa in 1943. One of the fighters in his battalion was 21-year-old Yaakov Natkowicz from Koziany who brought 20 young people to the fighting unit and was a platoon commander and fell in January 1944 while mining a railway. Baruch Cimmer, who was 22 years old, was also a platoon commander and participated in rescuing 40 Jews from Glubok. He fell in the battle for Miory in 1943.[9]

The Jewish partisans' efforts sometimes failed because of objective circumstances or because the Jews in the ghettos hesitated to act. The day after they had escaped, five young men returned to Dolhinov ghetto to extricate the remaining underground members. That same day a large German force arrived in the town. Despite that, Sigalczyk succeeded in getting out with a group of 11 persons. In the forest they met Timczuk, a commander of a partisan unit who maintained a positive attitude towards the Jews and, with his aid, they established a Jewish unit of 26 Dolhinov men. Timczuk suggested to the Jewish fighters that they join in an attack on Dolhinov where there were still some 400 Jews. Sigalczyk's Jewish unit joined the partisan force going to attack Dolhinov. When they penetrated the town the Jewish partisans hurried to the ghetto and urged the Jews to flee to the forest. To their surprise, the ghetto's inhabitants hesitated. The day after the partisans left the town the Jews were charged with assisting the partisan attack and executed.[10]

We may assume that the motives deterring the last Dolhinov Jews from escaping to the forest were the same ones that existed among most of the Jews of Mir, and in other towns in similar circumstances. What is astonishing is that even if these remaining Jews of Dolhinov still hoped that their being skilled workers might yet somehow keep them alive, how could they not comprehend that the partisans coming to them would construed by the Germans as a form of cooperation and thereby seal their fate?

Jewish partisans continued to take risks and to come to the ghettos even when these missions more than once cost them their lives. On the night of 17 September 1943 the Jews of Lida were assembled in the square in preparation for deportation. A group of Jewish partisans came to the ghetto to take Jews to the forest but their retreat was blocked by the Germans and they were unable to leave.[11] Three partisans — Nachmanovicz, Kantorowicz and Frenkel — penetrated into Zhetl ghetto before it was surrounded by the Germans. With iron rods and rocks they stormed the German ranks and were killed in this desperate fight.[12]

Vengeance

At the end of 1942 Jewish existence was undergoing its death pangs in Western Bielorussia. Many ghettos had already been liquidated and only in a few did there remain a small remnant. The ghettos, for the most part, were piles of ashes. Only in the vast forest were there still any Jews. Loneliness, bereavement and longings prevailed. Baruch Levin, the fighting partisan saboteur, related that one day he entered a peasant's house: "... Suddenly the infant in the cradle began to cry and wail, to my eyes there suddenly came the memory of my daughters and home. I felt my hands failing. Tears flooded my face."[13]

A.L. Poliak, who had fled from Motele to Janow near Pinsk, related: "... How much I now envied the Janow Jews, most of whom still had their children with them... My longings for my child and infant grew; to embrace it and press it to my heart and to give it all the warmth that had accumulated in a heart growing hard, turning to stone..."[14]

With the years, concepts are eroded, lose their vitality and these remain only the skeleton of words. We must distill into these concepts the contents and fervor they had then, and relate to them according to the values given them in those days when vengeance was the only elixir for the spirits of the fighting Jews. There was nothing greater than that, and there was nothing more than just that, and it alone justified remaining alive after all that had transpired. Vengeance: that was the Jewish aim in this war. Jews, Jewish fighters, lusted to take revenge on the murderous German, the Bielorussian, the Pole and the Lithuanian who had collaborated, robbed and murdered, and on all those who had stood by while Jewish blood was shed and had kept silent.

The Jewish partisans in the Jewish units and in the mixed ones were subordinate to the partisan command which did not view Jewish vengeance as a value in itself. What motivated them were the usual concepts of war: enemy, invader, allies, etc. What is more, the Jewish consideration, especially settling accounts with the collaborators among the local population, in many cases did not match the interests of the partisan command and, in its view, only disturbed the relations between the peasants and the partisans. Great efforts were invested by Jewish partisans to persuade the commanders of the partisan units to carry out the acts of vengeance they desired and, in the large majority of cases, these efforts were to no avail.

About two weeks after the liquidation of the Dereczyn Jews, Dr. Atlas' Jewish unit, numbering 40 men, and Bulak's non-Jewish unit, with some 80 men, attacked the German forces in Dereczyn with the Jewish unit spearheading the attack. Five Germans were killed and six wounded. Dozens of Bielorussian and Polish policemen were captured and led to the Jewish common grave, where they were shot.

Two Jewish partisans came to Baranowicze from the forest in December 1942 when there were still many Jews in the ghetto. They burst into a German's house and killed him. While they were searching for weapons in the house, some Germans suddenly arrived. One partisan succeeded in escaping, but his comrade, Issy Ozochovsky, was killed together with some Germans by the grenade he threw at them.[15] On the road from Glubok to Polissa, Romka Gnicnowicz killed a German, Kuffenberg, in revenge for his father's murder; together with his comrades he also carried out the execution of the wife of a volksdeutsche, Aditzke, who had taken part in the murder of Jews.

At the initiative of Jewish partisans from Rubzhewicz, a number of partisan units attacked the local German police in the middle of July 1942. They captured some 40 policemen with their commander, and shot them in the market square. Wiszniewo was also attacked by some 200 partisans at Jewish initiative; they captured the collaborators Stankvicz and Torinsky and sentenced them to death by court-martial. In a second attack by some 300 partisans, the town was set on fire.

A few days after the deportation of the Pruzhany Jews at the end of January 1943, a group of Jewish partisans entered the city and blew up the Gestapo building. On the night of 6 February 1944, David Epstein, together with 80 partisans, attacked Lubieszow: ten Germans were killed and 35 Ukrainian policemen were captured. For six weeks Lubieszow was in partisan hands. Eight Ukrainians who had killed Jews were captured by David Epstein. In the spring of 1943, three Jewish partisans volunteered to serve as guides for a partisan attack on Kobylnik. They blew up the railway station, set fire to the home of the mayor, a sworn enemy of the Jews, and left the city in flames. In April 1943 the two Ginzberg brothers blew up the sawmill in the town of Iwje. Sernik was attacked by the "Misiura" partisan unit, in which there were many Jews from that town. They captured local collaborators and executed them. The same unit also attacked the town of Wysock in November 1942.[16]

Noah Volpin, a scout in his partisan unit, made a survey in January 1943 of the town of Stolin and mapped the locations of the German forces in the town. He brought the maps to his commander, Saburov, and a few days later the unit set out to attack Stolin, with Volpin leading the way. Nineteen policemen were captured. Volpin was severely wounded in this battle and it was necessary to amputate both his feet.[17] In January 1943 Czkalow's brigade attacked Horodok. A Jewish partisan, Alterman, was one of the first to break into the town and threw a grenade into the German headquarters. The partisans asked the remaining Jews in the town, 12 in all, to join them, but they refused. In March 1943 a partisan group again broke into the town, captured the mayor and shot him.[18]

The acts of revenge we have mentioned here are only a few examples of a large number of such acts of vengeance by many thousands of Jewish partisans. This provides the wide background and forms the very essence of Jewish partisan combat and goes beyond our limits here. These acts of vengeance produced a tremendous repercussion in the hearts of the Jews in the town, the partisan camps and the family camps, and provided some meaning for their continued existence and desire to fight. Rescue and revenge were at the very heart of the Jewish underground's activities in the ghettos and the partisans' actions in these areas were a natural continuation of that war.

Notes

1. Moshe Shutan, *Ghetto un Wald* (Ghetto and Forest) (Tel Aviv, 1971), p. 175; Ruzhka Korczak, *Lehavot Ba'efer* (Flames in Ash) (Tel Aviv, 1965), p. 159.
2. Shalom Cholawski, *Ir Vaya'ar Bamatzor* (A Town and a Forest under Siege) (Tel Aviv, 1973), pp. 104–106.

3. Moreshet Archive (MA) A-73 (Chjena Lifshin).
4. Mordechai Sajczyk, *Miyomano shel Partizan Nitzol Hasho'ah* (From the Diary of a Partisan Survivor) (Tel Aviv, 1971), pp. 56–56.
5. Moshe Meierson, testimony in *Fun Letztn Churben* (From the recent Destruction), no. 4 (March 1947).
6. Yad Vashem (YV) 03/727 (Yitzhak Friedberg).
7. Dov Amit, testimony in *Sefer Zikaron likehillat Kamin-Koshirsk* (Memorial Book for the Community of Kamin-Koshirsk and Its Environs) (loc. date), pp. 146, 244.
8. Zalman Roichman, testimony in *Churban Glubok, etc ...* (The Destruction of Glubok, etc ...) (Buenos Aires, 1956), p. 370; YV 03/3498 (Shmuel Zaslavsky).
9. MA A-73 (Yossef and Chjena Lifshin).
10. MA A-331 (Ya'akov Sigalczyk); YV 2304/224-P (Moshe Furman).
11. YV 2086/195 (Chana Berkowicz).
12. Yehiel Yosselewicz, testimony in *Pinkas Zhetl* (Zhetl Diary) (Tel Aviv, 1957), p. 404.
13. Baruch Levin, testimony in *Sefer Zholudok veOrlova* (Memorial Book of the Communities of Zhulodok and Orlova) (Tel Aviv, 1967), p. 182.
14. A.L. Poliak, testimony in *Churban Motele* (The Destruction of Motele) (Jerusalem, 1957), p. 73.
15. Avraham Lidovsky, *Bayearot* (In the Forests) (Kibbutz Meuchad, 1946), p. 117. (?)
16. Shaike Osherowicz, testimony in *Sefer Rubzhewicze* (Rubzhewicze Memorial Book) (loc. date), pp. 327–329; *Wiszniewo kefi shehaita ve'einena od* (Wiszniewo, as she was and is no more) (Tel Aviv, 1072), p. 148; Zalman Oriewicz, testimony in *Pinkas Pruzhane, etc ...* (Diary of Pruzhany, etc ...) (Buenos Aires, 1958), p. 599; YV E/48 (David Epstein); Meir Svirsky, testimony in *Sefer Kobylnik* (Kobylnik Memorial Book) (loc. date), p. 248; Mordechai Ginzburg, testimony in *Sefer Zikaron Likehillat Iwje* (Memorial Book of the Iwje Community) (loc. date), p. 571; YV M-1/E 2776/2306 (Shalom Galecki).
17. YV Matzker Collection 0–22 (Noah Volpin); *Forwerts*, 27 August 1947.
18. Moshe Meierson, loc. cit.

CHAPTER 13

Underground and Judenrat

In this chapter we shall examine the complex relationships between the various Judenräte and the Jewish underground organizations. In the previous chapters we have already mentioned the conflicts as well as the positive relationships that existed between them.

In Heydrich's instructions of 21 September 1939, he had declared: "In every Jewish community a council is to be chosen, composed as far as possible of important personalities and rabbis who have remained."[1]

These instructions were further elaborated upon in an order by Hans Frank, Governor-General of the General Government, on 28 November 1939, as follows:

> ... Clause 2: The Judenräte (Jewish councils) are to be elected by members of that community ...
>
> Clause 3: The Judenrat will elect a chairman and vice-chairman from amongst its members.
>
> Clause 4: ... (2) The district head or mayor will decide whether to ratify the suggested composition of the Judenrat. He is empowered also to decide on some other composition.
>
> Clause 5: The Judenrat is obliged to receive, through its chairman or vice-chairman, the German orders. The Judenrat bears responsibility for the full implementation of these orders. The Jewish men and women must accept the Judenrat's authority and fill its instructions with the aim of implementing the Germans' orders.[2]

It appears, then, from the Germans' explicit definition, that the Judenrat was intended to receive German orders and bear responsibility for their implementation. We do not know of instructions given the *reichskommissar* in the eastern region concerning the establishment of Judenräte in the area under his control, but in a secret document labeled: "Temporary instructions for the treatment of the Jews in the eastern region," of 13 August 1941, we read: "... The ghetto inmates shall conduct their internal affairs themselves under the supervision of the district or town commissar or his authorized representative."[3]

In some places in Western Bielorussia, the Jews themselves initiated arrangements with the Germans in order to prevent haphazard kidnappings to forced labor and for a more equitable distribution of the burden of contributions imposed by the Germans upon the Jewish communities. In the main, it was the former public personalities who urged the establishment of "Jewish committees." This happened in Baranowicze, Glubok and Novogrudok.

In Ejszyszky, after Rabbi Shimon Rozovsky was ordered by the German military command to establish a Judenrat, he assembled all the men in the synagogue and informed them of the commander's demand. No candidates volunteered for an election. It was decided, therefore, to choose the twelve persons by lot.[4]

In Zholudok the German authorities demanded in October 1941 that the Jews assemble and elect a Judenrat. A meeting was held, but "actually no one wanted to be a member of the Judenrat. All wanted to escape serving the bloody regime. Despite this, a list of candidates was prepared; the first on the list was Mendel Galai."[5] When Avraham Meir Drewiansky was ordered to join the Judenrat he considered it a great injustice and went to consult his sister-in-law Devorah, an outstanding woman with great moral influence in the town. She supported his joining the Judenrat "because we should thereby be close to the burning events and will be able to watch that they do not cause injustice or make mistakes."[6]

After the heads of the first Lida Judenrat — Kalman Lichtman, Simcha Kotok and the advocates, Israel Kreczner and Benjamin Cederowicz — were murdered, the Germans issued an order for the election of a second Judenrat. No one was found eager to enter the Judenrat ... There was, however, no choice, and a new Judenrat was somehow established. It was Dr. Charny's lot to be elected chairman of the second Judenrat.[7] In Michaliczky the chairman of the existing council, the *gemina* Ora Bleicher, was ordered to choose the Judenrat. When the matter came to elections it appeared that no one desired the honor. All were afraid of the responsibility connected with the position."[8]

After the members of the first Judenrat in Slonim were executed, it was not easy to form a second one. People feared to be part of the Judenrat lest they share the fate of the first members. In the great *aktzia* of 14 November 1941, all the members of the second Judenrat were killed. When Jeliszewicz volunteered for the Judenrat, people considered this a very strange act. In Radun "People did not willingly to be members of the Judenrat and to meet the Germans, but they recognized the necessity of leading the town and of representing it before the tyrant …"[9]

In Janow near Pinsk the former chairman of the Jewish community, Alter Dubinsky, was called to German headquarters and ordered to establish a Judenrat. Since he had previously always been the community chairman, they asked Dubinsky to accept the role of chairman this time as well. At first he refused, but finally yielded.[10] After the Judenrat appeared in the German headquarters and heard what its members could expect in the event of their not fulfilling orders, the men returned to the general meeting. When Dubinsky completed his remarks, he burst into tears and all the assembly wept with him.

In Drohyczyn, too, Jews refused to be elected to the Judenrat. There were places where members of a candidate's family were opposed to his election and he deferred to their opinion.[11] In many other cases the persons who joined the Judenrat, either by election or appointment, did so with much reluctance and real fears. There were reasons for this: the degree of responsibility; the heavy presentiments concerning the Germans' intentions; the fears of conflict within the Jewish community and personal fear of the Germans, with their demands and the possible consequences of not implementing them.

According to Frank's instructions, as mentioned above, the Judenrat's election required the ratification of the authorities, who could also alter its composition. Actually, in most cases, the authorities made no changes in the list of members submitted to them. The Germans imposed both personal and collective responsibility upon the Jewish representatives.

We may assume that Heydrich wanted respected personalities in the Judenräte for two reasons: one to exploit those with executive ability among the Jews; and secondly to discredit the Jewish leadership in the eyes of their community.[12] The Judenräte were established in order to serve as a tool for the implementation of the Germans' plans and their functions lay in three fields:

1. Tasks imposed upon them by the Germans as for example to prepare lists for compulsory labor, deportations, the collection of money, clothing, jewelry and other articles for the Germans;
2. Social functions within the ghetto; and
3. Responsibility for food supplies for the ghetto, for the police, etc.

Immediately after the establishment of the Judenräte in 1939 in Poland in the area of the General-Government, the German authorities demanded lists of the Jewish population. At that time, the Germans' intentions concerning the Jews were still unclear. Some of the Judenräte; however, had later to play a terrible and tragic role by preparing lists for deportations after rumors began to filter through concerning the murder camps to which the deportees were being sent.

In Western Bielorussia (as in other regions in the east), except for isolated cases like Oszmiana, Lida and Pruzhany, the Germans carried out their *aktzias* of annihilation against the Jews near the places where they lived and did not send them to murder camps. The Judenräte in Western Bielorussia and in most of the ghettos that had previously been under the Soviet regime, were therefore not given orders to prepare lists for deportation. The mass executions in Western Bielorussia were carried out soon after the occupation by leading the Jews, after the *selektzia*, directly from the town square to nearby murder sites. The terrible chasm created in other places, in central and western Poland, in western Europe and other occupied lands, between the Judenrat that prepared the lists and the people who were eventually murdered was therefore avoided here. That was a very important factor affecting the Judenrat's image in the eyes of the Jewish population in the ghettos of Western Bielorussia.

After the wave of *aktzias* in the Western Bielorussia ghettos, a considerable number of Judenräte tended to accept the view that it was still possible to save something. Some Judenräte even came to terms with the idea that there was a need to sacrifice part of the Jewish population in order to save the rest. A fundamental element in much of the Judenrate's thinking was the illusion that, by working for the Germans, they could save those who had remained. Another element in this conception was the assumption that was still held by a considerable section of the Judenrat members that bargaining and bribes might avert the evil decree. The Germans helped to strengthen these ideas.

At the same time, however, there was some reassessment among the Judenräte, up to the point of their beginning to maintain ties with the underground movements in the ghettos, by cultivating links, providing limited support and assistance or by cooperating with them to a certain degree which varied from time to time. In some cases there was even full identification.

We will examine the Judenräte or the Judenrat members here not only according to their direct cooperation with the underground. For example, Yehoshua Izikson of Baranowicze, who was murdered on 4 March 1942, even before the underground had come into being, won the admiration of his fellow Jews for his activities to the benefit of the ghetto population and his refusal to send young Jews to the Germans.[13]

There were Judenräte where the chairman's personality and approach determined, in practice, the attitude of the Judenrat as a whole to the problems of the ghetto and the underground. In many cases, however, there were members with differing approaches within the same Judenrat. There were Judenräte which had an ambivalent attitude towards the underground; sometimes this attitude prevailed throughout the ghetto's existence, sometimes they opposed the underground at the beginning and, as time passed, came to terms with reality, aiding it and even cooperating with it. In attempting to classify the Judenrate we must not ignore the fact that the spectrum of views was varying and a very broad one, and obviously some views were in the center. We shall classify the Judenrate into three groups:

1. Those Judenräte and Judenrat members who opposed the underground;
2. Judenräte and Judenrat members with an ambivalent attitude towards it;
3. Judenräte and Judenrat members who stood at the forefront in the underground movement.

Judenräte which Opposed the Underground

The Iwje Judenrat, which had been elected on 12 August 1941 in keeping with the order received by Rabbi Perlman, was headed by Moshe Kopold, a refugee from Krakow. The police was headed by Yoel Girshowicz. The Iwje Judenrat was opposed to the underground's activities and argued that they were endangering the ghetto.[14] The Judenrat and some of the Jewish policemen were very severe with the ghetto population in collecting goods and money for the Germans. When the Ginzberg brothers planned to get two Bielorussian policemen intoxicated in order to kill them and take their weapons, Libman, a Judenrat member intervened and prevented them from doing so. The families of the Judenrat members were moved from Iwje to Lida, something that aroused the anger of the other Jews. Some of the policemen, however, including their commander, Girshowicz, supported the underground.

In Oszmiana, the city rabbi had been ordered to establish a Judenrat and its chairman was a refugee, Grop.[15] When the Germans decided, in October of 1942, to "narrow" the ghetto and Jewish policemen came from the Vilno ghetto to carry out the deportation, it was the Judenrat that prepared the list of elderly persons to be "deported".

After the first *aktzia* in Baranowicze on 3 March 1942, and after Yehoshua Izikson's murder, a second Judenrat was formed, headed by Shmuel Jankelevicz. His influence was limited and two other Judenrat members, who were strong in their opposition to the underground, had great influence. In July 1942 these Judenrat members arrested two members of the underground and threatened to hand them over to the Gestapo if the underground were not disbanded. During the second *aktzia*, in September 1942, a member of the Judenrat issued an ultimatum to the underground that they hand over their arms or the membership would be turned over to the German police. The underground suggested the compromise of hiding the weapons in the ghetto and in this way settled the dispute.[16] The Judenrat headed by Jankelevicz stopped the growing flight to the forest. The chairman attempted to explain this conduct by his being between the hammer and the anvil — between partisans' and the Gestapo's threats.

The Glubok Judenrat headed by Gershon Lederman imprisoned in a basement all Jews who were suspected of planning to escape to the forest. The Judenrat even stationed guards to prevent people from escaping at night. One group of 30 Jews who had fled the ghetto was discovered by police in the cemetery and returned to the ghetto.[17] Hinde and Shabtai Gutkin were arrested and shot by the Germans because members of their family had escaped. The attitude of the Jewish police towards the Jews of the ghetto was not all of one piece. There were some who believed that it was permissible to sacrifice the individual for the "general welfare". They therefore provided the Germans with Jews, sometimes for labor and sometimes — for execution.

The Dolhinov Judenrat chairman, Niomka Ryer, imposed all of his influence upon the hundreds of Jews who still remained in the ghetto; when partisans attacked the town, he did not permit them to escape to the forest.[18] The chairman of the Lachowicz Judenrat threatened a group of Jews about to escape to the forest that he would betray them to the Germans.[19]

The Swienciany Judenrat refused to accede to the underground's request for money with which to purchase weapons; only under the pressure of underground members who came armed to the Judenrat, did it yield. There were other Judenrat members, however, who had a positive attitude towards the underground organization's acquiring weapons and saw the fighting organization's presence in the ghetto as a prospect of saving at least a few.[20]

The Novogrudok Judenrat and police were opposed to fleeing to the forest and thwarted it. The police used to take the shoes of suspected persons for the night and return them in the morning. A second Judenrat was organized after the first *aktzia* and most of its members were executed during the second one. Then Daniel Ostashinsky was appointed Judenrat chairman. He was later to be active in organizing the escape via the tunnel.

Members of the Pinsk Judenrat, established in the middle of July 1941, took an active part in assembling the Jews before the murder in the first *aktzia* on 5 August 1941.[21] Some of the Judenrat members died in that *aktzia*, but there was strong hostility toward those Judenrat members who had remained with their children. "You and your children did not go to the roll call, but our husbands and fathers you sent to be killed," was hurled at them. When the Judenrat learned that the underground was organizing in the ghetto, its members warned the underground not to endanger the ghetto by ill-considered actions and persuaded young people not to escape. When a group of young workers fled outside the city from their places of work, Judenrat members came to their families and threatened that the parents would be taken in their children's place if they did not bring them back to the ghetto. Indeed, under the pressure of the Judenrat and the parents and because of the lack of any contact with the partisans, the young people returned to the ghetto after two days. When rumors were spread in October 1942 of pits being dug, the German commander had invited the Judenrat chairman Minsky and his colleagues come to him and calmed them with a story that the pits were to be used to store fuel and that the Jews were working for the German war effort. Minsky and his colleagues passed on the soothing words verbatim without any warning or reservations. Two attempts to organized escapes were postponed because of these calming words. The Jewish police's second commander, Goldberg, however maintained contacts with the ghetto underground.

The Kurzeniec Judenrat chairman, Szaf, a refugee, requested that parents prevent their children from escaping, since it endangered all the ghetto's Jews. Otherwise, he would hand over to the Gestapo the members of the families of those escaping. In Rubzhewicze the Judenrat and its chairman were opposed to any escape to the forest or armed resistance, since these would hasten the ghetto's liquidation. Six Jews who had escaped from Kajdanow reached Rubzhewicze and the police demanded that the Judenrat surrender them. Despite the local rabbi's decision relying on a biblical precedent that, according to *Halakha*, these refugees should be turned over in order not to bring death to the ghetto's inhabitants, the Judenrat members refused to heed this decision but instead bribed the German commander and did not betray the refugees.[22]

During the last period of the Lida ghetto's existence the two foremen, Altman and Alperstein, practically ran the ghetto's affairs. They knew of the partisan emissaries who had reached the ghetto and warned against any escaping to the forest. Altman assembled all the shopworkers, told them how valued they were, spoke of the ghetto's prospects of surviving and in sharp words condemned the irresponsibility of those escaping to the forest and thus endangering all the ghetto's inhabitants in their desire to save their own lives. He also went on to describe the sad lot of Jews who had gone to the forest. The bitter dispute with Alperstein has been described by the partisan and underground member, Baruch Levin. This was after news had reached Alperstein that Levin was preparing weapons and organizing the underground for an escape. Levin relates:

> I was invited to him one day and he began to speak to me very seriously and with great concern. "You must know," Alperstein said to me, "that if we still have any dream left us, it is the dream that some few of us will remain; believe me, I do not hope to be among those few. Let us hope that someone will remain to tell about what happened here, when the time comes." I remember that he was very emotional in talking and he began to walk back and forth in the room ... "And now someone comes," Alperstein hurled at me, "and with his actions is destroying that small prospect. The whole world ... a

great and tremendous world, is bowing before the Germans and here someone comes who has already lost his family and his father's house and has only one thing left — a rusty rifle, and that man will get up and suddenly shoot one pif-paf from his rifle and seal the end of the one and only prospect."

I sat sunken into myself and listened silently to his words, uttered with pain and sorrow and great emotion, but I knew that I must not be moved, not become confused but reply strongly and vigorously."

Levin's reply was that he had more than one rusty rifle, and especially the necessary courage, when his heart would tell him to act. He promised that he would not cause any provocation liable to cause harm to others and said that he had not exploited such opportunities that there had been, when *generalkommissar* Kube and his company had visited Lida. Levin ended his words with a sharp warning that if Alperstein decided to betray him to the Germans he would not be deterred from killing him.

The underground continued its activity in Lida until the ghetto's last day on 18 September 1943. When Lida's last Jews were being carried away by train, Dr. Grow, the last Judenrat chairman, went from car to car to convince the Jews that "there was no reason not to believe the Germans that they were moving them to a different place of work."

Sympathetic or Ambivalent Attitudes towards the Underground

We will now study those Judenräte who assisted or cooperated with the underground or maintained an ambivalent attitude towards it, that is — that had a sympathetic attitude at some stages of its activity and a reserved one at others. The Germans demanded of the Ostrin Judenrat chairman, Josef Vigdorovicz, that he prepare a list of all the young Jews fit for work. He replied: "I have no young Jews; if you like, take me to work in their stead." He was arrested on the spot and sent to a concentration camp, where traces of him disappeared. In May 1942 the Germans demanded 100 Jews of Finger, chairman of the Volozhin Judenrat. He refused and was shot in public.[24]

When rumors reached the Kleck ghetto on 21 July 1942 of an impending *aktzia*, some 200 young people met in order to prepare for an escape from the ghetto. Judenrat chairman Cerkowicz came and asked them not to do anything liable to lead the ghetto's annihilation. After he heard their refusal he told them to act as they saw fit, began to weep and went away.[25]

The chairman was convinced of the correctness of the young people's intentions, while they were impressed by his arguments — and remained.

Yitzhak Janovitz was appointed Judenrat chairman in Pruzhany. He was assisted by Z. Segal, a local man who lived a long time in Danzig. The Judenrat members were known for their efforts on behalf of the public welfare and their decency and therefore won the appreciation of the ghetto's inhabitants. The Judenrat carried on wide activities — it received wages for the residents' labor, imposed taxes and even engaged in smuggling for the inhabitants' benefit. Janovitz saw a danger to the ghetto in the underground's existence. He rejected the underground's suggestion of escaping from the ghetto, but as more rumors began arriving of Jews being murdered in other ghettos, his attitude towards the underground changed and became more positive. The advocate Shreibman, the Judenrat vice-chairman, became the head of the underground's arms stores. Wooden stocks for the rifles were even prepared in his home. The Judenrat, that now agreed to young people leaving for the forest, only asked that they leave as individuals or small groups so as not to arouse too much attention. On the night of the deportation (27 January 1943), Shreibman suggested that the ghetto resist but his proposal was rejected by all the other Judenrat members.

In Stolpce the Judenrat chairman cooperated with the underground and refused to hand young Jewish women over to the Germans. The ghetto inhabitants' refusal to respond to the Germans demands for clothing and money served as the background for conflicts between them and the Judenrat.[26] The chairman of the first Judenrat in Slonim, Wolf Berman, enjoyed great prestige in the ghetto. Members of the Judenrat assisted the underground in providing clothes and shoes that had been sewn and manufactured in the ghetto for the partisans.[27] The first Judenrat in Lida, that was headed by Kalman Lichtman, assisted many Jewish refugees who had fled from Vilno, by providing forged papers and other aid. After some incidents the members of this Judenrat were executed by the Germans. Of the Judenrat which followed headed by Dr. Czarny, the partisan Dr. Alpert writes:

> ... I want to stress the active assistance of the Lida Judenrat and of the police commanders there to anyone desiring to leave for the forest ... In my meeting with the Judenrat chairman I told him that I was leaving for the forest. He only wondered, 'How will you exist in the forest?' because of the problems of water and shelter in the hard winter ...[28]

In Mir the members of the underground looked upon the Judenrat people as decent persons. There was cooperation between the underground and the Judenrat in the field of intelligence at the time of an escape, but there was a sharp dispute between them in the fields of weapons and plans for self-defence.

Yehoshua Izikson, chairman of the first Baranowicze Judenrat, believed that he could avert the German schemes through bribes. He did indeed succeed in doing so a number of times. He provided the Germans with many things, but when he was asked to provide Jews on the eve of the *aktzia*, he replied: "I have given you everything you asked for, but Jews I will not give you because I am not the master of human lives." For that, he and his secretary were sentenced to death. The members of the Baranowicze underground held the first Judenrat in high esteem as "people with a clear conscience who worked with great devotion."[29]

Judenrat in the Forefront of Revolt

This third group of Judenrate who lead the revolt, existed in only a few ghettos, where Judenrat members were active in the underground or played a central role in the spontaneous uprisings by the ghetto's Jews. They also maintained continuing cooperation with the underground or initiated resistance activities.

In June 1942 rumors reached Szarkowszczyzna of a possible *aktzia* in the neighborhood. The German commander soothed Judenrat chairman Berman by saying that the army movements in the region were connected with military exercises. The Judenrat, however, doubted this and issued instructions to the Jews to escape to the forest. Some 1,200 Jews fled outside the ghetto.[30]

The Germans ordered the Disna Judenrat chairman, Rochlin, to assemble the old and weak. The Judenrat refused to obey these instructions and when the ghetto was surrounded in the middle of June 1942 by German and local forces, the Judenrat members set fire to the ghetto's houses. The Germans opened fire with rifles and machine guns and there were many casualties but some succeeded in escaping.[31]

Alter Dvorecky was the outstanding personality in the Zhetl Judenrat. His intuition led him to establish a fighting underground. He also had eleven underground members enlisted into the local police. In actuality, Dvorecky headed the underground activity in the ghetto; he initiated its activities and organized them.[32]

In the Lachwa ghetto (see also Chapter 9 on the revolt in the ghettos) there was a cooperation between the Judenrat headed by Dov Lopatin and the underground even before the revolt, but this cooperation was limited. The underground's yielding to the Judenrat's request to postpone the uprising's zero hour (set for midnight of 2 September 1942) to the morning of the next day, when it would become clear whether there was any other way out, reinforced the cooperation between the Judenrat and the underground and they became one rebellious body standing at the head of the Jewish population. The problems that divided the underground and the Judenräte and created bitter disputes and even hostility, were life and death issues, of salvation and paths to salvation, and they are the very essence of our discussion of this relationship of undergrounds and Judenräte. The frictions between the Judenrat and the ghetto population were very great particularly since they took place in so densely populated a place as the ghetto and its difficult conditions. These involved problems of housing, food, contributions and the like, problems which, while they were not of the first priority, were nonetheless important.

There are Judenräte about which we have no documentation relating directly to their relationships with the underground but only to their relationships with the people in the ghetto, in detail or in general evaluations. Despite the measure of subjectivity of these testimonies and despite there not necessarily being any identification between Judenrat-underground and Judenrat-population relationships, we can sometimes find in the Judenräte conduct in everyday ghetto life some indirect indication of their attitudes towards the underground and its activities.

Judenräte where the Population Attitude to them was Negative because of their Conduct

In Berezna, Judenrat chairman Yoel Gilber, a one-time public figure, exploited his status in the ghetto for his own benefit and the benefit of the other Judenrat members. He received food for the ghetto but gave only part to the population, taking the rest for himself and his colleagues. He sent the poorer persons to compulsory labor and accepted payment in order to register someone as a craftsmen. The Jewish police, which was headed by Meir Keiler, who considered himself the ghetto ruler, conducted itself with severeness towards the Jewish population.

In Lubieszow, Judenrat chairman Jacob Pelczuk and police commander Shmuel Levin also dealt severely with the ghetto population.

In Brzesc there was a conflict between the Judenrat and the Jewish police. The Judenrat, headed by Rosenblum, acted decently towards the ghetto's population, but the Jewish police headed by a refugee from Biela-Podlaska, Moshe Feldman; and his second, a refugee from Warsaw, inflicted fear upon the Jewish public. Particularly harsh was their attitude towards refugees coming from nearby towns or from the other side of the Bug River. The police deputy commander handed Jewish Communists and other Jews over to the Germans. He also prevented attempts at underground organization or contacts with the Russian partisans. He was murdered by a Jewish policeman in the ghetto and the Judenrat had to bribe the Germans with gifts in order to pass over the incident.[34]

In many other ghettos, too, there were Judenrat members and policemen who were known for their inflexibility, their indifference toward other people's suffering, their heavy handed methods and their concern only for themselves.

Judenräte Held in Esteem because of their Conduct

The Ilja Judenrat, headed by city rabbi Avraham Eli Remez, "conducted itself in the most decent way and took upon itself all the needs of the Jewish population ..." And from another testimony it is clear that: "The Judenrat, under the existing circumstances, did the best it could to avert the evil decree. It acted with honesty and supreme objectivity."[35]

In Bereza-Kartuska the Judenrat and the police conducted themselves fairly towards the Jews of the ghetto. "They were compelled to fulfil the Germans orders but together with that, whenever they could do favors for the Jews they did so." There is an appreciation of the Dokszyce Judenrat headed by Jacob Botvinik: "The ghetto did not suffer from the Judenrat; on the contrary, the Judenrat defended the ghetto."

The Horodok Judenrat, headed by Ephraim Rackin, who had formerly been chairman of the local Jewish *kehilla*, worked to prevent harsh decrees. In order to distribute the burden fairly, it called the Jews to Rabbi Halpern to declare before him the extent of their property.[36] The Jewish police helped to smuggle food into the ghetto. When information was received of arms being brought into the ghetto it warned the smugglers about the dangers of this.

In the spring of 1942 Chaim Bruk, Lubcz's Judenrat chairman, and the policemen Naftali Alperszein and Yitzhak Rosenblum were executed for their refusal to carried out a German order. The chairman of the Lenin Judenrat, Aharon Milner, was very much respected in his city and was known to be honest. The Judenrat was under great pressure of the Germans' demands for goods and money, and some of the Jews revealed their bitterness towards the Judenrat when they were asked to meet the Germans' demands. However, when Milner decided to join the Jews being sent to the Hancevicz work camp, the ghetto Jews pleaded with him to stay with them. Shmuel Verble, chairman of the Kamen-Koshirsk Judenrat, who was known for his fairness, joined 80 Jews who were afterwards executed. He departed from his children with the words: "Children, be good Jews; if you can, take revenge!"[37]

We have documents testifying to the positive attitudes of the Judenrat chairmen and members to ghetto populations in Byten, Rozhanka, Olszany, Braslav, Wasyliszky, the Hancewicz camp, Korelicz, Michaliczky, Wiszniewo, Donilovicz, Druja, Kobryn, Parafianowo, and Szczuczyn.

In Janow-Polesky there was a sharp difference between the Judenrat's positive attitude towards the ghetto population and its negative attitude towards underground organization for escape. On the day of the ghetto's extermination Judenrat chairman Alter Dubinsky was brought before the Germans. He addressed them and said: "Know that your end is near. This will not be forgiven you and I am confident that you will reap your punishment." In the middle of his speech he was shot and fell.[38]

In the course of our study we have attempted to differentiate between the ways the Judenräte and their members operated — in many cases against their will — within the organization into which they had been thrust and which had been established by the Germans to carry out German orders. Did they work for or against the welfare of the ghetto Jews in their everyday lives? To what degree did they face the ghetto Jews' problems of physical existence? Did they oppose or lend their hands to the underground?

We have found various views coming from the Judenräte, even though almost certainly many other views have not come to us and we are aware of the measure of subjectivity on the part of the witnesses in replying to these questions. There were a number of factors that distinguished the characters of the Judenräte in Western Bielorussia:

1. Despite the tragic changes that took place in the life of its Jews with the Nazi invasion and all the other consequences, with the concentration of the Jews in the ghettos, that same way of life, the same moral norms and values that had existed in personal life, in the Jewish home and in Bielorussian Judaism prior to the Holocaust, remained in effect,

sometimes with even greater strength. Almost certainly these qualities were present among many Judenrat members in times of great stress, in the difficult decisions of conscience they faced.
2. There was in this region no assimilated strata of persons like the many who entered the Judenräte in other parts of Poland and in other European countries, particularly in the larger cities, and who served as a murky source of alienation and even of hatred, not a little due to self-hatred, towards the ghetto Jews.
3. The existence of the Jewish towns in which most of the Western Bielorussian Jews lived was within compact and not too large communities, where everybody had known everyone else for years as neighbors and relatives. This had a stimulating effect on the one hand, and a moderating and restraining one on the other, on the Judenräte and their members' attitudes towards the ghetto's problems, the problems of rescuing Jewish individuals and the community as a whole, as also in their sense of responsibility towards their communities. To the Judenräte of this region were also elected Jews of the popular strata, even though in most cases those elected were individuals with a past of public activity, and among them some who had won reputations for their devoted public service.

This is the reason for the ghetto Jews' great sensitivity and their suspicions towards the refugees who worked with the Judenräte and in many cases filled the role of chairman or the ghetto's representative to the Germans, often because they knew the German language. In many cases they worked in some estrangement from a public they had not known previously (e.g., in the ghettos of Iwje and Oszmiana) and sometimes they clearly gave priority to their own personal interests before public ones.

Still, we must emphasize the fact that there were, among the refugees, persons who worked for the general welfare as members of the underground and cooperated with the underground when they were Judenrat members. Ghetto life and its unbearable pressures were, of course, sufficient to cause deviations in people's behavior in keeping with their characters. Still, the essential elements of moral conduct and norms were not without their weight. The significant fact that Judenräte in this region were not called upon to prepare lists for deportation, in addition to the factors we have listed above, can help more than a little to explain the image of Judenräte in the eyes of the inhabitants of these ghettos.

There were very few Judenräte in this region which operated in blind obedience to German orders, in full indifference to the fate of the Jews. There were cases where the Judenräte turned Jews over to the Germans but there were very few.

There were cases where the Judenräte or Judenrat members threatened to hand over members of the underground. The very threat of betrayal to the Germans placed the threatened on the other side of the barricade, no matter whether the threat was a real one or only intended to prevent an escape to the forest or the introduction of arms into the ghetto. In almost all cases, however, these remained only threats and were not carried out. We must distinguish between threats which were really meant and threats of a possible or potential act, no matter how serious the latter were in themselves. These latter potential threats had their serious implications for the underground because, in some cases, they inhibited the flight to the forest, prevented the acquisition of arms, narrowed, slowed down and sometimes ended all hopes of smaller or larger groups escaping from the ghetto.

We have previously classified the Judenräte into those which opposed the underground and even threatened to betray it to the Germans, those which cooperated with the underground in some areas and disagreed with in others, and those which took their places at the head of the revolt. We have also distinguished between Judenräte which helped the ghetto Jews and those which were alienated from them.

We should not overlook personal decency and all that it involves as regards honesty and devotion towards the ghetto population, but we must be aware of its limitations given the ghetto's problems. We must distinguish between a Judenrat's decent attitude towards the population and its attitude towards the underground, and especially towards the ghetto's fundamental problems. These, the questions of life and death, of rescue and resistance, were subject to differences, sometimes to dispute, sometimes with divided hearts and sometimes with hostility. Sometimes both paths coincided, at least partly, sometimes almost wholly; sometimes they were completely divergent.

In their confrontation with the underground most of the Judenräte argued that they wanted not to endanger the ghetto's existence. For most of the Judenräte this was a genuine answer; for some — only an argument, since more than a few Judenrat members, in their hearts at least, had come to terms with the fact that in those days there was no avoiding saving what could be saved, even at the terrible price of sacrificing a part in order to save the rest. We should not look upon the division into the first and the second groups as a clear-cut one, since many Judenrat members lived their heavy spiritual crises in a wide gamut of shades between the two extremes.

Let us see what the condition "not to endanger the ghetto's existence" meant. Was not the ghetto, its very existence, in a permanent state of potential danger? What, then, does "endangering mean?" In using the term "the ghetto's existence", the people in the ghetto referred to two concepts. The first: an existential situation of "present existence." Of living from one day to the next. The second: estimating the prospects of human existence, while living in a dangerous situation, for continuity or continuation. In other words: existence in the future by looking for some way out beyond "present existence." The first concept is, of course, the basis for the search for the second.

Concerning the first component — "present existence" in the ghetto, there were hardly any essential differences between the Judenräte which raised this argument honestly and the underground, though the underground found itself facing a not very simple problem in many ghettos: how to act according to its conscience without endangering the lives of the Jews in the ghetto. They, however, saw this imperative and faced it. The history of the underground is one of difficult and tortured deliberations in facing this terrible problem of conscience and more than once the activity itself suffered in order not to put the lives of the ghetto Jews in jeopardy. The Jewish underground in the ghetto, everywhere, had to assume the heavy responsibility of deciding for itself, since there was no central leadership that could make decisions for it and give orders from above.

On the question of the ghetto's "existence in the future," beyond its existence in the present, however, a sharp confrontation developed between most of the Judenräte and the underground. In the course of time the doctrines of the Judenräte were shaken: that "work could save us," that bribery could help, that "ghettos might be made smaller but would not be liquidated." The underground's evaluation of the situation was more frequently proven correct. The underground had dared to ask: what next?

The Judenräte were busy putting out the everyday fires. Some Judenräte, or their leaders, out of an exaggerated self-confidence based perhaps on past experience as public officials, did not grasp the fathomless difference between "then" and "now", and attempted to employ the conventional Jewish diaspora weapons of intervention which in the past had had their small achievements and no less — failures towards a new enemy of a very different kind, who had come to kill. The underground, on the other hand, asked for a solution and provided a daring partial answer.

The underground did not come with an inclusive alternative for all the Jews in the ghetto because it did not have such an alternative. However, in its day-by-day battle in the ghetto to move groups of young people to the forest, to arm them, to establish resistance to the Germans, to rescue Jews or at least some of them, the underground was the alternative force waging a bitter battle against its opponents, showing a way to fight and even opening some prospects, though perhaps only limited ones, for salvation.

The local compositions of the Judenräte and the underground organizations affected the relationships between them in each location. We should also not ignore the accumulating effect of a situation in which two opposing organizations sought the support of the ghetto's Jews.

In not a few ghettos there was cooperation between the Judenrat and the underground, as mentioned previously; in most of these cases this was between individual Judenrat members or group of Judenrat members, and the underground, with the former providing their assistance in some specific field. This cooperation was sometimes accompanied by reservations concerning other underground activities. In more than a few cases, Judenrat members were also active in the underground. In a number of places Judenrat members led the revolt and escape from the ghetto.

On the issue of escaping there was strong opposition on the part of some of the Judenräte, but also agreement on the part of others. Some of the latter looked aside, some provided active assistance, on condition only that it be controlled and carried out in small groups. A large section of the Judenräte reacted very vigorously against bringing arms into the ghetto either for fighting in the forest or combat within the ghetto itself. The sharpest confrontation between the large majority of the Judenräte and the underground was on the subject of the revolt in the ghetto.

The composition of the Judenrat generally influenced the ability of the underground to act in this area. Judenräte which opposed the underground's activities worked against escape and acts of revolt. The Judenräte for the most part did not interpret the situation correctly. They either did not grasp its unique nature, attempted to ignore what they understood, or refused to face it. They thereby came into essential conflict with the underground, which had very clearly seen the aims of the Germans' annihilation policies, warned against them and mobilized Jews in the ghettos to fight and save themselves.

Notes

1. Nuremberg Documents (IMT) PS-3363.
2. Yad Vashem (YV), *Verordnunqsblatt G-G, Polen* (Official Gazette, Generalgouvernment of Poland), Verordnug veber die Einsetzung von Judenraeten vom. 28 (translation), (November 1939).
3. Isaiah trunk, *Judenrat* (New York, 1972), p. 6.
4. Ribak Ben-Shemesh (Shalom Sonnensohn), testimony in *Eishishok, Koroteha Vechurbana* (Eiszyszky, Its History and Its Destruction) (Jerusalem, 1950), p. 61.
5. Moshe Beirach, testimony in *Sefer Zholudok ve Orlova* (Memorial Book of the Communities of Zhulodok and Orlova) (Tel Aviv, 1967), p. 243.
6. YV 3458/311 (Moshe Beirach).
7. Leizer Engelshtern, testimony in *Sefer Lida* (Lida Memorial Book) (Tel Aviv, 1970), p. 325.
8. YV E/286 (Ore Bloicher).
9. YV 03/508 (Avraham Aviel).
10. Symposium of Yanov Survivors at Yad Vashem, 7 June 1964, YV 2622/67-N.
11. Yaffa Plotnik, testimony in *Sefer Zikaron likehillat Kamin-Koshirsk Vahasvivah* (Memorial Book for the Community of Kamin-Koshirsk and Its Environs) (loc. date), p. 743.
12. Aharon Weiss, *The Jewish Police in the General Government and Upper Silesia during the Holocaust*, PhD Thesis (Hebrew University, 1973).
13. Elizer Lidovsky, testimony in *Sefer Zikaron Baranowicz* (Baranowicze Memorial Book) (loc. date), p. 467.
14. YV M-1/E 2338/2387 (David Baksht); YV 1772/96 (Elimelech Melamed); Moshe Kaganowicz, testimony in *Sefer Zikaron likehillat Iwje* (Memorial Book of the Iwje Community) (loc. date), p. 530.
15. Shraga Faiwushewicz, testimony in *Sefer Oszmiane* (Osmiane Memorial Book) (Tel Aviv, 1969), p. 335.
16. Lidovksy, loc. cit.
17. Michael Z. Rayak, testimony in *Churban Glubok, etc* … (The Destruction of Glubok, etc …) (Buenos Aires, 1956), p. 155.
18. YV 03/3483 (Avraham Klorin).
19. Yossef Pecker & Zalman Rabinowicz, testimonies in *Sefer Zikaron Lachowicze* (Lachowicz Memorial Book) (Tel Aviv, 1969), p. 315.
20. Yisrael Kochalski, in *Undzer Weg* (Our Path) (Munich, 4 January 1946).
21. Nachum Boneh, testimony in *Sefer Zikaron Pinsk* (Pinsk Memorial Book) (Tel Aviv, 1969), p. 328. Judenrat members went out into the streets and declared: "all those above the age of 16 have to present themselves".

Thousands came, but many refused and hid. Parents and wives also urged the men: "you have to go. You will work for a few days and then return. Why should you endanger our lives? Surely we will all die if you refuse to go."

22. The Halakha ruling related Samuel 2, 20:1; see YV 03/725 (Shalom Yoran); Moreshet Archive (MA) A-7 (Rivka Gewint); Ze'ev Rabunsky, testimony in *Meqillat Kurnitz* (Kurzeniec) (translation) (Tel Aviv, 1956), p.155; Yehiel Sigalowicz, testimony in *Sefer Rubzhewicze* (Rubzhewicze Memorial Book) (location, date), p. 351.
23. Baruch Levin, testimony in *Sefer Zholudok veOrlova*, op. cit., p. 117.
24. YV 1009/106-P (Hersh Perski).
25. YV 2214/24-P (Yitzhak Preiss).
26. YV 723/39-M (Eliezer Melamed).
27. Kalman Lichtenstein, testimony in *Pinkas Slonim* (Slonim Diary) (Tel Aviv, 1962), p. 68.
28. YV 2838/207-A (Dr. Alpert).
29. Lidovsky, op. cit., p. 467.
30. Rayak, op. cit., p. 105.
31. YV M-1/E 1573/1448 (Eliahu Abramson).
32. MA D. 2. 105/16 (Shalom Gerling).
33. Of. Dr Bigl (ed.), *Mein Stettele Berezne* (My Shtetl Brezna) (Tel Aviv, 1954).
34. L. Gluzman, testimony in *Sefer Brisk* (Brzezc Memorial Book) (Tel Aviv, 1954), p. 485; Sh. Winograd, ibid., p. 522.
35. Yonah Rier, testimony in *Sefer Ilja, Yizkor-Buch* (Ilja Memorial Book) (Tel Aviv, 1962), p. 427.
36. YV 216/204-F (Batya Fren): YV 2938/63-T (Moshe Tuchman).
37. YV 1038/921 (Lipe Misholow); also, *Sefer Zikaron Kehillat Lenin* (Memorial Book for the Community of Lenin) (Tel Aviv, 1957), pp. 51, 198; Shoshana Partchik, testimony *in Sefer Zikaron likehillat Kamin-Koshirsk Vahasvivah*, op. cit., p. 637.
38. Symposium of Yanov Survivors, op. cit.

CHAPTER 14

The Non-Jewish Population's Attitude Towards the Jews During the Holocaust

The non-Jewish population's attitudes toward the Jews in Western Bielorussia were determined by the national and ethnic characters of the various population groups residing in the region, the political changes they had gone through and the neighborly relations that had been formed in the course of generations of living together. These relations had been replete with both crises and periods of relaxation but were relatively better than in the neighboring regions of Ukraine and Lithuania. The period of Polish independence had aggravated the attitudes of the non-Jews towards the Jews and the period of the Soviet regime, 1939–1941, saw the growth of antisemitic tensions that had previously lain dormant beneath the surface. With the German's arrival, Nazi ideology found fertile soil for its propaganda and infected the non-Jewish population with a racialist antisemitism in its own spirit.

Before the German's Arrival

During the short interim period between the Red Army's retreat at the end of June 1941 and the German's arrival, members of the non-Jewish town population and peasants from the surrounding villages carried out acts of robbery, pogroms and murder against the Jewish population. Here are some examples:

In Iwje hundreds of peasants in groups invaded Jewish homes and looted property — goods, furniture, and other articles, loaded them onto wagons and brought it to their homes. The same happened in Novogrudok,

Korelicz, Wasyliszky, Kamen-Koshirsk, Szarkowszczyzna, Kurzeniec. The self-defense exercised by groups of young Szarkowszczyzna Jews caused the rioter to retreat.

In Naliboky the bands broke into Jews homes, robbed, mistreated the aged and the women to the sound of music, hit at the Jews with wet whips and commanded them to dance. The local priest, who in the past had been known as a notorious antisemite, asked his people to stop but was not obeyed.[2] The Polish doctor and a group of Polish intellectuals led the attack on the Jews of Miory. When the Jews of Lubcz returned to their town from the fields to which they had fled because of the German air-raids, they saw peasants rushing away with their wagons loaded with stolen Jewish property and preparing for a second attack. "Their faces were excited, their eyes burned with wild hatred and the lust for revenge. We immediately understood that our fates had been sealed to destruction and death."[3]

One day after the Russians' retreat from Lubieszow, the Ukrainians, with the help of the Poles, conducted a pogrom and killed 24 Jews. The Ukrainians announced: "We know what the Germans are going to do to you; we'll help them!" A Jewish "self-defense" group, armed with axes and iron bars, battled with the Ukraninas and, after an extended struggle, the rioters were compelled to retreat. The night after that the rioters went to the neighboring village of Lubiezh and murdered all six Jewish families there, 20 persons in all. The Germans afterwards executed three of the murderers.[4] Pogroms were conducted by the non-Jewish population also in Sernik, Stolin and Pniewa.

The Germans Arrive

When the Germans arrived part of the population received them with demonstrative enthusiasm and bitter hatred for the Jews. In Dolhinov, for example, the inhabitants erected an arch of honor for the German invaders and received the soldiers with flowers.[5] The non-Jewish population received the Germans with joy in Slonim and Rubla. Peasants raised glasses in honor of the first two Germans to reach Kobylnik. One peasant, Krolak, who had worked for many years for Jews and knew Yiddish, made a speech in the Germans' honor and promised to help them in any way he could to rule out Jewish rule. On 11 July 1941, the local inhabitants conducted a pogrom against the Jews. In some places the inhabitants went on with a pogrom they had begun before the Germans' arrival (Kurzeniec and Stolin), and in other places renewed it after a pause (Lubcz, Szarkowszczyzna, Iwje, Zuszky).

Jews had fled from some places to Russia at the outbreak of the war, but most had returned to their towns worn out by the difficulties they had undergone. Their abandoned homes had served as objects for looting by the local inhabitants and the neighboring peasants. However, after having broken into these homes, which had been abandoned temporarily, they moved on to other populated homes which were still occupied. In one place the Germans deliberately drove the Jews into an open field in order to provide the local populace with an opportunity to riot and rob, which they did.

The acts of robbery and the pogroms conducted by the non-Jewish population both before and after the Germans' arrival, reflected the Bielorussians' previously restrained hatred. These acts were the beginning of a dynamic process and a portent of what was to come, according to the axiom of one crime leading to a still greater crime. The members of the non-Jewish population who committed the robberies, who had been intent at first only on the loot, began, in the depths of their hearts, to think of removing the Jews in any way possible in order to ensure the stolen property remained permanently in their possession. "Those who robbed Jewish property, hoped for their deaths," testifies Chaim Ben-Aryeh of Braslav and these words some partial explanation for future events.

The pogroms took places in regions that had been surfeited with anti-Jewish feeling even before the Germans' arrival but we can recognize German inspiration. The slogan of "One Jew less", matched the Germans' "purification goals". The aspect of the non-Jewish population participating in the *aktzias* against the Jews was important for the Germans. They were interested in the civilian population taking an active role, on its own initiative, in the murder operations. They considered this important for foreign propaganda. Dr. Stahlecker, commander of Einsatzgruppe A, wrote:

> It is not less important for our future goals to establish the irrefutable fact that the liberated population had adopted the most serious measures against the Bolshevist and Jewish enemy on its own initiative and without any instructions of the German authorities."[6]

Nonetheless, the scope of the pogroms in Bielorussia did not satisfy *Einsatzgruppen* and they blamed this on the Bielorussians' political "passivity and indifference". The Germans were happy to discover the non-Jewish population's negative attitude towards the Jews' "leading role at the time of the Soviet regime," but at first were not satisfied by the support provided by the local population to the German authorities in the measures adopted by them against the Jews.[7]

From the standpoint of current security, however, the German Army units had a different approach. These did not view the pogroms too favorably: "We must by all means prevent 'lynch' trials against the Jews and all other terror." The military forces will not tolerate one terror (Soviet) to be replaced by another, the German Army commanders declared. This of course did not reflect any love for the Jews or any basically different approach towards the Jews. Almost certainly the German Army, which was responsible for security in the rear too, saw a potential danger in the existence of armed and unruly bands which might begin with action against the Jews and in the course of time were liable to serve as nuclei for partisan warfare against the Germans themselves. The German authorities also believed that the Jews must be liquidated, but only with their permission.[8]

Hatred, Alienation, Mockery and Spite

As German propaganda against the Jews increased and also the acts of degradation and mistreatment, the hostility of wide sections of the non-Jewish population towards the Jews also intensified. "All the peasants have been poisoned; they feel great hatred towards us." That hatred was reflected at the very beginning of the German occupation and bore the seeds of the criminal actions in the future. The expressions of this attitude towards the Jews were varied: alienation, mockery, spiteful joy at their misfortune, and sometimes a combination of all these together. "On the part of the surrounding population there was total alienation towards the Jews and even towards former friends. Many had their eyes on the Jewish property."[9] Non-Jews ceased greeting their Jewish neighbors. They mistreated Jews in the streets. The wicked and brutal attitude of the large sections of the non-Jewish population towards the Jews was revealed in many places in this region.

> The hatred surrounding the ghetto was very dense. You sensed that something latent had come to the surface. The Polish settlers were almost all of them antisemitic and in the Soviet era that hatred had become even deeper. The Germans reinforced that hatred. If a western people like Germans consider hatred of the Jews so important a goal, then there must be something in it … The Bielorussians were no better than the Poles.

> A short time ago they carried us to work in Kleck by car ... Suddenly we saw someone running towards us and shouting ... We discovered that he was cursing the Jews in Bielorussian; cursing wildly by the automobile. I, wondered where that man had gotten that accumulation of hatred. His eyes were burning. The German accompanying us pushed him away; he was our 'defender!'[10]

Sometimes the hatred expressed itself in mockery and sometimes in humiliating actions: "A frightened dog was running alongside us, a pair of *Tefilin* (phylacteries) bound to his head and back. A gentile came up to me and asked, half-seriously and half in mockery: 'So, where is your God?'[11] When the Germans were leading the Volozhin Jews to the death pits through the Christian streets, young Christian men and women came out of their houses and played enthusiastically on their accordions, sang songs, began to dance and to insult the Jews. After the *aktzia* in Nieswiez, in which 4,000 Jews were murdered, the rest were compelled to move to the ghetto.

> The Jews hurried, eyes filled with tears. They could not look into the eyes of those standing in the streets, most of whom were indifferent and some spiteful happy. By my house on the corner of the street stood my neighbor, young M ... leaning on a telephone pole, and when he saw me he began to whistle his pleasure. That whistling cut into my flesh and to this day echoes in my ears ...[2]

Settling Past Accounts

Members of the non-Jewish population found it a propitious time to revenge themselves on the Jews and ran to Germans with every past complaint — against a Jew teacher who had given his Polish student a bad mark once; against a Jew in Oszmiana who had dismissed a non-Jewish watchman; against a young Jew in Pinsk who during the Soviet era had caught a Christian woman stealing wooden boards, for which she had been sentenced to imprisonment. Informers told the Germans about that the Jews had carried work out for the Soviets during their regime in the Western Bielorussian region.

Property in Trust

When the acts of robbery began, as well as the collection of valuables and jewelry for the Germans, Jews turned to their former neighbors and wanted to entrust their property to them until times changed. Some even hoped to find shelter with their gentile friends because of that property. Members of the local population, including former friends, began to visit Jewish homes and to urge them not to leave their property to the Germans but rather to deposit it in their hands. There were also those who spread rumors of anti-Jewish killing operations in other places in order to encourage Jews to entrust them with their property. The wiser Jews were careful not to entrust them with their property to the Christians since the trustees could turn on them and might be the first to seek their elimination in order to enjoy the spoils. When the Jews came to peasants they reported that these Jews were Communists and they were executed. Christians came to Jewish families and attempted to convince them: "In any case they are going to murder you, at least let your houses remain in our hands." There were some few cases of peasants who concealed Jews in return for their property until the arrival of the liberating Red Army.

Informing, Betrayal and Incitement to Murder Jews

Informing against Jews was a common phenomenon. One Lithuanian, Rakocky, informed on Berl Lipkonsky of Radun saying that he was a Communist because a bicycle had once been stolen from in front of his house. Lipkonsky and the members of his family were executed.[13] Peasants from Rubla went to Luniniec and informed the Germans that the Jews of David-Horodok possessed weapons and were plotting with the partisans. The Germans conducted an *aktzia* in David-Horodok and the non-Jewish population enjoyed the spoils.

"All around everybody is hostile to you and if you succeed in escaping from the camp the first gentile will recognize you by your meager Jewish looks and, happy at your end, will turn you over immediately to the Germans or the local police."[14]

Many of the Disna Jews, who had revolted, set fire to their homes and fled; the Kobryn Jews who had escaped to the fields and forest, and Jews of other towns, were betrayed to the Germans by peasants. In return they received sugar and salt. Sometimes it was the peasants who had undertaken to hide the Jews who betrayed or killed them themselves.

Part of the non-Jewish population displayed both insensitivity and brutality. Leah Levin, who was standing by the deportation cars, was approached by a Lithuanian woman who asked her if she was prepared to give her shoes in return for some cheeses. "I motioned to her to go away. She said that I didn't have to be stingy since they were taking us to our death. I spat in her face ..."[15] Non-Jewish inhabitants pressed the German authorities and wrote petitions to the occupation forces to accelerate the execution of the Jews.[16]

Helping the Germans Murder Jews

In many places members of the local population actively assisted the Germans in murdering Jews. That happened in Pinsk, in Braslav, in Motele, Oszmiana, Dereczyn, Novogrudok, Lachwa, Miory and many other towns. In Pruzhany a crowd of Christians gathered at the ghetto gate before the *aktzia* and waited impatiently for the looting to begin. "Their eyes gleamed like beasts of prey on the hunt."[17] In Kurzeniec a large crowd went to look for hidden Jews, shouting as they did so: "Kill the Jews!" In Szarkowszczyzna peasants from the village of Palileik murdered Jews who were fleeing to the forest. In Kurzeniec the Russian Orthodox priest made inflammatory sermons in the church on Sundays: "Take axes, take hoes, destroy the Jews!"[18]

In Slonim, and in Wiszniewo, Dvorec, Zholudok, Nieswiezh, and other towns, crowds of neighborhood peasants assembled neared the ghetto on the day of the *aktzia* in order to gain the property of the Jews being murdered before their eyes. When Jews found shelter, they killed them. In Donilovicz they even desecrated the bodies of the Jews they found in the shelters, pulled out gold teeth and opened a dirt-covered common grave in order to look for gold.[19] On the day of the second *aktzia* in the Baranowicze ghetto peasants, women and children rushed to take the loot and even stripped the bodies of the dead. Even after the Jews in the ghetto were all dead, their former Christian neighbors continued to look for booty. In Janow near Pinsk peasants returning from town passed a field strewn with corpses and they sat happily in their plunder-laden wagons. Jews who returned to their towns after liberation were welcomed by the peasants with the question: "Are you still alive?"[20]

The Friends

In all this tremendous sea of hatred there were also persons with consciences who expressed their sentiments in encouraging words, in acts if assistance and rescue at the risk of their own lives, and there were those who paid for this with their lives.

Moral Encouragement

To say a good word in favor of the Jews was also sometimes no less dangerous than active assistance.

> ... The miller in the Zholudok region was a man with a heart who was troubled by the Jews' suffering and desired to help them. More than once I was troubled by the Jews' suffering and desired to help them. More than once I heard him preach morality to the villagers coming to his mill: "You must reveal a measure of mercy. As long as the Jews exist you can be sure that you too will live. But after they liquidate the Jews the Germans will turn their death weapons at you." These arguments were very practical ones but he also had moral arguments which he employed."[21]

Rivka Dudik and her family fled from Kurzeniec to a village and were received by the Smitenko peasant family with warm words: "You are not miserable, you are heroes ..." In Nieswiezh there were a number of Poles who maintained friendly relations with Jews.

> The Polish teacher, Volodka, a number of times left small packages of food by the fence near our house. The geography teacher, Tomaka, when we met him in the street, would come off the sidewalk and walk towards me on the street, take off his hat and bow. That act meant more in my eyes than any help ... The same is true for the principal of the former Polish high school, the pastor Grodis, who was beloved by his students and especially the Jewish ones ... and who expressed his deep shock at the German policies towards the Jews and respected the Jewish suffering; but these were so frightfully few ...[22]

Assistance and Shelter for Refugees

There were isolated cases where Jews received shelter for a day or a short time among the peasants, but in most cases the Jews were requested because of fear of discovery (sometimes with expressions of sympathy for their trouble) to leave the hiding place in the barn or some pit and go to the forest. There were, however, cases where peasants risked their lives and maintained Jewish families for longer periods.

Bakacz, an inhabitant of Kurzeniec, defended Jews against the rioters and rescued Torah scrolls. After the war he even came to one of the surviving partisans, Alperovicz, with two scrolls and said: "When the others were robbing I did not want their filthy hands to desecrate your holy things, your

Torah. I have kept them as the apple of my eye ... Now I'm giving back to you."[23] In Iwje, in return for a Jewish family's help during the Soviet regime, a Polish shoemaker named Korbat concealed 15 persons in a hidden pit. In the Kobylnik district Josef Tonkewicz concealed 14 Jews. In a village near Stolpce one woman hid six Jews two years under her storehouse floor.

Among the priests, too, there were those who rescued Jews or helped them. There were pastors who attempted to persuade their flocks to cease doing evil to the Jews since no one knew what the morrow might bring, but there were also those among them who were motivated by religious values. The priest Smorczevsky said to a Christian who had saved two Jews: "Save them, that will be the most Christian act."[24] There were religious peasants who hid Jews at their own risk. Especially noteworthy for this attitude were the Baptists, who lived in various places in Western Bielorussia. Posesorsky, who had fled from the Stolpce ghetto found his way to a Baptist's home:

> We were impressed by the nobility prevailing in this house ... They did not give us our bread to eat the way you give it to miserable persons who have aroused your mercy, but treated us with hospitality, the way you receive important persons bringing pleasure and honor to their hosts.
>
> We asked them if they were not afraid because of our being in their house. They replied that they feared only God. "Hitler will not destroy you for you are eternity and Israel is immortal. He is only punishing you for your sins and testing your faithfulness."
>
> We asked him if our sins were greater than the gentiles' sins he replied simply: "No, but you are God's beloved children, the chosen people, and that is why He is punishing you. God chose you purify the world of evil and bring salvation to mankind ..."
>
> He told us he was a blacksmith and that all his family were practicing Baptists ... The landlord read to us parts from a book he had on the mission of the people of Israel in the future, as the leader of all the nations ...
>
> I did not believe in the contents of what he was saying, but listened closely to how a pleasant and warm voice was telling us, the persecuted and unwanted, with deep faith, completely earnestly, that we were the redeeming people, for whom everything had been created ... God's elect and precious children ... We sat there and our eyes shone.[25]

There were those who paid with their lives for helping Jews. That is what happened to the Russian Orthodox priest in Kobylnik who was shot by

Germans when he responded to the request for aid by some Jews after his Catholic colleague had turned them away.

Summing up

The non-Jewish population of Western Bielorussia was composed of Bielorussians, Poles, Ukrainians and Lithuanians. The Bielorussians were less clear in their national consciousness than the other nationalities in this area. Relations between Jews and Bielorussians were generally better than the relations between Jews and the other ethnic groups, and there were a number of reasons for this.

1. The Bielorussians' national consciousness had developed comparatively late and had affected only parts of the population, mainly members of the intellectual class who formed only a thin stratum in Bielorussian society; even among them it was not too strong. This was to the benefit of the mutual relations between the Jewish and Bielorussian populations.
2. In addition, the social distress of the Bielorussian peasant, though very great, had not been implanted on extremist nationalist goals and this too moderated their hatred towards the Jews and to a certain degree even served as a bridge between the poor of both populations and led to some cooperation in the struggle against social injustice.
3. Finally, the cultural differences between the Jews and Bielorussians in language and cultural creativity were very great. The factor of assimilation did not exist at all and that of national competition was weak, and this situation, too, worked to moderate relationships and not to exacerbate them.

Bielorussian antisemitism was nourished mainly from traditional Christian sources and was free to a large extent of any "leading force" bearing ideological or practical goals, even though in this area, there were elements that could worsen relations — such as Catholicism and the Polish settlers. There was, however, a much larger degree of personal contact between Jews and other nationalities in the region. There are historians who speak of a "period of living together" of Jews and Bielorussians, which was better than between Jews and members of the other nationalities in the region.[26] One example of this is the poem by the Bielorussian poet Yanka Kupala entitled *Jews* which describes the closeness between the Jews and the Bielorussians and finds a common attribute in the Jews' longing for Eretz Israel and the Bielorussians' for a country of their own with freedom and equality. Though the poem possesses a large measure of idealization and exaggeration, it certainly does have an element of truth.

During the Soviet period Jewish-Bielorussian relations worsened, with the Jews as a group being identified with the Soviet regime and the Bielorussians viewing the Jews as playing a leading role in the government. With the arrival of Germans and under the influence of their propaganda, the attitudes of the Bielorussians and of other sectors of the populations toward the Jews deteriorated drastically. The annihilation of the Bielorussian Jews took place at a time when large sections of the population still nourished hopes of establishing an independent Bielorussian state and the cooperation between Nazi Germany and Bielorussian circles was at its height. This cooperation, of course, had its effect upon the attitudes towards the Jews, but with the Red Army's victories at the front and the German retreat, the growing strength of the partisan movement, and the harsh measures adopted by the Germans towards the gentile civilian population, especially from the beginning of the spring 1943, large section of the Bielorussian population began to change its attitude towards the Germans. By then, however, the annihilation of Bielorussian Jewry was almost complete. The increasingly negative attitude towards the Germans might perhaps have led to a change towards a more positive attitude towards the Jews if there still had been many Jews living in the region at that time, but this is difficult to prove.

The Bielorussian population's attitude towards the Jewish partisans from the spring of 1943 and until the end of the war does not supply an answer to this question. These attitudes were formed of many components and it is difficult to isolate the one component of "attitude towards Jewish partisans." It is quite reasonable to assume that those attitudes were not the results of any principles but primarily, and perhaps totally, of pragmatic and utilitarian considerations in view of the approaching Red Army.

The attitudes of the Poles towards the Jews in that period were complex. On the one hand, the Germans were the enemy who had attacked Poland and ended its independence. This led to some ties with the Jews (more theoretical than practical), who were the Germans' victims. However, during the German occupation's first stage, except for some limited circles, the Poles' hatred for the Soviets was stronger than their hostility towards Germans, and during this stage most Poles adopted a hostile attitude towards the Jews as having been "collaborators with the former Soviet regime," as they termed it. At a later stage, upon the formation of a Polish underground and after the Germans had adapted sharp measures against patriotic Poles, some circles of the Polish population began to develop a more positive attitude towards the Jews, but then, again, only very few Jews were still living.

The Ukrainians in southern Polesie and the Lithuanians in the southwest part of the Vilna district had always possessed inimical attitudes towards the Jews.

The influence of religion on the population's attitudes towards the Jews was ambivalent. On the one hand, the dominant churches of the region — the Russian Orthodox and the Roman Catholic (but not the Baptists) nourished Jew-hatred; priests led riots and preached against the Jews. On the other hand, there were many cases where Jews were assisted by religious people drawing their inspiration from a Christianity in which Jews were to be degraded but not annihilated.

A small part of the gentile population stretched their hands out to the Jews and tried to save them; some, as mentioned before, paid for this with their lives. In some cases, simple people, at great risk, in prevailing atmosphere of suspicion and betrayal, displayed nobility and human fraternity. Here, too, it was sometimes not their attitudes towards the Jews in general was decisive, but their personal relationship towards the specific refugee.

Michael Nusanczik of Rubla (near Stolin) hid on a small island in a river when the Jews of his village were murdered. The peasants plundered all the Jewish property. When Nusanczik afterwards came to the village he met the peasant's wife. When she saw him she fell at his feet weeping: "My son, don't be afraid. Now everything is all right. Thank God it is quiet." Such was the spiritual world of one good person who wanted to console and aid this one Jew but yet came to terms with a world where Jews were killed, because "everybody does it."

Here, too, there were different degrees of assistance: not betraying Jews to the Germans and the local police; opening one's door to the refugee and providing a piece of bread; providing food and a hiding place in the nearby forest for an extended period of time; providing a hiding place in one's home for a short period until it became too dangerous; and providing a hiding place for a long period of time at great risk.

The motives for providing assistance to Jews, to make an effort to save them, were simple human conscience or religious faith or a combination of two; a sense of obligation or friendship, or previous acquaintance or material benefits in the past or present.

These acts of assistance were dangerous but there was at least one form of help that could have saved many thousands of Jews without any risk at all, and that was — the neutrality of non-betrayal. The temptation that carried people away and brought them into the camp of enemies and informers was the kilogram of salt and sugar promised for every Jew betrayed. There was still a great distance between non-betrayal and taking a risk.

How many members of the non-Jewish population took part in helping Jews? This is a question without statistical answer. There are witnesses who dealt with the question and what they said is important from the viewpoint of the witness' subjective view, and we must not ignore these impressions, but they cannot be considered objective evaluations. "The attitude of 95 percent of the population towards the Jews was very bad. They faithfully helped to annihilate the Jews. The remaining five percent stood aside." says Zalman Rabinowicz of Lachowicz. Another witness from the same ghetto testifies that peasants helped the ghetto.[27] One witness from the Baranowicze ghetto writes: "We must point out that in the course of the annihilation we had to face not only the Gestapo but also almost all of the civilian population, who almost without exception collaborated with the Germans."[28] Another survivor testifies; "Unfortunately, the 'Vladeks' [a peasant who helped this witness] were few and the hooligans numbered millions."[29]

The isolated witness saw only his part of the action: the man standing in the market square at the time of the *selektzia* saw the faces all around — watching them waiting to die. The man saved by finding a hiding place saw the single peasant, his savior. Though both saw only parts of the whole picture, there is a difference in the one seeing a crowd of rioting peasants, that is numerically a lot of hostile people, while the second saw only one savior.

There are two aspects of the problem we are discussing — that of the quantitative measure of the non-Jewish populations' attitudes: good and bad, the prevalence of these attitudes, and secondly to what results these attitudes could have led to, or did actually lead?

As we have said, this problem has no statistical answer even though, paradoxically, its quantitative dimensions have more than a little weight in determining the question's essential qualitative answer. We can, however, find a verbal, proportional answer to this problem that had more than a little effect in deciding the fate of the Jewish population. We might say, first, that in fixing the proportions between the murderers, informers, betrayers and the simply indifferent, one the one hand, and the saviors on the other, we face the fact that the murdered do not speak and the murderers are silent, and the only survivors and the saviors speak and justly praise.

A historian must be careful in fixing the correct proportions between the hatred and murder and the mercy and assistance, and we shall be closer to historical truth if we estimate that the large majority of the non-Jewish population related to the fate of the Jews of Western Bielorussia with hostile indifference. Many of them murdered Jews. A few — and be their deeds as shining, bright and noble as they were — only terribly few helped and did something to save them.

Notes

1. Yad Vashem (YV) 1556/112 (Shmuel Geller)
2. YV 204/18-A (Shabtai Esterow)
3. Yisrael G. Yankelewicz, testimony in *Sefer Lubcz-Delatycz* (Lubecz-Delatycz memorial Book) (Tel Aviv, 1971), p. 334; Shifra Solomiansky, ibid., p. 380.
4. YV 1251/39-D Y. Dawidowicz).
5. YV M-1/E 1572/1441 (Zlata Dokszycka)
6. Nuremberg Documents (IMT) L-180, Stahlecker Report, 15 October 1941.
7. YV DDN/58/2-E.M.67, of 29 August 1941. the criticism was directed primarily against the civilian population in Eastern Bielorussia, where the German murder campaign in the early months of their occupation of the area aroused unease among some circles, who judged the German behavior to be inhuman.
8. IMT NOKW-2628, 8 November 1941.
9. Rivka Yosselevska, testimony in *Yizkor Kehillot Luniniec/Kozhanhorodok* (In Memory of the Communities of Luniniec/Kozhanhorodok) (Tel Aviv, 1952), p. 68.
10. Shalom Cholawski, "Mahteret Ba'ir" (An underground in Town), *Hedim: A Journal for Kibbutz Problems,* no. 53 (April 1957), p. 64.
11. Moreshet Archieve (MA) A-461 (Shaike Osherowicz).
12. Cholawski, op. cit., p. 54.
13. YV 03/508 (Avraham Aviel).
14. Isik Berkowicz, testimony in *Sefer Zikaron Stoipc Swierezhne veha' ayarot hasmuchot* (Memorial Book of Stoipc-Swerzhna and the Ajoining Townships) (Tel Aviv, 1965), p. ?.
15. Leah Omanuti, testimony in *Sefer Oszmiana* (Oszmiana Memorial Book) (Tel Aviv, 1969), p. 344.

16. YV 2718/196 (Moshe Abramowicz).
17. Shmariahu Elman, testimony in *Pinkas Pruzhane*, etc ... (Diary of Pruzhany, etc ...) (Buenos Aires, 1958), p. 668.
18. Ze'ev Rabunsky, testimony in *Megillat Kurnitz* (Kurzeniec) (translation of title) (Tel Aviv, 1956), p.310.
19. YV 1900/181-F (Boris Friedman).
20. YV 2829/206 (Ya' akov Abramowicz).
21. YV 3458/311 (Moshe Beirach), p. 250; Lyuba Yudin, testimony in *Sefer Druja* (Drujsk memorial Book) (Tel Aviv, 1973), p. 193.
22. Cholawski, op. cit., pp. 63–64.
23. YV M-1/E 990/863 (Mottl Alperowicz).
24. YV 187/66 (Marian Poznanski); Shmuel Slutsky, testimony in *Sefer Iwieniec, Kamen Vehasviva* (Memorial Book of Iwieniec, Kamen and Environs) (Tel Aviv, 1973), p. 401.
25. Cholawski, op. cit., p. 113.
26. Wiktor Ostrowski, *Antisemitism in Belorussia and Its Origins* (London, 1960)
27. YV M-1/Q/212 (Zalman Rabinowicz)
28. Eliezer Lidovsky, testimony in *Sefer Zikaron Baranowicz* (Baranowicze Memorial Book) (loc. date), p. 489.
29. YV 1556/112-G (Shmuel Geller).

CHAPTER 15
In Conclusion

When the Germans invaded Western Bielorussia in June 1941 the Jews there found themselves in the midst of a process, one that had been imposed upon them during the past two years, of a crumbling Jewish public life, eroding leadership, weakening foundation at home, and surrounded by non-Jewish population that had, on the eve of the war, reached one of its peaks of hostility to Jews. Now it was face to face with Nazi policy that was stunning in its method and in its practical implementation of the Final Solution. We have devoted as much space as possible in this work to the time when the Western Bielorussian Jews were subject to Soviet rule from 1939 to 1941 because of its importance and implications for the Holocaust period. The dismantled frameworks of the real, even if only limited, autonomy, with its range of institutions, that the Jewish national minority had enjoyed, the arrest of public leaders, the ban on welfare, cultural and intellectual activities during the period of the Soviet occupation, had led to the paralysis of Jewish life. In many towns, leaders, teachers and older members of the Zionist youth movement had left and wandered on to other places, among them to the 'center' in Vilno. This fact had its great influence upon the composition and character of Jewish leadership during the Holocaust, upon Jewish response and first and foremost upon the formation and activity of the Jewish underground.

Knowing as we do, the importance to the underground movement in our region of those who had remained in their places or had returned in some way, we can estimate the loss to the Jewish resistance movement of those who had left. In those critical moments of soul searching deliberations faced by the underground in the various ghettos, one individual with the power to decide might have tipped the scale, as had happened in other ghettos. "One man could have ignited the revolt," complained one underground member from the Stolpce ghetto, when the members of the underground were waiting at the gate and prepared to break out. The local underground leadership did not always have that one man who could have assumed the responsibility of decision and decided the fate of many people in the ghetto.[1] Similarly, another underground member,[2] from Kamen-Koshirsk, argued: "Only the organizing hand and commander were lacking." The processes that Jewish youth had undergone during the Soviet period had led to a decline in mutual trust. Adaptation to the Soviet regime on the part of some of the youth on the other hand, and loyalty to their people on the other, led to some alienation among various sections of the youth who previously had been close; and unfortunately, suspicion of each other increased. This had a negative effect when the underground began to organize in the ghettos.

The Zionist undergrounds that had been established in some places during the Soviet era, provided the nucleus for the anti-German underground. The pogroms that had taken place in many Western Bielorussian towns with the Red Army's retreat and before the arrival of the Germans had stimulated the organization of a Jewish defense in many places which had more than a little success in repelling attacks.

Many Jews, and especially young people, fled eastward towards the Soviet Union, from the towns during the first days of the war, but many returned to their homes. Some had found their way blocked by Red Army Military Police or parachuted German troops. A very small part succeeded in getting into Russia. The older generation, for the most part, did not flee.[3] Many Jews were deterred from leaving their homes, livelihoods and gardens, and taking the wanderer's path to an unknown country, far from family and friends. They preferred to stay at home. Those Jews who remained at home generally assumed that the Red Army was the strongest in the world and would return to liberate them in a few weeks, after it recovered from the shock of the treacherous Nazi attack.

With the Barbarossa Operation, the Germans began to implement their Final Solution — total annihilation of the Jews in the occupied territories, one of the chief goals of Nazi ideology. The annihilation process in this region was a relatively prolonged one — except for Hancevicz, all of whose Jews were murdered between 13–15 August 1941. Even after the first wave of *aktzias,* ending at the close of 1941, many Jews still remained in the ghettos. These formed the basis for the formation of the Jewish underground.

Four days were required by the Germans in order to traverse all of Western Bielorussia and to come to within 20 kilometers from Minsk, a fact that was itself a shock for the Jewish population. The Germans began a campaign of decrees against Jews who were isolated from their environment, with their communities cut off from each other, starved, humiliated, impoverished and placed in constant danger of death, in order to stun them, to depress them and bring them to despair. All this was done consistently so that the victim would not recover and gather his wits even a little. Parallel to these came the first wave of the mass bloody killing operations, the *aktzias*, that began after the invasion and went on until the end of 1941, destroying a large part of the Jewish population, in some places almost all.

The Germans appreciated the Jews' potential behavior and activity as a stimulating force behind the partisan movement. In many places immediately after their arrival, they wiped out the Jewish intellectuals. They felt that Polesie was destined to support partisan movements and therefore, they killed most of the Jewish men during the first months. This murder of tens of thousands of Jews in this region at the outset of the German invasion decided the fate of the Jewish underground and of its offspring, the Jewish partisan movement in the Polesie district.

In the autumn months of 1941 the Germans conducted *aktzias* in order to annihilate the ghetto inhabitants in most of the region's towns.

There was a tragic paradox in the proximity of the dates of the partisans' appearance and the Germans' implementation of their annihilation policies. The Jews' hopes and prospects lay in the partisans, but when these appeared on a large scale in the forests, the Germans hastened the implementation of their already planned annihilation policies in the Western Bielorussia ghettos.

Deportations

Jews were deported from many small towns and concentrated in larger ghettos. These deportations uprooted the Jews from their native places, from the villagers and the peasants, with whom many of them had ties, some of them good ones, too; where they knew the forests and in time of distress could obtain food and shelter from their neighbors. They were suddenly uprooted and moved to a new place, a larger ghetto, with their only desire to find a roof over their heads and food for their families: they were occupied with the concerns of daily existence in a new and strange place. Their moving deprived these Jews suddenly of many opportunities for underground activities, for acquiring arms, for escaping (as was the case, for instance in Naliboky, Rubzhewicze, Iwieniec and other places). Some of these deported Jews did indeed integrate swiftly into the underground in their new homes and even formed a fermenting element, but their activities lacked the advantages they had enjoyed in their old homes. The Nazi deportation policies prevented the growth of Jewish underground organization in this region.

Despair, Hope and Illusion

The Jews in the ghetto were flung from despair to hope and illusion and back again. What is more, despair and hope prevailed among them at one and the same time. It was impossible to continue to exist in the ghetto, to maintain a family and to function among the daily risks by the power of despair alone: "… I want to emphasize that people finding themselves face-to-face with death call on illusion to assist them so that they can comfort themselves that the danger is not threatening them, that it will not happen, that under all circumstances it is impossible for it to happen."[4] The illusions prevailing in the ghetto, however, also formed a very serious barrier to the establishment of the underground.

Defending their Lives

Anyone studying the testimonies from the ghettos in the region cannot help coming to the conclusion that most of the ghetto Jews, with the exception of a small minority, revolted in their hearts and with all their might against Nazism, and conducted anti-Nazi activities in their everyday lives, were concerned to live as Jews, and would have been potential armed fighters if they had had the necessary conditions — more precisely, if it were not for the very difficult conditions that prevented revolt, including direct activities in conflict with the enemy's goals. In view of the Nazi's goal of annihilating the Jews, the Jews' very efforts to stay alive as human beings and Jews, at great risk and against the enemy's intentions, by hiding, escaping, forming underground organizations, fighting in the ghetto and with the partisans, are all qualitatively different variations of a general Jewish revolt during the Holocaust.

The customary terminology of sociological research in ordinary human society cannot be applied to the reality of ghetto life. The use of terms borrowed from non-ghetto reality in dealing with ghetto reality leads to an essential distortion. The vocabulary used today for the Jews' battle in the ghettos has led us to lose sight of a central area of their battle.

Let us take one form, only one of the various forms of Jewish resistance to his murderers; the story of one man, one of many, who fought under his circumstances in his own way. Yehoshua Swidler escaped from the *aktzia* in his town, Kobylnik, to Swir, and his wife and two daughters followed him. They fled from the *aktzia* in Swir to Michaliszky, where the Judenrat demanded that they leave since they were refugees. They reached Vilno and there continued their struggle to live.[5] This simple story of one ordinary Jew, with its dangers and courage, must be included in the story of the Jewish revolt and is worthy of the name.

To the story of the revolt belong the stories of Jews, ordinary Jews, who emerged out of the ghetto, like Chaya Bloch from Dokszyce who gave herself up to the Germans in the place of her sister who had a baby, and was then tortured and killed. Like 62-year old Beila Reichel from Koziany, who roamed the villages in order to obtain food, brought arms and information to the ghetto and took Jews out of the ghetto and condemned the Germans for their actions on the day of deportation. Like Devora Drewiansky from Zholudok, who went from house to house in the ghetto, quietly bringing aid to the needy and became one of the ghetto's leaders in its hours of distress.

These kind of activities may be termed fighting for life and include the everyday struggles of the ghetto Jews, the hiding places, the escapes, and the armed Jewish underground. The daily struggle of the ghetto Jews is a stirring epic of a people who under the ghetto conditions held on to the prospect of life and fought as human beings and as Jews, at times with great self-sacrifice, for their own and their families' lives as well as the lives of other Jews. There is a great deal of documentary evidence about this type of reaction which deserves a separate study.

Hiding places

One of the forms of rebellious reaction were the hiding places that Jews prepared with great difficulty and secrecy despite the lack of materials and tools. The sudden surrounding of the ghetto, by the Germans and the police, the informing and betrayal on the part of the non-Jewish population, obliged many Jews to build bunkers, shelters for themselves and their families, according to detailed calculations, with minimum supplies and maximum camouflage. In this field Jews revealed great initiative and varied stratagems. The more hiding places there were in the crowded ghetto the harder it was to prepare them.

When the Germans entered the Zhetl ghetto on 6 August 1942 in order to destroy Jews, the ghetto streets were empty. Some 4,000 Zhetl Jews were "underground" in the bunkers. In Pruzhany more than 2,000 Jews hid on the day of deportation (28 January 1943); in Horodok — 900; in Dvore — 800; in Kosov-Polesky — 200, and so on for many other places.

Escape

Escape from the ghetto was an act of revolt that involved great risk, heavy soul-searching and family separation. Escape generally began after the first wave of *aktzias*. It started with an activity at initiative of the underground organizations, in organized and sometimes armed groups. After them came groups of Jews who had not worked in underground, individuals, whole communities working spontaneously or under the direction of Jewish partisans. Most of the testimonies mention that the number of those who fled was actually much larger than those who reached the forest. Many of those who fled from the ghetto were killed during their escape or were betrayed. We are interested in the number of those who attempted to escape from the ghetto even if a large part never reached their destinations. The man who escaped from the ghetto — was a rebel.

The Armed Underground

The underground organizations in the Western Bielorussian ghettos arose in most cases after the first wave of *aktzias* that took place in the large majority of ghettos. In some places groups of young people began to meet clandestinely before the first *aktzia*, especially in those places where there had been ideologically-minded pioneering Zionist underground organizations in the Soviet period. They met to examine the new situation created with the Germans' arrival, to consult together, to look for paths of action, and to organize once again the young people they had once led, but they still did not draw up any clear lines of action to react to the Nazi conquest (as was the case in Kremeniec, Nieswiezh, Swienciany).

The heavy blow of the first wave of *aktzias* plunged the Jews into deep depression. In some ghettos most of the Jewish population was killed and many single persons remained, among them young people who had lost all their families. It was in this atmosphere of depression that the underground organizations came into being. At their beginnings the organizations talked of a "fitting reply," of "fighting with arms," of "revenge," of "no more going the path of the selection," "no more *aktzias*," without the young people knowing clearly how to implement these ideas. There was a strong inner urge to find a way to live and to fight back. The reaction sometimes followed the depression and its effect was then even greater.[6]

Underground organizations arose and were established in many towns. We have the numbers at hand: of the 111 ghettos and other communities in Western Bielorussia of which we have some documentation (excluding the Bialystok region and the city of Vilno, which are not included in this study), and including the ghettos from which Jews were expelled to other larger ghettos shortly after their establishment, 64 ghettos and work camps had underground movements and in 30 more there were manifestations of revolt that undoubtedly testify to some underground organization within them, too, though the evidence we possesses does not permit us to affirm their existence with certainty. Therefore, in 94 out of 111 ghettos, work camps and communities, there were underground organizations and signs of revolt (85 percent).

In ten[7] of the other 17 ghettos and communities, most of which were small communities sometimes numbering some dozens of families alone, the Jews were deported to larger ghettos and had no time to organize a local underground. We have, however, information about their activities in the undergrounds of the ghettos to which they were sent. On the basis of this material we may conclude that there was hardly any ghetto or work camp in Western Bielorussia where there were no underground organizations or signs of revolt.

The Numerical Dimensions of the Underground

* See also Table on undergrounds, weapons, weapons and organizations.

District	No. of ghettos	No. of members
Polesie	8	520
Vilno	14	600
Novogrudok	13	945
Total	35	2,065

We may assume that the 64 underground organizations in the region actually numbered close to 4,000 members. The figures in our possession for most part are the figures of the numbers at the beginning; they more or less reflect the situation during the period between the end of 1941 and the spring of 1942.[8] In the summer of 1942 the organizations expanded their ranks.

The underground was the initiative of young people — most of them members of the pioneering Zionist youth movements, and partly persons of a Communist inclination and other young people not from the movements. In some places the organizers' ages ranged from 17 to 19 (Kurzeniec and Swienciany), and in some — between 19 and 25 (Nieswiezh, Slonim, Lachwa, Pinsk, etc.). The members of the underground basically came from two important sources: the pioneering Zionist youth movements and the Hebrew schools, especially the "Tarbut" schools and to some degree also from the Yiddish schools.

In the course of time, and sometimes even at the very beginning, the youth were joined by an older element coming from the broad laboring strata and the intellectuals. The intense fear of the *aktzias*, the depressing effect of the *selektzias*, the young peoples' strong will to live and to avenge, the need to resist that impelled them to take up arms as Jews and human beings, the pride they had absorbed from the Bielorussian Jewish environment and their Jewish, Zionist and/or Socialist educations, were the psychological and ideological motives of the underground's organizers. "Thanks to our Zionist and Hebrew teachers our consciousness had been impenetrated with the total rejection of the Galut (Exile) and a deep national identification, the basis for human pride, that served as the impulse to revolt."[9]

The role and the personal and ideological influence of the youth movements' members were very large in almost all of the ghetto undergrounds. This was reflected in the initiative behind their formation, their activities and ideological motivations they brought with them. However, we have documentary material about movement affiliation only for 30, underground organizations (see Table below). The older and more general section grew and expanded within the underground organizations in the later stages and particularly with the increasing escapes from the ghettos.

From their initially unclear ideas of resistance, the underground organizations arrived at the recognition of the need to fight with arms. Their

Youth Movements in Underground Organizations in 30 Ghettos

Movement	No. of ghettos	Percentage
Hashomer Hatzair	20	67
Hechalutz (including Hechalutz Hatzair)	12	40
Betar (including Brit Hechayal)	9	30
Hanoar Hatzioni	5	17
Gordonia	4	13
Poalei Zion	5	17

devotion to this was more than once accompanied by sober scepticism,[10] but they were strong enough psychologically to withstand that scepticism. In the course of time the underground organizations were compelled to set targets and programs for implementation. Throughout their existences the underground organizations were engaged in debating their aims and programs, and this — because of the specific conditions of their battle. The surprising fact is that most of the organizations, working almost completely isolated and without any contacts between them, arrived, after all the intensive internal argument, at the same conclusions: to fight with the aim of rescuing as many people as possible. It was that principle which determined their goals.

There were underground organizations which, because of their proximity to the forests or the inclinations of their leader, tended from the outset towards going to the forest, and organized themselves for that. There were organizations which tended from the beginning towards resisting the Germans within the ghetto area. However, they were to a very extent similar in viewing both the uprising and the escape to the forest as integral elements of their programs, though the emphasis on the one or the other varied. Sometimes the underground organizations had to improvise changes in their emphasis in keeping with the changing situations. The Zhetl underground drew up a plan for an uprising in the ghetto and prepared weapons for that purpose, but because of the changing situation and the partisans' appearance in the region went over to preparing only for an escape to the forest, in order to build a large partisan force. The underground organization in Nieswiezh had plans to establish contacts with the partisans and to leave for the forest but in view of the situation decided on a revolt in the ghetto.

The plans of most of the inderground organizations, including both the uprising in the ghetto and the escape to the forest, generally followed the following lines: on the day that the ghetto was surrounded, the houses would be set on fire by the organizations' members. In the ensuing confusion and in the course of the fires and battle, Jews would flee the ghetto for the forest. The organization's units would cover the escape with their gun fire.

In some of the underground organizations, as we have said, the members prepared to leave for the forest in groups and to establish partisan bases for the absorption of the Jews still in the ghetto. In those underground organization that were under Communist influence the dominant tendency was to escape to the forest. They pinned all their hopes on partisan combat alone.

Arms

In 42 ghettos[11] the underground organizations had weapons in their possession. In 21 other ghettos, they either had no weapons or we have no information of their having them. Acquiring firearms in the ghetto was only one, even if the most important, of the marks of the intensity of the underground's activities. Some undergrounds had only few weapons but still engaged in intensive activity and even carried out revolts in the ghettos. Whether they had firearms or not, all the underground organizations were armed with such weapons as iron bars, knives, axes, and, in some places, also bottles of acid. Weapons were acquired mainly by underground members who worked in the Germans arsenals, but also in other ways. Here are some figures in our possession:

In five ghettos in the Vilno district the underground possessed 30 rifles, 15 pistols, 1 machine gun, 1 Maxim heavy machine gun, and an unknown number of grenades and bullets. In 6 ghettos of the Polesie district there were 105 rifles, 20 pistols, 2 machine guns, 2 automatic rifles (PPDs) grenades and bullets. In 14 ghettos of the Novogrudok district there were 211 rifles, 70 pistols, 27 machine guns, 13 automatic rifles (PPDs), and an unknown number of grenades and bullets. In total, 25 of 42 armed underground organizations possessed 346 rifles, 105 pistols, 30 machine guns, 15 automatic rifles, 1 Maxim, grenades and ammunition. We may assume that in the 42 armed ghettos the underground organizations possessed close to 500 rifles, some 150 pistols, about 35 machine guns, some 20 automatic rifles and some Maxims.

The numbers of weapons given here are not all of the same date; they changed in accordance with the possibilities of acquiring them and taking them to the forest with the groups escaping. There is a striking difference between the numbers of weapons in some of the larger ghettos (Baranowicze and Slonim) and the others.

The Underground's Opponents

The underground's formation and activities led to a dispute between these organizations and those who opposed them completely or conditionally, a dispute that to a large measure coincided with the debates between generations, between the younger and older people. The opponents may be divided into two groups:

1. Those who totally opposed underground organization in itself, the acquisition of arms and the links with the partisans, because these acts "were liable to endanger the ghetto's existence."[12] This argument was raised by many Judenrat members and large parts of the ghetto population, especially the older people. These opposed, attempted to prevent and fought underground organization. There were even some who threatened to turn the members of the underground over to the Germans, although except for a few cases they did not carry out their threats. The threat themselves, however, were sufficient to create ill-feeling.
2. Opponents whose views on the underground revolved about the question of the measure of salvation the underground activity could promise. These people had no great illusions concerning the Germans' intentions and would have been prepared to come to terms with the underground if its proposals had promised an even partial way to save Jews. There were those who argued: either all go to the forest or none.[13] Some employed this argument none too honestly since one of the alternatives — that all go to the forest — was an almost impossible one and by their condition they sealed any second and possible alternative. Some, however, raised this argument in all honesty.

Pliskin, one-time chairman of the Dokszyce Jewish *kehilla* came to complain to Josef Shapira, a Hechalutz member and underground leader who was about to leave for the forest with a large group of young people. If, he said, the ghetto were asked to take the risk in order for people to go to Eretz Israel, they would agree to that; but he warned against endangering the ghetto in order to escape to the forest, which, he estimated, meant death in 99 percent of the cases.

From these remarks we can also draw some conclusions concerning two other aspects: what Eretz Israel meant to the ghetto Jews and what the forest's prospects looked like in older eyes. However, despite the bitter disputes between the underground and its opponents of all kinds, they were not always deaf to what the other side said.[14]

The decisions the underground organizations faced were very difficult from the viewpoint of conscience because of the situation of the Jewish population, as often the very parents of the underground's members would have to be abandoned to their fate. The Jewish public in the ghetto identified itself partly with the underground, partly with the Judenrat, and partly found itself of a divided heart. That part of the population that supported the underground related to it with hope, respect and fear.

The Dilemma, Ghetto or Forest?

Escape as a realistic prospect stood at the center of the underground organizations' battles and was the core of all their programs in Western Bielorussia, though they never deluded themselves that a whole ghetto population could be saved. Among the facts that determined the underground's character in this region were the presence of the forest proximity of the ghettos and the presence of quite a few Jews who possessed a close acquaintanceship with their town's physical and demographic neighborhood; escape meant the forest.

As we have seen above, there were many ghettos which did not face the dilemma of ghetto or forest though the question certainly existed. The decision in these ghettos was almost self-understood. There were mainly small ghettos whose dwelling areas had been narrowed to some dozens of wooden houses, with the possibilities of planning to fight within them very limited. On the other hand, the forest's proximity held out hopes of flight and escape.

Eretz Israel: The Pride of the Jews

In the spiritual world of the ghetto Jews, fighting for existence was identified with Eretz Israel as the symbol of a secure Jewish existence. Parents who had children in Palestine were the happiest persons in the ghetto. Nowhere did Jews ever long for Eretz Israel the way the ghetto Jews in this region longed for it.

Under the degrading ghetto conditions, on the verge of death, Jews cultivated their pride in their Judaism. "Here, I see my dear father, his eyes filled with tears. "This is our fate, children, we must be proud we are Jews … Do not lose your hope."[15]

Concern for the Family

Life and death coexisted permanently in the ghetto. There was the feeling of the impending end but with this feeling, and growing out of it, there was another phenomenon that was extraordinary in its force: the supreme concern for existence. Out of the feeling that the flood of blood had erased human culture and the Jewish people in Europe, there awoke a fierce desire that somebody remain … We have a wealth of documentation of the Jews' concern, at the last moments, that "somebody remain alive".

The core of the struggle for existence was the idea of "My Family" expressed in extraordinary devotion and readiness for self-sacrifice for the members of one's family; the individual's concern for his own life was often pushed aside by his worry about the existence of the "family unit". With the last of their strength, mothers and fathers standing at the pits encouraged their children to flee. Parents did what they could so that not all the members of the family would reside in the same ghetto, but instead were dispersed in a number of ghettos in order to increase the prospects of someone surviving. Many sadly found no point in remaining alive without their families. Chava Feldman from Drohiczyn, who alone of her family survived, confessed many years after the war: "Many times Dr. Schachter's words come to my mind: 'What good will it be if you are saved alone? What kind of life will you have if you are saved and all your relatives and dear ones die?' Now I feel that. It was not worthwhile my torture which I have, and remaining alive …"[16]

For their devotion to their families very many Jews paid with their lives even though they knew that their self-sacrifice would not save their families. The family was, then, the subject of heavy problems of conscience for the Jewish underground and was its Achilles' heel in terms of carrying out its goals.

"… Mother worried about me very much. I and my brother tried to convince father that we mustn't wait, but mother didn't want to give herself to flight and suffering … Father didn't want to leave mother alone and we remained and waited."[17]

Jews with skills to whom the Germans offered life, alone and without their families, refused to accept the Germans' offers and joined their families on the last road. The dilemma that faced the ghetto Jew was whether to leave his family, as against the very poor prospects of living after escaping, given the terrors and dangers lurking outside.

> ... However, It is no simple thing to flee with a family and little children and on the other hand — what Jewish head of a family could agree to abandon his family and try to save his own life. In that way the close family ties made the task easier for the enemy ... The prospects of help from the outside were weak and they saw no point in taking the risk, in suffering tortures and separating from their families in order to be killed somewhere among the gentiles in some unknown place.[18]

Jews preferred to remain with the members of their family.

> ... The solution of mass flight to the forest was not to be considered at that time ... That step meant premature suicide.
> How could we demand of a crowd of weary old people and children that they cut the wire and go out at night under a rain of German and (local) police bullets? ...[19]

There were even cases where Jews who had fled to the forest heard that their families in the ghetto were being subjected to an *aktzia*, returned to their towns and accepted death with their families. The family, and concern for its fate, was a central problem for underground members themselves and played an important role in deciding their fate and activities. Not a few among them who had planned flight at great risk, were deterred at the last moment from fleeing when the time came to separate from their families.

The organizer of the underground in Bereza-Kartuska asked young people to join him in escaping. Some preferred to remain with their parents. Young people in Pinsk replied to the suggestion that they go to the forest: "Why should we separate ourselves from our families? What happens to them will happen to us too."[20] Given the dilemma of fleeing to the forest or going with their deported families, most of the Pruzhany youth decided to go with their parents, in January 1943. Sometimes an underground member made his going to the forest conditional upon his family going with him. Two members of the Swienciany underground returned their arms to the underground on the day of the escape and remained with their widow mothers.

Responsibility for the Whole: "To act at the decisive moment"

One of the fundamentals of underground activity was responsibility for the Jewish collective. This responsibility imposed limits upon the underground's activity. Escape from the ghetto also involved soul-searching over responsibility for the whole. The members of the Judenrat feared that escapes might bring the *aktzia* closer. More than once ghettos were ordered to bring back Jews who had escaped. Many young people were deterred from escaping because they did not want to bear on their consciences having placed other Jews in jeopardy. One young man who fled from Voronowa said: "Escape suddenly turned into a kind of 'I'm going to save my own life,' a kind of salvation at the price of betrayal."[21]

The price seemed high in the eyes of some of those who fled and the flight itself seemed in the eyes of many Jews to offer only the poorest prospects of saving one's own life. "The town's Jews began to think of escaping, but only to think. Actually, there was no place to flee to. Outside the town the danger was many times greater. We were surrounded by enemies who were lusting for our property."[22] Indeed, in many cases Jews viewed escape as only an emergency way out. There were debates in the ghettos between individuals who insisted on the necessity of fleeing and the family heads. There were differences of opinion between refugees and local people even within the underground organization.

Sometimes underground members were deterred from escaping because of the situation in the ghetto, sometimes the young people took the Judenrat's request into consideration and left only individually or in small groups. There were also cases where, after persons had fled to the forest, the Germans took the Jewish hostages and demanded that those who had fled be turned over to them. Those who had escaped returned to the ghetto and surrendered to the Germans in order to free the hostages. That happened in Antopol (the case of Josef Friedman) and in Kobylnik (Dimenstein) (see Chapter 7).

A member of the Pinsk underground testified about the underground avoiding a ghetto uprising because it did not want to take upon itself the responsibility of being the direct case of thousands being killed. At the time of the deportation from Olkeniky, the young people wanted to fall upon the guards at the head of the column, but yielded to arguments that the Germans would take their revenge on women and children.

Their responsibility for the whole community was the reason for the members of the underground remaining in Swienciany despite the great risk they thereby took, after the executions in Miadzolsky and Beck; for their postponing the date of the uprising in Baranowicze; for hundreds of young people of Janow near Pinsk it meant avoiding an uprising and escape.

In the course of this debate within the underground organizations over an uprising in the ghetto and their responsibility for the communities, some undergrounds formulated an approach that was termed: to act at the decisive moment. This meant that the underground would take arms in hand only at the moment it discovered that the Germans were about to annihilate the Jews in the ghetto. This was a logical and seemingly practical answer to the two distressing considerations: the urge to act and the responsibility for the whole community. In its formulation, however, this approach did not sufficiently take into account the Germans' methods of annihilation and their forms of camouflage and deceit.

An order for all to assemble in order to carry out an *aktzia* was often disguised as "moving to a new place of work." Then the problems began: was the move really to work or perhaps to annihilation? If it was to work, how could they endanger all these people, the aged and the children, because of one hasty act? What is more, the *aktzia* came suddenly and the underground's possibilities of preparing were very limited. The gap between the Germans' surprise and their precise organization, and the underground organization's limiting conditions avoided the possibility of an "action at the decisive moment." The need to combine a fighting Jewish response with responsibility for all the Jews was another of the Jewish underground's weak points. The decision to revolt in the ghetto (e.g., in Nieswiezh, Lachwa) came after all hopes of saving anybody had disappeared.

Ties between Ghetto and Forest

The Jewish partisan movement in Western Bielorussia is, as pointed out at the outset, a subject in itself and is not included in this study. Our interest here is in the ties between the ghettos and the partisans, and in the manifestations of partisan and, especially Jewish partisan, aid to the ghetto. The underground never ceased seeking contacts with partisan units in the forest. In most of the ghettos these contacts formed one of the central elements in the underground's plans. The underground's real ties with the partisan units never matched its expectations. The timetable took its own fatal path: the beginning of the partisans' expansion came together with the final annihilation of the ghettos in the region. The Germans were intent upon preventing the ghettos and the partisans existing together.

Despite the dangers, the underground organizations established contacts with the partisans at the end of 1941 and members even left for the forest in spring of 1942. The search for these contacts intensified towards the summer of 1942 and the end of the year. In a few places, refugees from the ghettos were the pioneers of the partisan movement in their area (e.g., Rubzhewicze, Novogrudok, Dereczyn, Kurzeniec, Vilejka, Zhetl, Nieswiezh, Stolpce, etc.). In Kurzeniec, Wilejka and Zhetl the underground carried out widespread anti-German propaganda among the general population. After Dvorecky of Zhetl dreamed of establishing a large partisan center in the Zhetl area, with the Jews as its nucleus.

Jews who fled the ghettos felt a sense of mission, responsibility and duty to save the rest and the main task of their lives was to bring Jews to the forest. These were the lines of interaction between the ghettos and the forest. Jewish partisans came at great risk to the ghettos, sometimes even a number of times, in order to organize and take Jews to the forest (e.g., in Bereza-Kartuska, Kamin-Koshirsk, Pruzhany, Lida, Novogrudok, Glubok, Dolhinov, Horodok, Miadl, Stolpce, etc.).

Under pressure, and at the initiative of their Jewish members, partisan units engaged in attacks on a number of towns in the course of which Jews were taken out of the forest (as in Kosov-Polesky, Miadl). The Jewish partisans' aspirations for vengeance moved them, together with other partisan units, to attack towns whose Jews had already been annihilated. They waged battle against Germans and also settled accounts with members of the local population who had collaborated with the murderers.

Hiding Places and Escapes in Numbers

In the 16 ghettos for which we have details, a total of 12,600 Jews hid. From those 16 ghettos, 4,240 Jews fled to the forest. In some places, some of those escaping were the same as those who had gone into hiding.

If we assume that the total number of Jews who found concealment in all the 111 ghettos and other communities we have examined in our study was only double that of the 16 ghettos mentioned above, we arrive at a minimum of 21,000. We have figures concerning the escapes to the forest from these 111 ghettos. Close to 16,000 Jews fled from 80 of the ghettos (72 percent).

If we consider that this figure applies to only 72 percent of the ghettos, that there were escapes which for we have no documentation, that many of the testimonies give figures for those who reached the forest and not the actual number of those who had fled (and there is a great difference). We can assume that the number of those fleeing from the Western Bielorussian ghettos came to at least 25,000.

As we have said above, the flight began mainly in the spring of 1942 and went on until the final annihilation of all the Jews in the ghettos. In the 86 ghettos of our region for which we have numerical data, about 210,000 Jews had remained after the first wave of *aktzias*. The proportion of Jews who hid (21,000) was then at least 10 percent. The percentage of Jews who fled to the forest in proportion to all those living in the ghettos at that time, is at least 12. The Jews who hid and those who escaped to the forest together come to at least 22 percent. That is, every fourth or fifth Jew, at least, of the total ghetto population, took some active step to save himself and resist — by hiding or fleeing to the forest.

Every Jew concealing himself was a potential escapee unable to do so because of the conditions in which he was situated. In the same way, every Jew fleeing intended to fight with a partisan unit. Many of those who fled were killed in flight by the Germans, were murdered on their way or were betrayed by the non-Jewish population. Those who did reach the forest established a series of autonomous Jewish partisan units or joined non-Jewish units as groups or individuals. Jews who were not accepted into the partisan units (because antisemitism, the lack of weapons or the unwillingness to accept families into the unit, etc.) established family camps which to some small part were armed and were supported by Jewish partisans from the combat units.

Do we not have an obligation to ask how many Western Bielorussian Jews might have taken the path of active resistance if there had not been so many difficulties preventing them from so doing?

Particularity and Comparisons

The Jewish underground was different from all the non-Jewish underground movements. The differences dominate in this comparison; we can list some of them:

1. **The fear of annihilation prevailed in all the ghettos;** the Jewish individual feared death for any act;

2. **Strategic bases:** the Jews in the ghettos lacked any such base; they did not obtain such a base even when they went to the forest for partisan combat;
3. **Arms were a *sine qua non* for the underground.** The ghetto Jews were severely lacked weapons;
4. **Leadership:** some of the Jewish leaders had fled, some had been deported (by the Soviets), some — the intellectuals — were murdered by the Germans immediately upon their arrival.

The phenomenon of "fighting for their lives" which included the armed underground, was unique in its background and fate under ghetto conditions. Despite all these, we shall attempt to find some points of comparison.

As we have pointed out, there were 21,000 persons who hid (10 percent of the ghetto population) and at least 25,000 (12 percent of the same population) who fled to the forest; together at least 22 percent of the total Jewish ghetto population at that time.

The total population of all Bielorussia (Eastern and Western) was 10,589,000[23] in June 1941. Armstrong[24] quotes an estimate from a Russian source that the number of partisans in Bielorussia — classic partisan country — came to 360,000, of the 700,000 partisans in Nazi-occupied Soviet territory. According to the estimate of the head of the Bielorussian partisan command, there were in all of Bielorussia at the end of 1941, some 5,000 partisans and officers; in 1942 — 73,000 (0.69 percent of the total Bielorussian population); in 1943 — 243,000 (2.3 percent); and in 1944 — 374,000 partisans and officers[25] (3.53 percent of the total Bielorussian population); but this number also includes the non-Jewish family camps, the couriers and those villagers providing provisions to the partisans.[22]

To these figures we might add:

1. The Bielorussian partisan movement enjoyed conditions for living and fighting denied the ghetto Jews (no fear of any general annihilation, the strategic base of a people on its own soil, freedom of movement, a sympathetic civilian population, etc.);
2. Throughout the war, large partisan forces, arms, supplies and equipment were flown to the fighters in the rear in the partisan movement;
3. In 1944, as a result of the "scorched earth" policies adopted by the Germans in their retreat and the deportation of labor forces to Germany, many of the Bielorussian villagers fled to the forests and established new

family camps or villages under partisan protection. These camps formed a large proportion of the 130,000 partisans who were added to the partisan movement in 1944.

By the close of 1942 more than 20,000 Jews had already fled from the ghettos to the forest and the Jews formed a large proportion of the partisan movement.[26] One student of the Polish partisan movement in Polesie, Zbigniew Malyszczycki, wrote of the situation of the Poles in the forests and formation of the Polish "Tadeusz Kosciuszko" unit in the middle of 1943: "The circumstances impelled towards the formation of a Polish partisan unit if only for the purpose of defending the lives of the Polish families ... The situation was a difficult one because the Poles had no arms ..."[27] If that was the situation of the Poles in the forest, how shall we describe the situation of the Jews there?

To further compare, let us see what happened in *other* occupied countries. In summing up the Danish underground, Haestrup said:

> In the Second World War occupation did not mean isolation. Thanks to modern inventions — especially the radio and the air force — the occupied peoples had opportunities to maintain contact with the free world. When the distress grew stronger — they could use the opportunity to fight for freedom and to conduct battle even within a country where ordinary war seemed hopeless.[28]

It was especially in those countries where ordinary war did not seem "hopeless" that the occupied nations had an opportunity to maintain close ties with the free world.

On 9 April 1940 the Germans invaded Denmark and eventually occupied it. After the capitulation the Danes were permitted to maintain an army of 5,000 men. In spirit the government was anti-Nazi and popular sentiment was anti-German. Still, the government attempt to adapt itself in its desire to save its people from "too great suffering."

Only a few Danes thought it possible to establish an underground. In 1941 an underground did appear. From 1942 to 1945 the number of acts of sabotage increased. An intelligence network appeared. Thanks to the underground's links with Sweden, the great mass rescue operation was possible and some 7,000 Danish Jews were saved by being transferred to Sweden. Beginning with the spring of 1943, underground groups began to receive equipment, sabotage materials and highly effective weapons from the British through the SOE (Special Operation Executive) and, from 1944, also from the American Office of Strategic Services — (the OSS). Denmark's underground army of 45,000 men received supplies and equipment by air from the allies.[29]

Dutch opposition to the Nazi occupation regime was expressed in three large strikes: at the end of February 1941, in protest against the arrest of 400 Jews who had been sent to Mathausen in April 1943, against Hitler's order to rearrest Dutch prisoners who had been liberated and to send them back to Germany; and the railway strike of September 1944, as a service for the allies.

In addition to these strikes many Dutch hid Jews and provided them with false papers. In September 1944 all the underground units in Amsterdam possessed some dozens of pistols. In April, the Allied forces airdropped 30,000 Sten submachine guns; the outstanding student of the Dutch underground under the Nazis, Louis de Jong, asked: "Was that enough in order to revolt — that is a question," and notes that the commanders of the Dutch forces did not believe that people with only light arms could revolt.[27]

Alongside the Norwegian Milorg (Military Organization) there was a British organization (the SOE), providing the Norwegian underground with instructors, equipment and interactions. Both the Americans and the Russians supplied weapons to the Norwegian underground that numbered 32,000 men in 1944.[28]

The Greek underground organizations were assisted by outside forces and especially by the British.[29]

The Bielorussian Jews, as part of all the Jews within occupied Soviet territory, faced the actual implementation of the Final Solution with its terrifying effects and methodicity alone. Despite the frightful and bloody *aktzias*, the spirit of the Bielorussian Jews were not broken. Despite their depression and despair, they maintained their spiritual forces, their human and Jewish norms of living and morals, throughout their tortured road. It was out of their very feelings of impotence that the underground fighters arose and found their strength. If Jewish life in the ghettos wavered between terror and hope, it was the underground that faced that terror and gave some reality to the hope.

The movement of revolt in the ghettos of Western Bielorussia comprised a wide range: from simple Jews to rabbis, various youth groups — from the non-Zionist left, the socialist-Zionists and the nationalistic Zionists. Unlike the underground among the other European nations in the Second World

War, the Jewish underground in the ghettos was surrounded by walls of hatred, in frightful isolation, without any outside assistance, orphaned and bereaved. It also had to conduct its battle within the ghetto as to how to lead to salvation.

Though the Jewish underground worked without any centralizing hand, it was guided by one common principle: to fight the enemy while rescuing fellows Jews, and with maximal responsibility for the lives of the Jews as a whole. When hopes for salvation disappeared, Jews revolted and fought within the ghettos. After most of its members had been cut away and only a few remained in the work camps, these revealed astounding vitality in their very desire to stay alive and in planning ways to escape.

The tragedy of the Jewish underground lay in the terrible disproportion between the fierce desire to fight, something very real in the hearts of the ghetto Jews, and the conditions of the ghetto. Despite the great spirit of sacrifice, salvation was very small.

Notes

1. Izik Berkowicz, testimony in *Sefer Zikaron Stoipc-Swierezhne veha'ayarot hasmuchot* (Memorial Book of Stolpce-Swerezhna and the Adjoining Townships) (Tel Aviv, 1965), p. 140.
2. Dov Amit, testimony in *Sefer Zikaron likehillat Kamin-Koshirsk* (Memorial Book for the Community of Kamin-Koshirsk and Its Environs) (loc. date), p. 152.
3. Yad Vashem (YV) 2381/174-G (Yitzhak Gordon).
4. G. Bill, testimony in *Megilat Chayim Vechurban* (The Scroll of Life and Destruction — Kobryn) (Tel Aviv, 1951), p. 320.
5. Yehoshua Swidler, testimony in *Sefer Kobylnik* (Kobylnik Memorial Book) (loc. date), p. 151.
6. YV 2910/44-P (Pinchas Czerniak).
7. Our figures for the underground organizations refer in most cases to the first period of existence. After the spring of 1942, they increased in numbers despite the fact that more and more groups left for the forests.
8. Moniek Yosselewicz, testimony in *Sefer Zikaron Stoipc-Swierezhne ...,* op. cit., p. 468.
9. YV 2987/258-SH (Arieh Shevach).
10. This includes the ghettos of Antopol and Dunilowice, where there were weapons, but we have no information regarding an organized underground there.

11. *Sefer Motele* (Motele Memorial Book) (loc. date), pp. 14–15; Michael Z. Rayak, testimony in *Churban Glubok, etc ...* (The Destruction of Glubok, etc ...) (Buenos Aires, 1956), p. 378.
12. Yosselewicz, op. cit., p. 470.
13. Fruma Einhorn, testimony in *Sefer Druya* (Drujsk Memorial Book) (Tel Aviv, 1973), p. 124.
14. Chava Feldman, in *Drohiczyn* (Chicago, 1958), p. 305.
15. Sonia Czernia, testimony in *Sefer Zikaron Lekehillah* (Memorial Book for a Town — Disna) (Tel Aviv, 1969), p. 160.
16. YV 03/508 (Avraham Aviel).
17. Meir Yaffe, testimony in *Sefer Byten* (Byten Memorial Book) (loc. date), pp. 446–447.
18. Fanny Solomian-Lutz, *Na'ara Mul Gardom* (A Girl Facing the Gallows) (Tel Aviv, 1971), p. 74.
19. Yitzhak Ben-Amin, testimony in *Sefer Zikaron Likdoshei Woronowa Shenispu Basho'ah* (Memorial Book for the Martyrs Who Perished in the Holocaust) (Tel Aviv, 1971), p. 127.
20. YV 3059/226 (Avraham Alperowicz).
21. Nicholas Vakar, *Bielorussia: The Making of a Nation* (Cambridge, Mass., 1956), p. 14.
22. John Amstrong (ed.), *Soviet Partisans in World War II* (Madison, 1964), p. 35.
23. Mieczyslaw Juchniewicz, *Polacy w Radzieckim Ruchu Podziemnym i Partyzanskim 1941–1945* (Poles in the Underground and Partisan Movement 1941–1945) (Warsaw, 1973), pp. 53–60. According to Juchniewicz, there were 20,489 partisans in Bielorussia in September 1942.
24. Zbigniew Malszyczycki, *Partyzanci z Polesia* (Partisans from Polesia) (Warsaw, 1974), pp. 22, 28.
25. (Author's name), *European Resistance Movements 1939–1945* (Oxford, 1960), p. 160.
26. Ibid., pp. 150–160.
27. Ibid., pp. 137–146.
28. Ibid., pp. 324–339.
29. Ibid., p. 374.

Index

Abilevitz, Lolik 23, 104, 185
Abramovsky, Dr. 106–7, 112, 171–2, 174
Acksenbaum (of Brzesc) 107
Aditzke (volkdeutsche) 247
agriculture xv–xvii
Aharon, Rabbi xxiii
aid, mutual xx–xxi, 20
aims of underground organizations 110–5
A.K. *see Armia Krajowa*
Akselrod, Z. 19
aktzias 41–3, 50, 83–4, 254, 288–9, 292–3, 302
   conflict among German authorities 59–64
   disbelief in 91–2
   first wave 69–72, 86–91
   non-Jewish population 273
   pause between first and second waves 72–3
   resistance 110
   return from the forest 300
   rumors about 140–1
   second wave 73–4, 150–4
   to prevent Jews joining partisans 56, 177
   see also under name of individual ghetto
Alperovicz (partisan) 278
Alperovicz, Herzl 126
Alperovicz, Nachum 104, 136–7
Alperovicz, Rivka 137
Alperoviez, Berl 186
Alperovitz, Yaakov 228
Alperstein (of Lida) 129–30, 258–9
Alperszein, Naftali 263
Alpert (of Zhetl) 218
Alpert, Dr. 260
Alterman, Chanan 242, 248
Altman (of Lida) 129–30, 258
Angelowiez, Dr. Yaakov 162
Antek (Kopelowicz), Moma 107, 112, 170
anti-Jewish policies xiv–xv, xv, xvi, xviii, 57–8, 82
anti-partisan warfare: differences over 60–1
antisemitism xv, xvii, 13–4, 210–1, 271, 274, 280
Antopol 93, 143, 206–7, 301
Appelbaum (partisan) 243
Arad (Rudnicky), Yitzhak 104, 120, 240
Arluk, Shabtai 144
Armia Krajowa (A.K.) 108, 139, 180–1, 216
arms 117–27, 144, 204, 294–7
Aron, Yitzhak 90
arrests: under Soviet rule 27
assistance for Jews 278–80, 282–3
Atlas partisan unit 218, 228, 235, 247

311

attitude towards Jews: of the
    non-Jewish population   12–4,
    204, 271–84
attitude towards Soviet regime   3–7,
    10–1
Auerbach (of Vilna F.P.O.)   231–2,
    240
"Aunt Pescke" (of Kurzeniec)   119,
    148–9
Auschwitz   167, 243

Backe (responsible for "gas-vans")   42
Bakacz (of Kurzeniec)   278–9
Bakalczuk, Ephraim   217
Bakaler (partisan)   243
Band, Aharon   228
Banszczyk, Dov   152, 192
Baptists   279
"Bar Kochba" (Halkin)   18, 23
Baran, Binyamin   241–2
Baranowicze   282
    aktzias   83, 145, 152, 171–3,
        227–8, 256, 277
    deportations   168, 171, 177
    escapes   242
    hiding places   141
    Judenrat   145, 252, 255–6, 261
    Koldiczevo crematorium   109
    opposition to underground
        activity   133
    partisan attack   247
    partisans' paper   138
    skilled workers   63
    underground   106–7, 110, 112, 119,
        121, 123, 145, 170–4, 226–8,
        242, 256, 261, 297, 302
    yeshiva   xx
Barbakov, Fania   93
Barbarossa Operation   35–45, 288
Barchash, Gershon   120
Beck, Gershon   123–4
Beckman, Isser   166
Beder, Yosef   148
Begun, Chanoch   207

Begun, Mottel   207
Beirach (of Dvorec camp)   111
Beirach (Levit), Pesya   203
Beit Hamidrash   xxi–xxii
Ben-Aryeh, Chaim   273
Benes, Zusia   152
Benkin, Leah   152
Benz (German commander)   207
Beresina River   47
Bereza-Kartuska
    deportations to   86
    escapes   230, 243, 300, 303
    Judenrat   263
    underground   110, 118–9, 161
Berezna: Judenrat   262
Berezov: resistance   204–5
Berkowicz, Danny   218
Berkowicz, Isik   168
Berman (of Szarkowszczyzna)   261
Berman, Wolf   260
Bet-Hamidrash   xxi–xxii
Betar   xxiv, xxv, 25–6, 97, 104, 108–9,
    229, 295
betrayal of Jews   276, 283
Bialik (poet)   23
Bialoskurnik (of Baranowicze)   170–1
Bialystok district   9, 228
Bialystoker Shtern   18
Biberstein (E.G. commander)   40
Biegma Brigade   218
Biegomel area   164
Bielica   202
Bielorussia   2, 44–5, 47
    "independence"   49–51
Bielorussian Committee   49
Bielorussian Defense Corps   50
Bielorussian National Defense
    Forces   51
Bielorussian Scientific Society   50
Bielorussians   10, 12–4, 47–9, 280–1,
    305–6
Bielsky, Asael   108
Bielsky, Tuviya   108, 227, 241
Bielsky, Zusya   108

Bielsky partisan unit 108, 120, 218, 222, 227, 235, 239, 242
Bildugy 164
Bill, G. 159
Birkan, Hirsh 216
Blatt, Yitzhak 229
Bleicher, Ora 252
Blobel, Paul 75
Bloch, Chaya 291
Bobruisk xx
Bokszycze 164
Bolshevism/Bolsheviks 37–8, 40, 45
"Borba" partisan unit 218
Border and Friendship Pact between Germany and the USSR 1
Borecky, M. 225
Borelom forest 235
Borenstein (of Nieswiezh) 186, 188
Borishanska, Chilke 121
Borisov 202
Borowica forest 149
Boryszansky, Hilka 171
Botrimanz 92
Botvinik, Jacob 263
Botwa forest 217
Boyarsky, Yekutiel 121
Braslav 109–10, 163–4, 205, 264, 277
Braune Mappe, Die ("Brown Book") 57–8, 59
Bräutigam, Dr. Otto 59
Bresk *see* Brzesc
Breznick, Mottel 162
Brit Hechayal 295
Broderson, R. 18
Brodes, Manis 193
"Brown Book" (*Die Braune Mappe*) 57–9
Bruk, Chaim 263
Brzesc 47
  aktzia 70
  escapes 234–5
  German invasion 39
  Judenrat and Jewish police 263
  pogrom xv
  resistance 147
  underground 107, 110, 120, 126, 139, 167
Brzesc-Gomel area 74
Budownic, Reuven 214
Bulak partisan unit 235, 247
Bund xxiii, xxiv, xxv, 19, 192
bunkers *see* hiding places
burial pits 73, 87, 89–90, 149–51
  see also aktzias
burning of villages 60–1
Burstein, Moshe 108, 175
Busel (of Baranowicze) 222
Bussel, Michael 162
Bussel, Shlomo 218
Buzin (of Nieswiezh) 186
Buzin (of Warsaw) 96
Byten 264
  escapes 235
  German reprisals 140
  hiding places 141
  opposition to underground activity 133
  underground 109–10

Carl (commissar of Slutzk) 62
Caucasus 43, 45
Cederowicz, Benjamin 252
Central Bielorussian Council 50–1
Cerinsky, Munia 106
Cerkowicz (of Kleck) 192, 259–60
Chacia, Edward 242
Chadash, M. 230
Chadash, Rabbi Reuven 161
Chaim, Rabbi xx
Chana (of Dakszyce) 83–4
Charchas, Shlomo 106, 221, 223
Charny, Dr. 252
Charny, Solly 222
Chaya (of Dakszyce) 83–4
Chefetz, Asher ben Zalman 104, 194, 196
Chefetz, Basha-Leah 197
Chefetz, Chaim 196

Chefetz, Moshe Leib 104, 194, 196, 198
Chefetz, Shimon 194
Chefetz, Zalman 193
Chenczynsky, Max 148
Cholawsky, Shalom 104, 185–9, 191, 241
Chomsk 148
Chwediuk, Mottel 162
Ciklik, Yehuda 242
Cimmer, Baruch 245
Cimmer, Zalman 242
Cirulnik, Shimon 104
Cirynsky, Nionia 228
citizenship, Soviet 2–3, 8–10
civil government (*Zivilverwaltung*) 43–4
civil rights *see* anti-Jewish policies
civil service xvii, 12
collective responsibility 132–6, 143, 174, 253, 301–2
"Communist" Jews 83–4
Communists xxiii, xxiv, 4–5, 10, 104, 106, 109, 114–5, 164
compulsory labor *see* forced labor
concentration camps 75
conflict among the German authorities 58–65
crafts/craftsmen xv–xvi, xix, 58, 63
culture 18–9
"Czapajew" partisan regiment 229
Czarny, Dr. 260
Czech Jews 171
Czernia, Sonia 100
Czernia, Sonie 94
Czerniak, Dr. 93
Czestochowa xv, 8
Czkalow partisan brigade 248
Czorny, Moma 107, 242, 227
Czwiertak (of Swierzen) 128–9

Dakszyce 83–4
Damesek, Eliahu 138
Damesek, Moshe 186, 191
Danish underground 306–7
Dasky, Josef 147
David, Shmuel 123

David-Horodok 207
 aktzias 70, 73, 204, 276
 anti-Jewish slogans 13
 Communists 5
 German invasion 69
 Jewish men killed 202
 Red Army arrival 6
 resistance 85
defence of one's life 290–1
de Jong, Louis 307
Delaticky, Anshel 114–5
deportations 10, 27–9, 86, 164–5, 167, 177, 202, 243, 254, 289–90
Dereczyn 277
 escapes 228, 235
 German invasion 69
 hiding places 142
 partisan attack 247
 partisans 303
 Red Army arrival 4
 underground 110, 226
Derzhinsky partisan unit 228
despair 290
Diadia Vasva partisan group 137
Dimenstein, Berta 119, 137
Dimenstein, Chanan 134–5
Dinerstein, Noah 119, 136–7
Dirlewanger, Oskar 54
Disna 80
 aktzia 163
 escapes 138, 276
 resistance 152
 underground 110, 261
Dobroshin (Soviet Jewish writer) 19
Dobrowelia airfield 169
doctors xvii, 58
Dokszyce 23
 aktzias 141, 234
 escapes 234
 hiding places 141
 Judenrat 263
 opposition to underground activity 132
 Red Army arrival 7

resistance   291
underground   23, 106, 138, 142
Dolhinov   23
  aktzia   92, 135
  deportations from   164
  escapes   245–6, 303
  German invasion   272
  underground   106, 109, 136, 257
Dolinko, Aryeh   107
Dolinsky, Henya   153
Dombrowsky, Benjamin   235
Dombrowsky, David   235
Dombrowsky partisan brigade   234
Donbas mining region   16
Donilovicz   201–2, 264, 277
  aktzia   203–4
  resistance   204
Drabsky, Israel   193, 196
Drabsky-Levin, Pnina   197–8
Drewiansky, Avraham Meir   252
Drewiansky, Devora (Devorele)   98–9, 252, 291
Drewiansky, Zippa   98–9
Drohyczyn   205
  Judenrat   253
Dror   21–4
Drug, Dov   213–4, 243
Druisk   164
Druja   264
  aktzia   234
  escapes   212, 234
  underground   109–10
Druk, Yaakov   242
Dubinsky, Alter   132, 152, 253, 264
Dubkovsky, Monik   170
Duckar, Leah   120, 187, 190
Dudik, Rivka   278
Dugaliszky   206
Dukadowo   206
Dukszty   205
Dutch soldiers   121
Dvorec work camp   86
  aktzia   165–6, 277
  escape committee   109

escape/return   219, 225
hiding places   292
underground   109
opposition to underground activity   131
resistance   85, 146–7
Dvorecky, Alter   105, 111–2, 124–6, 176, 261, 303
Dweig: *aktzia*   92
Dzankovsky partisan unit   206
Dziewieniszky   23

east: escape to   28–9, 80–1, 202, 288
Ebner (German commander)   169
economic situation   xiii–xv, 14–6, 58, 71
education   xvii, xxiv, 18–20, 48–9, 97–8
  see also schools
E.G. *see* Einsatzgruppen
Ehrenleiter (Slonim deputy *Gebietskommissar*)   60
Eichorn (of Mir)   221
Einbinder, Yitzhak   137, 148–9
Einsatzgruppen (E.G.)   39–43, 59–60, 69–70, 82
Einstein, Mirel   153
Eishishok *see* Ejszyszki
Ejszyszki   105, 216
  calls for resistance   160–1
  escapes   161
  Judenrat   252
  underground   109–10
  yeshiva   xx
emigration   xii, xvii, 8
employment   xv–xvii, xix, 12, 14–6, 58
Enlightenment   xxiii
Epstein, David   87–9, 114–5, 247–8
Epstein, Feige   88
Epstein, Velvele   88–9
Eretz Israel   7, 19–20, 24, 96–7, 298–9
Erren, Gerhard   63, 72, 127, 142
escape committees   109
escapes   80–1, 142–4, 166–7, 169, 174, 176–9, 209–35, 292, 295–6, 300–1, 303–4

Estonia 44, 47
Ethics movement xxiii
executions, mass see *aktzias*
Eyszyszki 69

family: concern for 213–4, 222, 224, 299–300
Farber, Benjamin 105
Farfel, David 191–2
Farfel, Mottel 191
Farfel, Siomka 185–6, 188, 241
Farmer (*Rolnik*) xvii
farming see agriculture
Feigelman, Avner 229
Feigelson family (of Glubok) 229
Fein, Monish 153
Feinberg, David 104, 194, 196
Feivel (tailor) 85
Feldman, Chava 299
Feldman, Moshe 263
Feldman, Shepsel 123
Fella (girl friend of Dr. Offerman) 114
Fialkow, Leib 218
Final Solution 41, 57, 62–3, 65, 73, 288
Finger (of Volozhin) 259
Finkel, Yitzhak 192
Fiodorov partisan unit 89
Fiolun, Shalom 125
firearms see arms
"First Anti-Fascist Brigade" 164
Fisher (of Braslaw) 163
Fishkin, Josef 105, 119, 229
Fishkin, Sarah 94
Fishkin, Shabtai 229
For the Homeland (*Za Rodinu*) 138
forced labor 54–5, 61, 63–4, 71–2, 74, 82
forest, escape to 127, 159, 209–35, 297–8
  see also escapes
Fort, Reuven 85
Forty days of Musa Dagh, The (Werfel) 95

F.P.O. (United Partisan Organization) 231, 240
Frank, Hans 251, 253
free professions xvii, xix, 58
Freiheit xxiv, xxv
Frenkel (partisan) 246
Friedberg, Yitzhak 144
Friedman, Avraham 134, 244
Friedman, Boris 203
Friedman, Josef 134, 301
Friedstein, Saul 26
friends of Jews 277
From the Depths 22–3
Fuksman (of Kobryn) 226
Funt, Moshe 166

Gach, Aharon 190
Galai, Mendel 252
Galecky, Sh. 230
Galicia xiv, 44
Gaon of Vilno xxii, xxiii
Garbuz (Reznik), Rachel 94
Garmiza, Judel 105, 119
"gas-vans" 42
Gelberstein, Ida 228
Geller, Chaim 22
Geller, Eliezer 180
Gendel, Baruch Shalom 152
Gendel, Hirsh 244
"General Bielorussian Congress" 51
Gens (of Vilno) 231–2, 240
Gercowski (of Novogrudok) 95
Gerling, Shalom 106, 124–6, 218
German occupation 80–3, 289
  see also Nazi policies; Operation Barbarossa
German regime: and Bielorussian partisan movement 51–4
Germany
  invasion of Poland 1
  pacts with USSR 1, 8
Gershon (from Dweig) 92
Gershuny, Sarah 121
Gertman, S. 104

Gertman, Shaike 240
ghettos 56, 71, 246
    change to concentration camps 75
    deportations 86
    establishment 71–2, 82, 289–90
    life in 94–8
    liquidations 73, 75–6, 150–4
    resistance 110
    see also under names of individual ghettos
Gilber, Yoel 262
Gilboa, Yehoshua A. 25
Gilerevicz, Zila 185
Gilerovits, Cila 104
Gilinsky, Mottel 143
Ginsberg, Bezalel 235, 248, 256
Ginsberg, Mordechai 235, 248, 256
Girshowicz, Yoel 255–6
Gittelman, Berl 197
Glazer, Feivel 217
Glazman, Yosef 240
Glebokie 23, 204
    aktzia 150, 164–5
    deportations to 164
    escapes 149, 163–4
    liquidation of ghetto 75
    underground 106, 110
Glebokie area: partisan units 164
Gleibman (of Pinsk) 107
Glubok 205, 216
    aktzia 230
    escapes 229–30, 242, 245, 303
    Judenrat 252
    Judenrat and underground 256
Gnicnowicz, Romka 247
Goebbels, Joseph 44
Goering, Hermann 37, 41, 44, 60
Goldberg (of Nieswiezh) 188–9
Goldberg (of Pinsk) 258
Goldberg, Dr. Chaim 161–2
Goldberg, Shaike 207
Goldfein, Dr. Olga 98, 152
Goldin, Rachel 161
Goldstein, Natan 119

Golz, Emil 48
Gordonia xxiv, xxv, 97, 104, 295
Gorodecka, Avraham 150
Gorodecka, Chaim 149–50
Gorodecka, Chana 149–50, 234
Gorodecka, Israel 150
Gorodecka, Yehuda 150
Gorsky, Aharon 171
Gotein (village council head) 11
Graf, Yehudit 228
Grajewer's wife (of Motele) 153–4
graves of murdered Jews 75
Grazhevsky family 203
Greek underground 307
Grinboim (of Hancewicz) 109
Grinwald, S. 185
Grodis (of Nieswiezh) 278
Grodno xv, xx, 39
Grodno district: agriculture xvi
Groll, Tuviya 203
Grop (of Oszmiana) 256
Grow, Dr. 259
Gudagei 231
Guderian, General 36
Gulkowicz, Ben-Zion 100
Gursky, Aharon 107
Gurvicz, Chaya 230
Gurvicz, Zalman Uri 104, 136–7, 148–9
Gutkin, Hinde 256
Gutkin, Shabtai 256
Guzewicz, Yehuda 194
Guzewicz, Yosef 193

Ha'am Ahad 23
Hajduciszki 164
Hajdukowsky, Aharon 219
Halder, Chief-of-Staff 36, 39
Halib, Yosef 85
Halkin: "Bar Kochba" 18, 23
Halkin, Sh. 19
Halpern, Rabbi 263
Hancewicz 264
    aktzia 72, 87, 288
    deportations to 109

Hancewicz (*continued*)
  escape committee   109
  escapes   219
  underground   110
Hanger, Josef   203
Hanishak   92
Hanoar Hatzair   295
Hanoar Hatzioni   xxiv, 25, 97
Hanveg, *gebietskommissar*   129
Harkawy, Josef   109, 229
Harlap, Yaakov   23
Harmonowicz   164
Harp, Riwa   85
Hase (Vilejka *gebietskommissar*)   74
Hashomer Haleumi   104
Hashomer Hatzair   xxiv, xxv, 97, 104, 108–9, 136, 185–6, 224, 229, 295
  activity under Soviet rule   21–3, 25
  attempt to cross Romanian border   21
  Jutrznia   179–80
  transfer of older members to Vilno   21
Hassidism   xxii–xxiii
hatred of Jews   274–5
Hebrew language   11, 18–9, 23–6
Hechalutz   xxiv, 24–5, 104, 186, 295
Hechalutz Hatzair   xxiv, 97, 138, 295
Heit (German commander)   216
Helman, Yudke   24
Herman, Abrasha   162
Hermonowicz   86
Heschel, Joshua   xx
Heydrich, Reinhard   39–41, 61, 251, 253
Hibat Zion   xxiii
hiding places   140–2, 204, 291–2, 303–4
Himmelfarb, Moshe   170
Himmler, Heinrich   40, 42–4, 48–9, 54, 61, 63, 65, 74–5, 169
Hirocz   125
Hirsh Kaplinsky partisan unit   218
Hitachdut   xxv
Hitler, Adolf   43–5, 53, 59, 63
  Operation Barbarossa   35–9

Hoeppner, Oberst-General   42
Höhere SS and Polizefuehrer (HSSPF)   43, 59, 63, 70
hope   290
Horodok
  escapes   230, 234, 242, 303
  hiding places   141, 292
  Judenrat   263
  partisan attack   248
  underground   109, 118, 138
Horodzei   140, 188
Hotnick, Dr.   243
Hryczyn marshes   198
HSSPF (*Höhere SS and Polizefuehrer*)   43, 59, 63, 70
humiliation of Jews   82, 275

Igalnik, Dr.   196–7
Ignalino: deportations from   86
Ignatka camp   207
Ilja
  aktzia   211–2
  Judenrat   263
  underground   109, 138
illusion   290
Imber, Aviezer   106
incitement to murder Jews   277
"independence" for Bielorussia   49–51
industry   xv–xvi, xix, 58
informing   16–7, 275
intelligence on German activities   142
intimidation   16
"Iskra" partisan unit   120, 235
Ivanovsky (mayor of Minsk)   50
Iwacewicze   86
Iwieniec   69, 71, 82, 290
  Armia Krajowa   139
  deportations from   86
  murders of Jews   86
Iwje   279
  attacks on Jews   82
  escapes   225, 235
  humiliation of Jews   82
  Judenrat   255–6, 265

Index

murder of Jews 84
partisan attack 248
pogroms 271, 273
underground 110, 127, 142, 255–6
Izikson, Yehoshua 145, 255, 261

Jaeckeln, HSSPF 43
Jakobowicz, Dr. 175, 177
Jankelevicz, Shmuel 145, 256
Janow 17, 277
   aktzia 70, 73, 149, 234
   escapes 225, 230, 234
   Judenrat 253
   opposition to underground activity 132
   resistance 152, 160
   underground 109, 138, 302
Janow-Polesky: Judenrat 264
Janowitz, Yitzhak 260
Janson, Welwke 227
Jarockin (partisan) 225
Jazersky (of Ostryn) 207
Jeliszewicz (of Slonim) 253
Jewish police 105–6, 108, 121, 231–2, 263
Jews (Kupala) 280–1
Jews of Shklov, The (Schneor) xxi
Jody 205
Johaj (of Swienciany) 123–4
Jokow (of Nieswiezh) 189, 191
Jokton, Cila 152
Joselevicz, Berl 108, 176, 178
Joselevicz, Yechiel 218
Joselewsky, Monik 105, 131
Josselevsky, Lipa 109
Judenräte (Jewish councils)
   aktzias 254–5
   escapes 301
   establishment 40, 58, 82, 251–4
   food/medical care 98
   Lachwa 193–6
   Mir 221
   Nieswiezh 185, 187–8
   requests for money for arms 127

   and underground 128–30, 143–6, 255–68
Jutrznia 179–80

Kacelenbogen, Luba 152
Kaczanowsky, Shalom 107
Kagan, Dr. 108, 112, 175–6, 178
Kagan, Aharon 138
Kagan, Rachel 120, 187
Kaganovics partisan unit 164
Kaganowicz, Shlomo 153
Kaganowicz partisan unit 234
Kajdanow 258
Kalinin, P. 54
Kalmanovicz, Josef 207
Kamen-Koshirsk
   aktzia 153
   attacks on Jews 82
   escapes 213–4, 228, 234, 243, 303
   Judenrat 264
   pogroms 272
   resistance 152
   underground 110, 122–3, 226, 288
Kamieniecka, Zirl 213
Kamieniecki (of Volozhin) 161
Kandlik, Shlomo 107, 235
Kantarowitz (of Novogrudok) 108
Kantorowicz (partisan) 246
Kaplan, Devorah 120
Kaplan, Moshe 144
Kaplan, Yitzhak 144
Kaplan, Yosef 23, 121, 129
Kaplinsky (daughter of Hershl) 95
Kaplinsky, Hirsh 218
Kapusta partisan unit 191
Karol (of Kimielishky) 203
Karona forests 205
Katzav, Yitzhak 90
Kazian 104–5
Kaziany forest 215
kehilla 18–9
Keiler, Meir 262
Keitel, Wilhelm 38, 40, 42–3, 48, 53–4
Kessel, Dr. 188

Kessler, Israel 109, 225
Kienc (Sejm delegate) xv
Kiev 19, 42–4
Kimieliszky 203, 205
Kiwielecky, Dr. 147
Kiwielewiez, Dr. 188
Klaczko (of Nieswiezh) 191
Kleck 17
  aktzias 91, 192
  German invasion 69
  resistance 152
  revolt 168, 192–3
  underground 110
Klinghofer (*Vorkommando Moskau* head) 40
Knianinina 137
Kobryn 159, 264
  aktzia 161–2, 219
  escapes 219, 226, 276
  underground 110, 120, 126, 143
Kobryn district: population xii
Kobylnik 135, 279–80
  aktzia 83–4, 147
  escapes 81, 230, 301
  German invasion 272
  partisan attack 248
  resistance 85
Kobylnik district 279
Koch, Erich 44
Koifman, Liebl 185
Koldyczevo
  aktzia 150
  escape committee 109
  escapes 219–20, 225
  last of the Jews flee from 75
  resistance 85
  underground 110, 119
kolkhozes 10
Kolodny, Shaike 107
Kolpanicky, Moshe 194
Konarsky, Dr. 203
Konskowolsky, Chana 97
Konskowolsky, Yaakov 97
Kopelowicz (Antek), Moma 107, 112, 170

Koplinsky, Moshe 194
Kopold, Moshe 255
Kopyl forest 193, 229
Kopyl region 220, 241
Korbat (of Iwje) 279
Korelicz 264
  attacks on Jews 82
  escapes 225
  pogroms 272
  underground 134, 138–9
Korelicze
  resistance 85
  underground 110
Koresman, HSSPF 43
Korfish forest 125
Kosov-Polesky 110, 218, 230, 292, 303
Kotok, Simcha 252
"Kovalov" partisan unit 218
Kovno 19, 63
  deportations to 86, 202, 234
Kovno district: agriculture xvi
Kovpak partisan unit 205
Kowiensky, Eliahu 106, 124, 218
Kozhuchovsky (of Novogrudok) 178
Koziany
  escapes 244
  resistance 149, 291
  underground 110, 119
Koziany forest 230, 244
Kozlovsky (*Belaruskaja Gazeta* editor) 50
Krashinsky, Shalom 218
Krasna 234
  deportations to 202
  escapes 230, 242
  Judenräte and the underground 144
  underground 110, 120
Kraviecz, Jehoshua 187
Krawiec, Zalman 153
Kreczner, Israel 252
Kremen, Zorach 106, 127, 228
Kremeniec 292
Krilovshzczyna 85
Krivicz 134, 136
Krolak (of Kobylnik) 272

Krulewicki, Aryeh   121
Krupsky, Velvel   121, 242
Kube, Wilhelm   47–8, 50, 52, 55–7, 61–5, 73–4, 259
Kuffenberg (German)   247
Kulik forests   135
Kupala, Yanka: *Jews*   280–1
Kupperszhmit (partisan)   243
Kurzeniec   277
  aktzia   152–3
  attacks on Jews   82
  escapes   228–9, 233–4
  partisans   303
  pogroms   272–3
  resistance   148
  underground   23, 103–4, 110, 119, 136–7, 233–4, 258, 294, 303
Kushnir, Shlomo   109, 220
Kushnirov (Soviet Jewish writer)   19
Kusze (of Volozhin)   161
Kuzmick, Anton   140
Kwint, Gershon   146
Kwitko, Leib   19

labor *see* forced labor
laborers: manual   xvii–xviii
Lachowcizka, Chedva   188
Lachowicky, Moshe   191
Lachowicz   282
  aktzia   87, 91, 162
  escapes   215
  German invasion   69
  Judenrat and underground   257
Lachowicz
  forests   205
  resistance   85
  underground   110
Lachowiczky, Chedva   104, 185–6
Lachwa   277
  aktzia   73, 195
  deportations from   109
  Judenrat   193–6, 262
  revolt   193–8, 302
  underground   25, 103–4, 110, 119, 262, 294

Lammers, Heinrich   43, 59
land: ownership   xvi, xvii
Landau, Linka   95
Langman, Yosef   188, 190–1
language   xxi, 18, 48
Lareczka bridge   137
Latvia   44, 47
laws: Soviet   11–2
Lederman (of Glebokie)   164
Lederman (of Glubok)   216, 230
Lederman, Gershon   256
Lederman's sons (of Glubok)   230
Left Poalei Zion   104
Leizerke, Rabbi   193
Leizerovsky, Moshe   108
Lenin   6, 219
  aktzia   242
  deportations from   109
  escapes   230, 242
  German invasion   69
  Judenrat   263–4
  resistance   152
"Leninsky Komsomol" partisan unit   206
Levin, Baruch   118, 121, 130, 133, 214, 246, 258–9
Levin, Hershl   85, 107
Levin, Leah   276
Levin, Moshe   214
Levin, Reb Aharon   186
Levin, Shmuel   133, 262
Levinbuk, Dr.   225
Levit (Beirach), Pesya   203
Libman (of Iwje)   256
Lichtenberg, Yitzhak   193–4
Lichtman, Kalman   252, 260
Lida
  aktzia   150–1, 177, 254
  deportations   86, 97, 150, 202, 256
  escapes   206, 212–4, 226–7, 235, 241–2, 303
  gebietskommissar Hanveg's speech   129
  German invasion   39
  Judenrat   252, 258–60
  liquidation of ghetto   75

Lida (*continued*)
  opposition to underground
    activity 129–30
  partisans 246
  resistance 26, 151
  underground 23, 109, 119–21, 138,
    226, 258–60
  yeshiva xx
Lida district: population xii
Lidovsky, Avraham 145
Lidovsky, Eliezer 106–7, 112, 170–3
Lidsky, Eliahu 118, 230
Lidsky, Yerachmiel 206
Liebke (of Postavy) 134
lifestyle xix–xxv
Lifszyc (of Koziany) 244
Lifszyc, Chaim 138
Lifszyc, David 225
Ligumsky, Kosha 214
Liker, Natan 228
Lipczany forest 226, 235
Lipkonsky, Berl 276
Lipshovicz, Chaim Yehoshua 235
Lipshovicz, Eliahu 235
Lipshovicz, Gershon 235
Lipshovicz, Taibe 235
Lithuania 1–2, 44, 47
Lithuanians xix, 204, 216, 282
Litwakova (of Nieswiezh) 187
Litwaks xix
livelihoods *see* employment
Lohse, Heinrich 44, 52, 59, 61–3, 73–4
Lopatin, Dov 193–6, 198, 262
Lubawicz (of Braslaw) 163
Lubcz 263, 272–3
Lubcz-Delaticz 203
Lubetkin, Zivia 25
Lubieszow 83
  aktzia 87–9
  Judenrat 262
  partisan attack 247–8
  pogroms 272
  self-defense groups 82
  underground 109–10

Lubiezh 272
Lunin, Israel 161
Luniniec 73, 276
  deportations from 109
  Jews flee east 202
  murder of Jews 202
Luszky 164, 207
Luszky area 229
Lvov 9, 21, 24
Lyntupy 86, 141, 147–8

Maccabbee 108
Maceikin, Yerachmiel 104
Machandler (of Lubieszow) 89
Machtey, Elimelech 241
Mackewicz (of Kurzeniec) 136
Magalif (of Nieswiezh) 185–90
maggidism xxii
Magun, Liza 180, 231
Mal'ach, Heniek 228
Malik, Benzion 243
malines see hiding places
Malka (daughter of Beila Reichel) 149
Malyszczycki, Zbigniew 306
Mansky, Yitzhak 214
manual laborers xvii–xviii
Margolin, Yaakov 162
Marhvinsky partisan unit 191
Mark, Berl 180
Markish, Peretz 19
Markman, Shmuel 207
Markov partisan brigade 229, 240
Markowsky (of Nieswiezh) 97
mass deportations 27–8
mass escapes 215–25
mass executions *see aktzias*
Master, Yaakov 193, 195
Masuot Polin (Poland's Flames) 25
Matusow, Leib 100
Mayevska, Pesya 95
Mazin, Yishai 191
Meiczet 162, 225, 229
Meir (son-in-law of Beila Reichel)
  149

Meirowicz, Meir 134
Mejerowicz (of Kleck) 193
Melinkov partisan brigade 234
Menches, Gedalya 123
Mendelovicz (of Lachwa) 194
Mesita (of Nieswiezh) 187
Messer, Natan 186
Miadel 147
Miadenek 97
Miadl 60, 109–10, 303
Miadziol 218
Miadzolsky (of Swienciany) 123–4
Michaliczky 147, 231, 264
  deportations to 86, 202
  escapes 80, 212, 234
  Judenrat 252–3
  underground 109–10
Michalowski, Moshe 216
Mickiewicz, Adam 180–1
Migdalovicz, Tuviya 196
Mikashevicz 109
Mikulicz forest 105, 119
Milcenson, Elyakim 168
Milikovsky, Zelig 122
Milikyn family (of Glubok) 229
Miller, *Gebietskommissar* 56
miller of Zholudok region 278
Milman, Nachum 193
Milner, Aharon 263–4
Milstein, Rabbi 152
Milszstein, Chana 203
Mincel (of Dolhinov) 135
Minsk xix, 43, 47, 63, 73, 289
  anti-German activity 50
  gebietskommissars council 64, 74
  German invasion 39, 82
  yeshiva xx
Minsk district
  agriculture xvi
  sherele 19
Minsk forest 138
Minsk-Mazowiecki xv
Minsky (of Pinsk) 257–8
Minsky (of Stolpce) 169

Miory 205, 245, 277
  aktzia 90, 215
  escapes 215
  pogroms 272
  underground 109–10
Mir
  aktzia 83, 144, 221–2
  escapes 214, 221–4
  Judenrat 144–5, 221, 261
  underground 103, 106, 110, 123,
    144–5, 174, 192, 261
  yeshiva xx, 17
Mirowszczyna forest 125
Mirsky, Moshe 95
Misiura (Communist peasant) 217
Misiura partisan unit 218, 248
Missura (of Sernik) 113
Mizrachi xxv
mockery of Jews 275
Molczad 106, 110, 127
Moldevezna 171
Molotov, Vyacheslav Mikailovich 1, 79
Molotov brigade 220
moral encouragement 278
Morashkin (of Swienciany) 152
Mordokovsky, Noah 162
Moscow 19
Moshin, Shlomo 234
Moshkovsky, Rivka 122
Mosser, Natan 188
Motele 128, 150–1, 153–4, 206, 277
Mudrik (of Lida) 130
Mukasey, Rita 122
Müller 75
murders of Jews *see aktzias*
Mushinsky, Monik 123, 170
Mussar (Ethics) movement xxiii
Mustafa (partisan) 243
mutual aid xx–xxi, 20
Myth of the twentieth century, The
  (Rosenberg) 44

Nachmanovicz (partisan) 246
Nachumovsky (of Novogrudok) 108

Nachumovsky's sister-in-law (of Baranowicze) 152
Nacza forest 226
Nadel, Gershon 120, 214
Naliboky 86, 108, 139, 272, 290
Naliboky forest 220, 226, 228
Narocki, Zelig 85
Narocz region 233
Nashrishky forest 125
"National Bielorussian Self-Aid" 50
nationalization 10, 14–5
Natkowicz, Yaakov 245
Nazi policies 65–6
   attitude towards Bielorussians 47–9
   Bielorussian Jews as potential partisans 55–7
   Bielorussian partisan movement 51–4
   "Brown Book" 57–9
   conflict among German authorities 58–65
   establishment of "independent" Bielorussia 49–51
   evacuation of labor to Germany 54–5
Nebe, Arthur 40
Neika 136
Nekama (Vengeance) 107
Neufeld, Boria 109, 119
Niemenczyn 204–5
Nieswiezh 221, 275
   aktzia 91, 140, 186, 277
   Judenrat 185, 187–8
   partisans 303
   Poles 278
   revolt 168, 185–92, 302
   selektzia 186
   underground 23, 103–4, 110, 119–20, 292, 294–5
   Zionism 26
Nissboim, Shmuel 190
Nivichowicz, Yaakov 108, 178
NKVD (Soviet Secret police) 10, 16–7
Noah Pandre (Schneor) xxi
Noar Hatzioni 26
non-Jewish population
   aktzias 71

   attitude towards Jews 12–4, 204, 271–84
Norman, Joseph 137, 230
Norwegian underground 307
Novik (of Dworec) 131, 165–6
Novogrudok xx, 277
   aktzia 175–6, 178
   attacks on Jews 82
   deportations 86, 177
   escapes 227, 242, 303
   ghetto life 95
   Judenrat 252, 257
   partisans 303
   pogroms 271–2
   underground 107–8, 110, 112, 138, 142, 175–9, 226, 257
   and Warsaw ghetto revolt 179–81
   yeshiva xx
Novogrudok district
   agriculture xvi
   aktzias 70, 73, 150
   Armia Krajowa 139
   craftsmen xvi
   doctors xvii
   emigration xii
   Jews' share in trade xiv
   liquidation of ghettos 75–6
   population xiii, 3, 28, 70, 76
   underground 293, 296
Novoprocky (of Iwje) 84
Novy-Pohost: deportations from 86
Nusanczik, Michael 282

occupations *see* employment
Odzhibul xv
Offerman, Dr. 114
Ohlendorf, Otto 40–1
Okienczyc, Fabian 50
Oliker, Ruchama 204–5
Olkeniky 153, 301
   aktzia 92
   calls for resistance 160
   deportations 216
   escapes 225
   underground 105, 110

Olszany 202, 264
Omalinski, Michael 107, 167, 235
Operation Barbarossa 35–45, 288–9
opposition to the underground 128–36, 297–8
Opsa 245
Ordiansky, Michael 187
Oriol district 47
Orliansky (of Novogrudok) 178
Ormland, Pinchas 122, 212
ORT 19–20
Oshman, Aharon 194
Oshman, Chaim 107, 170, 172
Oshmianka 231
Ost program 48
Ostapczuk 139, 230, 206
Ostashinsky, Daniel 108, 257
Ostrin 259
Ostrovsky, Radoslabel 50–1
Ostrowiec 231
Ostryn 205, 207
Oswald (Mir underground's contact) 123, 145, 174, 221–4
Oszman, Aharon 104, 194
Oszmiana 275, 277
  aktzias 83, 231–2, 254
  deportations 86, 150, 202, 234
  escapes 231–2
  Judenrat 256, 265
  resistance 85
  underground 109, 136
Our Life 23
ownership of land xvi, xvii
Ozochovsky, Issy 121, 247

Palevsky (of Kobryn) 226
Palileik 277
Parafianowo 164, 264
  aktzia 205
"partisan attack" exercises 109
partisans 38, 50, 73, 209–11, 235, 303, 305–6
  and *aktzias* 74
  attack on Kossov-Polesky 218
  contact with 136–40, 224, 226, 302–3

differences over anti-partisan warfare 60–1
and German regime 51–4
Jewish 55–7, 108, 207, 211, 227, 233, 239–48, 296, 303
and Jews 107–8, 118, 210–1, 233, 239–40, 247
Novogrudok escapees 178
numbers 54
Polesie region 289
supplies sent by the Jews 127
Zhetl area 111–2, 124–6, 218–9
see also anti-partisan warfare
peasants: murder of Jews 226
Pecker, Josef 162
Pelczuk, Jacob 262
"people's militia" 5
Percowiez, Yitzhak 119
Perelman, Rabbi 84
Perlin, Zirl 97
Perlman, Rabbi 255
personal responsibility: Judenräte 253
"Peshke, Aunt" (of Kurzeniec) 119, 148–9
Petrovicz work camp 206
physicians xvii, 58
Piernikow, Hirsh 106
Pinczov, David 164
Pinsk 18, 47, 205, 275
  aktzias 70–1, 73–4, 169, 257–8
  Betar 25
  craftsmen xvi
  escapes 226, 230, 300
  Hebrew gymnasium 19
  Judenrat 143–4, 257–8
  population xii
  resistance 85, 151
  Soviet intimidation 16–7
  underground 26, 107, 110, 112–3, 143–4, 169, 257–8, 294, 301
Pinsk district: population xii
Piotrkov 8
pits, burial *see* burial pits
Pleszczenice forest 138
Pliskin (of Dokszyce) 132–3, 297

Plotnik, Yeshaya 85
Plotnitzka, Chantshe 25
Plotnitzka, Frumka 25
Pniewa 272
Poalei Zion xxiii, xxv, 104, 108, 295
Pobieda partisan unit 218, 235
Podberezky, Batya 162
Podboresky, N. 230
Podbrodzh 164
pogroms xv, 6, 42, 69, 88, 271–4, 288
Pohost 87, 89–90, 109–10, 234
Polaczek, Eliahu 187, 190
Poland's Flames (*Masuot Polin*) 25
Poles
  aktzias 48
  and Jews 12–4, 272, 278, 281–2
  public service 48, 50
  and Soviet regime 10
Polesie
  agriculture xvi
  craftsmen xvi
Polesie district 47
  agriculture xvi
  aktzias 70, 73, 87, 150, 202, 289
  Armia Krajowa 139
  doctors xvii
  emigration xii
  German invasion 39, 69, 82
  liquidation of ghettos 75–6
  population xiii, 3, 28, 70, 76
  underground 293, 296
Poliak, A.L. 128, 153–4, 206, 246
Poliakov (partisan) 194
police, Jewish 105–6, 108, 121, 231–2, 263
policies against Jews *see* anti-Jewish policies
Polish Delegation 13, 28
Polish underground 139
Polygon camp 104–5, 149
Pomerantz, Berl 234
Ponar 231, 233
Popko, Chana 153
population
  Bielorussia 47, 74, 305
  Novogrudok district ghettos 70, 76
  occupied territories 28
  Poland xi–xiii
  Polesie district ghettos 70, 76
  territories annexed to USSR 2–3, 8–9
  Vilno district ghettos 70, 76
Pordes (of Nieswiezh) 119
Pordess (of Nieswiezh) 189
Port, Garmiza 229
Port, Reuven 229
Porush (of Swienciany) 240
Posesorsky, Hersh 109, 114, 220, 241, 279
Postavy
  escapes 138, 230, 234, 244
  underground 110, 134
Pozdonsky, Moshe 106, 126
Pozharik, Avraham 192
Prager, Dr. 107
Priluztky, Noah 18
Prinovo 195
Pripet marshes 39, 54, 69, 74, 198
prisoners-of-war 38
Pritzmann, Hans 43, 74
professions xvii, xix, 58
Proniagin (partisan) 127
property in trust 275–6
Pruzhany 98, 205
  aktzia 254, 277
  deportations from 150, 167, 243
  escapes 230, 234, 300, 303
  group revolt 85–6
  hiding places 292
  Judenrat 144, 260
  partisan attack 247
  partisans 243
  resistance 152
  underground 109, 113, 139, 142, 144
Pruzhany district: population xii
Pszytyk xv
public life 12, 19–20, 86
Pupko, Shmuel 227
Pupok, Michael 222

Rabinowicz, Dr. 203
Rabinowicz, Aharon 151
Rabinowicz, Max 146
Rabinowicz, Velvel 123
Rabinowicz, Zalman 282
Rachmilevicz, Josef 228
Racionzh xv
Rackin, Ephraim 263
Radom 8
Radostov work camp 205–6
Radun 105, 276
  aktzia 216–7
  calls for resistance 160
  escapes 216–7
  Judenrat 253
  underground 110
  yeshiva xx
Raduszkowicze
  escape to Russia 81
  escapes 226, 233
  opposition to underground activity 130
  resistance 152
  underground 109–10
Radyonov, Gil 164
Raeder, Admiral 35–6
Ragutner, S. 230
Raishkes, Velvel 6
Rakocky (of Radun) 276
Rakov 71, 203–4, 207
Rakovsky (of Novogrudok) 108
Rasch, Otto 40
Rasp (S.D. commander) 73
Ravic, Sevek 242
Rawic, Zehava 228
Rayak, Michael 164
Rayak, Ziv 164
Rechtman (of Nieswiezh) 186–7
Red Army 1, 288
  and fleeing Jews 80
  Jews' receipt of 3–6, 12
  and partisans 52–3
  retreat 79
refugees 5, 7–10, 113–4, 265, 278–80
Reichel, Avraham 149

Reichel, Beila 119, 149, 291
religion 17–8, 282
Remez, Rabbi Avraham Eli 263
resistance 290–1, 304–8
  organized 159–81
  unorganized 84–6, 146–54, 201–7
  see also escapes; hiding places
responsibility
  Judenräte 253
  see also collective responsibility
return to the ghetto after escape 225–6, 300
Rev, Shlomo 170
Reval 63
revolts 198–9, 290–1
  in ghettos without undergrounds 201–7
  Kleck 192–3
  Lachwa 193–8
  Nieswiezh 185–92
  preparations 166–9
Reznik, Berl 106, 214, 221
Reznik (Garbuz), Rachel 94
Ribak, Jacob 105
Ribbentrop-Molotov Pact 1
Riga 42–4, 63, 73
Ritter von Leeb, Wilhelm 38
Rivka (daughter of Beila Reichel) 149
Riyer, Niomka 135
Rochczyn, Yitzhak 194–6
Rochlin (of Disna) 261
Rochzin, Yitzhak 104
Rodes, Leah 121
Rogovin, Chanan 230
Rolnik (Farmer) xvii
Roman Catholic church 282
Romek (of Koldiczevo work camp) 109
Ronkin, Eliezer 85
Rosaky forest 233
Rosenberg, Alfred 36–7, 43–5, 59, 61–3
  "Brown Book" 57–9
  The myth of the twentieth century 44
Rosenblum (of Brzesc) 263
Rosenblum, Yitzhak 263
Rosovsky, Shimon 160–1

Rotman, Noah 242
Rowno 21–2
Rozhanka 84, 205, 264
Rozovsky, Rabbi Shimon 126, 252
Rubin, David 213
Rubinowicz (Schiff), Sarah 145, 228, 242
Rubinstein (of Postav) 244
Rubla 272, 276, 282
Rubzhevsky, Baruch 166
Rubzhewicze
   deportations to 86
   escapes 229, 290
   Judenrat and underground 258
   partisan attack 247
   partisans 303
   underground 105, 110, 119
Rudicky, Benjamin 165–6
Rudnicki, D. Yohai Yoske 104
Rudnicky (Arad), Yitzhak 104, 120, 240
Rufeisen, Oswald 123, 145, 174, 221–4
Rundstedt, Field Marshal 39
Russia: escape to 80–1
Russian Orthodox church 282
Russian Orthodox priest (of Kobylnik) 279–80
Russians: Jews' receipt of 3–7
Ryer, Niomka 257

sabotage 142–3, 248
Saburov (partisan) 248
Salanter, Israel xxiii
Samec forest 230
Sapczyc (of Baranowicze) 170–1
"Sashka" (partisan) 139, 235
Sauckel, Fritz 55
Saurer (German commander) 151
Schacter, Dr. 299
Schectman (of Lachwa) 194
Schiff (Rubinowitz), Sarah 145, 228, 242
Schlossberg, P'nina 146
Schneider, Moshe 206
Schneour, Zalman xix
   Noah Pandre xxi
   The Jews of Shklov xxi

schools xvii, 17–20, 294
   underground activity 26–7
   see also education
Schroeder, *Oberliutnant* 142
Schultz (German commander) 222–3
Schusterman, Israel 189–91
Schwartz, Mina 153
Schwartz, Yehuda 153
"scorched earth" policy 60–1
Sczors, Dr. 49
Segal, Berl 243
Segal, Josef 243
Segal, Z. 260
Segalowicz, Yehiel 85
Seger, Esther Leah 203
selections (*selektzia*) 72, 87, 110, 186
self-defense 82, 88, 161–6
"self-government": Bielorussia 49–51
Sernik
   aktzias 70, 83
   escapes 217–8, 230
   partisan attack 248
   pogroms 272
   underground 110, 112–3
Shapir (Shtopper), Zev 205
Shapira, Josef 132, 234, 297
Shayak, Gedalyahu 106
Shechtman, Eliahu 193
Sheinman, Aryeh 107
shelter for Jews 278–80
Shelubsky (of Slonim) 122
Shevkovsky, Reuven 175
Shifmanovicz, Shlomo 219
Shimonowicz, Ben-Zion 123
Shklar, Yerachmiel 186, 188
Shkolnik (of Miory) 215
Shkoncyki 207
Shmuel-Yossol (of Michaliszok) 5
Shreibman (of Pruzhany) 260
shtetls (towns) xvii–xix
Shtopper (Shapir), Zev 205
Shulman, Benjamin 136–7, 221
Shuster, Chaim 106
Shuster, Shimon 105
Shusterowicz (of Slonim) 122

Shutan, Moshe   240
Sielec: deportations from   86
Sigalczyk (of Dolhinov)   135, 245
Sigalczyk (Jewish partisan)   218
Silber, Zalman   138
Skif   xxiv
skilled Jewish workers   61, 63–4, 71–2, 87, 128–9, 233
Skladkovsky, Florian Slavoi   xv
Skwarczynski, Stanislav   xv
Slobodka   xx
Slonim
  aktzias   106, 141, 162–3, 253, 277
  assaults on Jews   6
  deportations to   86
  escapes   228
  forced labor   72
  German invasion   39, 272
  Hashomer Hatzair   22
  Judenrat   146, 253, 260
  Red Army arrival   3
  resistance   152
  theater   18
  underground   23, 106, 110, 114–5, 122, 127, 142, 146, 226, 260, 294, 297
  yeshiva   xx, 17
Slonim district: population   xii
Slucky, Yitzhak   194
Slutzk   xx, 62
Slutzky, Lolik   107
Smitenko family   278
Smolensk district   47
Smorczevsky (priest)   279
Smorgon   86, 136
social origin   12, 15–6
socialist Jewish parties   xxiii
Sokoly   23
Soly   86, 136, 231
Sosensky, Dania   152–3
Sosnovik (of Miory)   215
Soviet citizenship   2–3, 8–10
Soviet Jews   11, 58
Soviet rule   1–31, 287–8
Soviet Secret police (NKVD)   10, 16–7

Soviet Socialist Republic of Bielorussia   2
Sovietization   2–3, 10, 12–4
"Spartak" partisan brigade   244–5
Spector, Koppel   104
Speigel, Jacob   109, 113
SS   59, 61, 82
Stahlecker, Dr.   273
Stahlecker, Franz   40, 42, 70
"Stalinsky" partisan unit   198
Stankevicz   108
Stankvicz (of Wiszniewo)   247
Stapf, General   55
Steimle (E.G. head)   40
Stein, Arik   106, 122, 228
Stein, Riwa   85
Stobla river   218
Stolin
  aktzia   73
  attacks on Jews   82
  escapes   234
  partisan attack   248
  pogroms   272–3
  self-defense groups   82
  student resistance   26
  underground   110, 138, 167
Stolovicky, Chaim   121, 170
Stolowicky, Zimmel   229
Stolpce   168, 279
  aktzia   168
  escapes   229, 303
  German invasion   48
  Judenrat   145–6, 260
  Koldiczevo crematorium   109
  partisans   211, 241, 303
  underground   23, 106, 108–10, 113–4, 145–6, 167–9, 192, 260, 288
Strauch, Edward   56, 64–5, 73–5
Stryjer's wife (of Kamen-Koshirsk)   152
Stryjer (of Kamen-Koshirsk)   213–4
Sucharsky, Natan   176
Suckever, Chaim   148, 152
Suvalki   xv
  district: agriculture   xvi
"Suworow" partisan brigade   164

Index

Svir 69, 205, 207
 aktzia 147
 deportations from 86, 202
 Jews fell east 202
Svirsky (Vidz escape guide) 230
Svirsky, Noah 138
Swidler, Yehoshua 147, 291
Swiecicka, Roza 121
Swienciany
 aktzia 231–3
 deportations 86, 148, 150, 164, 240
 escapes 214, 232–3, 300
 hiding places 141
 Judenrat 143, 257
 murder of Jews 83
 resistance 152
 underground 103–4, 110, 120, 123–4, 127, 133–4, 143, 240, 257, 292, 294, 302
Swierzhen
 escapes 220
 Jewish fighter in Palestine 96
 murder of Jews 83
 opposition to underground activity 130–1
 resistance 85
 partisans 241
 underground 105, 110, 114, 119, 123
synagogues xxi–xxii, 17–8
Szaf (of Kurzeniec) 258
Szarkowszczyzna 205, 277
 aktzia 216
 deportations to 86
 escapes 149, 216
 Judenrat and underground 261
 pogroms 272–3
 self-defense group 82
 underground 110
"Szczors 51" Jewish partisan unit 228
Szczuczyn 84, 202, 264
Szelubsky, Chaim 162
Szkonciky 164
Szotan, Moshe 104

"Tadeusz Kosciuszko" partisan unit 306
Tanpel, Fruma 235
"Tarbut" schools 20, 26, 294
taxation 15, 17
Tchernichovsky 23, 178
Tennenbaum, Gershon 126, 161
Timczuk (partisan) 245
Timolovicz 207
Tomaka (of Nieswiezh) 278
Tonkewicz, Josef 279
Top, Moshe 121, 145, 172, 242
Torah study xix–xx, xxi–xxii
Torinsky (of Wiszniewo) 247
towns xvii–xix
TOZ 19–20
trades see crafts/craftsmen
transfer of Bielorussians 48
Traub (German commander) 177
Treblinka 207
Tuchman, Moshe 118–9, 230
Tunik, Azriel 109

Ukraine 44–5
Ukrainians 272, 282
underground 97, 117, 287–8, 290, 292–6, 304–8
 aims 110–5
 aktzias 150–4
 arms 117–27
 beginnings 103–10
 collective responsibility 301–2
 contacts with partisans 136–40, 224, 226, 302–3
 hiding places 140–2
 intelligence 142–3
 and Judenräte 143–6, 255–68
 opposition to 128–36, 297–8
 resistance 146–50
 revolts 185–99
 sabotage 142–3
 under Soviet rule 20–7
underground bunkers see hiding places
"Unit 1005" 75

United Partisan organization
   (F.P.O.)   231, 240
universities   xvii
Untershul, Yosef   230
USSR: occupied territories   1–3

Vant, Reuven   244
Vanya (partisan)   125
Varman, Eliezer   105
Velitovska, Doba   85
Velitovsky, Benjamin   119, 130
vengeance   246–8
Vengeance (*Nekama*)   107
Verapajewo: deportations from   164
Verble, Shmuel   264
Victor (partisan)   178
Vidz   138, 230, 244
   underground   110
Vielitovsky, Benjamin   105
Vigdorczyk, Mirka   173
Vigdorovicz, Josef   259
Vilejka   23
   deportations to   202
   escapes   219, 230
   escape committee   109
   opposition to underground
      activity   130
   partisans   303
   synagogue   17
   underground   106, 109–10, 126,
      136–7, 303
Vilejka region   47
Vilno   xix, 19, 147, 231
   deportations to   86, 202, 234, 240
   escapes   240
   underground   21–3, 25
   yeshiva   xx
Vilno, Gaon of   xxii, xxiii
Vilno district
   agriculture   xvi
   aktzias   70, 73, 150, 204, 231–3
   Armia Krajowa   139
   calls for resistance   160
   craftsmen   xvi

   emigration   xii
   Jews' share in trade   xiv
   liquidation of ghettos   75–6
   Lithuanians   204
   population   xiii, 28, 70, 76
   underground   293, 296
Vilno University   18
Visoky   73, 203, 205
Vitovsky, Melech   206
Vittenberg, Itzik   240
Vladek (peasant)   282
Vohlynia district   xii, xiv, xvii
Volfovicz, Esther   121
Voliak, Leib   105, 244–5
Volkovisk   xxiv–xxv, 39
Volochoviansky, Shalom   23
Volodka (of Nieswiezh)   278
Volodya (partisan)   136, 148
Volodya partisan unit   119
Volozhin
   aktzia   161, 275
   deportations to   202
   escapes   213, 235
   Judenrat   259
   ritual bath   19
   underground   109–10
   yeshiva   xx, 17
Volozhin forest   231
Volpin, Noah   248
von Bock, Fedor   38
von dem Bach Zalevsky, HSSPF   43,
   54–5, 64–5, 75
von Gottberg, *generalkommissar*   50, 55,
   74
Von Reichenau, Field Marshal
   General   37
Voronowa   25, 301
   deportations from   86
Voroshilov partisan brigade   234
voting   12
Vujca (Glubok courier)   242

Wagner, General   40
Wanckovicz (mayor of Kobylnik)   84

Wannsee Conference 45, 73
Warsaw: emigration xii
Warsaw ghetto revolt 176, 179–81
Warshavsky (of Baranowicze) 106–7, 171
Wasyliszky 82, 264
  aktzia 153
  escapes 242
  pogroms 272
  resistance 152
  underground 109
ways of life xix–xxv
weapons *see* arms
Wehrmacht 42–3, 54, 59, 74
Weiner, Noah 107
Weinman (E.G. commander) 40
welfare institutions xx–xxi, 20
Werfel, Franz: *The forty days of Musa Dagh* 95
Western Bielorussian National Assembly 2
Western Ukraine 1–2
Wetzel, Dr. 48
"White Ruthenia" 47
Wicenberg, Josef 161
Wiszniewo 264
  aktzias 83, 162, 277
  calls for resistance 160
  escapes 230
  partisan attack 247
  underground 25, 109–10, 139
Wolak, Leib 138
Wolfson, Israel 240
Wysock 248

Yaffe, Dr. 147
Yanov 25
Yanovicz, Yitzhak 167
Yelin, Yeshaya David 162
Yermatzenko, Dr. 50
yeshivas xx, 17
Yiddish schools 294
Yitzhak (of Baranowicze) 171
Yoffe, Meir 133
Yoslevska, Markele 89–90

Yoslevska, Rivka 89–90
youth movements xxiv, 97, 103–4, 110, 292–5
Yozhelewsky (of Byten) 140
Yukov (of Nieswiezh) 190
Yurshan, Chaim 222

Za Rodinu (For the Homeland) 138
Zaglembia 180
Zakin, Abba 133
Zalman, Rabbi Avraham 193
Zalmanovicz, Moshe 107, 171–3, 242
Zalmanson, Yitzhak 22
Zamosz 153
Zarecky, Moshe 241
Zaryckevicz, Alyosha 112
Zaryckevicz, Elyosha 107, 170–1
Zaslavsky, Shmuel 134, 230, 244
Zeitlin (of Baranowicze) 171–3
Zelikson, Dr. 147
Zezmary: deportations to 202
Zhetl 246
  aktzia 84, 105, 218, 292
  deportations 105, 202
  escapes 218–9, 228, 242
  hiding places 141–2
  Judenrat and underground 261
  partisans 303
  underground 105–6, 110–1, 124–6, 174, 226, 295, 303
Zholudok 98
  aktzia 203, 277
  Judenrat 252
  murder of the Jews 83
  resistance 203, 291
  underground 110, 142
Zhukov partisan unit 114, 191, 193, 205, 228, 241
Zigelbaum (of Baranowicze) 170
Zilberberg, Zorach 106
Zilberfarb, Nachman 217
Zimmer, Baruch 164, 216
Zionists/Zionism xxiii, xxiv, 7, 19, 21–7, 97, 103–4, 106, 185–6, 287–8, 292, 294

Zippora (of Dweig) 92
Zkubacky, Hershl 162
Zolotov partisan unit 162, 229
Zowisky, Batya 92
Zubak (of Baranowicze) 172
Zuckerman, Yitzhak 23
Zukunft xxv
Zusky: pogroms 273